EUROPEAN CITIES
AND TOWNS
400–2000

PETER CLARK

OXFORD

UNIVERSITY PRESS

OXFORD
UNIVERSITY PRESS

Great Clarendon Street, Oxford OX2 6DP

Oxford University Press is a department of the University of Oxford.
It furthers the University's objective of excellence in research, scholarship,
and education by publishing worldwide in

Oxford New York

Auckland Cape Town Dar es Salaam Hong Kong Karachi
Kuala Lumpur Madrid Melbourne Mexico City Nairobi
New Delhi Shanghai Taipei Toronto

With offices in

Argentina Austria Brazil Chile Czech Republic France Greece
Guatemala Hungary Italy Japan Poland Portugal Singapore
South Korea Switzerland Thailand Turkey Ukraine Vietnam

Oxford is a registered trade mark of Oxford University Press
in the UK and in certain other countries

Published in the United States
by Oxford University Press Inc., New York

British Library Cataloguing in Publication Data

Data available

Library of Congress Cataloging in Publication Data

Clark, Peter, 1944-
European cities and towns: 400-2000/Peter Clark.
p. cm.
Includes bibliographical references and index.
ISBN 978-0-19-870054-8 (pbk.: acid-free paper)—ISBN 978-0-19-956273-2 (hbk.: acid-free paper)
1. Cities and towns—Europe—History. 2. Urbanization—Europe—History. I. Title.
HT131.C53 2009
307.76094—dc22   2008043466

Typeset by Laserwords Private Limited, Chennai, India
Printed in Great Britain
on acid-free paper by
CPI Antony Rowe

ISBN 978-0-19-956273-2 (Hbk.)
ISBN 978-0-19-870054-8 (Pbk.)

1 3 5 7 9 10 8 6 4 2

For Marja Holmila

EUROPEAN CITIES AND TOWNS

400–2000

EUROPEAN CITIES AND TOWNS

300–1300

Contents

Figures and Tables

Figures

Tables

Preface

The idea for this book came from Peter Burke over a friendly lunch at Cambridge in the late 1990s, and I am grateful to Peter for his suggestion. But the gestation and orientation of this survey started rather earlier: in the collaboration with Peter Burke, Paul Slack, Penelope Corfield and others in the early 1970s in an Open University course on urban history which led to my first attempt to sketch out European trends in *The Early Modern Town* (1976); in my involvement with the Pre-Modern Towns Group (along with Peter Borsay, Caroline Barron and others) and the British Urban History Group (led by Jim Dyos and David Reeder) in the 1970s and 1980s when we explored together a widening arc of new themes and periods in urban history; and in my work at the Centre for Urban History, University of Leicester, where I was director between 1985 and 1999. Particularly valuable at that time was the cooperation with Herman Diederiks, Herman van der Wee, Walter Prevenier, Anngret Simms, Toshio Sakata, Adriaan Verhulst, and Bernard Lepetit which led to numerous conferences and publications on many aspects of European urban history. In the 1980s the first international workshops on urban history were held at the Maison des Sciences de l'Homme in Paris under the splendid leadership of Maurice Aymard; and 1989 saw the creation of the European Association for Urban History, whose biennial conferences, attended by many hundreds of scholars from all parts of Europe and beyond, provide an exciting forum for the latest research on many aspects of European urban history.

This book is an attempt to summarize and provide a structure and argument for much of the comparative and interdisciplinary research on the European city since the Middle Ages that has appeared in recent decades. It examines urbanization trends and types of town as well as key economic, social, political, and cultural developments in European cities between about 400 and 2000. For strategic reasons the book is divided into three conventional parts: the first up to the end of the Middle Ages, the second from the Reformation to the French Revolution; and the last covering the nineteenth and twentieth centuries. At the same time, there is a concern to explore key themes and questions over the long *durée*. There are no footnotes but a select bibliography is appended. An early decision was taken with the publisher not to have plates (and only a limited number of figures) because of the ready availability of numerous illustrated histories of European towns.

I began preparing the book as a Visiting Fellow (1999–2000) at the Netherlands Institute for Advanced Study, Wassenaar, and I am grateful to the then rector, Professor Henk Wesseling, and his colleagues for that opportunity. In 2000 I came to the University of Helsinki and the move advanced the study in two major ways: firstly, it gave me the chance to work with other professors in the urban studies network (notably Jussi Jauhiainen and Jari Niemelä), and to carry out detailed comparative research on the modern city; secondly, it gave my work a new geographical perspective. From the Finnish shore with Russia to the east and the Baltic states and Poland to the west, Europe spreading southwards appears a rather different continent to the stereotypical vision from the Atlantic seaboard. I am heavily indebted to my good friends Marjatta Hietala and Marjaana Niemi at the University of Tampere, to Eero Holstila and Asta Manninen, successive directors of Urban Facts Helsinki City, the city research office, and to Henrik Meinander, Henrik Stenius and other Finnish friends for welcoming me to Helsinki and supporting my research here. My postgraduate students in the History Department have also been an invaluable source of critical ideas, fresh approaches, and sociable friendship.

In a work of this kind one is inevitably indebted to a host of organizations and individuals. I am grateful to the University of Leicester and its Centre for Urban History for continuing to support my research; in particular, I am indebted to Sue Smith and other staff of the University Library, Leicester, for answering many queries from afar. Thanks are likewise due to the staff of the Parliament Library, Helsinki. Research has also been generously helped by short-term visiting fellowships at the Flemish Academic Centre for Science and the Arts, Royal Flemish Academy in 2002 and 2003, where Inez Dua and numerous colleagues there and at Antwerp, Leuven, and Brussels made my stay especially sociable and productive. The University of Helsinki has no sabbatical leave arrangements, but in 2007 the Academy of Finland gave me a six-month Senior Scientist Fellowship to work abroad and complete the book, and I am obliged to that body and to the excellent researchers who assisted me to carry out revisions to the text: Stephanie Van Houtven and Annelore Brantegem in Brussels; Peter Jones in Oxford; and Jyrki Hakapää and Suvi Talja in Helsinki.

Among the many friends and colleagues who have helped over the years, I would like to thank Marc Boone, Neil Christie, Hugo Soly, Rina Lis, Richard Rodger, and Pim Koij for reading major sections of the book and making valuable suggestions. I am no less indebted to Peter Borsay, who read the book for the publisher, for his excellent comments and ideas. Thanks also to Vera Bacskai, the doyenne of Hungarian historians, for her advice on Hungarian towns, Robin Briggs who greatly facilitated my stay in Oxford in May 2007, Dr Stephanie Hovland who gave me the story of Alice Hermendesworth in Chapter 4, and the late Kathleen (Kay) McLoughlin for her life story in Chapter 14. I am also indebted to Donatella Calabi, Luda Klusakova, Denis Menjot, Alan Kreider, Sven Lilja, Lars Nilsson, Peter Johanek, Anngret Simms, Heinz Reif, David Mattingly, Leonard Schwarz, the late David Reeder, Anne Hardy, Bas van Bavel, Isabel Holowaty, Derek Keene, Katalin Szende, Anne Winter, Renato Sansa, Erik Aerts, Robert Lee, Ute Lotz-Heumann, Heinz Schilling, John Walton, Clive Emsley, Jussi Wacklin, Wolfgang Hoffman, Patrizia Battilani, and Caroline Barron for a miscellany of kindnesses.

Mathew Cotton at Oxford University Press has been both a patient and supportive publisher. I am also grateful to Andrew McLennan and Keith Thomas in the initial discussions with the Press. Last but not least, the book could never have been finished without the encouragement of my wife, Marja, and our lively discussions of the contemporary urban scene.

I

Introduction

Since the Middle Ages, Europe has been one of the most urbanized continents on the planet and its cities have stamped their imprint on the European economy, as well as on European social, political, and cultural life. Rarely sprawling mega-cities like those of present-day Latin America or Asia, mostly compact and coherent, they have been communities of heavy mortality (until the twentieth century) and of high immigration. Endowed often with administrative functions and political privileges, they have always functioned as commercial and business centres, while religion (up to recent times), education, leisure activity, and a distinctive townscape have helped define urban cultural identity. Often perceived as chaotic and threatening—noisy, stinking, crowded, and anonymous—they have also been pillars of European continuity and stability, serving as the interface between European regions and states and as springboards to the non-European world.

The development of European cities was hammered out in a forge of individual urban experiences—of slow or rapid growth, of stagnation or decline, sometimes (but less frequently) of disappearance. We must never forget that the motor of Europe's urban expansion was to be found at the level of the local urban community. Many towns were never more than bit-players in the urbanization process, but others had starring parts, which resonate in the European consciousness and illustrate broader urban themes. Three case stories are illustrative here. The first is of Venice on the Northern Adriatic, among the most brilliant and prosperous of Europe's medieval cities. Rising in the eighth century out of the ruins of the Roman and later Byzantine Empires, Venice profited from its trade in spices, silks, and other luxury commodities from the Near East and beyond, from its provisioning of the Crusades, and from growing commerce over the Alps to Western Europe. As Martino da Canale declared

in the late thirteenth century, 'merchandise passes through this noble city
as water flows through fountains'. Commercial success was seconded by
political ruthlessness as the Venetians outmanoeuvred and overcame, often
by military force, their rivals: in the war of Chioggia from 1378 to 1381,
the Venetian fleet defeated the besieging Genoese, and forced thousands
to surrender, bringing their arch-enemies' battered galleys and abject crews
in triumph into Venice. Crowded on to the islands of the lagoon, with a
population of about 100,000 in the fifteenth century, Venice's tolerance
and acceptance of foreigners—Florentines, Jews, Greeks, Slavs, Turks,
Germans, and Flemings—created an environment that not only promoted
trade, crafts, and economic dynamism but also generated an extraordinary
cultural efflorescence, in which Tuscan, Byzantine, and Flemish traditions
flowed together to shape the distinctive Venetian style of high Renaissance
art. Underpinning this economic and cultural creativity was an autonomous political regime that displayed flexibility, administrative innovation,
and permeability to wider political interests across the community. The
Venetian success story lasted 700 years but by the seventeenth century
the city was in long-term decline. Internally less open, less tolerant, more
rigid economically, it also suffered overwhelming external challenges from
the ships and merchants of Atlantic cities like Amsterdam and London,
engaged in the new oceanic commerce to Asia and America. A tourist
attraction before the eighteenth century, Venice at the end of our period
had become an international icon, archetype of Europe's urban heritage,
its beauty smiling as its population faded.

By the Enlightenment period, London, our second case story, had
succeeded Venice as one of the most famous and successful cities in
Europe, impressing a flurry of fascinated foreign visitors from Voltaire to
Haydn. Founded by the Romans, strategically located on the country's
largest river, and already the English capital and a major European city
by the time of the Black Death in the 1340s, London enjoyed a meteoric
rise during the early modern period. As a great Atlantic port and the
capital of a leading European power, by 1750 it was the biggest city in
Europe, probably the biggest in the world, and its highly mobile and
increasingly well-educated workforce was employed in a kaleidoscope
of commerce, industry, and services. Like Venice, London welcomed
not only a tidal wave of English migrants, but also a growing army of
foreigners—French, Germans, Jews, Irish, and blacks. Women—the wives
of landowners, country girls who worked in shops and crafts, and domestic

service—formed the majority of the population and brought about a feminization of public and private space. Londoners took full advantage of the religious and political freedoms that followed the Glorious Revolution of 1688, and an innovative cultural world burst on the European scene, famous for its newspapers and magazines, smart coffee-houses, convivial clubs, concerts, and cricket matches.

London raced ahead during the nineteenth century as a world port, imperial capital, and commercial and manufacturing centre, but by 1900 its ascendancy was challenged by other metropolitan cities—Paris and Berlin in Europe, New York, Chicago, and Tokyo beyond. In the later part of the twentieth century, losing much of its manufacturing and port activity, and bereft of a metropolitan government between 1985 and 2000, London had to fight hard to maintain its international ranking against a rising cohort of other global cities.

The last three decades of the twentieth century have seen the growing dynamism, influence, and affluence of cities in Northern Europe, among them, as our final example, Helsinki, the Finnish metropolis, located in the Eastern Baltic, with its coastal situation protected by an archipelago of small islands. A small town from the seventeenth century, Helsinki was established as the capital of the new archduchy of Finland under Russian rule after 1812. Planned in a classical Russian style, growth was slow until the late nineteenth century when the rapid expansion of the Finnish economy transformed Helsinki into a major port and industrial and financial centre for the Russian Empire. After 1917, the city became the capital of an independent state. The urban elite acted aggressively to introduce innovations from abroad, importing the best ideas and practices from the leading cities of Western Europe. In the later twentieth century, Helsinki grew rapidly as a headquarters for advanced technology, information industries, and services. With the country badly affected by the collapse of the Soviet Union in 1990, Helsinki quickly bounced back through new economic and cultural strategies. The city and its region became one of Europe's leading centres of growth in information and communication technologies. After the country joined the European Union in 1995, the city was populated by a growing number of international companies and foreign residents. Civic initiative and fiscal autonomy ensured heavy investment in urban infrastructure, world-class education, and specialist services (such as public libraries), creating a dynamic 'information society', which was also remarkable for its relatively high levels of social integration. On many international measures, greater Helsinki at the start of the twenty-first century, with 1.2 million people resident in the metropolitan area, was coherent, economically creative, and well governed. With Helsinki as its epicentre, Finland was ranked in 2003 as the most competitive economy in the world by the World Economic Forum, Davos. Nonetheless, given the competition from other cities in the region and beyond, Helsinki's leaders recognize that the city will constantly need to adapt, to innovate, to become more open and cosmopolitan, if it is to stay ahead.

I

Our case histories not only show the range of individual urban experiences, and the mix of economic, political, and other variables shaping them, but also highlight three of the wider realities of European urban development. One is the important continuity of urban settlements over a long period of time. From the Balkans to Iberia many cities and towns date back to the Roman Empire or before, while across much of Western Europe most urban communities were founded by the high Middle Ages. Only in outer Northern Europe and Eastern Europe do we find large numbers of urban centres established after 1500. Europe is thus a continent with a complex urban heritage. Secondly, our three city histories illustrate the powerful changes over time in the network of Europe's urban communities, with many of these changes having a geographical dimension. Indeed a major concern of this book is with the changing rank of different urban regions during the centuries from 400 to 2000 (see Figure 1.1). Certainly, as we shall see, there was no single European urban system as such until perhaps the end of our period.

Chapters 2–6 detail how European urbanization in the medieval era was led by the resurgence of cities in the Mediterranean countries, particularly in Italy and Iberia. Such cities—not just Venice but Cordoba, Florence, Naples, Pisa, and Barcelona—were often at the forefront of developing long-distance commerce and specialist industries, as well as inventing new services such as banking. They innovated in forms of urban government and created a strong sense of civic identity. Influenced by Byzantine and Islamic traditions, they generated a vibrant and distinctive cultural voice, not just as religious centres, but also through their ceremonies and

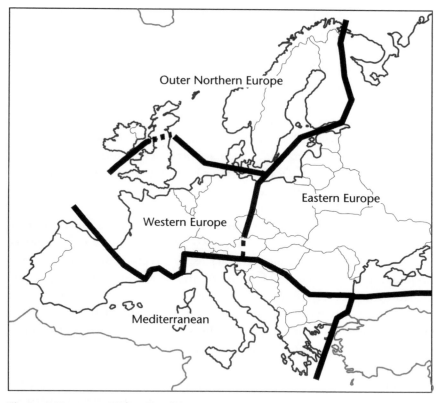

Fig. 1.1 European Urban Regions.
Basemap reproduced from http://www.hist-geo.co.uk

processions, through public art and civic histories, and through a distinctive architecture of city walls, churches, piazzas, and public and private buildings (such as looming tower houses—early skyscrapers). Despite the European contraction after the Black Death, the Mediterranean network retained its primacy.

Yet, as we will discover in Chapters 7–11, by the seventeenth century many Mediterranean cities were in relative decline, praised still for their architecture and artists, but no longer for their merchants or craftsmen. For all its spectacular success, London was only one of a cluster of West European cities that took over the Mediterranean mantle as centres of innovation, economic and social dynamism, and cultural efflorescence. For much of the sixteenth century, the cities and towns of the Southern

Netherlands under the leadership of Antwerp were at the cutting edge
of urban advances in finance, craft specialization, long-distance trade, and
consumer culture. After the Netherlands Revolt against Spain, it was the
turn of the cities of the new Dutch Republic to grow rich on the back of
the colonial trades, specialist textile, and consumer production (including
fine art and mapmaking), and financial services. But, within a generation
or so, Dutch cities were outshone by British ones. Here, London's growth
was echoed by regional capitals like Norwich and Newcastle, by new
industrial and commercial cities such as Birmingham and Liverpool, and,
as the classical Georgian facades of their high streets still disclose, by large
numbers of English country towns, enjoying unprecedented prosperity as
craft, commercial, and cultural hubs for their local areas.

Though the upheavals of the French Revolution gave a shock to urban
growth in Western Europe, by the 1850s the momentum of industrial
urbanization was advancing right across the region, and by the early
twentieth century more and more of the West European population
resided in towns. The factors behind this decisive transformation will be
discussed in Chapters 12–16, but there can be no doubt that in terms of
the conquest of mortality, large-scale heavy industry, the rise of retailing
and the service sector, governance, cultural vitality, and the remodelling of
the urban landscape—no longer dominated by city walls and churches but
by grandiose railway stations, brilliantly lit department stores, monumental
town halls, green boulevards and parks—the major cities of Western
Europe, from London to Berlin, became exciting laboratories and models
for the rest of urban Europe and beyond.

After 1900, urbanization in other European regions, led by the Nordic
countries, started to catch up. Even so, the urban ascendancy of Western
Europe remained unchallenged until after the Second World War. At
this time, social scientists pointed to an 'urban banana' of metropolitan
expansion stretching from Britain via the Low Countries, Northern France,
and Western Germany into Northern Italy. From the 1960s, however,
urban decentralization (as residents moved to the suburbs and beyond), and
the dramatic crisis in large-scale manufacturing affected many of the bigger
cities of the region, especially old industrial centres like Sheffield and Liège
and once great ports such as Liverpool and Marseille, a crisis that bred
oppressive levels of unemployment and social deprivation.

At the end of the twentieth century, many West European cities began
to recover, but their effortless superiority, their pre-eminence as urban

models, over the rest of Europe was lost for good. Increasingly, the new focus of urban growth and innovation moved away to outer Northern Europe. Growing urban prosperity has been notable in Ireland (Dublin and Cork), and the Nordic countries, where Helsinki's success has been flanked by that of Stockholm, Oslo, and Copenhagen, and by the achievements of regional centres such as Malmö, Oulu, and Tampere. In Chapters 12–16, we shall try and evaluate the significance of these advances and explore the factors behind them. However, since the late 1990s, a number of East European cities like Prague, Budapest, and Warsaw have enjoyed revived growth and vitality, while Moscow at the end of our period was the largest European city.

A third general point about the European urban order needs to be reiterated. While primate cities like Venice, London, and, most recently, Helsinki have been star performers in European urban development, many of Europe's townspeople from the medieval to modern period had their homes in much smaller places—in market towns and regional centres. In 1500, small towns with fewer than 2,000 inhabitants may have comprised over 90 per cent of all urban communities in Western and Northern Europe. Into the twentieth century, small towns were the places where many Europeans had their first experience of urban society. In this book we shall need to ask why small towns have been such a prominent feature of the European urban network (unlike elsewhere in the world) and what their impact has been on the urbanization process. Because of the limited scale of current research on small towns, the answers will often be incomplete; for some issues we simply do not know the facts. Hopefully, this book may stimulate greater research.

No less important, and better documented, are the larger regional centres like Norwich in East Anglia, Rouen in Normandy, Groningen in the northern Netherlands, or Gothenburg in southern Sweden. These have also shown striking resilience over time, often founded in the medieval period, stagnating at certain points, but usually recovering strongly, particularly in the late twentieth century. Across Europe, this evolving hierarchy of primate cities, regional centres, and market towns with their wide range of central place functions—as commercial, political, and cultural hubs for their hinterlands—constituted the spinal structure of the European urban network from the high Middle Ages.

However, the evolving urban order also included an important group of more specialist urban communities, among them ports, manufacturing towns, and resort towns, and we will need to ask when and why they emerged and what was special about them. Port cities, whether Mediterranean Genoa and Barcelona or Atlantic Rotterdam and Bordeaux, were clearly important in the expansion of specialist international trades, but we also need to look at their role as gateway cities, their polyglot communities stimulating new industries, and new forms of networking. Manufacturing centres—some older towns such as Leeds or Lille, others completely new places like Burslem or Seraing—emerged in Western Europe from the later eighteenth century, and massively reconfigured the urban landscape of the late nineteenth and early twentieth centuries. The rise and nature of these specialist manufacturing towns will be an important theme of later chapters. Another important urban type were the spa and seaside towns which surfaced in a few places like Spa, Bath, Brighton, and Ostend before 1800, and then multiplied along the Atlantic, Baltic, and, later, Mediterranean shores. Already, in the 1890s, Europe had approximately 400 seaside resorts and thereafter numbers soared. In the late twentieth century many specialist towns, whether heavy industry centres in the Ruhr or Poland, ports like Liverpool and Marseille, or seaside resorts such as Blackpool, Boulogne, and those on the Black Sea, seem to have found it more difficult to adapt to economic and social change than more conventional multi-functional towns. If this is true, how do we explain it?

II

To try and answer these and other questions about the dynamism of individual cities, about changing regional trends in urban growth, and about the typology of cities, this book will draw on the large and exciting increase of literature on the European city in all its forms which has appeared in recent times. While city chronicles and early town histories appear in the Middle Ages, urban history as an academic subject began in Germany during the nineteenth century, with scholars such as Carl von Savigny, Heinrich Brunner, and Ferdinand Tönnies writing on the institutional and communal history of cities. German influence spread to England where the legal historian F. W. Maitland promoted the subject, and, more importantly, to Belgium. Here, Henri Pirenne gave a new economic and international impetus to the study of urban development through his famous book *Medieval Cities: Their Origins and the Revival of Trade*

(1925). In the 1930s the French *Annales* school launched systematic research on the demographic, economic, and social development of communities. Initially, their interests were primarily rural, but in the decades after the Second World War French scholars penned a series of pioneering studies of early modern French cities—for instance, Pierre Goubert on Beauvais and Maurice Garden on Lyon—setting a new high standard for urban research. By the 1970s, British historians and other researchers were attacking the subject on two fronts: through work on the Victorian city led by H. J. Dyos and Asa Briggs and an interdisciplinary group of scholars (notably Brian Robson, Ray Pahl, and David Reeder); and through the study of the early modern town largely inspired by W. G. Hoskins and F. J. Fisher. The dynamic of British collaborative work led to the production of the *Cambridge Urban History of Britain* (2000), whose three volumes cover the period from 600 to the 1950s. However, the last years have seen a parallel advance of research activity in most European countries, evinced by the formation of national urban history societies, an upsurge of international projects and international meetings (such as the biennial conferences since 1992 of the European Association for Urban History), and an outpouring of books, journals, and articles. European cities have equally attracted multifaceted research by North American and Asian scholars.

In each country, the research community has usually had a different agenda of interests and different chronological priorities, often reflecting the specific character of national urban processes as well as institutional, academic, and other factors. Nonetheless, recognition is growing that the study of urban history in Europe shares a number of core, underlying, approaches and concerns. One is that urban history (unlike the local town biography) is concerned with seeing cities and towns in comparative perspective. Even in the study of a single community, we need to take into account its interaction with the wider urban network, whether regional, national, or transnational. Another belief is that the subject is interdisciplinary: the city is so complex an entity that it needs to draw on the concepts and methods of a wide range of disciplines—not only geography, sociology, and anthropology, but also archaeology, art history, architecture, and literary studies, as well as urban ecology.

Thematically, urban historians are concerned, above all, with three key relationships. The first is that *between* the urban community and the host society, whether represented by the hinterland, the nation-state, or the global economy, and the interactions and flows—economic, political, or environmental—that take place between them. A second relationship is that *between* cities; here one needs to think of communities in local urban networks, in the national urban hierarchy, or in the increasingly global systems of cities. The third relationship we need to understand is *intra-urban* and involves the interaction of the different functions and structures of the urban world: hence the way that population changes affect the economy, social problems impact on urban governance, power shapes cultural life, and how the complex spaces of the city—physical, social, meta-physical; built-up grey, open space green, and sometimes water-front blue—are constantly contested and reconfigured through an array of economic, political, and other processes.

It is from these perspectives that we can best understand what we mean by a city or town in Europe between the fifth century and the present day. Many varied definitions of the urban community or urbanization have been offered by scholars from different disciplines—from the narrowly demographic, to the institutional and communal, to a stress on spatial zoning. As we try to compare different urban levels from widely different geographical contexts over a long period of time, it would be simplistic to rely on a 'one club' approach, a single definitional prescription, with all the risks of semantic nominalism. Demographic definitions by themselves are particularly tricky, given that for much of the period up to the nineteenth century population statistics are at best indicative and population thresholds for urban communities deceptive. Here, a more sensible approach would be catholic and non-prescriptive, recognizing the multi-functionality of urban communities over time. On this basis, one might suggest that towns and cities usually—though not invariably—have a relatively dense concentration of population, specialist economic functions, complex social and political structures, a cultural influence extending beyond their boundaries, and a distinctive built environment. At the same time, as we have argued, towns are also defined by their close, fluid interaction with other towns, and with the wider economic and political society. In some sense, urban communities are identified and driven both by opportunity—greater job openings, the hope of more social mobility, more freedom of ideas and behaviour—and by risk, with high mortality for much of our period, greater economic and political instability, and the danger of destitution. Above all, the European city between 400 and 2000 was a dynamic phenomenon, adapting and responding to change, and any meaningful definition must take account of this.

III

At the core of this book is an attempt to describe and explain the successive advances (and retreats) of urbanization across Europe, from the collapse of the Roman Empire to the end of the twentieth century, looking at the urban momentum building slowly from the eighth century and reaching a climax in the decades before the Black Death; at the widespread downturn of the late Middle Ages, the urban revival of the sixteenth and early seventeenth centuries, and the subsequent stagnation or decline; at the renewed if selective urban growth before the French Revolution, that eventually led to the urban explosion of the second half of the nineteenth century; an expansion that continued, despite the disruptions of the two world wars, until the 1970s and 1980s, when once again stagnation and even de-urbanization returned to parts of Europe. In examining and explaining these oscillating trends, the analysis will focus on regional and national shifts, but also on the different levels of the urban hierarchy, the different types of town, identifying (where possible) the winners and losers.

Already, we have caught sight of some of the factors at work shaping the course of European urban history. Throughout the period, fierce competition fuelled the interaction between cities. As in the case of Venice, during the medieval period this erupted in naval wars and bloody battles between Italian city-states. Very different in its nature was the rivalry of metropolitan cities like London and Paris, that emerged in the age of Louis XIV and reached its height in the half-century before the First World War when the European capitals competed over public infrastructure, international exhibitions, fashion, department stores, hotels, cultural monuments, and much else. In this sense, the present-day struggle between European cities to be successful players in the global economy is nothing new. Along with inter-urban rivalry over the centuries has come strong emulation. In Chapter 6, we see how the Mediterranean cities copied one another during the eleventh and twelfth centuries in their new forms of civic government, while new agencies of poor relief spread quickly between European cities during the sixteenth century by the same process. In the modern era, ambitious municipal leaders at Helsinki and elsewhere sent their officials and experts to tour foreign cities to learn about the latest innovations in sewerage, utilities, and electric trams, just as there was a copycat adoption of urban privatization policies towards the end of the twentieth century.

Yet, as will be seen, if competition and emulation often dominate the urban agenda, cooperation is also a recurrent and necessary motif in inter-city relations. Already, in the Middle Ages, there were many city leagues in the Holy Roman Empire (one of the most important serving as the basis of the Swiss Confederation). In the seventeenth century, Dutch cities in Holland and Zeeland moved to develop an economic network of complementary industrial and commercial centres (the so-called Randstad), and this model of urban networking was also later adopted in the industrial regions of Britain and Germany. In 1913, the Union Internationale des Villes was founded in Ghent (the historian Henri Pirenne playing a key role), with the aim of promoting cooperation on a European and worldwide level, to help solve the problems caused by urbanization. In the late twentieth century, the creation of the European Union encouraged the formation of consortia of European cities to try to influence Commission policies, as well as to promote municipal best practice (see Chapter 16).

Migration is another variable that is essential for understanding the evolution of European cities since the Middle Ages. In almost all periods until the late twentieth century, immigration from the countryside, from the region or abroad, has been vital for the demographic growth of towns, given the way that plague epidemics and later outbreaks of smallpox, typhoid, and cholera, turned cities into killing fields. But we also need to explore the role of migration (including that of women and ethnic minorities) in economic innovation and for political and cultural renewal. High levels of immigration often pose severe challenges to urban society and government—exacerbating problems of poverty, housing, social differentiation, and public order. We will need to examine how these problems were managed, and also look at how newcomers sought to find a foothold in society, and how far they could convert physical into social mobility.

Heavy flows of newcomers raise the issue not simply of urban integration but also of urban identity, with problems of social cohesion and stability compounded by high mortality rates and recurrent economic crises. How in this environment did communities manage to create a sense of civic or communal identity? Already, in the early Middle Ages, city walls and ecclesiastical buildings had become defining features of the urban community, and over succeeding generations other public buildings such as townhalls, market houses, and in the nineteenth century art galleries, museums, and public libraries were used to buttress civic pride and urban status. But what were the other strategies for affirming civic identity and visibility? When did cities start to resort to inter-city competitions, festivals, and those other spectacles that we associate with contemporary urban marketing?

One proposition that will be examined in this book is that those European cities that were most successful in generating urban identity, as well as managing their economic and social problems, have been those with an effective level of municipal autonomy. Power is fundamental to understanding the difficult evolution of European urban communities from early times to the present day. In the Middle Ages, civic privileges were rather like teeth, only slowly extracted from rulers—usually when they needed urban support against the nobility. From the time of the Reformation, the expansion of early modern states increasingly encroached upon urban autonomy, but cities might negotiate economic and political benefits in return. Those cities that did best were often capital cities or residential towns under the sway of the state. How far did this trade-off between urban autonomy and civic authority continue into the modern era? To what extent did the rise of national governments in the late nineteenth century offer new opportunities for European municipalities to expand their activities? And what was the effect of the social welfare society after the Second World War on local autonomy? As will be discovered, throughout our period trends in urban governance varied between countries and cities. How crucial for urban success were the role of finance and the extent of municipal territory? The achievement of urban government also needs to be assessed in the context of urban elites, raising the question: do more open elites promote more innovative policies in cities?

This book will contend that from the high Middle Ages cities have been an essential driving force in European transformation. We need to investigate why cities became such crucibles for new ideas in banking, manufacturing, patterns of consumption, voluntary and leisure activity, radicalism, architecture, and the use of space and time. What were the factors contributing to the distinctive role of the European city as a creative milieu? How do we evaluate the contribution of migration and ethnicity, the relative openness of the social order, urban leadership, and other factors? The question of the creativity and innovativeness of the European city brings together many of the concerns of this study. It may also be one of the factors helping to define what is distinctive about the city in Europe compared to its counterparts in other parts of the world.

The central focus of this book is the European city and town in all their guises (here, because of the difficulty of hard and fast definition, the terms city and town are used more or less interchangeably), taking the urban continent west of Constantinople and including the Balkans and western Russia. At the same time, we must be aware of the recurrent effects of non-European influences: of the influence on medieval European urban society of Byzantine cities and the Islamic world; of the commercial effect of Asia in the eighteenth century and again in the late twentieth century; of the powerful economic, cultural, and political influence of North American cities after around 1900. Conversely, it is important to recognize the impact of European cities outside Europe from the sixteenth century onwards—shaping the development of colonial and neo-colonial cities in the Americas, Asia, and Australasia.

The book is organized in three parts: the first, on the period from the break-up of the Roman Empire to the end of the Middle Ages; the second, taking the story from the sixteenth to the start of the nineteenth century; the last, covering developments until 2000. Inevitably, such chronological caesurae are not watertight; themes and processes recur and spill over between the different parts of the book. Yet this kind of structure enables the analysis to focus on the temporal specificity of certain developments and that crucial interaction of key urban functions. In each part of the book, chapters are devoted to the pattern of urbanization, including regional variations and the experience of particular types of city; economic trends; social developments; cultural life and landscape; and governance. A concluding chapter will attempt to address some of the questions and issues raised in this introduction.

There is no ambition to provide an encyclopedia of European urban history, or to cover every part of the continent in the same detail (the current literature is heavily biased towards Western Europe, though that is starting to change). Rather, the objective is to try to understand the origins, processes, and nature of European urban development from the fifth century to the present times. At the start of the twenty-first century, when the apparently inexorable momentum of urban growth of Asia and Latin America raises questions about the future of the European city, the scale of its achievements can only be evaluated through a sustained historical analysis.

IV

One point is clear: the Europeans did not invent the city. Cities date from the mists of time, when definitions of what we mean by a town are often quite problematic. Nonetheless, it looks as if the first cities evolved in the Middle East as a result of advances in irrigation, agriculture, and trade. Sumerian cities like Eridu in present-day Iraq probably date from about 3200 BC, and there may have been several dozen city-states in southern Mesopotamia, some of them reaching 30–40,000 inhabitants and exercising significant religious, administrative, and commercial functions. Inter-urban warfare led to the decline of the Sumerian cities, and, by 1800 BC, they had been eclipsed by the rise of Babylon as the dominant centre of an extensive empire. On the Mediterranean coast, Phoenician port cities such as Acre, Beirut, Sidon, and Tyre enjoyed their most dynamic phase of evolution from 1200 BC–700 BC, marked by extensive commercial and cultural activity as well as some industrial production. Tyre, in particular, created a string of Phoenician colonies (the most important being Carthage) around the Mediterranean as far as Iberia.

After 1450 BC, cities also emerged in the Aegean (for example, Mycenae and Troy), linked to long-distance trade, and, by the eighth century BC, the Greeks too showed a strong preference for urban settlements: two centuries later the Greek city-states had emerged. Like the Phoenicians, the Greeks established a number of colonies in the Mediterranean region. How far these early ancient cities, many of them with important agrarian functions, were really urban remains uncertain: before the sixth century BC, many settlements might be described more accurately as proto-urban. Among the Greek city-states, most, apart from Athens, were relatively small in size, with a significant part of the population engaged in agriculture. But the cities acquired financial and commercial roles, developed craft sectors, and functioned as political and cultural centres—with cults, civic festivals, and inter-city competitions. By the fourth century BC, urbanization was accelerating in the Mediterranean region, town walls and grid pattern layouts became common, and an urban way of life emerged.

The proximity of Greek colonies, along with Phoenician influences, may well have helped shape Etruscan urbanization from 800 BC onwards in central and southern Italy, leading to the evolution of about a dozen city-states that possessed industrial crafts, cult sites, town walls, and agricultural territory. Though significant local proto-urban centres may already have existed by 1000 BC in Etruria, Latium, and Apulia, the impetus for change was strongest in Campania where Greek and Etruscan communities interacted.

The rise of Rome—urbanizing from the seventh and sixth centuries BC—led to the conquest of existing Etruscan and other cities in most of Italy by the third century BC, and the planting of many new urban centres which were populated by colonists (and rather later by army veterans). Roman Italy had more than 400 towns, and across the empire there were probably several thousand—constituting the primary level of civil administration. For the first time in European history a recognizable urban hierarchy was erected. The Romans identified distinct categories of city—*municipia, coloniae*, and *civitates*—depending on their political rights, but a functional hierarchy is also visible. The imperial capital, Rome, Europe's first truly primate city, had more than a million inhabitants at its height, a powerful consumer economy with a huge demand for foodstuffs (above 400,000 metric tons of grain, oil, and wine per year, much shipped from across the Mediterranean) and with 200 crafts and trades, a massive building industry employing around 15 per cent of adult males, a multitude of services, extensive political, religious and entertainment functions, a high level of imperial control, a heavily visible military presence (up to 31,000 troops under Severus), and an impressive array of urban infrastructure (including eleven great aqueducts). A major regional centre like Trier, serving as an imperial capital for the north-west of the empire, was endowed with an extensive imperial palace, circus, amphitheatre, and a wide array of other secular buildings, and an early cathedral built by Constantine. Lower down the hierarchy came middle-rank provincial cities with fewer monumental buildings, smaller populations, and more limited territories, and a myriad of lesser towns.

Yet, if there was a Roman urban system, it covered both more and less than Europe. While it reached out to incorporate many ancient cities in North Africa and the Middle East (including the great metropolis of Alexandria with perhaps a million inhabitants), large parts of the continent were left outside its orbit: outer Northern Europe from Ireland to Scotland and Scandinavia; and most of Eastern and Central Europe north of the Danube and east of the Rhine. Even in the provinces under Roman rule, the quality and nature of urbanization was highly variable. In the Mediterranean region, urban society reached an advanced level and there was a relatively dense network of larger and smaller towns. Here, cities often had complex economies, sustained by a greater or smaller manufacturing sector, local markets, and frequently longer-distance regional trade catering for elites. They were also important religious communities with temples, shrines, and other sacred places integrated into the urban infrastructure, alongside extensive civil buildings. A city like Pompeii near Naples, occupied by 20,000 inhabitants at its destruction in AD 67, had a rich tapestry of public buildings, including an elaborate basilica, seven temples and other religious sites, several theatres and public baths, a grand amphitheatre for many thousands of spectators, as well as a multiplicity of shops, markets, brothels, public laundries, and traders in wool and fish, while better-off citizens occupied elegantly decorated private dwellings with gardens and green space. Cities were notable for their civic pride and patriotism, with leading citizens making generous benefactions of public buildings, and there was a good deal of inter-city rivalry. Centralizing imperial rule was mediated by a measure of urban autonomy.

In other parts of the empire the urban culture was more shallow. In the West, Roman Britain had only twenty to twenty-four major towns, with another hundred minor settlements of varying degrees of urbanness. The development of towns was closely linked to military control and civil administration, as imperial government sought to maximize its exploitation of resources. Crafts were varied and widespread, even in small towns, but long-distance commerce was limited; and civic autonomy was never robust. The urban network was strongest in the lowland south, weakest in the uplands. Already, by the end of the third century AD, there are suggestions of urban failure, of the disintegration of infrastructure and urban functions. In Gaul, the south was Romanized largely by means of colonies planted by Caesar and Augustus, with earlier settlements boosted and transformed by new populations of army veterans; further north, there was less continuity with existing Celtic *oppida*. The biggest cities, those of a truly Roman type, were in the south either along the Mediterranean coast or in the Rhone Valley, with another cluster enjoying privileged status in the Rhineland led by Trier. But, elsewhere, cities were generally small-scale and urbanization levels low. Though never just parasitic settlements, their marketing and industrial functions were weak, and by the third century they were often reduced to being government or ecclesiastical centres. Even in the core areas of Roman rule, Gaul's cities were less wealthy and enjoyed less political influence than their Italian or Iberian counterparts. Further east, the organization of *civitates* to administer Roman rule occurred not long after the establishment of Roman provinces in the middle Danube. Initially, such towns were under the supervision of military officials and only later did they acquire political privileges with Hadrian's creation of twelve *municipia*. Roman rule was promoted by colonization from Italy and other parts of the empire, including Syria; but the urban elites show only limited Romanization, economic development was limited, and with the military and political dislocation of the later empire the cities were swept aside.

Although there is a long-running debate among ancient historians about this, it is arguable that the Roman city was a top-down creation by a powerful centralizing state: its structures, institutions, and even urban layout were broadly homogeneous. Its function was essentially administrative rather than economic: municipal elites were officials rather than businessmen. Within this framework, however, as we have seen, there was a good deal of regional variation in the quality and nature of Roman urbanization. Moreover, the urban system of the ancient world was always fluid. Like their predecessors, Roman cities often decayed, and needed to be refounded or relocated. City-history writing, with its stress on foundation myths or legends, sought to create a sense of urban continuity when discontinuity was frequently the norm. From the third and fourth centuries, the Roman Empire in the West was under intense pressure from military invasion by Germanic and other Central European tribes, demographic setbacks, and economic decline: the urban order likewise faced mounting crisis. The regional divergences of the Roman period not only influenced the way the urban order responded to this crisis—the core cities, mainly in the Mediterranean, usually surviving best, the others overwhelmed—but also, as we shall see, had a powerful and lasting impact on the shape of the post-Roman landscape of European towns.

PART
I

2

Urban Trends 400–1500

M ost of the foundations of the European urban order were laid in the medieval period, but the process was difficult and uneven, characterized by surges of growth (as between the eleventh and thirteenth centuries) and contraction (such as the late fourteenth and fifteenth centuries), by variations between different European regions, and by the instability of individual cities and towns. Towns disappeared. Not just embryonic trading centres like the emporia of the eighth and ninth centuries or small market towns badly affected by the late medieval de-urbanization, but even large cities such as Kiev, one of the leading European commercial centres, which the Tartars destroyed in 1240. Other places, not least ancient cities in Western Europe, had discontinuous development after the collapse of the Roman Empire, disappearing as cities for a time before resurfacing. This chapter looks first at the natural and man-made threats to European cities and then investigates the main phases of urban growth and decline before 1500.

I

Early urban communities faced many threats. As in developing countries nowadays, natural disasters could have a disproportionate effect. In the Mediterranean world, earthquakes were a special problem, with seismic activity badly affecting Cadiz in 881, Cordoba in 944 and 955, and a wide swathe of Andalusian towns in 1024. Seven communities in the kingdom of Naples lost half their populations after the earthquake of 1456. In other parts of Europe, where many towns had wooden houses, fire posed the greatest hazard. Conflagrations devastated Frankish towns in the sixth century, while great fires were common in Flemish and English towns during the high Middle Ages. In 1212, many hundreds of Londoners were trapped on London Bridge by a blaze that jumped the river and engulfed both ends of the crossing. Without even rudimentary fire services, a community might suffer repeated infernos. Devastating as they were, such disasters might have positive consequences. They provided opportunities for urban improvement, and, in the case of fire, cleansed the site of accumulations of debris and natural and human waste. Increasingly, cities introduced building regulations to reduce the risk of fire: for instance, in the Low Countries from the fourteenth century, town rulers required the construction of housing in brick and tile.

Epidemic disease represented another powerful threat to urban society. Outbreaks of smallpox or measles decimated cities in the late Roman era, while the pandemic of bubonic plague that broke out in 541 in Egypt and spread to Asia Minor, Italy, Iberia, Gaul, and elsewhere had a devastating effect, with renewed eruptions over the next two centuries. Around Clermont in the 570s, it was said 'the dead bodies were so numerous it was not even possible to count them'. The pandemic caused population decline, labour shortages, and trade recession. Though the period of large-scale urbanization from the eleventh century seems to have been largely free from major epidemics, the return of plague in the 1340s, and the recurrent outbreaks thereafter, played a key role in the urban contraction and economic instability of the late Middle Ages. As well as plague, malaria was common in Mediterranean cities, contributing, for example, to the decline of late medieval Pisa and other places on the Tuscan coast.

High mortality might also derive from another natural threat to the urban community—harvest failure. Inefficient agriculture and poor transport systems meant that many European cities were vulnerable to subsistence crises. In the famine that afflicted the Rus city of Novgorod in 1128, we hear that 'many died of hunger and corpses lay about in the streets'. The great crisis of 1315–17 affected large parts of Europe. In Dublin it was said 'many heads of families...became beggars and many perished', while at Tournai, Bruges, and Ypres in the Southern Netherlands starvation swept away one in ten of the inhabitants. Not only were death rates pushed up, but also poor harvests drastically affected consumption and so caused economic disruption, unemployment, and poverty. As we shall see, by the late Middle Ages town authorities were starting to construct civic granaries to store food reserves and these probably alleviated the worst effects of famine.

The most serious man-made threat to the European city in medieval times was war. While the invasions by Germanic and other Central European tribes into the late- and post-Roman Empire are now regarded by scholars as less disastrous for cities than was once thought, still they undoubtedly exacerbated existing economic difficulties. After the Muslim invasion of Iberia during the late seventh and eighth centuries, many cities quickly revived and flourished under Islamic rule. More ruinous were the Viking attacks on Western Europe during the ninth century, not least because the invaders had little prior experience of urban society. In the east, Moscow suffered six military assaults by the Tartars and Lithuanians between the twelfth and fifteenth centuries, and Polish towns were targeted by foreign forces of Mongols, Tartars, Teutonic knights, and Cossacks during the same period. The Ottoman advance into Europe in the fifteenth century involved not just the fall of Constantinople in 1453, but also the siege of many Balkan towns and the deportation eastward of some of their unlucky inhabitants.

Even so, medieval cities probably suffered as much from local warfare as from foreign invasion. While the German Holy Roman Emperors besieged and laid waste North Italian cities in the eleventh and twelfth centuries during the internecine conflict between the Papacy and the empire, such communities were hardly any better behaved when they fought one another over trade or territory: thus, Milan, Pisa, Florence, and other cities did their best to destroy and eradicate towns that opposed them. Later, medieval princes—increasingly armed with gunpowder and cannon—sought to hand out fierce punishment to recalcitrant towns. However, by then cities had stronger defences, more adapted to the new warfare, and greater resilience to ward off or limit the effects of military attack than in the earlier Middle Ages.

II

Turning now to examine the fortunes of European cities in the transition from Antiquity to the early Middle Ages, during the fourth to sixth centuries when the break-up of the Roman Empire in the West was underway, it is evident that cities suffered not only from natural disasters and military assault, but also from long-term economic and political crises. Sources for this period are fragmentary, fragile, and divergent: we have to rely on a mixture of documentary, archaeological, numismatic, and other material that is not always easy to reconcile. However, already in the third century, there is evidence that Roman towns in Gaul and Italy were losing population, that fortifications were being raised but covering a reduced area of the urban site, and that economic power was moving to the countryside. By the fourth and fifth centuries, a major shift was occurring from cities dominated by temples, forums, and amphitheatres to ones in which churches, episcopal palaces, and monasteries were the key features of the urban landscape.

Thus, the so-called barbarian invasions from the fourth century by Germanic and other tribes compounded a deteriorating urban situation. The crisis was most acute in those parts of the empire—in Britain and Western Europe—where, as we saw in the previous chapter, the Roman urban order was least robust. By the fifth century, the network of Roman towns in Britain had virtually disappeared: though urban sites probably remained, as at Canterbury, London, and York, they had ceased to function in any real urban sense. In Gaul and Germany, the eclipse may have been less total, but there was widespread abandonment of towns, as the aristocracy became embedded in the countryside. At best, a limited number of centres may have retained a shadowy half-life focused around their churches. Tours seems to have functioned mainly as a symbolic and religious centre without much urban life; Lyon, one of the principal cities of Gaul, was still inhabited by members of the Gallo-Roman aristocracy, but the city was in decline under Burgundian rule. Even so, cities in the south probably showed greater continuity, albeit at a relatively low level, than those further north where heavy taxation and plundering by the Frankish kings drove out many of the remaining residents of towns.

In the east, in the provinces south of the Danube, from which the Romans finally withdrew in 488, the old urban network broke down completely; here, churches failed to offer the minimal urban continuity found in other regions. Indeed, it is striking that most of the Hungarian episcopal sees set up in the tenth and eleventh centuries were not located at sites of Roman towns. Likewise, the Balkans and Dalmatia were over-run by the sixth century by Huns, Bulgars, and others, and only a few coastal towns were left to function under Byzantine control.

In the Mediterranean, cities displayed a higher survival rate, though usually on a lower scale of urbanity. No longer the imperial capital, Rome was sacked by the Goths and saw its population fall by a half between the fourth and sixth centuries, while its built-up area contracted sharply. Ravenna did better as the capital of the Ostrogothic king Theodoric and later as the centre of Byzantine power in Italy, though under Lombard rule from the eighth century the city's population declined and it was marginalized politically. Elsewhere, cities like Padua and Cremona were destroyed and other places saw their inhabitants moving outside the old city walls, though, overall, few Roman towns disappeared. A profound crisis, it has been argued, enveloped many Italian cities. Roads were abandoned, sewage systems collapsed, and there may have been a rustication of urban housing, with the spread of poor-quality wooden houses (churches alone were stone-built). Cities became poorer and even the idea of the classical city suffered eclipse, but the Lombards eventually adopted elements of Roman administration centred on towns, and the aristocracy in areas under Lombard and Byzantine rule remained overwhelmingly urban. Before 800, a number of cities like Lucca, Pisa, and Brescia had networks of prosperous landowning families.

The dialogue of continuity and change was not dissimilar in Iberia. Already, in the fourth century, a modest decline in urban prosperity had taken place, and the next century saw cities damaged by invaders (thus, Seville by the Vandals in the 420s). However, the Visigoths based their rule first in Barcelona and then from the mid-sixth century in Toledo, where the Court enjoyed a lively cultural scene, even though the urban population probably numbered just a few thousand. Buoyed up by an expansion of Mediterranean trade, a new wave of urbanization occurred from the late sixth century, and, in the south at least, aristocrats preferred to live in cities; even so, seventh-century Spanish cities were almost certainly poorer and less impressive than their Roman predecessors.

Divisions in the Visigothic kingdom opened the door to Arab invasion and conquest during the eighth century. But only limited urban disruption took place since Islamic rule was based on towns. An early description of Islamic Andalusia tells of it being 'composed of fortified towns' as well as castles and palaces. Well situated on sloping hills, Cordoba, capital of the caliphate, witnessed a massive growth of population (up to perhaps 400,000 in the tenth century), matched by large-scale public works and a flourishing city life: one Arab writer in the tenth century declared that it exceeded all other cities of the Muslim world in its 'population, extent of its territory, area of its markets, cleanliness of its inhabitants, mosques, ... baths and hostelries'. In both Spain and Portugal, the elites lived in cities that dominated decision-making. Not all older Roman towns survived: Mérida was suppressed for its opposition to Islamic rule. Yet, in general, Muslim control heralded an important renewal of the Iberian urban network, stimulated by expanding trade with North Africa, and new towns were established, including Murcia and Madrid. At the same time, the townscape was reconfigured in the Muslim city: old street patterns were abandoned, new public buildings—mosques, *souks* (markets) and *alcabala* (fortresses)—erected, and new private dwelling complexes, often quite elaborate with their own water supply, laid out.

If the centuries from the fourth to the seventh century were ones of urban retreat, more or less disastrous, across the Roman West, the eighth century saw the start of an urban revival, as the trend in Islamic Spain was mirrored, to a greater or lesser extent, elsewhere in Europe. In Sicily, Palermo, under Islamic sway from the eighth to ninth centuries, prospered as a great cosmopolitan port, while north Italian towns consolidated their position under Carolingian rule. Urbanization was boosted by demographic resurgence, agricultural and trade expansion, and greater political stability. Rome, under papal control, benefited from the upturn in pilgrimage traffic and its connection with the Emperor Charlemagne. As we noted in Chapter 1, Venice, a new settlement on the Adriatic, used privileges from the Byzantine emperor and an expanding fleet to build up a powerful stake in Levantine and Black Sea trade; by the ninth century, it had proclaimed itself an independent *civitas*, enhancing its status by stealing the relics of St Mark from Alexandria and installing them in the cathedral. Other cities revived as places of secular and ecclesiastical administration, attracting a growing number of landowners to live there. Poems were written in praise of the cityscapes of Milan and Verona, though some of the descriptions may have been idealistic (see Chapter 5).

Across the Alps, urban recovery was more selective. Commercial entrepots or emporia, almost all new towns like Hamwic, Quentovic, and Dorestad, appear from the seventh and eighth centuries in England and North-West Europe, engaged in river and sea traffic around the North Sea. Most were quite small, probably unfortified and located in places where it was easy to beach boats. Among the more important was Dorestad, in the Low Countries, with perhaps 1,000–2,000 inhabitants and a wide range of industrial and commercial activity. All the emporia seem to have enjoyed royal sanction as a way of promoting and taxing trade. Elsewhere in the region, urban growth was directly linked to the Church, or royal or aristocratic residence. At Metz, in Germany, the old Roman city revived as a royal centre after the sixth century, with fifteen known churches in the next century and forty-three in the eighth, but its population fluctuated, boosted at particular times by religious festivals or royal visits. Cologne also appears to have enjoyed considerable prosperity as a trading and episcopal centre on the Rhine, with some measure of Roman continuity. As well as the renewal of old Roman sites, new towns emerged in the Rhine Valley and its tributaries such as Duisburg, linked to a royal palace. Further east, Erfurt developed from a pre-Frankish fortress and royal abbey; by the ninth century it was trading with the Slavs.

One of the most important early medieval cities in Western Europe was Paris, the leading royal centre in North-West Gaul, which seems to have had numerous shops, churches, and artisans. From the eighth century, old episcopal cities like Tours were joined by a flurry of towns in western France linked to seigneurial castles such as Thouars (762), Loudun (799—800), and Amboise and Barbezieux (ninth century). In the Low Countries, the period saw the rise of new towns at Deventer, Tiel, Bruges, Antwerp, and Ghent, encouraged by growing land reclamation as well as demographic and economic expansion. In England, the urban renewal visible from the seventh century was (except for a few emporia like Hamwic near Southampton) associated with former Roman sites such as Canterbury, London, and York which had been adopted by bishops as their sees after the Roman mission and return of Christianity in 597. Population growth and trade revival steadily fuelled urban recovery. London's trading settlement, expanding after the mid-seventh century, had moved by the ninth century into the area of the old Roman walled city. By then, the country had a growing collection of markets engaged in local and regional trade and a number of these, quite often associated with royal or ecclesiastical estates, turned into towns. Thus, Northampton's initial growth from the eighth century was due in part to the large palace there, though by the tenth century signs of economic progress are evident with pottery production and a mint. Expanding royal administration under the English kings further encouraged the development of towns. By 1000, England may have had up to two hundred urban communities, including an increasing number of middle-rank and smaller market towns.

Viking attacks in the ninth century—as on Antwerp (836), Hamwic (837), London (839), Rouen (841), and Paris (besieged 885—6)—posed a serious threat to this nascent urban revival. The emporia, with their

minimal fortifications and exposed locations, were particularly vulnerable
to destruction and several, like Hamwic, Dorestad, and Quentovic, disappeared or were relocated. By contrast, the administrative and ecclesiastical
centres fared better, often aided by new fortifications. For example, Rouen,
its new defences sheltering many refugees from Viking-occupied areas, saw
its position consolidated as a major city after about 890. Moreover, the
Vikings soon urbanized. After the Danish host settled in eastern England
and established the Danelaw in 878, they adopted and developed older
urban centres. York became the capital of the Danelaw, and a series of
Viking kings resided there until their expulsion in 954; in the Midlands, the
principal towns—the Five Boroughs—expanded under Danish control.
A similar trend is visible in Normandy where the invaders were granted
control of the lower Seine settlements.

Outside the old areas of Roman rule, in Northern and Eastern Europe,
where there had been no earlier urban settlement, the development of
towns came at a snail's pace and was very localized. The first embryonic
urban centre in Sweden, Birka, was established in the ninth century and
had no more than 900 inhabitants, while early Hedeby in Denmark may
have sheltered 1,500. Such population figures are highly speculative. The
first Northern towns have been described as little more than 'congested
countryside' having few urban functions. By the tenth century, a number
of urban centres had emerged, often as a result of royal intervention. Thus,
in Sweden, Sigtuna on Lake Mälaren was probably a royal foundation in
about 980, to replace Birka. In Denmark and Norway, the new foundations
included Lund, Oslo, Bergen, and Trondheim. Along with growing royal
and Church support for towns, the expansion of trade—not least the rise of
the long-distance route through the Baltic and Russia to the east—played
its part in promoting urban growth (many of the new towns were on
the coast). In Ireland, the Viking attacks of the ninth century initially
involved plundering, but by the next generation the invaders had turned
into merchants and craftsmen and had set up the major port of Dublin (first
fortified in 950−1000) and other coastal havens at Wexford, Waterford,
Cork, and Limerick. Early Irish towns, it has been argued, may have served
as an inspiration for the development of towns in the Nordic countries.

In Eastern Europe progress was equally patchy and tardy. The small
number of towns by 1000 sprang mainly from the nascent long-distance
traffic through the Baltic. Among perhaps a score of urban centres across
Ancient Rus, Kiev developed from the ninth century into an important

fortified settlement, enjoying a key position on the Dnieper trade route to Byzantium, as well as developing as a political centre. Under Yaroslav the Wise (1016—54), the city saw a brilliant flowering of craftsmanship, architecture (St Sophia Cathedral), and literature. Also on the Baltic—Byzantine trade route was Novgorod, established by the Boyar lords about 930, which became the leading urban stronghold in northern Russia. Westward, we find early Slavic towns at Lübeck (from the ninth century), Wolin, and Gdansk (after the tenth century). Southward, Cracow was an important point in the Christianization of the region, supporting a bishopric after 969. In the Danube region, the rise of the Árpádians as kings of Hungary during the tenth century led to new episcopal sees, royal residences (like Esztergom), and county administrative centres that served as poles for groups of traders and foreigners. In Bohemia, Prague, the seat of the Premsyl dynasty from the ninth century, soon acquired an important role in European trade.

In sum, after the urban recession of the post-Roman era, the centuries from the eighth to the eleventh marked a time of urban renewal and development, as trade and lords created a mesh of cities and towns across Europe. The mesh was thickest in the Mediterranean world, weaker but still visible in Western Europe, and most tenuous in Northern and Eastern Europe, where there had been little or no previous urban experience. Despite these variations, an underpinning had been wrought for the sustained urbanization of the twelfth and thirteenth centuries—probably the most dynamic phase of urban take-off in Europe before the modern era.

III

The great wave of urban growth during the high Middle Ages was stimulated by widespread population increase and advances in agricultural output. Greater local and regional trade in foodstuffs and basic goods was complemented by rising demand for luxury products for the landed and elite classes. Such demand was supplied by the growing volume of long-distance trade, involving imports of silks and spices from the Middle and Far East, and textiles and other high-quality manufactured products from the Southern Netherlands and northern Italy. Urban growth also gained momentum from political changes: the advance of stronger states in France, England, and Northern Europe; the political rivalry between the popes and Holy Roman Emperors in Germany and Italy; and the Christian reconquest of Iberia.

Expansion of cities and towns was greatest in the Mediterranean world, particularly in Italy, building on the momentum achieved before 1000. Up to 1100, southern Italy had probably the greatest concentration of large cities in Europe. Rome may have housed about 35,000 inhabitants, Naples (under the Normans) perhaps 30,000, and Palermo over 50,000. From the twelfth century, however, urban leadership moved northward. In Tuscany and Lombardy, several dozen large and medium-size towns, most of Roman origin, extended their walls, diversified their economies, and, in the case of ports like Pisa, Genoa, and Venice, acquired extensive commercial networks in the eastern Mediterranean. Trading with the Levant, Sicily, and North Africa, Pisa trebled its population to about 38,000 in 1293; Florence, in 1200, had about 50,000 inhabitants and Milan about 90,000. Initially, the Church and landowners were the key economic actors but, after the twelfth century, cities enjoyed mounting mercantile prosperity, seconded by a growing range of specialist craft guilds and services. Economic diversification and new-found affluence were reflected, as we shall see in Chapter 6, by mounting civic self-confidence, as cities asserted their claim to political autonomy and representative institutions, and sought to control their hinterlands, whether on land or beyond the seas—hence Venice's growing necklace of colonial possessions included Dalmatia, islands in the Ionian Sea, Crete and various Aegean islands, and territory in the Peloponnese.

Cities were also heavily engaged in the reconquest of Islamic Spain. Already, from the ninth and tenth centuries, advances from the north by the Christian kings of Oviedo-Léon had involved both the resettlement of older cities and the establishment of new relay towns like Puente la Reina en route to Santiago de Compostela. Here, the shrine of St James (founded in the early ninth century) attracted a growing procession of European pilgrims, whose devotions helped to finance and promote the Christian march southward. By the twelfth and thirteenth centuries, parts of northern Spain saw intense urbanization, with the Castilian kings establishing many new towns. Meantime, a growing number of the Islamic cities of central Spain fell under Catholic control. Often some of the Muslim population remained, but Christian settlers of both sexes were attracted to such frontier towns by the offer of generous privileges and civic autonomy.

In Western Europe the dominant themes were, firstly, consolidation of the urban network and, secondly, urban colonization—with thousands of new towns, many of them small, being founded in the two centuries before the Black Death. Existing urban communities witnessed considerable expansion. Rhineland cities prospered from the overland trade via the Alps to northern Italy, while across the Southern Netherlands centres like Ghent, Bruges, Tournai, Cambrai, Arras, and Ypres benefited from the rising output of their industries, especially textiles, and growing trade in cloth and other goods to Germany, England, and (increasingly) to the Baltic and Italy. Under successful French kings, Paris saw its population rise to over 150,000 on the eve of the Black Death and there was an advance both of regional centres such as Toulouse and Bordeaux, and middle-rank towns like Besancon, communities that displayed a growing sense of identity by the thirteenth century. In eastern France, trade with Italy stimulated international fairs located in towns such as Lagny sur Marne and Troyes. In Provence, urban growth was led by Marseille and Arles (which extended its walls, and acquired new suburbs and monasteries), but by the thirteenth century all the towns of the province exhibited signs of expansion, including new ecclesiastical buildings.

Despite the disruption caused by the Norman Conquest in 1066, England's urban progress was no less remarkable. Finally becoming the capital of the Anglo-Norman kingdom after the 1230s, London increased its population from about 20,000 in 1100 to perhaps 80,000−100,000 in 1300. Regional centres, including Norwich, York, Bristol, and Newcastle, consolidated their position (Norwich's population may have reached over 20,000 in the early fourteenth century); so did middle-rank county towns and larger market communities. Equally striking was the multiplication of new towns, most of them small seigneurial market centres, founded by lay and ecclesiastical lords hoping to exploit buoyant local trade. Some planted settlements proved abortive, but by 1300 around 600 small market towns were functioning. A not untypical example was Stratford upon Avon, which was chartered and laid out by the Bishop of Worcester in 1196; within sixty years the population numbered over 1,000 and rose to 2,000 before the Black Death. New foundations sprang up in other countries too. In France, the military struggle between the French and English kings contributed to a rash of fortified *bastide* towns, planned or semi-planned, with the greatest number founded between 1250 and 1350. Four to five hundred were established, mainly across southern and south-west France, though not all survived. As well as their military function, places like Navarrenx, Mirepoix, and Cordes served to promote local trade and agriculture.

In such ways, the urban network in Western Europe evolved and was reinforced. Growth was accompanied by the acquisition of civic privileges, though only in the Low Countries and Germany were there real strides forward with regard to urban autonomy (see Chapter 6). In terms of acquiring a distinctive cultural identity, most West European cities and towns remained poor cousins of the Italian communes.

Expansion of West European cities and states supported urban colonization elsewhere. In the British Isles, the Anglo-Norman kings used the establishment of new towns in Ireland and Wales (often with settlers from England), to attempt to impose their control over those countries. After the Anglo-Norman invasion of Ireland, Henry II chartered a number of existing Hiberno-Norse towns such as Dublin, Waterford, Cork, and Limerick. As part of the settlement process, Anglo-Norman lords established a network of new towns in the east and south-east of the island, including Drogheda, Carlow, Kilkenny, Clonmell, and New Ross, though urbanization in the north had to wait until the early modern period. Similarly, in Wales a hundred towns and chartered boroughs were established by 1300, often fortified and situated near the coast. To the east of the Elbe, a similar process took place as the German emperors sanctioned a host of new towns as part of a sustained move to annexe and convert the Slavic lands; upwards of 1,500 new towns were established in the period 1200−1400. The old Slavic town of Lübeck was refounded in 1143 and 1157, and a series of Baltic port towns followed (for instance, Tallinn in 1248), all of them subject to the Lübeck law of municipal government. Inland cities were established or refounded (often with German settlers), their charters generally modelled on that of Magdeburg. Wroclaw, destroyed by the Mongols in 1241, was rebuilt and repopulated by German immigrants, the city getting a new charter under Magdeburg law. In all, perhaps 700−800 Magdeburg-law towns were founded—about 82 in Prussia and 445 in greater Poland (including the Ukraine and Belarus).

In Northern Europe, port towns flourished and multiplied. Benefiting from the general growth of population and the new political stability created by increased royal power, they also took advantage of technical improvements in shipping, the building of quays, and the vitality of the northern trade route from the Low Countries (via the Baltic) to the Black Sea, which was complemented by strong intra-regional and North Sea trade.

After the 1260s, the power of the Northern ports was buttressed by the emergence of the Hanseatic League, linking first communities of German merchants and then towns in Germany, the Baltic, and Western Europe—a network that stretched from Tallinn and Lübeck to Bruges and London. By comparison, inland towns in the area were slow to develop, linked to the limited advance of commercial agriculture. In Norway and Finland, few inland towns were established, though elsewhere districts like the Mälaren Valley in central Sweden and Skäne in the Danish kingdom saw greater urbanization due to royal intervention. Certainly, up to the fourteenth century it is difficult to speak of any urban hierarchy in the region.

In Eastern Europe, numerous small towns sprang up in Rus during the eleventh and twelfth centuries, mainly as agrarian centres, but most disappeared after the Mongol invasions of the thirteenth century. Another casualty was the international trade route through Novgorod to Kiev and the Black Sea, which came to an end when Kiev was destroyed by the hordes of Khan Batiya. This led to a reorientation of trade, in turn stimulating the expansion of towns on the Volga like Nizhnii Novgorod, trading to the east. At the same time, towns further north like Novgorod and Pskov increased their ties to the Hanse, while Moscow (established by 1147) became powerful as a political centre.

By the twelfth century, Poland had an urban hierarchy led by Cracow, the royal capital, along with several regional strongholds of 4–5,000 inhabitants, about ten middle-rank towns, and twenty small centres having less than 1,000 inhabitants but considerable local trade. There were always urban swings and roundabouts. The important city of Wolin declined, but its rival Szczecin flourished as an administrative town and port on the Baltic coast, joining the Hanseatic League in 1278. In Hungary, the urban network was restructured during the thirteenth century, in part due to the upturn of traffic on the Danube, and in part due to royal policy. New towns were chartered and several of them fortified, including Nagyszombat, Zagreb, and the Transylvanian Saxon towns; some already existing centres were also transformed to meet new needs, like Pozsony, Sopron, and Györ. On a high promontory overlooking the Danube, Buda was established by royal order after the Mongol invasion in the 1240s and soon attracted German, Jewish, and, later, Italian settlers. Smaller central place towns like Kassa and Bártfa also sprang up.

On the eve of the Black Death, at the start of the fourteenth century, the total urban population of Europe, boosted by the foundation of many new towns, may have reached 10–15 per cent, but this figure masked enormous disparities across the continent: from high levels, reaching perhaps 30–40 per cent in parts of northern Italy, Spain and the Southern Netherlands; possibly 15 per cent in France, western Germany, and England; but as low as 3 or 4 per cent in Northern and Eastern Europe. Because the data are very meagre, such figures are only speculative, but we are on surer ground in terms of the quality of urban life, which, as we shall see in later chapters, also varied greatly: from the relatively sophisticated economic, social, and cultural worlds of Italian, Spanish, and Flemish cities to the more spotty development in Western Europe as a whole, where urban institutions were heavily concentrated in the royal capitals and bigger cities; and the still rather tenuous urbanity of the north and east of Europe.

IV

After the 1340s, Europe's urban networks experienced severe shocks. The pandemic of bubonic plague that swept across Europe, with renewed outbreaks over the following decades and indeed centuries, caused a long-term decline of population (though in some places the downturn may already have started before the end of the thirteenth century). Demographic contraction reduced demand for foodstuffs, and depressed rents and prices, but increased the concentration of wealth. Thus, the volume of local and regional trade probably diminished, though demand for luxury products may have held up better. Demographic and economic problems were aggravated by warfare. In France and the Netherlands, the Hundred Years War between the English and French kings and the dukes of Burgundy disrupted trade, damaged towns, and imposed heavy military and financial burdens. In Germany and England, outbreaks of civil war caused local difficulty, and in the east the Ottoman advance, particularly after the fall of Constantinople, had significant demographic and economic implications.

In the late Middle Ages Europe's urban population contracted. How far there was a decline in urbanization rates is more debatable, because of the uncertainty about overall population levels, but it is possible some downturn occurred, at least during the fifteenth century. Certainly, the number of late medieval towns stagnated or fell, relatively few new towns being founded, and a number of the smaller market towns set up in the heyday of urban growth during the twelfth and thirteenth centuries falling by the wayside. The trends were broadly similar across the continent, affecting most regions. In the Mediterranean region, Catalan towns generally lost population, that of Barcelona slumping from 50,000 in 1340 to 20,000 in 1477, although Castilian towns may have fared somewhat better, helped by an increase in exports of wool, iron, and other products to Western Europe. In northern Italy, virtually all the cities suffered demographic setbacks: Florence's population dwindled by 80,000 after the Black Death, while that of middle-rank Pistoia slipped from about 11,000 in 1340 to 4,000 in 1401.

In Western Europe, towns suffered badly. In France, Albi shed over a half of its inhabitants, and Montpellier more than 80 per cent. Across Provence towns were hit by serious demographic losses, while a third of the houses in Paris were abandoned. English towns saw a similar downturn. Though the evidence is scrappy, London's population may have declined from 100,000 in the early fourteenth century to about 50,000 in 1500. The east coast port of Grimsby had about 2,000 inhabitants before the Black Death, but less than 900 by the end of the Middle Ages. On the other hand, towns in western England may have experienced less severe problems than those in the east, and in the Low Countries the picture was likewise mixed. Even if many towns suffered decline in the fourteenth century (as military conflict aggravated the disruption caused by pandemics), the next century saw greater variation. Towns in the north, like Amsterdam and Leiden, benefited from commercial expansion in the Baltic, the development of the fisheries, and the rise of linen and textile manufactures: by 1470, Holland was the most urbanized province in the Netherlands, 44 per cent of its population living in towns. In the south, the port and fair city of Antwerp grew in the later Middle Ages, along with small towns like Dendermonde, Aalst, and Oudenaarde, beneficiaries of commercial expansion and new specialist industries, but other places such as Bruges, Ypres, and Dixmunde stagnated or contracted. In fifteenth-century Germany, southern cities with transalpine trade connections to Italy, including Nuremberg, Ravensburg, and Augsburg, grew more strongly than those further north.

In Northern Europe, the general fall of population and decline of agriculture in Scandinavia led to the stagnation of the urban network with few new towns being established. Continuing long-distance trade with Germany and the Low Countries may have benefited larger ports like Bergen, Copenhagen, Malmö, and Kalmar, though smaller havens dependent on local traffic did worse. In Eastern Europe, overland trade routes were disrupted by wars and the Ottoman advance, but the impact of these (and plague) was variable. Bigger centres such as the Polish Court and commercial city of Cracow, the trade city of Wroclaw, and the imperial capital at Prague flourished, while Hungary witnessed a growth of *oppida* or markets in the Carpathian basin during the fourteenth and fifteenth centuries. In the Balkans, the Ottoman advance could be critical for towns, but the impact was not universally negative, and some Serbian towns recovered quickly from the occupation.

Indeed, despite the general demographic recession after the Black Death, the late medieval scenario was by no means pessimistic. As we will see in the next chapters, falling prices (and interest rates) and rising incomes for a good part of the surviving European population created new economic opportunities for towns. In a number of respects cities responded to the crisis through innovation: in manufacturing they cut costs by developing links with rural producers; in the service sector they expanded activities such as education (establishing schools and universities), hospitality (inns and taverns), and cultural tourism (supporting new ceremonies, public buildings, and cultural competitions to attract visitors); as for the environment, they took steps to improve water supply, street maintenance, and public hygiene. Reduced density of habitation may have contributed to an improved quality of urban life, including better housing, for ordinary citizens.

Overall, two points are clear. Firstly, there were winners and losers in the more competitive climate of the late Middle Ages, as leading urban centres generally improved their relative position and power at the expense of smaller or weaker ones. By 1500 about twenty-five European cities had 40,000 or more inhabitants, according to Paul Bairoch (see Table 2.1). These included a mixture of capital cities (for example, Paris, Prague, and London), provincial capitals (Rouen), trading cities (Florence, Cologne), and ports (Venice, Genoa, Malaga, Lisbon).

Predictably, the greatest number of major cities (see Figure 2.1) were in the Mediterranean region, with Western Europe (especially the Low Countries) next, and only one or two elsewhere. In Tuscany and the Lombard plain, Florence, Milan, Genoa, and Venice strengthened their grip over their hinterlands or *contados,* as well as their control over middle-rank and smaller subject towns, in this way creating dominant city-states. Competition between cities was strong. In Provence, the old leading centre of Arles was steadily eclipsed by the rise of Aix as the capital of the Count of Provence and by the growth of Avignon as a papal city. Across Europe,

Table 2.1. Leading European cities about 1500

Paris	225
Naples	125
Milan	100
Venice	100
Granada	70
Prague	70
Lisbon	65
Genoa	58
Florence	55
Palermo	55
Ghent	55
Rome	55
Bologna	50
London	50
Antwerp	50
Verona	50
Brescia	49
Cologne	45
Seville	45
Ferrara	42
Malaga	42
Valencia	40
Cremona	40
Rouen	40
Bruges	40
Nuremberg	38
Lyon	38
Cordoba	35
Tournai	35
Brussels	35

Source: Adapted from P. Bairoch et al., *La Population des Villes Européennes de 800 à 1850* (Geneva, 1988)

very small market towns often disappeared, their micro-scale making it difficult for them to adapt. However, as we have already noted, this was not invariably the case: a number of small towns in the Low Countries and elsewhere managed to manoeuvre through the economic shoals of the late Middle Ages with considerable success.

Secondly, by the fifteenth century, distinctive urban hierarchies are evident across several regions of Europe. Developments in northern Italy were matched by the delineation of a tiered urban network in Aragon and Castile. In France, the ascendancy of Paris as the capital of an

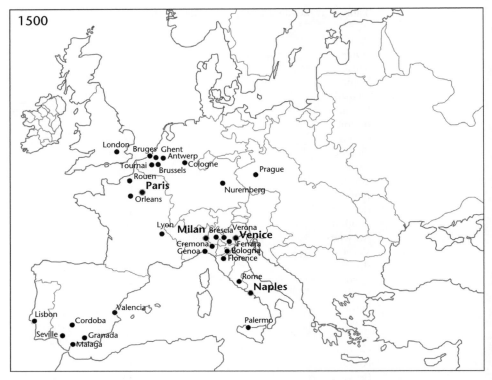

Fig. 2.1 Map of Leading European Cities about 1500. Cities in bold with over 100 000 inhabitants.
Population data adapted from Bairoch et al., *La Population des Villes Européennes de 800 à 1850* (Geneva, 1988). Basemap reproduced from *www.euratlas.com*, ©2003 Christos Nussli

expanding kingdom was complemented by the growing status of second-rank regional cities and middling towns—the 'bonnes villes'; and below them a third level of local small towns. A similar urban pyramid obtained in England where London, the only large city by European standards, stood head and shoulders above a half-dozen modestly sized regional cities scattered around the country—Newcastle, York, Norwich, Bristol, Exeter, Coventry, and possibly Chester; followed by several hundred smaller county and market towns. By contrast, in the Low Countries the network was more polycentric, embracing: a cluster of leading cities like Bruges, Ghent, Antwerp, and Brussels; major middle-rank cities, including a number in the Northern Netherlands (for instance, Amsterdam and Leiden); and a third level of populous lesser towns. In outer Northern Europe the urban network was more truncated: a few major cities, often ports or government centres, like Dublin, Edinburgh, Stockholm, or Copenhagen, towered over a handful of small regional towns, and very small ports and market towns. In Eastern Europe a cadre of larger cities, often administrative nodes like Prague, Cracow, Wroclaw, Magdeburg, Gdansk, and Moscow, was followed by a dozen or so middle-rank cities (for instance, Poznan, Buda, Kosice, and Bratislava), and a modest array of market centres. Strikingly, these broad hierarchic patterns were to endure, to a considerable extent, into the modern era.

If the vast majority of towns forming the new urban hierarchies of the late Middle Ages were multi-functional or spinal towns, a small minority of more specialist urban centres are visible. It has been argued that Italian cities like Venice or Florence, German imperial cities such as Augsburg, and Swiss cities, all with extensive dependent territories, formed a distinct, specialist category of city-state. But the argument is unproven. Apart from their hinterlands and high levels of political autonomy, such places conformed to wider patterns of urban typology. Arguably more important as specialist centres, were the great entrepôt cities that flourished in the high and late Middle Ages—ports like Lübeck, Bruges, Barcelona, Venice, and Genoa. Their large populations, often embracing foreigner communities, and their pivotal, gateway positions in long-distance continental and inter-continental trade, were matched by considerable levels of political independence and wealthy, often open and dynamic, mercantile elites. Another kind of distinctive specialist town visible by the late Middle Ages may have been the industrial town. A case can be made for Ghent as one of the world's first specialist manufacturing towns, since in 1356-8 over half of employment there was concentrated in textile-related occupations. Florence was another city with a high level of industrial employment, though across a greater range of trades. Both cities, however, had broader economic functions and neither was an industrial city *tout court*. Further examples may be found in small mining towns. From the thirteenth and fourteenth centuries, Hungary had several centres, including Selmecbánya and Besztercebánya, both chartered in 1255, and Körmöcbánya; their inhabitants comprised mainly German and Czech miners. Other mining towns included Goslar in the Harz mountains, which enjoyed a building boom after the re-opening of its ancient copper mines about 1460, Freiberg in Saxony, and Novo Brdo in Serbia. All were notable for their unstable populations of well-paid miners, their bursts of prosperity followed by decline, and their frontier-type social environment.

Another category of specialist town was the pilgrimage centre, or what might be termed the proto-tourist or leisure town. Here, the European prize went to Santiago de Compostela where the shrine of St James attracted many thousands of devout, penitential, and adventurous pilgrims who journeyed there via a complex network of sea routes and muddy trackways stretching across the continent: thus, during the early fifteenth century, over 15,000 English pilgrims may have visited the shrine. By comparison, Rome was less successful in this role, particularly after the Papacy moved to Avignon in the fourteenth century, followed by the Great Schism of 1378–1417; here, the upsurge of pilgrims came towards the end of the Middle Ages. Other minor pilgrimage centres like Chartres, Rouen, or Canterbury doubled as conventional regional or market towns.

Throughout this chapter, comparison has been made between the different European regions and by the late Middle Ages the distinctive urban character of these regions was clear. Around 1500 we have some tentative estimates of urbanization rates across Europe (see Table 2.2), though the median figures point to the variations within some regions.

In the Mediterranean region, important numbers of big cities dominated complex urban hierarchies and exhibited a striking economic and cultural dynamism, sustained, as we shall see, by long-distance trade, wealthy urban elites, and a high level of urban consciousness. Northern Italy was the most advanced urban area in Europe, having nine cities with 50,000 inhabitants or more by 1500. In Spain, the picture was broadly similar if less advanced: five cities had populations of 35,000 or above, though only one over 50,000. Portugese development was mainly on the coast, as in the Balkans where cities like Split and Dubrovnik were integrated

Table 2.2. European urbanization about 1500

	mean %	median %
Mediterranean	16.7	16.7
Western Europe	14.7	9.0
Outer Northern Europe	2.1	2.1
Eastern Europe	4.8	5.1

Source: Adapted from Bairoch et al., Population des Villes Européennes. Towns above 5,000 inhabitants

into long-distance Mediterranean commerce. In some measure, the Mediterranean region extended north of the Alps and cities with 'Mediterranean' features, including economic prosperity and strong civic identity, flourished in Provence and the Midi (for instance, Toulouse). Recent research has underlined the Italian parallels with the large, economically sophisticated and independently-minded cities of the Burgundian Netherlands like Ghent, Bruges, and Antwerp—parallels boosted by their important commercial exchange. Urbanization rates in the Netherlands may have vied with those in Italy.

In Western Europe as a whole, however, large cities were relatively few on the ground. Only a handful of communities had 50,000 or more inhabitants by 1500, and they were surrounded by a sea of middle-rank and small towns. Outside the Low Countries, economic activity was more localized in its character than in the Mediterranean region and civic autonomy was often menaced by the power of kings and nobility. In Northern Europe, newly urbanized from the ninth century, towns remained relatively few (mostly ports and capital cities), small (none over 35,000 in 1500), and mainly situated on the coast. Civic autonomy was generally exiguous, though the Hanseatic ports enjoyed greater freedom to negotiate their own affairs. The urban region of Eastern Europe was equally undeveloped, notable for a paucity of big urban centres (only Prague exceeding the 50,000 level). Life in many towns in Northern and Eastern Europe resembled that of the surrounding countryside.

So much then for the main phases of urban development in the Middle Ages. We have seen how European towns evolved from a half-life after the collapse of Roman rule to an increasingly complex, variegated, and resilient urban order by 1500. However, so far, we have only outlined the rattling skeleton of developments. Many issues that are fundamental to understanding how medieval cities and their citizens lived, such as the structure and diversification of the urban economy, social organization, the shaping of cultural life and the townscape, and the function and limits of urban governance, have only been touched upon. These key issues will be investigated in turn in the following chapters.

3
Economy 400–1500

I n the early Middle Ages evidence for the urban economy, as for towns in general, is sparse and fragmentary. We hear of merchants, but not of mercantile networks. There are references to shops in major cities, but it is not clear who their customers were. Towns where they existed had links to the countryside, as is implied in Gregory of Tours' comment that the town of Dijon was set 'in the centre of a pleasant plain. Its lands are fertile and so productive … a rich harvest soon follows', but it is not always sure whether markets functioned inside rather than outside towns. The same is true for craftsmen, given that many of their wealthy patrons resided in the countryside. More is known about the service sector of towns, since in the Mediterranean region and, to a lesser extent in Western Europe, they continued to function as ecclesiastical, administrative, and cultural hubs. Frequently, urban services and their maintenance must have constituted an important part of the surviving urban economy. Schools were significant in north Italian towns like Lucca in the seventh and eighth centuries, and tax collection may have generated dividends for urban residents.

It is only from the eighth century that we get a better view of the urban economy, as towns start to revive, though most information comes for the great era of economic expansion in the twelfth and thirteenth centuries, and the subsequent period of contraction during the late Middle Ages. Information is biased not just by period. We know more about the larger successful cities than about smaller towns that simply bumped along. Urban economies of the Mediterranean and West European regions have also attracted most attention, not least because only patchy documentation is available for the less developed cities and towns of Eastern and Northern Europe.

Allowing for such limitations, this chapter examines the economy of the medieval town from a thematic perspective, looking first at the fundamental relationship between town and hinterland, before moving on to consider trade, industry, the service sector, and finally institutional controls including guilds.

I

As seen above, the economic decline of the post-Roman and early medieval town was caused in part by an exodus of the elite classes to the countryside. When the ruling and landed classes came to town it was generally for short visits—for religious or royal festivities. Only in a minority of cities were there networks of prosperous landowning families resident in towns. By the tenth and eleventh centuries, however, the renewed interest of landowners in towns played a significant role in their revival. After 1000, minor nobles were moving back in considerable numbers into Italian cities, acquiring residence and power, and spending rural incomes on town houses, goods, and services. In Genoa, city leaders required the nobility of the *contado* to reside there, in order to keep an eye on them politically and also for the economic and fiscal dividends their presence brought. Elsewhere, town houses of lay and religious lords proliferated in capital cities after the twelfth century, as places to stay while attending the king or parliament, as sources of income, and as bases to purchase or store goods. By 1300, over forty abbots and bishops had town houses in London, and during the late medieval era growing numbers of town houses were owned by the nobility. In Vienna, at the end of the Middle Ages over a hundred nobles kept houses in the city. Other landowners, while preferring to live on their estates, established new towns or estates in towns, regarding them as a good way to profit from urban commercial expansion. In Northern and Eastern Europe urban properties were usually run as part of the landed estate.

Certainly, the relationship between town and countryside was fundamental to urban prosperity throughout the medieval and early modern periods. Rural produce fed urban populations, just as agrarian surpluses sold in town paid for the urban goods and services bought by consumers from the countryside. At Florence in the 1330s daily consumption of foodstuffs included, according to one report, 2,000 bushels of grain and 70,000 quarts of wine, while 40,000 cattle, 60,000 sheep and 30, 000 pigs were slaughtered annually to provision the city's inhabitants. Not all agricultural goods were imported from outside. Towns often had extensive areas of farm land within their limits, including commons and private farms and gardens. Such agricultural spaces may have declined in the high medieval period as population pressure rose, but they expanded again after the Black Death as populations waned. Farm stock was a noted feature of Frankish towns during the sixth century, and later in the period vineyards occupied an important part of the area of Provencal towns, while flocks of sheep grazed in the Low Country cities of Leuven and Antwerp. London's noble houses often had gardens where fruit and vegetables were grown commercially: thus, Robert, gardener to Henry de Lacy, Earl of Lincoln, cultivated vines, vegetables, hemp, green beans, and leeks at Holborn. In smaller towns, agricultural work constituted a significant part of urban employment: at Colchester, which had up to 4,000 inhabitants about 1300, two thirds of taxpayers were involved in agriculture, and substantial numbers went out to labour in the fields of the adjoining countryside. In late medieval Hungary, market towns were heavily involved in the specialist production of wine and livestock.

Nevertheless, accelerating urbanization from the eighth and ninth centuries was only made possible by increased agrarian imports from urban hinterlands and the growth of old and new markets and fairs to sell the produce. While fairs, frequently located in the countryside or outside towns, developed a growing role in longer-distance trade (see below), markets were primarily urban based. Bigger cities often had daily markets at a variety of sites within the walls, while small towns had at least one market a week (sometimes this preceded the existence of the town itself), often held (as in Finnish towns) on the main road, or else in a dedicated market place, commonly near the main church. At the market, peasants and townspeople jostled around open-air stalls to buy and sell food and livestock, as well as tools, basic wares, and locally brewed ale. Hinterlands of town markets varied greatly. In areas with a dense network of urban markets the trading hinterland might be quite localized, within walking distance—up to 10 kilometres. In less urbanized regions, the marketing zone could be much more extensive: in late medieval Hungary, for instance, market towns were often situated about 30 kilometres apart. Larger cities, with their major provisioning needs, depended on wide marketing zones. Already, by 1300, large north Italian cities relied on grain supplies from the south or abroad; London purchased grain from a radius of up to 80 kilometres; and the networks supplying livestock stretched further afield. By the fifteenth century, inhabitants of cities in the Low Countries and Western Germany ate meat supplied by the rise of pan-European cattle trades from the east and north. Even in the case of smaller towns, there are signs that their marketing hinterlands were expanding in the late Middle Ages.

In a world where, as we saw in Chapter 2, harvest failure could easily lead to famine as well as general economic disruption, civic magistrates were always concerned to protect their food supplies against scarcity. This concern was one of the factors driving the main Italian cities to extend and regulate their *contados*, or dependent hinterlands. Already, in the thirteenth century, Tuscan town councils elaborated policies of *divieto* (prohibition) as they closed their frontiers to the export of foodstuffs in times of scarcity. During the later Middle Ages, cities in the Low Countries tried to introduce similar policies. In 1438, the town of Dordrecht decreed that all grain in southern Holland should be sold in its markets within three days of harvesting; a few years later, the decree was extended to milk products. During the same period, Danish towns gained the right to force farmers to sell their produce in the urban marketplace. Such policies were widely adopted by European cities after 1500.

II

Agrarian commerce, whether local or regional, was the bread-and-butter trade for most medieval towns, but long-distance traffic in more specialist luxury wares was increasingly important by the ninth century, as shown by the rise of international trade routes to the Middle East and beyond. The Northern route, between the Low Countries, Baltic, and the East, involved the export of cloth, grain, timber, metal, and fish, and the import of spices, jewellery, cultural artefacts, and precious materials. As we saw in Chapter 2, the Mongol invasions of the thirteenth century pushed the main commerce further west and south, with growing trade down the Danube. At the same time, the network of Hanseatic ports, nascent from the late twelfth century, exploited the steady growth of the Nordic economies and technical advances (including the invention of the kogge ship) to develop a more westerly bulk trade between London and Bruges in the west, Bergen in the north, and Novgorod in the east, with the exchanges pivoting on Lübeck. Russian furs, wax, timber, and grain were exchanged for cloth and luxury goods from the Low Countries, with fish from the north traded everywhere. In ports like Bergen, Stockholm, Riga, and Tallinn, merchant communities, led by important groups of German traders, had their own guilds and other privileges. Significant differences existed between the ports: at London and Bruges the *kontore* were elaborate and merchants stayed for long periods (in London in an enclosed area; at Bruges the Steelyard dispersed through the city); whereas at Novgorod foreign residence was forbidden and Hanse merchants could only travel there once a year. Barter was common at Novgorod up to the fifteenth century: by contrast, at Bruges merchants traded on credit.

The Mediterranean trade route—to the Byzantine Empire, the Levant, and Egypt—had even wider ramifications. Here, the origins of the trade may date back to the fifth century or earlier, and by the eleventh century a clutch of Italian cities—Venice, Genoa, Pisa, and (on a smaller scale) Amalfi and Ancona—had secured privileged trading quarters (factories) in the main ports and cities in the Near East. Of the imported wares, spices, raw silk, and artefacts, an important share was sold to the wealthy elites in north Italian cities, but over time a growing volume was sold elsewhere. By the late thirteenth century, merchants from a great variety of Italian cities were engaged in this lucrative eastern trade, and Italian merchants even penetrated Persia and Asia. Outside Italy, Marseille and Montpellier developed commercial links with Egypt and Syria, and Barcelona grew swiftly from the twelfth century as a prominent commercial player. In the west, it competed hard with Genoa, strengthening its position through multilateral commerce with North Africa, Languedoc, and Sicily. After 1200, it moved into trade with the eastern Mediterranean, setting up a consulate at Alexandria, and acquired trading links with the Byzantine Empire, including Romania. Nor should we forget the southern cities of Islamic Spain: Malaga and Seville maintained a vigorous traffic with the eastern Mediterranean and North Africa in spices, foodstuffs, precious metals, and slaves—until they were overwhelmed by the Catholic reconquest. During the fifteenth century, many southern Spanish cities turned from overseas commerce to heavy involvement in the sheep, wool, and cattle trades.

Mediterranean trade also irrigated long-distance commerce beyond the Alps. Imported luxury goods from the Levant were re-exported from Venice and other north Italian cities overland to south German and Rhineland cities, and so onwards to the towns of the Southern Netherlands, which served as distribution hubs in North-West Europe. Barcelona likewise had important trading connections northwards to London and Bruges. After 1000 long-distance dealing was carried out at the growing number of international fairs. By the twelfth and thirteenth centuries, cycles of fairs had developed in Flanders (at Ypres, Lille, Bruges, and Torhout) and in Champagne (at Troyes, Provins, Lagny, and Bar sur Aube), which attracted traders and visitors from Flanders, Italy, England, Germany, and Spain and thrived as venues for the sale of silks, spices, and textiles, as well as for financial exchange. International fairs also functioned in eastern England—at Stamford, St Ives, and Boston; these brought merchants from the Low Countries and beyond to buy English wool. The decline of the Champagne fairs at the end of the thirteenth century allowed the rise of a new generation of international fairs at Besancon, Geneva, Lyon, and Medina del Campo. Alongside these international exchanges operated many national fairs (particularly important in Italy) and thousands of regional and local ones. Fairs were staged either outside the town walls or spread through the city, their temporary booths and stalls clogging the streets and churchyards, their foreign merchants, local traders, noisy entertainers, drink-sellers, and teeming crowds of visitors, including many sightseers up from the country, inundating the community for the days of the fair.

Expansion of long-distance trade fostered the rise of major trading firms in Tuscan cities, firms that had permanent partners, numerous branches, and diverse agents abroad: thus, the Cerchi and later the Bardi in Florence, the Riccardi in Lucca, and the Ammanti of Pistoia. International trade encouraged credit transactions and the bill of exchange had gained definitive format by the end of the thirteenth century. As already noted, the Champagne fairs became important as money markets, but merchant-banking networks spread from Italy to cities in Spain and the Low Countries. After the twelfth century, many Italian cities were already borrowing heavily from merchant banks, and in 1262 Venice established a permanent funded debt, an example which was soon followed by other Italian cities. From the following century, Italian merchant bankers were active in lending to the Papacy and other European rulers: Edward III, for instance, borrowed over 1.3 million gold florins from Italian financiers, mainly the Bardi and Peruzzi. International banking was underpinned by the growth of domestic banking as money-changing turned into deposit and transfer banking. Developing first at Genoa, banking of this type appeared later at Florence, Bologna, Piacenza, Barcelona, and Bruges: by the early fourteenth century, Florence had eighty banks.

Earlier writers like Henri Pirenne emphasized the function of long-distance commerce in the resurgence of European cities during the early and high Middle Ages. International trade was high profile and lucrative but always precarious, easily disrupted by warfare, conflict between princes, and the like. Even in the late Middle Ages, the volume of trade passing through major ports was relatively modest: for instance, in the mid-fifteenth century, London had only 450 vessel movements a year. More recent research has tended to stress the greater importance of local and regional commerce, particularly agrarian trade, which in volume terms was probably several hundred times greater than international commerce, and performed an undeniably crucial role not only in the growth of bigger urban centres, but also in the multiplying numbers of middle-rank and smaller market towns in medieval Europe.

III

Markets were the pivotal point of exchange between hinterlands and urban producers, not least because there town craftsmen sold their wares to peasants from the countryside. Initially, most of these urban products were basic wooden, metal, and ceramic wares, and in many small market towns trades remained limited in number—a couple of dozen or so, usually unspecialized—into the early modern period. More typical middle-rank towns might have several dozen trades. Common trades in medieval Oslo and Uppsala included bakers, belt-makers, crossbow-makers, tailors, joiners, goldsmiths, masons, shoemakers, smith, and tailors. However, after 1200, larger cities often had a wide array of occupations linked to greater urban affluence and the expansion of longer-distance trade. Spanish cities like Cordoba offered a wealth of sophisticated trades and specialist crafts, while high medieval London had at least 175 different occupations.

Food trades were always important. Bakers were numerous at York from the twelfth and thirteenth centuries; and butchers became increasingly prosperous in the late Middle Ages because of higher meat consumption. Small-scale ale brewing was a trade common in both town and countryside, but already in the later thirteenth century market towns of eastern England did a good trade selling better-quality ale to country customers. About the same time, German towns pioneered the infusion of hops to make cheaper, longer-lasting beer, and beer became a distinctly urban product in Western and Northern Europe. Already, in the mid-fourteenth century, Hamburg was producing about 25 million litres of beer a year, up to half for export (much to the Dutch market). By 1400, import substitution was under way and Dutch beer was flooding into Flemish and Brabantine towns; this in turn stimulated the growth of wholesale brewers in the Southern Netherlands, notably at Leuven. Brewers in southern England adopted the innovation soon after, and by 1500 large brewhouses were operating at London.

Construction was doubtless a key sector in the medieval town. Ecclesiastical building and, after the twelfth century, the erection of civic buildings in bigger towns often involved highly skilled, itinerant masons and glaziers. But the overwhelming mass of urban construction, mainly housebuilding, was done by local artisans, journeymen, and labourers who might also work on rural housing in the nearby countryside. By the thirteenth century, merchant houses were already quite elaborate, often several storeys high, but as living standards rose in late medieval towns, middle- and lower-class housing became more substantial and durable, and the industry probably employed more skilled workers.

Textiles became another core urban industry, developing mainly after 1000. By the twelfth and thirteenth centuries, West European cities such as Cologne, Ghent, St Omer, and Arras, and a number of Italian cities, had troops of inhabitants engaged in woollen-cloth manufacture. Certain localities began to specialize in high-quality output. At Florence, thousands of workers were employed in spinning, weaving, fulling, dyeing, and shearing: one contemporary account put the total figure at a third of the population but this was surely too high. At Pisa, the growth in textile output during the thirteenth century was due to an influx of skilled workers from the *contado* and Lombardy. In the Low Countries, Ghent was famous for its textiles: in 1356–8 over a quarter of its active population were weavers, 18 per cent fullers, and 12 per cent employed in related trades, while at the smaller town of Dendermonde 40 per cent of the 9,000 inhabitants was engaged in the manufacture of woollen cloth, using imported English wool.

During the late Middle Ages fluctuations in demand and trade disruption were compounded by fierce competition from rural producers, particularly at the cheaper end of the market—affecting not just textiles but many other urban products. Typically, the magistrates of the German town of

Freiburg im Breisgau complained how the trades there 'have markedly declined because all the trades and crafts in the countryside have increased'. In response, textile towns tried to specialize and move upmarket. Tuscan and Lombard towns, like those in Catalonia, shifted towards the greater output of fine cloths, as did towns of the Southern Netherlands such as Ghent, Ypres, and Bruges. In Holland, the fourteenth century marked the rise of the Leiden drapery, exporting luxury cloths to the Baltic region and Eastern Europe. Textile specialization became the rule. As one rhymer declared in the fifteenth century:

> In London fine scarlets,
> And at Malines vermilion cloths,
> And at Lincoln is the best white yarn,
> And at Ghent are good striped cloths,
> At Ypres are fine green and blue,
> At Reims are the good serges,
> And at Nevers are the good dyes
> Good grey cloths are at Montivilliers.

In some places, urban cloth manufacturers sought to reduce costs by teaming up with rural producers.

Other specialist industries included silk production. Silk was already well established in Islamic Spanish cities by the twelfth century: Almería, for instance, had 800 workshops devoted to silks and brocades. But there was growing competition from Italy. Palermo soon developed silk manufacture using Islamic weavers, and the industry spread to Lucca, where producers imported raw silk from the Byzantine Empire, Asia Minor, and beyond, and made costly cloths like damask, brocade, velvet, and cloth of gold and silver, as well as lighter silks for clothing—almost all for export across Europe. In the late Middle Ages, silk manufacture spread across northern Italy to Venice, Genoa, Bologna, and Florence: in the early fifteenth century, the last had up to fifty silk factories. Increased output reflected rising demand for high-quality products.

In the Southern Netherlands, specialization in high-quality luxury goods accelerated in the late medieval era as urban textile output suffered competition. In consequence, a number of places such as Oudenaarde, Alost, and Courtrai turned to the weaving of tapestries, many of which were exported. The same region also focused on the production of art works: thus, the painters guild at Bruges had 250 new members in the late fifteenth century, just as Ghent had a comparable number of painters, carvers, and glaziers after 1400. Altarpieces from Antwerp, Brussels, and Mechelen were exported to churches in north Germany, Poland, and Scandinavia. In northern Italy, too, art production on a commercial, workshop, basis was highly advanced (see Chapter 5). Here, and in the Low Countries, luxury manufacture meshed closely with the importance of the major cities as honey pots of international trade.

Improved urban living standards in the late medieval era (discussed in Chapter 4) may have encouraged the progress of more basic industries, such as the leather and tanning trades, hitherto largely rural based. From Poland westward, tanners and leather workers multiplied in European towns, developing a growing range of specialisms. In English cities, during the later fifteenth century leather trades ranked second, industrially, after textiles and clothing. At Cordoba, elaborately embossed and painted leather was made for wall decoration.

IV

Along with distribution and manufacturing, the service sector was another pillar of the medieval urban economy. Indeed, as we noted earlier, during the early Middle Ages towns were probably more significant as centres for ecclesiastical and administrative services, than for production or marketing. The role of Church and castle continued up to the tenth century, but, given the rapid expansion of urban trade and industry after 1000, the service sector may have diminished in relative importance. At Ghent, in the mid-fourteenth century the sector comprised only about 11 per cent of town occupations; at nearby Bruges, the comparable figure was about 14 per cent. From the twelfth and thirteenth centuries (as will be seen in Chapter 5) there was a flowering of new religious and quasi-religious bodies and services, including friaries, new religious orders, and hospitals, first in Mediterranean cities and then across Europe. During the high Middle Ages, Italian cities provided the forum for a rising number of professional men, led by notaries, linked to the expansion of trade and communal government. Bologna may have had 2,000 notaries at the end of the thirteenth century, Milan about 1,500, and Padua 600.

However, the main surge in urban services occurred in the late medieval period, partly in response to the problems of other economic sectors. Four main strands can be identified. Firstly, there was a continuing expansion of banking activity. Italian cities such as Florence and Venice remained influential, but a greater diffusion occurred north of the Alps in southern Germany, the Rhineland, and the Southern Netherlands. Such growth was encouraged by falling interest rates and the desperate need of European kings and princes to borrow to fund expensive wars. The financial relationship between rulers, city governments, merchants, and other leading citizens, became close. Already, before 1300, Bruges had inherited the financial role of the Champagne fairs and become prominent as a base for Italian banking firms. During the fourteenth century, the city accommodated a complex network of pawnbrokers (mostly foreign) who lent to rulers, nobility, and city governments, and offered other financial services associated with banking. Deposit-taking and small-scale lending and investment was provided by Bruges money-changers, though their numbers declined after 1400. As Bruges stagnated commercially in the later fifteenth century, Antwerp assumed its financial status. Banking was clearly a high-profile development, but it was always restricted to a small number of leading commercial cities.

A second, wider, trend was for the growth of professional services. In Italian cities, lawyers and notaries, already numerous earlier, acquired high civic office and status, because of their knowledge of humanist rhetoric as well as the law. Increasingly, legal practitioners crossed the Alps and multiplied in civic government in southern France. Arles had thirteen lawyers by 1270, Lyon thirty-three in 1363, and twice that number ten years later. By the fifteenth century, they were significant in small French towns in the Cevennes. Numbers of lawyers proliferated elsewhere too. Before the Black Death, Flemish towns recruited contingents of clerks and others trained in the law, and their influence advanced inexorably in the later Middle Ages. This growth of urban legal practitioners was connected to the institutionalization of municipal and state governments and the growing trend for citizens to resort to the courts to settle disputes. Also significant was the ability of better-off clients to hire legal advisers, and the attitude of magistrates, who saw the provision of legal services as a strategy to attract landed high spenders to town.

In a similar fashion, late medieval towns hosted an increase of medical services, mirroring urban concerns about health after the Black Death, as well as the greater spending power of townspeople. Already, by the early fourteenth century, Milan had over 180 medical men, while Florence in 1379 had about seventy doctors and sizeable groups were also found at

Venice and Pavia. In Spain, the picture was comparable: Barcelona, in the early fourteenth century, supported over sixty physicians and surgeons and more than eighty apothecaries, whilst Valencia had similar numbers at this time, and a full school of surgery in the fifteenth century. Italian towns began to hire physicians and surgeons to treat their citizens, and some were linked to the growing range of urban hospitals (discussed below). In English towns, elite medical practitioners enjoyed growing social status. Physicians and surgeons established their own guilds, both to distance themselves from other branches of the profession, but also to protect their superiority over herbalists and traditional practitioners (rural as well as urban), whose numbers were likewise on the rise.

A third development was the advance of towns as educational centres. Already, in the early Middle Ages, several Italian cities had important schools linked to cathedrals or monasteries, and by the eighth and ninth centuries we find schools and libraries in a number of West European cities, such as Tours, St Gall, Regensburg, Laon, and Auxerre—encouraged by Carolingian patronage. Further growth took place during the tenth and eleventh centuries when Chartres near Paris became a prominent scholastic centre. After the twelfth century, universities sprang up across Mediterranean and Western Europe: at Bologna (end of the twelfth century), Vicenza (1204), Paris, Montpellier, and Oxford (beginning of the thirteenth century), Cambridge (1209–25), Salamanca (before 1218–19), Padua, Naples, Vercelli, Toulouse, Orléans, and elsewhere. As for elementary schooling, the Florentine Villani claimed in 1338 that between eight and ten thousand boys and girls were at city schools learning to read and two thousand more were in higher schools. Though such claims were exaggerated, more and more children probably attended school both in Italian cities and also in the Low Countries.

Nonetheless, the breakthrough in urban education came during the later Middle Ages. Approximately fifty universities were established in European cities between 1340 and 1500. In Provence, universities were founded in most larger towns and a town without a new university and its assemblage of professors and students may well have suffered economically. In successful port cities like Venice and Dubrovnik magistrates could afford to reject the idea of university, fearful of student disorder, but other urban communities could not be so choosey. Meanwhile, municipal and privately endowed schools proliferated in European towns and by 1500 educational and information services were a recognized buttress of the urban economy.

Indicative of this was the rapid diffusion of the modern printing press, after its appearance at Mainz in 1439: by 1500, 236 European towns boasted a press.

A final strand in the growth of the service sector was retailing. Markets and fairs remained the principal channels of urban distribution long into the early modern period, and most shops in medieval towns combined production and retailing, craft workshops having boards or stalls outside, where the goods made indoors could be sold. However, permanent shops engaged in retailing, particularly of expensive wares, had existed in major cities by the twelfth century or earlier, and the number accelerated in the later Middle Ages. At Pisa, shops retailed the finest Florentine silks, while at Florence itself we hear of '83 shops of splendid and precious silks' between the Via di Maggio and San Martino. Even smaller towns, such as Prato, had numerous affluent shopkeepers in the fifteenth century. Though Italian cities were in the lead, clusters of goldsmiths, jewellers, mercers, apothecaries, and clothiers can also be found in Low Country and English towns by this time: London's Cheapside boasted fifty-two goldsmiths in the fifteenth century.

Arguably, the most successful and ubiquitous retail outlets in the late Middle Ages were drinking-houses, including elite taverns and inns and more popular alehouses or beer-shops, and cabarets, their growth driven by the profitability of the trade, and the strong demand for refreshment and other services from merchants, itinerants, and newcomers to town. Taverns selling wine were already well established in London by the early fourteenth century, and Milan may have had as many as a thousand. More popular ale-sellers increased in numbers in English towns during the fourteenth century, and by 1500 the trade was becoming more specialist and male-dominated. Particularly important in this period was the development of large inns or auberge-type establishments, with a growing range of economic functions, which were found in most parts of Europe. At Siena, in the fourteenth and fifteenth centuries, the main streets had many inns owned by wealthy men; at Prato, one inn kept by the di Cambio family over several generations had seventeen to twenty rooms and served customers and merchants from a medley of Italian cities. At Ghent and Bruges, innkeepers acted as brokers for their merchant customers at the cloth halls.

Traditionally, drinking-houses were linked to prostitutes and during the fourteenth and fifteenth centuries prostitution developed as a more organized service trade in town. Between 1350 and 1500, cities such as

Venice, Florence, Siena, Seville, Augsburg, Dijon, and London opened official brothels, both to discourage sexual crime and to promote urban income.

V

The growth of the tertiary sector in the late medieval town laid the foundations for the powerful take-off of urban services during the early modern period and after. At the same time, as we have seen, it was long-distance rather than local marketing, manufactures, or services that remained the most profitable if most risky economic sector until the end of the Middle Ages. Probably for these reasons it was one of the earliest areas of urban economic activity to become institutionalized and regulated. Though merchant guilds existed from the tenth century, by the twelfth century they had become widespread in larger and middle-rank towns, providing mercantile elites with mechanisms to regulate trade and to defend their commercial and political interests against princes and landlords, the Church, and craftsmen. In England, for instance, Canterbury and Dover had guilds by 1066 and within decades they are found in a wide variety of major and smaller towns, regulating trade. Kings and rulers had a growing interest in long-distance trade from the eighth century, anxious both to promote traffic and to boost their income from tolls and taxes. By the high Middle Ages, the counts of Champagne closely regulated the great international fairs in eastern France, while customs duties at English ports made a growing contribution to royal revenues after 1275.

In contrast, local trade was mainly controlled through municipal reg-ulation of markets. Venue, opening hours, prices, weights, and quality were already controlled by the twelfth and thirteenth centuries to create a level playing field for sellers and buyers and to prevent speculation. In the late Middle Ages, regulations may have become stricter as town markets competed with one another. In addition, as we noted above, growing attempts were made to interfere in the agrarian trade of the hinterland, which was paralleled by civic action against the rural textile industry. In the fourteenth century, for example, Ghent's civic militia invaded the ad-joining countryside and destroyed weaving equipment there. Other towns obtained bans on rural craft production.

From the thirteenth century, more and more craft guilds were organized in European cities to protect the interests of urban manufacturers. In 1287, Padua had over a dozen guilds for manufacturing crafts, and not long after we find 47 at Perugia, 73 at Florence, and 150 at Milan. In Provence, Marseille had 100 craft guilds by 1255, and Arles about 35. In the Low Countries, Leuven supported 25 craft guilds in the late thirteenth century, and Bruges 52. By 1400, well over 400 craft guilds had been established in the towns of the Southern Netherlands and over a hundred in the major cities of the north. Across the North Sea, Newcastle possessed a dozen craft guilds by the mid-fourteenth century and York 57 in 1415. In other regions they emerged later and were often fewer and less important. Thus, at Cracow and Lvov in Poland, only a minority of active inhabitants were members, while Stockholm's guilds needed royal permission to be established.

How far trade and craft guilds were protectionist, concerned to promote a narrow vision of their members' interests, and so serving as an obstacle to economic growth, remains a controversial question for this period as for later (see Chapter 8). Arguably, in the expansive economy of the high Middle Ages, guilds could afford to be more open and less restrictive than in the more unstable and competitive economic circumstances of the late Middle Ages. By the fifteenth century, there are widespread indications of greater restrictiveness. In Livonian towns, for instance, guilds became closed and membership compulsory. Within guilds, successful masters tightened their dominance. Another sign of a new rigidity was the growing trend to exclude women from guilds, or to reduce their participation, thereby undermining their position in key trades (see below Chapter 4).

At the same time, considerable variations are evident between towns not only in the incidence, membership, and effectiveness of guilds but also in their role in the economy, politics, and society. What we should not forget is that the particular configuration of guilds and guild policies in a community was caught up in the construction of a distinctive urban identity. That identity was as much cultural as economic, since the vitality of the guilds, like that of the wider spectrum of confraternities, owed much to their vital function in urban religious life (see Chapter 5). Even on the economic level, guilds were slow to move into the dynamic service sector during the late Middle Ages. Between 1400 and 1559, for instance, only 22 new guilds were founded for the service sector in Low Country towns, compared to 140 in the industrial sector.

VI

In conclusion, we can suggest that the urban economy before 1500 was hybrid. Leading cities, particularly those in the Mediterranean and Low Countries, exhibited advanced levels of sophistication in long-distance trade and finance; they also had a growing range of crafts, often increasingly specialist and smart, and, by the fifteenth century, an upsurge of professional, educational, and other services to complement the long-standing significance of religious ones. On the other hand, town economies, even those of the greatest cities, remained tied to the fortunes of the rural harvest, affecting both their supply of food and also what the rural population, the vast majority of European consumers, could afford to buy from town. Town economies might be strongly boosted when country landowners—grand tycoons by urban standards—took up residence in town and spent prodigiously, but depressed when they went elsewhere. Many of the jobs in the urban economy, particularly in smaller, more agrarian communities, were hardly different from those in the countryside. Here, urban production offered little added value. Moreover, the close, symbiotic relationship of town and countryside was sustained by a demographic constant: the great majority of town dwellers across Europe were recent migrants from the countryside, bringing their rural ways and customs, and even their pigs and other livestock to town. It is these migrants and the urban social order which they helped to create—and contest—which is the focus of Chapter 4.

4

Social Life 400–1500

In 1398, Alice Hermendesworth travelled the crowded highway to London to take up residence, probably as a servant girl, in the house of John de Bury in Old Fish Street, between St Paul's Cathedral and the River Thames. The young woman journeyed from her home in the Middlesex village of Harmondsworth, 25 kilometres to the west of the city. The move was helped by her older brother Robert, who the previous decade had become a monk of Westminster, outside the western walls of the city, and had risen to important office in the monastery. He paid her travel costs to London and a tailor to make her a dress with green cloth and a linen lining—more clothes were given to her later. In 1403 or 1404, Alice married a London baker, John Sakeville, and once again her generous brother bought her clothing for the wedding, gave her six capons for the feast, and a red box as a present. Alice was now settled in the English capital but she maintained her village links, getting her sister Matilda to collect money for her, perhaps from some property there.

In this chapter, we look first at the crucial role of migrants, like Alice, in urban society, then at the social structure and the position of marginal groups in the community, and finally at the ways the community sought to manage instability—through key structures like the family, neighbourhood, and community, as well as the growth of more formal controls.

I

Migrants, whether local movers like Alice or those coming from further afield, were the lifeblood of the medieval town. They not only revitalized the genetic pool, but powered the economy and society by bringing labour and consumers, as well as capital and know-how to the urban community. As we noted in Chapter 2, recurrent outbreaks of epidemic disease posed critical problems for European towns from the early medieval period onward. Even outside epidemic years, mortality levels in towns were generally high, especially in the bigger centres, due to environmental conditions. Heavy densities of population, cramped, overcrowded dwellings and problems of waste disposal and water supply all led to a high incidence of water-borne and other infections. Cemetery excavations and other sources indicate the prevalence of tuberculosis, leprosy, and Caffey's disease—characterized by bone and tissue swelling. Mortality was particularly high among children. In north Italian cities, during the early fifteenth century the mortality rate for children aged between one and five years was almost 18 per 100. Food shortages and malnutrition also contributed to mortality levels. At the same time, it is unlikely that the heavy death-rate in towns was offset by high birth-rates.

This demographic deficit meant that many bigger towns relied on substantial inflows of migrants to maintain their population. As we noted in Chapter 2, the decline of many towns in the post-Roman period was caused to a considerable extent by out-migration to the countryside, a process only reversed after the eighth century. The era of sustained urban expansion of the high Middle Ages depended on a heavy inflow of immigrants. At Pisa, in northern Italy, massive immigration occurred in the thirteenth century, with half the inhabitants of one parish new arrivals, while two thirds of the city's governing board after 1289 were men of rural origin; in the later Middle Ages, three-quarters of Vienna's city council were outsiders. Not surprisingly, given the close ties of towns with their hinterlands, the largest share of migrants came from the neighbouring countryside. At Arles, in the 1270s, 60 per cent of the newcomers to town had originated in Provence, 9 per cent from the wider region of Saone and Rhone, and only 19 per cent from elsewhere. This was a time when deteriorating rural conditions, including population pressure and agricultural difficulty, were pushing country people into town. In Ancient Rus, many of the movers to towns were fugitive slaves from the countryside. However, urban pull factors also played their part in attracting outsiders: cheaper living costs, greater personal freedom or tenurial rights, and more job opportunities. Although poorer country people doubtless represented the majority of new arrivals from the local countryside, other groups also travelled to town: craftsmen; professional men (two thirds of Pisa's notaries had a *contado* background); and landowners, increasingly numerous in Mediterranean cities after 1000.

Migration from the wider region and other towns could be significant too. In the thirteenth century, the influx of Lombard weavers into Tuscan towns gave an important stimulus to the growth of the cloth industry there. Professional men also moved between towns. In the thirteenth and fourteenth centuries, Venetians served as *podestàs*, or chief magistrates, in numerous cities of northern Italy—for example, at Padua, Treviso, Milan, Vicenza, and Ferrara—disseminating administrative and political ideas. During the fifteenth century, an influx of Tuscan merchant bankers to Rome helped transform papal government and the Roman economy and society.

Though native mobility predominated, there were also significant flows of ethnic migrants to medieval cities, not least to the larger port cities. Italian merchants who came to Barcelona in the early twelfth century brought expertise and contacts that helped to boost that city's commercial fortunes. Italian ports in their turn benefited from large and important groups of foreigners. In Northern Europe, German, English, Dutch, and other foreign merchants were prominent in the main ports: German merchants formed powerful communities with their own guilds and had extensive influence on the political and cultural life of Baltic cities. At Bruges, Italian merchants were organized according to 'nations' of Florentines, Genoese, Lucchesese and Venetians. Venice was probably the most multi-ethnic of Europe's great cities, but minorities were not confined to ports. Jews were numerous in the main European cities from the tenth century; already at this time a Jewish merchant from Mainz accompanied a diplomatic mission from the Frankish king to the Caliph of Cordoba. By the twelfth century, Jews were located in twenty major towns in England, and similar communities were found in many continental cities. As we saw in Chapter 3, Jews became heavily involved in money-lending to princes. Though largely expelled from the cities of Western Europe during the thirteenth and early fourteenth centuries, they maintained an important presence in Mediterranean and Eastern Europe. Jews, along with Germans, Flemings, Armenians, and Muslims, formed notable groups in Hungarian towns, while Balkan cities at the close of the Middle Ages welcomed Jewish residents along with Muslim settlers and gypsies.

Just as the social and ethnic composition of urban immigration was often significant, so was the changing gender balance. As the reconquest of Spain's Islamic towns swept southward during the twelfth century, the need for Christian colonists attracted large numbers of women who gained special legal rights and social advancement. Elsewhere, the industrial expansion of towns during the high Middle Ages probably encouraged a predominance of male movers to town. However, by the fifteenth century, shortages of labour caused by the plague and a growth of urban services seem to have brought about greater female immigration, with women (as at York in northern England) moving to the city from declining rural settlements.

Cities and towns in the Middle Ages (and later) churned migrants at high rates. Many newcomers left after short stays, either unable to gain a foothold in the community or taking back money or skills to their home in the countryside. Emigration could have as much impact as immigration. Like cities in the post-Roman era, late medieval towns such as Florence suffered from an exodus of skilled workers who took their craft secrets with them. However, those newcomers who stayed in the city played a vital part in shaping its social world. As we saw in the case of Alice Hermendesworth, they brought and often kept close links to the countryside. Incoming lords built their houses in the city in districts closest to their rural estates, while ordinary migrants clustered together spatially: for example, migrants to medieval Genoa from the same village often took up residence in the same urban neighbourhood. Migrant networks and alliances infiltrated the commercial community and civic politics. However, in general, newcomers reinforced rather than transformed the existing social structure of towns, translating their prior social standing, whether of the elite or labouring class, to their new community. The result was a paradox. While towns experienced high levels of physical mobility, social mobility remained much more restricted and only relatively small numbers of new arrivals—whether through exceptional talent, fortunate marriage, or the patronage of a town worthy—advanced very far or fast up the urban social hierarchy. If anything, downward social mobility was more common, due to bad luck, poor health, or business failure.

II

Medieval urban society was dominated by small elite groups. At Besançon, in the thirteenth century, they comprised only about 5 per cent of the population; two centuries later the comparable figure at Coventry in the English Midlands may have been even lower. But, if the urban leading group was almost invariably small, its composition and identity changed a good deal during the Middle Ages. In the earlier period when many towns were dependent on the Church or secular rulers, the principal townsmen were often their representatives and officials. At Pavia, in the late tenth century, *iudices* or *notari sacri palatti* were affirmed as masters of the city; at Cologne, the archbishop's *ministeriales*—sometimes also wealthy burghers—ruled the community up to the twelfth century. With the expansion of towns after 1000, local landowners established a prominent position in Mediterranean cities. Often they had a military role defending the community against attack, or (as in Spain) launching raids against Muslim cities. Catholic Segovia, for instance, was dominated by *caballeros* holding office and enjoying exemption from taxes.

By the thirteenth century, however, the ascendancy of landowners was eclipsed, at least in bigger communities, by the rise of merchant patricians. This was particularly notable in north Italian cities, but similar trends can be observed further north. The towns of Languedoc and Provence were formerly run by landed knights but after 1200 they were superseded by businessmen. At Cologne the city came to be ruled by a core of forty families, mostly engaged in trade; at Toulouse, Arras, and London similar powerful merchant groups emerged. Commercial elites were dominant in many West European cities until the end of the medieval era. At the same time, landed ties remained significant. Toulouse's new mercantile leadership included the offspring of landowners, the patricians of Mainz intermarried with the children of the lesser nobles of the region, and the new merchant rulers of Genoa, Marseille, Arles, and many other towns invested in rural property and agriculture.

Patrician groups varied greatly in power and were rarely stable. Considerable turnover of families was caused by high mortality, economic setbacks, and out-migration. Within some towns, political and jurisdictional divisions created a mosaic of different leading groups. Patrician ranks in north Italian cities during the twelfth and thirteenth centuries were bitterly split between factions supporting either the German Emperor or the Pope. Factionalism and conflict within elites persisted into the late Middle Ages (see Chapter 6). On the other hand, enhanced coherence and a greater sense of elite identity seem to have emerged by the fifteenth century. One reason was that urban elites were always defined by their relationship to power, and in the period after the Black Death not only did many cities and towns gain greater political autonomy, but also their civic elites were increasingly recognized by rulers who incorporated them into the processes of governance. No less important, as we shall see below, civic institutionalization increased and town leaders often monopolized administrative, political, and judicial offices in the community.

By the late Middle Ages, urban elites were further bolstered by their growing affluence. One fifteenth-century Florentine merchant adjured his colleagues: 'money is all the help you have. It is your defence, honour, profit and adornment'. Merchants, particularly those engaged in long-distance trade, appear to have flourished, despite the fluctuations of the late medieval economy. With affluence came greater family stability and the prospect of intermarriage with other elite families. At Dubrovnik, on the Adriatic coast, patrician endogamy became the rule: after 1462, marriage of a daughter outside the ruling class ended the family's noble status. Sons of patricians went to the growing number of schools and universities in European towns, and in Italian cities they were influenced by humanist notions of civic pride and responsibility. Elsewhere, however, elite identity was defined in other ways: German patricians often adopted a knightly lifestyle and in cities like Frankfurt am Main, Augsburg, and Lübeck reinforced solidarity through membership of social clubs or circles, which also helped settle disputes. Elite fraternities in English towns may have had a similar role. No less important, upper-class cohesion was forged by external pressures associated with growing middle- and lower-rank consciousness and organization in towns.

Farmers probably comprised the principal middling group in most towns up to the twelfth century, and held a significant position in smaller towns for much longer. Nonetheless, as we saw in Chapter 3, after about 1000, skilled craftsmen multiplied in towns, producing goods for the local hinterland and progressively for wider markets. In advanced manufacturing cities such as Florence or Ghent, manufacturing high-quality products for long-distance trade, craft masters numbered several thousand, and in larger regional centres possibly several hundred. Masters varied greatly in skill, wealth, and status, from the wealthy and prestigious pewterers and goldsmiths to poorer members of basic textile and building trades, but in the case of the better off their households might be of a substantial size, including several apprentices and journeymen. The social standing of such traders and craftsmen was underpinned by their significant influence in the urban neighbourhood or *quartier*, acting sometimes as minor officials, while, as burgesses and freemen, they might enjoy considerable economic and political rights in the urban community. In Picardy's towns, the status of such 'petits bourgeois' was formally recognized by the early fourteenth century. Crafts were more and more organized through guilds by the twelfth century (see Chapter 3) and during the next two centuries presented a recurrent political challenge to ruling elites.

Craftsmen may have improved their urban status in other ways. From the thirteenth century, Florentine artisans were frequently able to read and write, and by the 1500s this was increasingly the case among skilled workers in other principal cities of Southern and Western Europe. In the later medieval period, housing for masters and their families became more spacious and better constructed, and rooms displayed a small but growing number of consumer goods. Yet the economic position of middling townsmen was always precarious, vulnerable to trade reverses or sickness that might trigger business failure and so drive the craftsman and his family into destitution. The economic instability of the late Middle Ages may have aggravated competition and conflict between crafts, and craft guilds often lost out to merchant rule.

The bottom end of the social urban order comprised recent migrants from the countryside, day labourers, journeymen in poor trades, as well as the sick and unemployable poor, and formed around 60–70 per cent of the urban population during the expansive period of the twelfth and thirteenth centuries. Having few skills or assets of their own, they often lived in small households in shacks or sheds, not infrequently in slums outside the town walls. Few became burgesses of the town and so were excluded from the official political and economic life of the community. Predictably, they suffered badly both from short-term crises, such as harvest failure or trade disruption, and longer-term trends, like rising food prices or the growth of competition from rural workers. In consequence, many lower-class townspeople hung on the precipice of poverty. At Florence, before the Black Death, a skilled mason could just about make ends meet, but the unskilled labourer could never cover more than half his expenses. Frequently, they tumbled into destitution.

Stray references to the urban poor appear in the early medieval period, but the main evidence dates from the expansion of cities, with municipal government and urban record-keeping after the eleventh and twelfth centuries. There are suggestions that the proportion of poor was still relatively small in the twelfth century, but numbers almost certainly multiplied in the period before the Black Death, as the population surge outran food supply and demand for labour. Of the inhabitants of Carcassonne in 1304, a third were too poor to pay taxes, while the city of Siena counted 15,000 poor and indigent about this time. During the 1320s, the streets of Ghent and other Low Country towns were reportedly swamped with poor.

Demographic decline, following the Black Death, may have led to some improvement in the real wages of labourers and servants, as food prices, rents, and other costs abated. However, poverty levels were boosted by the demographic and economic disruption spawned by plague outbreaks, military conflict, and heavy taxation to pay for wars, and increased pressure on urban employment from rural competition (at Florence, for instance, wages fell sharply in the late fourteenth century). Poverty became a perpetual problem for many cities. During the English occupation of Paris, in 1420, one diarist recorded 'you might see all over [the city] ... here ten, there 20 or 30 children ... dying of hunger and of cold on the rubbish heaps'. At Dijon, in eastern France, over half of all households in the 1430s were classed as miserable and more than a quarter needed relief. In many Brabantine towns, the number of poor getting relief rose markedly between 1437 and 1480. Towards the end of the fifteenth century, Florence seemed overwhelmed by the suffering of the indigent. The shopkeeper Luca Landucci noted in early 1497, 'during all this time, men, women and children were collapsing from hunger, some dying from it, and many died in hospital from starvation'.

III

Beside the marginal or excluded lower orders, other social groups enjoyed a problematic status in urban society. The most important category consisted of women, in some instances the majority of townspeople. Across Europe, women suffered extensive disabilities. This was acutely the case in Italy, where under Lombard law public civic ceremonies and guild offices were closed to them. In general, the position of a married woman was defined by the status (or lack of it) of her husband. Wives of the urban elite might enjoy considerable autonomy, though few went so far as Margery Kempe (born 1373) from the East Anglian port of Lynn. Daughter of John Brunham, five times mayor of Lynn, and married to John Kempe, another member of the civic elite, Margery launched a number of business enterprises, including a brewery and corn-mill, both unsuccessful, and joined the prestigious

Guild of the Holy Trinity, before turning her back on her husband and espousing religious devotion, making pilgrimages to Rome, Jerusalem, and Santiago. Despite her elite status, she was criticized by neighbours and townspeople for her business ambitions, marital behaviour, and religious forwardness.

Middle-rank women might be involved in their husband's trade but in a number of cities could engage in business, including local and long-distance trade, on their own account. During the late Middle Ages, the social position of better-off townswomen seems to have been in flux. Greater public recognition may have come from their participation in fraternities and other religious activities (in Italian cities piety was feminized with the elevation of various female saints), but there seems to have been a trend against women being involved in business activity—reflected perhaps in the attitude to Margery Kempe. From the fourteenth century, guild restrictions at Frankfurt were tightened against women. At York, earlier guild ordinances allowed women to work in trades like weaving, but fifteenth-century regulations became more restrictive. In the Northern Netherlands, female inhabitants of Leiden were steadily excluded from a wide range of trades. Not that the trend was universal. At Cologne, women had access to prestigious and skilled activities, even able to engage in long-distance ventures and make their own deals. Throughout the period, life cycle was a significant variable. Prosperous widows might enjoy considerable status in their own right. Thus, Tuscan towns attracted widows of prosperous peasants or landowners, who lived a more independent life in urban society. For these, and other better-off women, fashionable clothes—sometimes of silk with gold ribbons and jewellery—could express and enhance their social standing in later medieval society.

Less is known about the social circumstances of lower-class women, but it was always hard and precarious. Many found work as domestic servants, washer women, nurses, or street traders. In the thirteenth and fourteenth centuries, townswomen (like their rural counterparts) were often drink-sellers. Here, as in other trades, there was pressure before 1500 for men to take over the business, at least officially. Poorer women might move to the suburbs to escape controls; others no doubt traded unofficially. Socially, they could try to buttress their position in various ways: by participation with other women in neighbourly activities; through kinship ties; and by religious activity. At least some lower-class women joined their better-off sisters in religious fraternities. In the Low Countries, single and widowed women combined employment in the textile industry with communal life in extensive *béguinages* (one at Dendermonde housed about 275 women, and another at Mechelen over 1,500).

Young people, often a large share of the total population, likewise held a marginal status in urban society. Those like Alice Hermendesworth, with whom we started this chapter, coming from better-off backgrounds might hope to join the established community through family support, marriage, or apprenticeship, but large numbers of young people from lesser families were always on the outside of the civic world trying to look in. Young men sometimes formed journeymen guilds or solidarity groups like abbeys of misrule, but often they were on verge of destitution, drifting into petty crime, moving from one place to another.

Marginality also defined ethnic minorities in European cities. Though Jews were numerous in Mediterranean cities, even after their expulsion from Western Europe, their fortunes deteriorated. In Spain, racist attacks spread from Andalusia, the first grisly murders occurring in Seville. In Catalan towns, pogroms took place in 1391 and those Jews who survived were forced to convert. Official persecution was ratcheted up. At Cordoba, Jews were confined to a special quarter by the Castilian king in 1478, and the following year they were forbidden to leave it. In 1483, there was a general expulsion of unconverted Jews and even Christian Jews suffered popular violence. In Italy, likewise, ghettoes became more common. The great Venetian ghetto created in 1516 had its precursors in the Venetian colonies. Muslim populations in Spanish cities also faced growing pressure. The capture of the last Islamic city of Granada in 1492 and the expulsion of its Muslim inhabitants marked only the latest stage in the repression of Muslims in Spanish cities. At Cordoba, one of the most important Islamic centres in Catholic Spain, the Muslim quarter and mosque were shut down in 1480, and the remaining Muslims driven out in 1502. Further north, in the Baltic region, the same process of ethnic discrimination led to the growing exclusion of Slavs from the citizenry of Livonian towns after 1400.

IV

In general, the social order of the medieval town was prone to instability and tension, swept by tidal waves of migrants, ruled by small, often factionalized elites, its middle-rank inhabitants divided by craft rivalries, and the great majority of the population—the lower classes and poor, women, young people and minorities—largely marginalized from the mainstream of community life. Though the trend in crime rates is unclear, violence seems to have been endemic. Siena, in 1350, complained of the great increase in violent crimes, and in the first part of the fifteenth century between a third and a half of all recorded crimes at Antwerp and Milan involved acts of violence; even small towns like Arboga in Sweden had a homicide rate similar to that of a big city. Individual acts of violence, usually between men in public places, often inflamed by alcohol, were only part of the picture. Rulers often responded to crime and conspiracy through violence and murder, while conflict within the ruling class in Mediterranean and Low Country cities regularly culminated in wider, often bloody, public disorder. As we will see in Chapter 6, by the end of the thirteenth century, European cities were affected by growing popular unrest and protests against the ruling elite as lesser artisans and smaller people felt alienated by a sense of political exclusion and worsening poverty.

Urban society sought to manage social instability and tension in diverse ways, both informal and (increasingly) formal and institutional. The corner stone of the informal social structure in towns (as in the countryside) was the family. Patrician families with their numerous servants and spacious houses were vital for the continuity of urban property ownership and wealth. Through their investments and contacts in the countryside, they served as a vital link between urban and rural society. Through marriage and service in their households, they absorbed outsiders into the urban community, and the *paterfamilias* regulated the social behaviour of household members and clients. In north Italian cities, patrician families formed clans of extended kin, clients, and other followers, who during the twelfth and thirteenth centuries clustered together in a particular urban district, not infrequently around the lord's tower house. Some principal families in Rome kept baths for their dependents, while at Naples in about 1309 Robert de Griffo maintained in his courtyard a fountain, fed by an underground channel, to supply relations and clients with water.

Middle-rank families were smaller in size and had fewer resources, but their household heads were often key figures in the neighbourhood or street, taking in servants, giving business or credit to neighbours, serving as minor officials, and acting as an anchor of local stability. The Bruges purse-maker, Jacob den Buersemaker, is a good example of a middling tradesman or shopkeeper, whose goods at his death included a sword and some armour (showing he served in the Bruges cavalry), had debts owed him by several people, probably customers and neighbours, and rented a house and paid taxes.

Poorer families were often very small and too fragile to function very effectively as independent social units. Lesser artisans at Venice in the fourteenth century had fewer than two children and in 1428 the average Florentine household counted only 3.8 members. Even so, through kin, client, servant, and neighbourly connections they might be networked to better-off families. God-parentage too cut across social boundaries and created secondary social networks.

Clearly, the social world and functions of the family overlapped with that of the street or neighbourhood: the border was porous, a great deal of domestic household activities taking place outside, on the street, and vice versa. In Florence, neighbourly controls became more institutionalized from the twelfth century through parish organizations, with councils of wealthier household heads maintaining social order and representing the locality to the community. But, generally, neighbourly norms were brought to bear informally through local ceremonies, games and rituals, gossiping, shared business dealing, marriage ties, life-cycle events, sociability, and the sanctions of solidarity. At the heart of many neighbourhoods was the parish church, the nexus of religious and communal gatherings, the repository of gifts by the living and dead, whose clerk took a significant part in social surveillance, watching over the behaviour of local residents. Neighbourliness was a mixed blessing: mutual help, fun, and support was conjoined with intrusive social pressure and constraint. As the Florentine Alberti advised his nephew in the fifteenth century: 'Please neighbours, [but] love kinsmen'.

By the late Middle Ages, the forum or space for elite social activity may have been moving away from the neighbourhood towards the wider urban community. Change probably occurred first of all in Mediterranean cities. At Venice, in the fourteenth century, patricians showed less interest in philanthropy at the parish level and were more active in community-based rituals and ceremonies; in death, they chose to be buried outside their home parish. Patrician families started to cluster more together—in Venice on the Grand Canal; in other cities in the centres of towns near the marketplace or town hall. Even so, evidence for sharp social segregation is lacking: throughout the Middle Ages, the spatial mixing of rich and poor was widespread and served to encourage social cohesion.

V

By the fourteenth and fifteenth centuries, more formal, institutional controls were becoming important in European towns to manage social problems. One major advance was the growth of public provision for the poor. In the early Middle Ages, the Church shouldered much of the burden of poor relief. From the sixth century, lists of poor were kept by Church officials at Ravenna, Rome, and Tours for relief purposes. Monasteries were prominent in charitable work, supplementing the contribution of neighbourly aid to poorer residents. As a consequence of greater urban poverty after the twelfth century, Church relief expanded alongside the rise of new secular charities, often on private initiative. The Franciscan friars and other mendicant orders shouldered a considerable part of relief work in bigger cities. Nursing orders like the Antonines became active and many new specialist hospitals and almshouses were founded, especially in cities in the Mediterranean region and the Low Countries. By the early thirteenth century, for instance, Toulouse had twelve hospitals and seven leper houses; Saragossa in about 1300 had eleven hospitals, and Leon nine. Civic intervention also began to develop: thus, Catalan towns from the late thirteenth century organized parish and civic relief. City authorities began to establish controls over new charitable institutions and a first effort was made to discriminate between the deserving poor—widows, orphans, and the sick—and able-bodied vagrants and scroungers. At Barcelona and Montpellier, vagrants were driven out of town.

In the late medieval period, poverty posed a serious challenge to the urban community. Church and hospital resources suffered from the decline of rents; traditional neighbourly almsgiving was unable to cope with the recurrent large numbers of indigent. The response was multi-pronged. Relief by confraternities expanded and lay-organized 'poor tables' spread in towns. Older hospitals, often in financial difficulty, were merged or reorganized, frequently taken over by civic governments. Relief turned more secular, though the religious dimension remained. In the Southern

Netherlands, city councils, like those at Mons and Huy, extended their control over the finances of hospitals and shared in their running. In Italy, general hospitals start to appear at Brescia (1447), and (Milan 1448), and in Spain at Saragossa (1425) and Lleida (1453). Mirroring the growing distinction between deserving and undeserving poor, a wave of new institutions concentrated aid on particular groups: the mad, the sick, occupational categories, orphans and foundlings. Monti di Pietà were established in Mediterranean cities to help the indebted poor. While it is difficult to quantify the overall scale of poor relief, it was probably modest: London before 1500 may have had 250–300 almshouses for the old and sick (in a population of about 50,000).

The trend towards more formal public relief and control of the poor was only part of a wider process of institutionalization in the late Middle Ages, led by Mediterranean cities. As we shall see in the following chapters, informal administrative controls enforced at the neighbourhood or parish level gave way to more concerted civic or community intervention across a number of sectors. Meantime, the political power and social cohesion of civic elites was strengthened, and there was a growing articulation of communal consciousness, whether in terms of architecture, art, ritual, or humanist historiography.

In various respects, a clearer definition of the social order of towns is visible by the fifteenth century, marked not just by more formal social control but by greater social stratification or social polarization, and by a sharper distinction between the mainstream hierarchy and other social groups. Arguably, a kind of social closure was taking place in European cities, as women, ethnic minorities, and undeserving poor came in turn under pressure. However, we should not exaggerate: the picture remained highly variegated. Some commercial cities like Cologne, Antwerp, or Barcelona were more socially open, less closed than others. On the Rhine, Cologne's city government remained welcoming to newcomers despite its domination by wealthy merchants, just as Antwerp hosted a medley of minority groups including religious heretics. After a visit to Barcelona, in 1512, Guiccardini remarked: 'its people have a saying: it is a city for everyone'.

As we have seen, tidal waves of migrants, social stratification, the growth of urban poverty, and the position of minorities all presented serious challenges to the social order and stability of European cities and town. In this chapter, we have been concerned to look at how communities and their leaders evolved a range of strategies and structures to contain those pressures, which also threatened the sense of communal and civic identity. In the next two chapters, we examine how European cities reacted to these and other problems through the transforming processes of urban culture, landscape, and governance.

5

Culture and Landscape
400–1500

T he Church was central to the urban identity and to the cultural world of the medieval town. That identity was also shaped by public buildings, especially, in the case of bigger cities, by town walls and gates. However, as towns expanded after the eleventh and twelfth centuries and faced growing pressures from high mobility, social tension, party factionalism, and spatial sprawl, communities (or at least their elites) sought to reinforce their sense of urban identity in further ways—through new patrician houses, new religious institutions, and new civic buildings. In the later Middle Ages, urban identity was re-forged again in response to changing economic and social pressures and rivalry between cities. New public and private buildings in cities, secularized ceremonies, schools and universities, and new historical and artistic representations of the community transformed the urban cultural world.

I

This chapter will examine in turn the processes of cultural and landscape transformation during the high and late Middle Ages, but first we need to sketch early medieval developments. In the wake of the collapse of the Roman Empire, from the third and fourth centuries civic identity was in short supply. As we know, in Western and Central Europe, the old Roman cities were struggling and lost most of their economic and political functions. Even in the Mediterranean region, demographic decline, the loss of wealth and administrative functions, as well as the partial withdrawal of the elite classes to the countryside, undermined the old vigour of urban life. Though civic fortifications were often built from the third and fourth centuries, in the following period when walls and public buildings were not razed or damaged by the invaders, they often lost their earlier *raison d'être*. Public monuments were sacrificed to rebuild city fortifications or were incorporated into defence works. At sixth-century Nîmes, for instance, the Roman amphitheatre was turned into a fortress with four towers. Urban space frequently relinquished its coherence and inhabitants lived in only one part of the fortified area or moved outside the walls, sometimes to cluster around suburban churches. Walls and gates were granted away to private individuals or organizations, and water and drainage systems often fell into decay. Palaces and patrician houses were used for 'squatting'. Thus, in 489, troops of Theodoric were billeted on Pavia and archaeology has shown how some of them made use of a big noble palace which was subdivided into little huts. In the former imperial capital, Rome, attempts were made to keep the main thoroughfares and public spaces open, but the street plan became increasingly irregular.

However, as the imperial and civil functions of towns diminished, their religious activities became ever more vital for urban identity. Christian churches had already become important in Roman towns from the fourth century. Now there was a Christianization of the urban landscape. As well as the continuation of late Roman basilicas, other public buildings might be converted to religious purposes. From the sixth century, further monasteries were built and cathedral complexes extended, while cults of saints and Christian festivals provided a revamped context for the expression of urban consciousness. At Verona, the city was encircled by a net of Christian shrines and churches. At Rome, from about the seventh century, the Pantheon became Santa Maria ad Martyres, and the temple of Apollo the Church of San Lorenzo in Miranda. Increasingly, the clergy took a leading role in efforts to restore parts of the urban infrastructure. Italian accounts of towns stressed how the civic walls, together with the Church and saints, defended city and citizens against an alien enemy. At Cahors, in southern France, Bishop Desiderius fortified his episcopal town, built new churches there, and set up a water system

The seventh and eighth centuries also saw growing royal support for the renewal of the urban infrastructure. In Spain, the city of Toledo and its churches benefited from the patronage of the Visigothic King Leovigold and his successors who also constructed a new set of city walls. Likewise, the Islamic rulers in Spain after the eighth century invested heavily in urban reconstruction, with new fortresses and mosques often adapted from earlier churches: thus, the Mezquita at Cordoba, remarkable for its beautifully vivid red and white, brick and stone interior, was built after 786 on the site of a Visigothic church, parts of which are still visible.

In Western Europe, too, the Church and rulers were crucial for the renewed sense of urban life from the seventh and eighth centuries. In a city such as Tours, religious buildings and the presence of clergy offered the main thread of continuity with the ancient urban community. In England, the arrival of missionaries from the Pope in Rome at the end of the sixth century stimulated the development of Canterbury, York, and London as ecclesiastical and administrative centres. York had a stone church by the 670s and a monastic school, as well as a royal palace. In the Merovingian city of Soissons, a new clerical quarter developed outside the walls (away from the Roman *castrum*), focused on funeral basilicas and chapels. Even so, we see at Metz how, despite considerable church building in the seventh century, the cultural life of the city was seasonal, fluctuating according to the times of liturgical festivals and when the king came there. However, by the ninth and tenth centuries, as urban life recovered, bishops and monasteries took a leading part in founding and laying out new towns (see Chapter 6).

As in the Mediterranean world, city walls were part of the revived urban identity. About 580, Gregory of Tours was surprised that Dijon with its wall and thirty towers (but without a bishop) was not deemed a city, and, though some of the new commercial emporia of the eighth century lacked fortifications, the threat of Viking invasion and attack led many civic leaders to build or reconstruct their walls. In general, though, the urban landscape of Western Europe before 1000 was unimpressive. At York, the former Roman site could boast little more than its small stone minster, a scattering of other ecclesiastical buildings, and a partially rebuilt town wall; inhabitants lived in tottering wooden buildings with earthen floors covered by straw or decayed vegetation, while the surrounding streets and yards smacked of the countryside.

Thus, the Church and urban fortifications were fundamental in the first phase of urban cultural revival after the seventh century, providing key elements of what has been termed 'salvage identity'. The cathedrals and monasteries promoted schools and education. Lombard Italy probably had a number of cathedral and clerical schools, and by the eleventh century the cathedral school at Chartres had become influential in North-Western Europe—linked to the city's importance as a pilgrimage centre.

Many churches had relics to attract pilgrims. The latter brought important benefits to towns, helping to fund the beautification of their churches and other forms of reconstruction—most notably on the pilgrimage route to Santiago de Compostela but also at Rome. In Iberia, mosques like the great Mezquita at Cordoba or the two beautiful, small, square ones at Toledo, both built about 1000, were essential elements in the Islamic remodelling and renewal of their cities.

By 1000, the reviving cultural confidence of European cities in the Mediterranean world started to be manifested in new ways. An early poem, lauding the city of Milan and dated about 789, was followed in about 800 by one in praise of Verona which began by bragging: 'This great and famous city is pre-eminent in Italy'. A prose description of Milan followed in the ninth or tenth centuries. Visual representations of cities also multiplied. An early tenth-century drawing of the splendours of Verona highlighted its circuit of walls and numerous churches. Elsewhere, particularly in Northern and Eastern Europe, developments were slower. In Ireland, the majority of towns were linked to religious houses but had only limited fortifications. In Hungary, almost all the early towns were seats of bishops. Across Europe as a whole, towns were more or less weak cultural stars blinking in a universe that was still predominantly rural in its values and ideas.

II

Urban revival after the eleventh century, when European cities grew strongly, extended their networks, and enlarged their economic and political significance, created a host of new issues in terms of the formation of a distinctive cultural identity. As we saw above, urbanization entailed a heavy influx of mainly rural outsiders, landowners and knights, as well as peasants and labourers. In north Italian cities, landowners established their own districts. Poorer people flooded in, often camping on the outskirts of town. In many places, there was a spatial extension of towns, new foci being created as well as suburbs. As a result, a considerable number of larger communities in the eleventh and twelfth centuries were polycentric in layout. Thus, at Toulouse, the city was divided between the old fortified Cité and the separate Bourg district linked to the monastery of St Servin. In Russia, major cities like Novgorod stretched over large areas with several distinct settlements. German towns frequently had three or four different foci, each sometimes with their own walls, reflecting the jurisdictions of different lords and different economic activities. At Gdansk, for example, there was the Altstadt, Neustadt, Rechstadt, and Vorstadt. Durham, in northern England, had four different boroughs, including areas which had grown up as independent communities at different times. Only slowly, over the following centuries, did these various centres or hubs coalesce to form a unified civic community. Elsewhere, however, particularly when towns were newly established or refounded (as in Eastern Europe), it was more normal for a simple gridiron plan to be laid out for the whole town in order to facilitate trade and traffic.

In this high medieval world of demographic, social, and spatial change, the Church continued to stand at the heart of urban cultural life, but the role of religion became more urbanized and pluralistic, at least in the larger cities. Reflecting the growth of population and increased significance of urban neighbourhoods, new parishes were defined and churches built, while a growing number of religious orders established their houses within the city rather than outside its limits. Quite often, as at Toulouse, new religious houses, such as those of the Templars and Hospitallers, were founded by lay families. Mendicant orders like the Franciscans and Dominicans took up residence in poorer sections of towns from the early thirteenth century, and this age of intense urban religious fervour witnessed an upsurge of other religious organizations. At Marseille, the townscape was crowded with a host of new foundations from the twelfth century, among them a house of Templars, a commandery of St Anthony, houses of Trinitarians, Carmelites, preachers, friars minor, Augustines, and Clares, and two hospitals. In Eastern Europe, cities like Wroclaw acquired friaries, houses of military orders, and hospitals, while in Orthodox Rus a similar proliferation of churches and religious houses occurred in and around towns, partly in response to the increased urban population.

As the political influence of bishops over towns waned, greater opportunities arose for the civic patronage of religion. North Italian cities took the lead during the thirteenth and fourteenth centuries in the promotion of civic religion through the construction of or support for cathedrals, oratories guarding the relics of a city's holy protector, and chapels that commemorated a key communal event. Florence, Siena, Bologna, and Verona, among others, all claimed to be new Jerusalems. Cities began to sponsor large civic processions. At Venice, the ceremony of the Purification of the Blessed Virgin Mary on 2 February was elaborated after the late twelfth century and lasted four days, with the procession crossing land and water (conveyed by a convoy of ships) and numerous parishes taking part, though the main focus was St Mark's Square. Here, as in other cities, almost the whole urban community was caught up in the ceremonial, either as participants or spectators, among the latter marginal groups like foreigners, women, and children.

Again in the high Middle Ages, town magistrates took action in the construction or extension of town walls. New walls were needed to incorporate parts of the community that now sprawled outside the old circuit of fortifications. Florence began building its second circuit of walls in 1172, enclosing 80 hectares, but new ones projected in 1284 and finished in 1333 enclosed 630 hectares. At Perpignan, the new wall raised in the early twelfth century enclosed an area six times greater than that of the old walled precinct. Across Germany, a third of city walls were erected between 1100 and 1300. Town walls and their gates had many functions. As well as their defensive role, they helped secure control of the urban population, both residents and the constant stream of immigrants and travellers; they were places where tolls were levied, while the gates sometimes doubled as prisons or guildhalls. But, above all, with their increasingly elaborate architecture and decoration they manifested civic pride and shaped the urban landscape, frequently enclosing earlier separate sections of the town. At Montpellier, for instance, the new wall of the twelfth century (completed in the thirteenth) brought together the two main quarters of the town to form a united nucleus. Near the walls, areas were laid out for parks and military exercise.

In the Mediterranean region, growing communal organization, rising public revenue, and fierce inter-city rivalry led to a wave of new civic palaces or town halls to house meetings of civic leaders and to accommodate the burgeoning civic bureaucracy: thus, we find them at Brescia and Verona from the 1170s, and at Padua, built between 1172 and 1219. The Palazzo Púbblico at Siena, built between 1288 and 1309, is especially splendid. An imposing Gothic building of travertine and brick, built on the south side of the Piazza del Campo, the facade is relieved by rows of elegant windows and cornices of round-headed arches and topped by battlements. The black-and-white escutcheon of Siena, the Balzana, is constantly repeated in the arches over the windows. North of the Alps, civic buildings appeared later and were more modest in scale. Belfries were built in Flemish towns from about 1170 and were regularly used as meeting places for civic officials. In England, town halls or guildhalls, often small and pokey, appear from the twelfth and thirteenth centuries, as towns strained towards self-government.

As urban government expanded and councils took greater responsibility for public water supply, we find Italian cities setting up elaborate fountains as symbols of communal pride. At great cost, Siena, for instance, installed a series of fountains not just in the city but also in the suburbs and even adjoining villages. More modest improvements in water supply took place elsewhere: Basel had new waterworks after 1260, the town of Périgueux in central France a water fountain in 1314, and several English towns had limited provision (often organized by monasteries) from the fourteenth century. However restricted, water supply was once more associated, as in the Roman period, with urban identity and civilization.

Slowly, the image of European cities was articulated not just by public buildings and facilities but by private housing. Most striking were the rural-style tower houses, up to 75 metres high, which appeared first in north Italian cities like Pisa, Florence, and Bologna from the twelfth century, mainly constructed by noble clans (though some by neighbourhood associations). Florence may have had 150 towers and Bologna nearly 200. Houses in this style also spread to the towns of southern France (as in Languedoc), and parts of Spain and Portugal (one or two survive in Oporto). Some tower houses were destroyed in clan fighting and others regulated by civic authorities, fearful of the threat to public order. In their place new, three-storey stone palaces were constructed by merchant patricians. In Western Europe, stone merchant houses appeared in the Low Countries, such as at Ghent, and in England (as at Lincoln). In general, however, the majority of elite housing in the area was still built of timber. Wooden construction was almost universal in Northern and Eastern Europe, including for many churches, and private housing remained basic and rural in style.

Even in the more advanced urban areas of Europe, it is important to remember that cultural ties with the countryside remained strong—mediated by the influential role of landowners. Thus, jousting and chivalric events constituted an important feature of the cultural year in Italian cities, and, in Low Country towns, jousts, tournaments, and passages of arms were regularly staged, associated with the counts but patronized by all levels of the urban community. However, we also start to find the growth of civic pride and cultural identity reflected in new ways. Following earlier precedents, a spate of literary works appeared praising and describing the city, whether Bergamo, Milan, Pavia, or Florence. Civic chronicles began to be compiled in Italy from the eleventh and twelfth centuries, often recording political and military conflicts as well as municipal officials and events, and several towns followed suit north of the Alps (for instance, London in 1173 and Paris 1323); but the main developments here came in the late medieval period.

III

Whereas the high Middle Ages marked the first flowering of a distinctive urban cultural identity, contributing to the new cohesion and self-importance of an expansive urban world, it was in the fourteenth and fifteenth centuries that the cultural life of European cities diversified and came into its own. This reshaping of the cultural image of the city reflected the pressures and problems affecting much of the European urban order in the later Middle Ages. Large-scale demographic contraction caused greater economic volatility, competition between urban centres, and tensions between town and countryside. Urban communities and their leaders recognized the need, perhaps explicitly for the first time, to promote themselves, regionally and beyond, through their civic image and the cultural services they offered. In this way, towns sought to attract and impress affluent outsiders. Moreover, as we know, social polarization and tension increased in late medieval towns, and the new cultural activities may have functioned to reconcile social groups and heal social divisions. New forms of civic identification constructed after the Black Death were also linked to the increased dynamic and institutionalization of municipal government.

Of course, religion remained at the core of cultural life in the late medieval city. Citizens like those of Venice saw their community as a city of God, one blessed by divine providence. Churches and other religious buildings were invariably mentioned by visitors to cities. On top of those many religious orders, houses, and institutions which had multiplied in the high Middle Ages, there was a crescendo of religious fraternities and guilds. Though some had appeared earlier, numbers of confraternities rose sharply across Europe during the fourteenth and fifteenth centuries: in the cities of northern Italy (over 150 at Florence, more than 130 in Genoa, 200 at Venice); in Spanish cities like Valladolid (100) and Toledo (140); in the Low Countries at Antwerp and Bruges; in English towns (150 in London); and in Sweden (20 guilds and fraternities at Stockholm). Confraternities were by no means limited to towns, as many spread to the countryside too, yet the most important and elaborate were located in urban communities. While some confraternities were more elitest than others, recruitment was often relatively open. In some Italian cities, between 10 and 30 per cent of the adult population had a confraternity member in their family. Those joining included landowners and upper clergy, the middling and artisan classes, and quite often women; but poorer folk seem to have been excluded, probably because they could not afford the costs of membership. Some confraternities included not only townspeople but also those from the nearby countryside, helping to integrate them into urban society.

Many different types of confraternity evolved. An important category comprised the trade and craft guilds (discussed in Chapters 3–4); but others included noble fraternities, youth guilds, women's guilds, archers' guilds, penitential groups, guilds of fools, ethnic fraternities, associations of pilgrims, and confraternities for philanthropic purposes (for instance, maintaining hospitals or bridges). On the other hand, shared functions are clear. One was a strong religious or spiritual purpose. A Spanish definition of a confraternity was 'a group of devout persons formed in order to perform works of piety and charity'. Masses and prayers were said for dead members; confraternities participated in the major liturgical festivities and processions of the Church year; and brethren attended and sometimes organized the burial of colleagues (for newcomers without an urban family the prospect of a fraternity burial was doubtless a membership attraction). A second, overlapping function was social solidarity and mutual support. In England, aid to poor members of London fraternities was 'casual and informal rather than automatic and regulated'; on the continent, it was often more organized and systematic, with loan funds for members down on their luck. Membership was also celebrated through rituals (feasts, processions), badges, symbolic artefacts, and special language and behaviour between brethren. Confraternities also played a significant part in the wider cultural life of the community, and sponsored sports events and literary competitions, commissioned works of arts, or patronized church building.

As we suggested before, the multiplication of confraternities can be construed in part as a response to the high mortality and preoccupation with disease and death in late medieval towns, but the phenomenon was also closely linked to the vitality of religious life at the parish and neighbourhood level. Popular religious fervour led to the widespread construction, rebuilding, and decoration of local churches. Voluntary religious activity included support for candles before altars, chantries, pilgrimages, and church maintenance. In Spanish cities, popular religious fervour may help explain the increasing animosity to Jews and Muslims during the fifteenth century.

Nonetheless, the religious identity of late medieval cities was not unproblematic. If heretical activity was more a rural than an urban phenomenon, there are signs of growing tension between lay and ecclesiastical authorities over jurisdictional rights, as municipal councils sought to extend their authority and control over urban territory. Meantime, religious activities acquired a more secular flavour. In English towns, liturgical processions on the feast of Corpus Christi were increasingly overlaid with plays and pageants organized by civic councils and guilds. At Venice, the long-established procession on the feast of the Blessed Virgin was drastically reformed and secularized by the city authorities towards the end of the fourteenth century; the festival was shortened to one day, involved the procession of the doge, and was linked to a supposed Venetian victory in 943. At Mons, the city authorities became heavily involved in the organization and finance of the Mystery of the Passion, with its large cast of local actors; they used the event to promote the community and invited ambassadors, bishops, and worthies from other places. Across the North Sea, not only larger English cities in the Midlands and North but small towns in the south like Lydd and New Romney organized play cycles to attract visitors to town and to assert their urban reputation. Political festivities such as royal and seigneurial entries could also help to boost civic identity and status. In Castile (and elsewhere in Europe), royal entries to cities were more and more lavish by the fifteenth century, the festivities (as at Valladolid in 1428) lasting for several days, including jousts and other chivalric entertainments that attracted large crowds from the region.

Cultural pluralism is also evident in other areas. In the Low Countries, confraternity chambers of rhetoric organized competitions in poetry and rhetoric, often with other towns, for all kinds of prizes. Competitions took place over several days and were heavily subsidized by the urban authorities. In the same way, guilds of archers and arquebusiers participated in military exercises, in competition with other towns; once again they were strongly supported by councils keen to market their civic image and reputation.

As well as sponsoring and managing new-style plays, pageants, and competitions, local councils financed town bands including trumpeters and other wind instruments. A number of German cities had bands after 1350 and within a generation they were widespread elsewhere—in the Netherlands, France, and Italy. Guilds of minstrels were established in Paris and other French and Low Country towns, and town bands played at civic processions, plays, public concerts, official serenades, confraternity feasts, and a host of private events. As well as traditional songs and dance, they also performed new style polyphony.

New forms of cultural identification were progressively linked to the rediscovery of classical models and the spread of civic humanism, especially in Italy. Here, an important role was played by the growth of education, including the proliferation of schools and universities (see Chapter 3). One development was the growth of historical literature. Though chronicles had existed for bigger cities since the twelfth century, in the late Middle Ages urban historiography became more sophisticated. In northern Italy, new forms of humanist writing evolved in the late fourteenth and early fifteenth centuries, under the influence of Petrarch, civic republicanism, and contact with Greek scholars. Among the major works was Bruni's 'History of the Florentine People', written after 1415, a strikingly original study based on historical research, while Bernardo Giustiniani's *History of the Origin of Venice* appeared posthumously in 1492. More traditional was the outpouring of town chronicles in Germany, hundreds being produced even for small towns, as communities competed with one another in their display of civic pride. Elsewhere in Europe (as in the Low Countries or England), historical writing seems to have been less important; here, other expressions of cultural identity may have been more crucial. For Dutch cities like Rotterdam and Haarlem, fifteenth-century humanists invented foundation legends that glorified their independence.

In Italian cities, the rediscovery of classicism was already reflected in the new literature on architecture and the design of new buildings. Patterned after the *De architectura* by the Roman architect and engineer Vitruvius, and written in the late 1440s, Alberti's *De re aedificatoria* (*Ten Books of Architecture*) was a seminal work that presented the idea of the planned city, with models for different levels of housing from the upper to lower classes. Meanwhile, after the late fourteenth century, Gothic influences were eclipsed in Florence (and other Italian cities) by a succession of neoclassical public buildings: among the most famous was Brunelleschi's dome of Florence Cathedral (1417−34) and the Old Sacristy of San Lorenzo. Alberti in turn designed neoclassical churches at Rimini and Florence. Also influential was the rediscovery of classical buildings at Rome, following the revival of the Papacy during the fifteenth century.

Classical influences spread to sculpture and painting. They were already visible in Sienese and Florentine religious paintings from the thirteenth century—in the works of Duccio and Giotto—and in the sculptures of Nicolo and Giovanni Pisani. Though early works were mostly commissioned by religious houses, after the late fourteenth century wealthy merchants started to have paintings in their houses, and before long there was a growing commercial market for many types of art—religious paintings, portraits, carvings, sculpture, town images, church furnishings, and the like. In Tuscan towns, output was organized on a workshop basis, with local artists developing their own styles. Art was increasingly traded (and exported) as a commercial commodity, involving protracted negotiations between clients, middlemen, and artists.

The Italian cultural renaissance had its strongest resonance in the cities of the Southern Netherlands. Here, close commercial links, and a flow of Flemish artists to Italy, chimed with the mounting prosperity of leading townsmen, especially those associated with the Burgundian Court, and painters, manuscript illuminators, silversmiths, and wood carvers multiplied. In contrast to Italy, the Gothic style remained stronger and most output was religious—altarpieces, religious paintings, and manuscripts: thus one Leuven mansion had nineteen religious paintings in 1489.

IV

Just as town walls (along with the Church) were key markers of European urbanity from the early medieval period, so they remained important features of urban identity through the fourteenth and fifteenth centuries. The Hundred Years Wars led to a wave of new expensive urban fortifications in France and the Low Countries. By the late fifteenth century, almost every French 'bonne ville' had its distinctive curtain wall. In Germany, a similar surge of wall construction occurred, and further east stronger and more complete fortifications guarded Russian cities like Moscow and Novgorod. From the 1420s, the deployment of cannon by besieging armies made older walls obsolete and forced reconstruction with defensive ports for artillery, new low thick walls, broad moats, and geometrical bastions. The defensive function of town walls and gates mingled with their symbolic importance as bulwarks of civic pride and urban autonomy. As one chronicler of Augsburg cried: 'dear men of Augsburg, man the gates with pious people, for you have many wicked neighbours who wish you dead'.

The cultural world of the late medieval town juxtaposed conservatism and innovation. Town seals, paintings, woodcuts, and tapestries revealed traditional visions of towns, their fortifications, and church spires, encircling and soaring over the city of God, and such visions remained vital for the identity of towns into the early modern era. But, in the real urban landscape, religious and other traditional edifices had to compete with a host of new secular buildings. Already on the scene in principal cities in the high Middle Ages, civic palaces and guildhalls became numerous, lavishly built and decorated. In London, the city's Guildhall, built in the early fifteenth century, was modelled on the royal Westminster Hall, one of the major buildings of medieval Europe. New town halls in France, England, and the Low Countries frequently combined a market space on the ground floor and the council chamber above.

Other infrastructure investment included a spate of new hospitals and almshouses (see Chapter 4). In addition, street improvement was more common, at least in the centres of towns, where paved or wooden roads were laid out. Spanish cities saw the design of new public squares. Public provision of water-supply cities expanded in Italian cities: thus, 39 per cent of Florentine houses had access to public and private wells, while Siena had an underground supply network. And similar improvements were adopted in other European cities, through greater provision of public wells and fountains and supplies channelled from outside springs; even so, provision varied greatly between towns and was rarely abundant. Likewise, attempts were made to improve and regulate sanitation and street cleaning. At Rome, after the return of the Pope, a powerful urban planning agency operated which was responsible for streets, squares, and water provision. The Flemish city of Bruges spent up to 16 per cent of its income in the late fourteenth century on urban improvement, including the markets, bell tower, town hall, bridges, and fortifications.

Public improvement in late medieval towns was matched by greater advances in private housing, and an emerging definition of public and private space. Though the decline of urban population and fall of rents probably led to the decay of some older wooden housing, parts of towns appearing derelict in consequence, the period saw the construction of new higher-quality houses. Architectural treatises designed model types of housing for different social classes, including the urban lower orders. In Italian cities like Florence or Venice new patrician houses were built in the classical style, spacious, and richly decorated. Though public rooms remained simply furnished before the late fifteenth century, the chamber of the owner might, according to Bruni, have 'fine furniture, gold, silver and brocaded hangings and precious carpets', as well as paintings. North of the Alps, new merchant houses at Augsburg and Cologne were several storeys high, often clustered together in particular areas of the city. In the Low Countries, patrician houses were built in brick from the thirteenth century, and, over the next two centuries, civic regulations made brick housing and tiles compulsory in the main streets of towns. Lower-class housing saw some improvement too, rows of tenement houses being built in English country towns like Tewksbury.

V

In sum, from a fragile and weakly defined cultural identity and reputation in the early Middle Ages, reliant in part on hazy memories of a classical past, by the late medieval era European towns had developed a complex of strategies—religious, ceremonial, educational, literary, and architectural—to foster a sense of communal cohesion and proclaim the community's cultural voice in the wider world. In the Mediterranean region, in particular, we have seen how the new cultural language of cities adopted neoclassical overtones. Certainly, by the fifteenth century, urban cultural life in the main cities of Mediterranean and Western Europe was more secular and multifaceted than in the past, helping to differentiate it more sharply from the countryside. At the same time, in much of Europe, particularly the north and east, towns were small and cultural life remained rudimentary and traditional, with strong rural continuities in housing, ceremonies, and religious belief.

Needless to say, townscape and cultural activities were not the only forces helping to furbish a sense of urban identity. No less important, was urban governance, including the development of internal political structures and organization and the changing relationship of urban communities with the external world—with their hinterlands, other cities, and local lords and princes. These topics must be explored in the next chapter.

6

Governance 400–1500

B y the close of the Middle Ages, the essential administrative and
political structures of towns, including municipal powers and civic
leadership, had been constructed, at least for the greater towns, in most
parts of Europe. As we shall see, the process was slow and difficult, but from
the twelfth century it proved incremental. The other main development in
medieval urban governance—the creation of civic autonomy from outside
control—was more problematic and fraught with difficulty. Here, there
were greater regional and national variations, depending on the strength of
external political forces—not just secular and ecclesiastical rulers but also
rival cities; and even when some measure of autonomy was achieved, it was
often precarious and might be overthrown. In this chapter, we examine
the two issues of municipal government and political autonomy together,
looking in turn at developments during the early medieval period, the high
Middle Ages, and the later medieval era.

I

Even before the collapse of the Roman Empire in the West, urban
institutional structures had begun to disintegrate. As many of the old urban
ruling elites withdrew to the countryside, growing financial problems
beset cities, and municipal bodies declined. Frequently, civic property and
responsibilities were granted away to private individuals. Civic provision
was increasingly limited to fortification and defence. Greater administrative
continuity occurred in the Mediterranean world—in Italy and Spain—but
almost everywhere municipal governance lost out to the militarization of
society.

Rule by city councils was steadily supplanted by government by notables (including local clergy), and the *defensor* emerged as the head of local administration. By the sixth century, civic functionaries in Gaul and Italy were increasingly supervised by the *comes civitatis*, the representative of the king. From the sixth and seventh centuries, most cities were in the hands of outsiders. Mainly residing outside cities, a succession of Gothic, Burgundian, Lombard, and Frankish rulers, as well as Anglo-Saxon kings, used former Roman cities as administrative centres, for tax collection, and as meeting places for royal and ecclesiastical councils. Where any local urban leadership survived, it was often provided by the Church, sometimes with links to local warlords or informal groups of city notables. From Rome to small provincial cities like Tours or Clermont, bishops struggled to shore up or salvage urban functions. From the end of the sixth century, the Popes began rebuilding parts of Rome and thereby attracted growing numbers of pilgrims. About the same time, Bishop Gregory of Tours was defending his own city from marauding armies.

As noted in Chapter 2, lay rulers and the Church were also important in the foundation of new towns from the ninth and tenth centuries, particularly in Western, Northern, and Eastern Europe. Often, they were located near royal palaces or monasteries. At Ghent, the abbey of St Bavo played a key part in the emergence of the town during the ninth century, through the activity of merchants in the abbey's service, which attracted independent merchants there; at Arras, the large abbey of St Vaast had a similar effect on the growth of the urban community. In England, the new tenth-century town of St Albans was located close to an abbey and a royal palace, while, in Eastern Europe, most of the new towns established by the eleventh and twelfth centuries were linked to castles, churches, or both.

Not surprisingly, the civic elites that started to emerge by 1000 were frequently dominated by servants or officials of secular or religious lords. Another group, especially influential in north Italian towns, were landowners, attracted there by the growing opportunities for trade; by the eleventh century, important clusters of merchants and craftsmen are also found, all with their own centres of activity. This mosaic of different political and economic interest groups was often mirrored on the ground, in the evolution of polycentric towns, with a mosaic of jurisdictions, as we noted in Chapter 5.

II

By the end of the tenth century, European cities had taken the first hesitant steps towards municipal autonomy—as evinced by the advent of the first guilds, and early grants of charters. In Italy, Genoa claimed its first charter in 958, Mantua in 1014, Brescia in 1038, and Ferrara in 1055. Over the next three centuries, urban communities acquired a growing array of institutions and powers that asserted their claim to autonomy from lay rulers and clergy. As in so much else, Mediterranean cities, especially those in northern Italy, were at the forefront of the new developments. Why? Partly because of their greater urban continuity and precocious economic resurgence, as well as cultural and educational revival; but also because of the specific political circumstances in Italy where the bitter conflict between the Holy Roman Emperors and the Papacy allowed cities to play off the two sides for their own municipal advantage.

In the first place, communes were established by urban landowners who were concerned to neutralize the authority of the Emperor and Church. Consuls appeared at Milan about 1081 and by the early twelfth century they were firmly in charge, even involved in the election of the archbishop. Similar developments occurred soon after at Pisa, Arezzo, Genoa, and elsewhere, as cities exploited the recurrent weakness of the emperors to gain imperial recognition. In 1183, the Treaty of Constance strengthened the powers of Italian cities and many of them enjoyed a growing measure of independence. However, noble feuding within cities, often linked to the cause of Pope or Emperor, led to mounting instability. To try and restore order, to overcome local factionalism, and to deal with outside powers, professional chief magistrates or *podestàs* were appointed, usually for short periods; such officials were usually recruited from another city (Venetians were a popular choice). Genoa had a series of *podestàs* from the 1190s to the 1240s and 1250s, Padua one in 1205, Florence in 1207, and at Milan *podestàs* alternated with consuls.

By the thirteenth century, Italian city government was broadened, as a result of the rise of the *populo*, which brought together armed companies from different parts of the city, led by well-to-do citizens, but also involving the guilds. Political instability remained a serious problem, however, because of tensions between the commercial and financial elites that dominated the urban economy, and the burgeoning demands of middling masters and artisans. At the same time, in northern Italy the new communes exploited the political vacuum created by the imperial–papal conflict to extend their jurisdiction over the hinterland or *contado*. Genoa and other cities concluded treaties with the local nobility that required them to live in the city for part of the year and to help in its military defence. At Pistoia, after 1100, the commune enlarged its superior jurisdiction over the countryside, following and moving out from the highways that led from the city. Though control over the *contado* was rarely stable or complete, often split by rival jurisdictions, it helped ensure urban food supplies, provided troops for civic armies, and had a major fiscal significance. Thus, Florence by 1093 was levying a tax on its *contado*, and in the late thirteenth century rural taxes levied by Pisa and other cities subsidized urban living costs and encouraged the movement of labour from countryside to town.

Aggressive policies towards the *contado*, along with rising urban wealth and pride, contributed to mounting conflict between cities, as major centres sought to extend control over smaller or weaker rivals. Thus, Florence attacked Fiesole, Milan moved against Lodi and Como, and Bologna asserted its influence over Imola. In 1135, Pisa waged war against Amalfi, Ravello, and Scalla in the south, reducing the last to near village status; but Pisa in turn was squeezed by its larger regional competitors, Genoa and Florence. Ferocious, inter-urban conflict was only part of the story, however. Cities could rally together against external threats, particularly from the Emperor: hence, for example, the league begun by Verona, Venice, Padua, and Treviso in 1164, which three years later was enlarged as the Lombard League, bringing together many of the major cities of northern Italy.

North Italian developments were mirrored to some extent elsewhere in the Mediterranean world, though not always for the same reasons. In Catalonia, consuls were elected in the 1180s at Cervera and Barcelona and other towns later on. Here the rise of burghers to civic power may have been encouraged by the Catalan counts as a check on local seigneurial lords. Elsewhere in Spain, the growing power of city governments from the end of the eleventh century was promoted by Catholic kings in the military advance against Islam. Since cities were central to Islamic power, Catholic rulers saw them as key battlegrounds in the reconquest struggle. Alfonso VI gave Leon an important charter in 1097, and those towns on the frontier with the Muslim power received grants of privileges, systems of municipal law, and extensive territory. Such grants reflected both the imperative to attract settlers and fighters to those places, and the financial and military weakness of the Spanish kings. In consequence, landowners and merchants gained a strong foothold in municipal government. In contrast to Italy, however, the role of the state in municipal empowerment made it easier for royal government to tighten its grip on town rulers after the thirteenth century.

While variations in urban political development are evident across the Mediterranean region, still what is striking is the impact of the concept of the commune, the relative precocity and scale of municipal privileges, and the importance of the civic hinterland. In Western Europe, similar variations are evident between countries, but in general municipal autonomy was more limited and came later, while few cities controlled a large urban territory. One important reason was that in Western Europe lay and religious rulers had played a more decisive role in the creation of the urban network, founding many new towns. Kings and princes were more powerful in the region, and cities were less populous and prosperous than their Mediterranean cousins.

Even so, by the twelfth and thirteenth centuries, towns across Western Europe were winning municipal recognition from princes or bishops. With their close ties to Italy, towns in Provence and Languedoc had consulates by the 1120s, often composed of local knights, and a century later Italian-style *podestàs* ruled towns like Arles; but the growing power of lords like the count of Provence, meant urban autonomy was acquired more gradually and partially than in the Mediterranean. Further north, Le Mans set up a commune against their seigneurial oppressor as early as 1070, and similar initiatives were vigorously supported by other towns. During the twelfth century, the term 'consul' was imported from Italy. Under Phillip Augustus (1180−1223), royal authority was extended over French towns through a spate of new charters which sought to control the commune movement by conceding some limited municipal autonomy in return for political loyalty and support. In England, as in France, some urban privileges probably dated back to the ninth and tenth centuries, but a series of royal charters from the twelfth century (thirty under Henry II) sought to prevent the spread of urban communes and to exploit prosperous towns to raise royal revenue. Privileges were often restricted and liable to be curtailed: thus, London's privileges granted by Henry I were probably curbed under Henry II, and in the thirteenth century discord with the Crown led to the repeated suspension of the city's charters, the longest period of direct rule lasting between 1285 and 1298.

In Germany, the roller-coaster fortunes of the emperors determined to a large extent the status of cities. Already, in the tenth century, Otto I granted numerous towns market rights, and in the next century towns battled to win further privileges to defend themselves against outside lords. In 1074, Cologne's merchants staged a rising against the archbishop and, though this was suppressed, the city acquired a civic seal under Emperor Frederick I. Here, and in other episcopal cities like Mainz, urban leaders used conflict between the Emperor and Pope to consolidate their position. While the Emperor Frederick II endeavoured to suppress civic institutions and autonomy in the 1230s, a growing cohort of cities developed elaborate forms of municipal government, including the office of consul. Confronted by the mounting power of territorial princes the Emperor became more dependent on the cities and a growing number—over half in some regions—acquired the status of imperial cities. Initially, this status was limited, but after the collapse of Hohenstaufen rule in 1250, imperial cities extended their rights. Before long, leagues of imperial cities (such as the Rhenish League) had sprung up to protect their privileges.

The Low Countries, notably Flanders and Brabant, witnessed the most advanced and sustained municipal development in Western Europe, a process stimulated by the large size and economic prosperity of many of the towns, their close commercial links to Italy, and the relative weakness of the princely rulers. Sworn communes appeared at the end of the eleventh century and start of the twelfth at Cambrai, Valenciennes, St Omer, Aire, and Tournai; they may also have existed at Ghent and Bruges. Though municipal privileges came under attack under Count Philip of Alsace, after his death in 1191 the towns regained their autonomy and maintained it throughout the thirteenth century.

Yet these municipal developments must be seen in perspective. In contrast to the more important centres that secured extensive rights, thousands of small towns enjoyed minimal privileges, often no more than a market charter, and stayed subject to local lords. In Northern and Eastern Europe progress was often limited, due to the low levels of urbanization and the relatively strong power of rulers. In Scandinavia, the kings had founded most towns and continued to run them through their officials and laws. On the southern side of the Baltic, major port cities and leading commercial towns acquired important privileges (as noted in Chapter 2) under Lübeck or Magdeburg law, but generally rulers kept close control over their urban communities. In Hungary, the thirteenth century Árpád kings sought to attract German and Saxon citizens by charters of privileges, but royal power over the towns remained considerable. In Ancient Rus, even major cities such as Kiev, Novgorod, and Smolensk struggled to obtain civic rights.

If considerable variation is evident across Europe in the pace and scale of the municipal advance, the broad trend was clear by 1300. Two related developments also occurred in the centuries before the Black Death. Firstly, we see the greater institutionalism of urban government, marked by the growth of civic powers and laws, along with an increased number of courts, civic bodies, magistrates and other officials, and the spread of civic record-keeping. Of particular significance was the advent of paid financial officials, often called chamberlains, and other financial reforms. In the van of innovation were the north Italian cities, where from the late thirteenth century a number like Venice and Genoa institutionalized their public debt. Further developments here included a flurry of specialist offices to control urban space and to deal with congestion and other problems caused by urban expansion. Venice's *Signori di Notte* were instituted, probably by the late thirteenth century, to regulate public order and the streets, and this move was accompanied by growing civic supervision of canals and water supply. Municipal regulation and officials multiplied in Provencal towns too: after 1246, Avignon had masters of the streets, whose activity was carefully regulated by ordinances. Growing pressure of royal taxation led to greater formalization of revenue collection by French town officials. As we saw in Chapter 4, high medieval cities undertook growing intervention in poor relief, to deal with the rising tide of indigence. Markets and crafts were other areas of greater communal regulation. True, the process of civic institutionalism must not be over-stated. In many cities, including Mediterranean ones, administration often retained a more traditional and informal dimension, linked to the neighbourhood, parish, or other jurisdictional divisions within town. Here, respectable householders were active in informal social surveillance. Even so, in thirteenth-century Florence, such informal arrangements became more formalized through the creation in each area of a *sindaco* or council of householders, which provided information for the city tribunals.

The second, related development was the institution of civic oligarchy. As we saw above, the urban economic and social order was dominated by small elites and, from the early Middle Ages, elite leaders, including lords and their agents, exercised a strong grip on urban administration. Whether in the communes established in the eleventh century or in the merchant guilds and sworn associations that frequently foreshadowed formal municipal government in Western Europe, the key actors belonged to the elite class. The idea of the municipal community was always restricted. Those poor inhabitants not paying taxes or fulfilling other requirements such as residence for a year and a day were excluded from citizenship, as were many ethnic minorities, and the large numbers of women and young people. When open assemblies of citizens of the commune had taken part in decision-making, their role was soon undermined by the rise of councils and the spread of indirect elections.

Power became concentrated. At Rouen, around 1200, city officials were chosen from a body of a hundred citizens, but at the end of the century the number had fallen to twenty-five. Likewise, at Ghent, the city was governed by three rotating boards of thirteen men—thirty-nine in all—chosen by cooption from the property-owners; but, in 1301, two benches of thirteen councillors were established, chosen by eight electors, four nominated by the count of Flanders, and four by the outgoing council. The rise of large and small councils reflected not only the increased social stratification of the high medieval town, and the ascendancy of mercantile interests, but also the need for more efficient governance as municipal authority expanded and civic officials and urban problems multiplied. Select rule was also supported by rulers who saw it as a mechanism for exercising leverage over urban communities. Consolidation of oligarchic power was strongly contested by craft guilds, more important economically by the early fourteenth century. Under pressure, individual elite families might be excluded from power, and greater representation was sometimes conceded to middling groups, but the structure of oligarchic control was rarely overturned. At Ghent, in 1302, the guilds won legal recognition and some broadening of city government took place, but within a short time patrician power was restored.

In conclusion, before the Black Death the basic foundations were laid for urban governance, through the emergence of many of the key concepts and practices—of municipal autonomy, civic community, citizenship, and elite rule—that would survive until the nineteenth century. Yet those ideas and structures were still fragile in 1300, more strongly established in larger centres and in the Mediterranean world, and parts of Western Europe, weakest in smaller towns and across Northern and Eastern Europe. In the late Middle Ages, recurrent demographic crisis and economic and social uncertainty posed many challenges for urban leaders but, despite this, everything indicates that many of the principal elements of civic government had become well entrenched by 1500.

III

With regard to the growth of municipal autonomy, the picture remained highly variable across Europe. In northern Italy, the leading cities extended their hinterlands and control over smaller cities. One of the most aggressive, Florence, acquired Arezzo, Pisa, Livorno, and other towns between 1384 and 1430, while it also launched a war of conquest against Lucca. Not content with a string of colonies in the Eastern Mediterranean, Venice sought to protect its overland trade routes and food supply by seizing Treviso in 1339, Vicenza, Verona, and Padua (1404–6), and later Brescia and Bergamo. By the close of the Middle Ages, the urban network of northern Italy was dominated by four city-states—Florence, Venice, Milan, and Genoa—often in fierce competition with one another. No less important, in three of these cities municipal rule was increasingly usurped by seigneurial lords—the Medici in Florence, the Visconti at Milan, and later the Sforzas at Milan and for a while at Genoa.

Although the rise of seigneurial lords in Italian cities had begun before the Black Death, the strong momentum of the late medieval period reflected the endemic factionalism of the urban elite and the severe problems and pressures created by economic volatility, territorial expansion, and inter-city rivalry. Seigneurial ascendancy often stripped the old ruling class of its political influence and created a closed clique of courtiers around the ruler. Cosimo de Medici's return to power in 1434 was associated with the political liquidation of dozens of elite families and the exile of many others.

In Spain, municipal government faced other challenges. After the four-teenth century, Castilian and Aragonese kings used their power to interfere in and regulate towns. With the reconquest of most Islamic territory, Spanish rulers had less need for urban goodwill, while feuding in elite circles gave the kings an excuse to nominate magistrates, suspend elections and choose new councils of *regidores* from the patrician class. At Burgos, in northern Spain, for example, the Castilian king appointed (in 1345) a *Regiemento* of sixteen non-noble knights to rule the city, all of them members of the *Real Hermandad*, a special brotherhood established by the king a few years before. Kin ties reinforced the new ruling caucus: nearly a fifth of the brotherhood came from the same family clan. As well as this internal remodelling, Castilian cities fell under the growing power of the royal *corregidor*. Up to the end of the fifteenth century, however, civic leaders accepted royal control as a defence against political threats from local aristocrats.

In Western Europe, the entanglement of rulers in foreign or civil wars gave cities more political space and helped them to consolidate their municipal privileges. In France, the earlier royal policy of recognizing limited urban autonomy in return for loyalty and support opened the door to growing involvement by the 'bonnes villes', mostly the larger provincial cities, in national government, as the Valois kings fought to defeat the English in the Hundred Years War. From the fourteenth century the 'bonnes villes' attended meetings of the States-General and carried out growing administrative, financial, and military duties. Cities such as Langres in eastern France used royal support during the war to throw off the control of local lords. Where royal interference occurred, it was mostly due to feuding within the civic elite or the government's desperate need for military finance: heavy royal taxation imposed growing strain on middle-rank towns.

In England, where most towns (other than London) were small by continental standards and the power of the Crown was relatively strong, the municipal advance was more hesitant. As late as 1392, Richard II cancelled the liberties of the city of London and Londoners had to pay £30,000 for their restoration. In the fifteenth century, the weakness of successive Lancastrian and Yorkist kings made them more dependent both on London and provincial cities. In the case of boroughs chartered by the Crown, there were advances on three fronts: the granting of shire status to cities, separating them from adjoining counties; the new concept of incorporation, confirming the borough as a legal body able to own property; and, lastly, the new right for city magistrates to act as justices of the peace. Under Richard III, a rash of new charters was approved as the king tried to shore up his political support, and, in consequence, the cities of York and Gloucester gained jurisdiction over extensive hinterlands. By contrast, towns under monastic or seigneurial lords secured few improvements in their status, despite recurrent popular agitation, including mob attacks on seigneurial officials during the Peasants' Revolt of 1381. Here we discover moves to create shadow urban governments separate from seigneurial control.

In the Holy Roman Empire, the power of the princes compelled the Emperor to make political alliance with the cities. As we saw above, a growing number of major centres had become imperial cities during the twelfth and thirteenth centuries. Initially, their status was limited, but during the later medieval period imperial control was further relaxed. At the same time, inter-city cooperation increased to defend urban interests against princes and Emperor. Leagues of imperial cities, already formed in the thirteenth century, multiplied in the later period, with several established by the 1340s. In 1376, the fourteen Swabian imperial cities set up a league to protect their privileges against the new Emperor Charles IV, and the next decade it united forty towns. In turn, the Swabian League made alliances with a Rhenish league of fourteen towns and with a league of Swiss towns. Alliances were promoted by the growing volume of contact and correspondence between towns. Most of the leagues proved temporary but two became more permanent: the Hanseatic League (discussed below) and the Swiss League whose membership eventually included 150 towns and hamlets, and which sought both to defend urban rights against the Emperor and to extend the towns' control over the countryside. In 1499, the Swiss League routed the imperial army of Maximilian I and raised the curtain for an independent state; under confederate rule, the leading Swiss towns of Basel, Berne, Fribourg, Lucerne, Schaffhausen, Solothurn, and Zürich enjoyed extensive territorial jurisdictions. Generally, however, only a few German imperial cities (such as Nuremberg) had large *contados* on the Italian model. One last point. Though German cities were concerned at the growing power of the princes, we should not exaggerate the level of conflict between the two sides: mutual interest dictated that many urban centres got on relatively well with neighbouring lords.

The relationship between privileged city and ruler was progressively recognized and encapsulated in the triumphal entries of princes into cities on their accession, marriage, and other festive or religious occasions, times when the prince could attempt to assert his authority but also try to conciliate the community through his human presence. Reflecting the tensions in the relationship, the ceremonial process was often difficult, fraught with misinterpretation on both sides. In the Low Countries, where *joyeuses entrées* start in Brabantine towns during the 1350s (and earlier in Flemish towns), and where large and prosperous cities like Bruges and Ghent had acquired extensive autonomy before the Black Death, the later Middle Ages saw the dukes of Burgundy and their imperial successors attempting to renegotiate the balance of power with the cities, to reassert control and consolidate the state. Initially, the Hundred Years War may have advantaged the Flemish towns, as rival forces needed to borrow from urban bankers and merchants, but the growing costs of military activity and the consequent disruption of trade and manufacturing led to a series of revolts by Flemish towns against the Burgundian government. That by Bruges in 1436–8 provoked heavy financial penalties which had serious economic consequences for the town. Ghent offered the strongest opposition to ducal power. In 1452, the city took to the field against the duke, but in the end its army was defeated, its troops massacred, and the city forced to submit to the humiliating Peace of Gavere (1453)—though at least Ghent escaped the sack of the town that Liège suffered in 1468. Not all towns in the Southern Netherlands experienced such reverses. More sensitive to the new political climate, more adept at negotiation with rulers, Antwerp, Brussels, and Lille benefited from the problems of their rivals and consolidated their political position.

In Northern and Eastern Europe, the relative power of rulers and landowners continued to restrict the growth of municipal autonomy in many areas (the Bohemian lands and Royal Prussia were exceptions). The most important development in the North was the rise of the Hanseatic League, creating a political network of major Nordic, Baltic, and German cities that controlled a large share of long-distance trade in the region. Formally established as a town league in 1336, its general assembly comprised nearly 200 members. Like the German leagues, the Hanse never constructed a strong institutional structure, but it was able to exploit conflicts between rulers to promote its commercial interests and buttress the position of individual towns.

If the progress of municipal autonomy was chequered across late medieval Europe, other developments followed a more consistent pattern. Processes of civic institutionalization, already under way in larger cities before the Black Death, accelerated in the following two centuries, spreading now to smaller centres. In Italian cities, the demographic and economic instability caused by the plague contributed to a decisive shift away from more traditional neighbourhood self-regulation, and neighbourhood organizations were incorporated into civic government under the control of the patrician class. At the same time, communal power was idealized in the growth of civic humanism and the passion for public life and public office that was one of the glories of late fourteenth-century Florence. Across Europe, as we have seen in previous chapters, increased municipal activity was evident in environmental policy (including the improved provision of water), economic regulation, social welfare, justice, education, and civic ceremony and ritual. Attempts by civic leaders to control the whole area of urban space led to pressure on separate liberties and other lesser jurisdictions within towns, notably ecclesiastical ones. Municipal activism was boosted by increased privileges (at least for some towns), and the professionalization of civic government. The number and power of civic officials expanded inexorably. In south Germany and Switzerland, 140 towns had town scribes by the late fifteenth century; in Spain, Cordoba employed a growing cohort of officials; and London's civic officials trebled to twenty-four by 1485. In Burgundian, as well as French towns, municipal clerks and legal *conseillers* contributed to greater municipal effectiveness.

Vital for the expansion of municipal activity and civic bureaucracy was the growing success of town governments in managing their finances. Spanish towns made greater use of tax farmers, often Jews or members of the elite, who helped to ensure a steady flow of urban revenue. Through funded debts, Italian cities like Venice and Florence were able to see their state debts rise tenfold while interest rates fell. In Burgundian towns, financial administration became more systematic, run by a hierarchy of officials. Civic taxes were levied in a more organized way, and detailed financial records survive for a growing number of towns after 1400.

Another widespread development of the late Middle Ages was the further entrenchment of town oligarchies. Pressures in favour of select rule, already evident in the thirteenth century, became more accentuated. Social stratification, the desire of central governments to have a knot of loyal agents in towns, economic and social pressures, and the expansion of municipal government, all played an influential role. In particular, the increasing complexity and cost of civic administration and negotiation with outside powers relied on prosperous burghers with time and money to spare for council meetings or long diplomatic missions to other cities or the royal Court.

Town rulers strengthened their position in a variety of ways, setting up new councils to whittle power away from ordinary burghers, reducing the size of councils, and increasing their own powers. Small groups of elite families moved to monopolize civic office. At Luxemburg, in the fifteenth century, a small group of families took over the offices of *echevin* and *justicier*. In Catalan towns, the magistracy was increasingly closed, though variations occurred between communities in the timing and scale. Ruling councillors in Hungarian towns sought to perpetuate their power through new electoral procedures which ignored the citizenry altogether. Moves also took place to expand civic control over the guilds, to enlarge the power of wealthy masters, and to exclude poorer inhabitants.

However, oligarchic controls were rarely set in cement. There was pressure for accountability from middle-rank burghers, and the most successful ruling elites responded to communal opinion. Feuding within the elite might lead to upheavals and sometimes the collapse of the ruling class, as at Brussels and Leuven during the fourteenth century. When the ruling elite closed its ears to communal opinion, middle-rank traders and craftsmen mobilized popular discontent over taxes and unemployment to challenge their exclusion from power. French towns in the Midi were the scene of insurrectional movements in 1330, 1380, and at the start of the fifteenth century. Large-scale risings erupted at Augsburg in 1368, at Florence in 1378, at Rouen and Paris in 1381–2, while popular urban discontent, led by Londoners, played a key part in the English Peasants Revolt of 1381.

Agitation sometimes led to limited reform. Opposition from Cologne weavers to the regime of the Council of Fifteen forced the widening of city government in 1370, with increased power for the Large Council, but the following year the elite staged a counter-coup and managed to restore the oligarchic regime. However, before the end of the century, lesser merchants, in alliance with the leading guilds, installed a new reformed order with wider elections. At Wroclaw, a rising by the trade guilds against the city council in 1418 climaxed in the execution of the mayor and six councillors, and the installation of a new council with guild representation, though the reforms were short-lived and the guild leaders were hanged. More lasting reform took place at King's Lynn, where conflict in the early fifteenth century drove the town's magnates to agree to political concessions to the town's *mediocres*, including the establishment of a council of twenty-seven to oversee the town's financial affairs. In contrast, at Venice towards the end of the Middle Ages, disastrous wars and political upheaval led to the reinforcement of oligarchy. In other North Italian city-states, now under seigneurial control, there was a similar trend. In sum, across Europe, the shift towards oligarchic power in cities was general, but there are indications that some cities, often more economically dynamic ones, such as Cologne and Barcelona, were less closed than others.

This raises one further issue: how far can we identify the evolution of a new kind of discursive political space in late medieval towns, linked to the enhanced role of drinking-houses, fraternities, guilds and fraternal societies? In the case of fraternities, there are some indications that the authorities feared that political intrigue was taking place at such meetings, but magistrates were quick to stifle such activity. In England, there is little evidence, for instance, that urban fraternities were involved in political agitation linked to the Peasants Revolt. As we know, craft guilds frequently led the protests against civic oligarchy, and both confraternities and guilds may have provided rudimentary political education for members, through their involvement in decision-making and office-holding. In towns under seigneurial control, such bodies sometimes served as shadow governments for the community. By the late Middle Ages, there are also indications of the importance of drinking-houses for the exchange and dissemination of news. But, while we should be wary of dismissing the idea of an embryonic political space in towns before 1500, it is difficult to see it having an important or coherent role. Rulers and civic officials were nervous of troublemaking and ready to stamp it out. Not only did guilds experience increased civic control, but also drinking-houses saw mounting official regulation and licensing, and the Church had a growing hand in the supervision of fraternities. Overall, the expansion of municipal government in the late Middle Ages was not accompanied by greater political pluralism.

IV

In this chapter and previous chapters we have examined how the disintegration of the urban order after the collapse of the Roman Empire with the disappearance of many towns, particularly in Western Europe, and the decay of population and economic and communal functions, began to be reversed by the tenth century, and how the three centuries before the Black Death saw strong and sustained urban growth, the foundation of many new towns, and the spread of towns to Northern and Eastern Europe, regions

which had previously lacked urban communities. Indeed, one might say
that the high Middle Ages was the first time that an urban Europe started
to exist. Propelled by demographic and agrarian expansion, local trade
and urban marketing flourished, and, largely on its back, industry and
long-distance trade took off. If earlier urban leaders were often outsiders,
by the twelfth and thirteenth centuries towns began to acquire their own
mercantile patriciates. At the same time, towns filled up with growing
numbers of craftworkers and poorer folk, as villagers flocked there from
an overcrowded countryside. Urban communities gained a renewed sense
of identity, associated as earlier with the Church and urban fortifications,
but now linked to new civic buildings, hospitals, and growing literary
and artistic representations. Municipal government, largely absent in the
early medieval era, was re-established; the fragile plant of civic autonomy
(minimal before) was nourished through grants of charters and privileges;
new governing institutions and laws developed. In one or two regions,
such as northern Italy, cities began to dominate the countryside rather than
the other way round.

Demographic crises and economic upheavals during the late Middle
Ages posed great challenges for the embryonic urban network. Many urban
populations declined, and some very small towns disappeared. Trade may
have contracted and increased competition from the countryside exerted
pressure on older urban industries, especially textiles, and stimulated greater
rivalry between cities and towns. Even so, many towns endeavoured
to overcome these difficulties by diversifying economically, through new
specialist industries and service activities. Social problems, particularly social
stratification and destitution, threatened social order, but towns responded
to the poverty issue by an expansion of civic as well as private relief. Cultural
life in the late medieval period became more secular and multi-layered with
cities developing a medley of initiatives—competitions, ceremonies, and
spectacles—to promote the idea of communal harmony, to bolster civic
pride, and to attract outside visitors. In a rudimentary way, urban or place
marketing had arrived.

Time and again, we have noted how during the medieval period
Mediterranean cities, notably those of northern Italy, led the way in terms
of political institutions and ideas, commercial and banking procedures,
luxury manufactures, and artistic and cultural innovation, reaching its
acme in the Renaissance rediscovery of classicism. As we have found,
of crucial significance was the relative continuity of the urban network,

the strong economic prosperity after the tenth century as Italians became the businessmen of Europe, high levels of immigration including the acceptance of ethnic minorities, important international interaction with the Eastern and Islamic World through migrants and trade, and the advanced educational skills of the urban population. No less important, the clustering of a number of relatively large, autonomous cities close to one another encouraged strong rivalry and emulation between cities, propelling the creative learning curve upwards.

By the close of the Middle Ages, however, there is evidence that the early dynamic of the Mediterranean city system was less assured, as the rise of city-states in northern Italy eclipsed the earlier polycentric network, as urban economies faltered, as civic autonomy was stifled by seigneurial rule or, as in Spain, by increased royal control, and as toleration of ethnic minorities began to fade. Already, before 1500, the urban networks in Western Europe show a growing resilience through economic specialization, increased elite prosperity and control, and enhanced civic and communal identity. Here, during the fifteenth and early sixteenth centuries, the cities of the southern Low Countries undoubtedly played a pivotal, bridging role linking Mediterranean and West European developments. But it was only in the seventeenth and eighteenth centuries that the cities of Western Europe, led in large measure by those of the Dutch Republic and later England, imposed their leadership on urban Europe.

PART
II

7
Urban Trends 1500–1800

The period from the Renaissance to the French Revolution was a time of critical transition for European cities. By the late eighteenth century, a loose urban network was becoming consolidated across the continent and new kinds of city had started to proliferate—powerful capital cities, Atlantic ports, industrial towns, and the first leisure resorts. Those centres were particularly important in Western Europe, which increasingly eclipsed the earlier urban brilliance of the Mediterranean world. New economic developments were under way after 1700, among them the initial stages of large-scale industrial growth, the expansion of the colonial trades to Asia and the Americas, the advance of retailing and the service sector—all of which had major implications for towns. The urban social order acquired greater potential stability through the growing status of middling social groups. During the Enlightenment era, cities and towns became the centre-stage for a repertoire of innovative and secular cultural activities, frequently performed against the backcloth of a redesigned, neoclassical townscape, while a more constructive dialogue opened between cities and states, and the first halting steps were taken for more effective civic administration.

However, the process of urban change was fraught and incomplete: it was not an easy ride. After the demographic downturn of the late Middle Ages, many urban centres grew rapidly during the sixteenth century, through an avalanche of immigration. In much of Europe, urban economies progressed relatively slowly and social conditions deteriorated. Civic institutional advances achieved in the medieval period were often overwhelmed by the new circumstances. Again, the cultural coherence and identity of the post-medieval city was frequently disrupted by the religious conflict of the Reformation. External forces—agrarian crisis in the countryside, recurrent warfare, and the growth of nation-states eager to tax towns and intrude in their government—contributed heavily to these problems. During the seventeenth century, the phase of strong urban demographic growth was quickly reversed and some urban decline occurred which lasted in most countries (but not England) until the early decades of the next century. Meantime, many of the earlier economic, social, political, and other problems continued to afflict cities. Only in the later part of the eighteenth century did urban momentum revive, as population growth was associated with strands of economic, social, cultural, and political change, notably in the major cities of Western Europe.

Three points are striking about the broad urban changes of the early modern era. Firstly, the urbanization cycles were relatively short compared to those in the Middle Ages. Secondly, there was a growing divergence in the patterns and chronology of urban development across the continent—both between the main urban regions but also, arguably, between national urban networks. Thirdly, even the urban achievements of the eighteenth century proved fragile, and in many countries they were thrown into the air by the political and economic upheavals of the French Revolution.

In this chapter, we look first at the common threats that cities faced; then at the main waves of urban growth and contraction; and, finally, at the experience of different types of towns, not only the more traditional, multi-functional centres, but also the growing numbers of more specialist communities like Atlantic port cities, and industrial, resort, and military towns, and the first advent of European colonial towns.

I

Urban growth in the early modern era was frequently menaced by the same natural and human threats that had confronted medieval towns (see Chapter 2). The important Balkan port of Izmir was largely destroyed by an earthquake in 1688 and 20,000 people killed, while the centre of Lisbon suffered a similar catastrophe in 1755. Fire remained a serious threat, as demonstrated by the great conflagration of London in September 1666 which burnt 13,200 houses, St Paul's cathedral and 87 parish churches, left 65,000 people homeless, and badly disrupted the city's commerce; the total cost of rebuilding may have approached £6 million. However, the spread of brick and stone building in Western Europe, following the model of Mediterranean cities, helped to reduce the risk of fire, while from the eighteenth century the formation of organized fire brigades in major European cities (in Britain linked to fire insurance) helped to contain the spread of fires.

Of the epidemic diseases, bubonic plague was the most damaging to towns, as we shall find in Chapter 9, but urban populations recovered relatively quickly from plague mortality, due to heavy immigration, and, after the late seventeenth century, plague had largely disappeared from urban Europe. While smallpox proved a terrible successor, by the end of the period the first medical steps had been taken to bring it under control. Harvest failures and food shortages were still a major problem for many Europe towns into the early eighteenth century, contributing to demographic crises, disrupting urban economies and generating large-scale poverty. Steadily, however, the most disastrous consequences of harvest failure were diminished, as a result of improvements in agriculture, trade, and communications—at least in Western Europe: in less developed regions urban subsistence crises continued into the nineteenth century.

Among all the scourges, warfare posed a mounting threat in the early modern period. Advances in military technology and organization, along with the rise of states and their funding capacity, meant that armies became much bigger and their campaigns longer, more extensive, and more devastating. The impact of high-level warfare involving large concentrated armies was compounded by the prevalence of chronic low-level conflict in which smaller marauding forces, often out of control, roamed and looted the countryside. The Netherlands Revolt and Spanish efforts to suppress it, the French Religious Wars, the Thirty Years War, the English Civil Wars, the French wars of conquest under Louis XIV, the Great Northern War between Sweden and Russia (1700–12), the Seven Years War, and the French revolutionary wars of the 1790s were highly disruptive to European towns and cities. Despite improved fortifications, cities suffered badly from sieges: Antwerp's population fell by a half as a result of the Spanish siege of 1585 and the consequent massive emigration, while at Rouen the siege of 1591–2 led to a great crisis of mortality, and it was said 'they die in every street and at every gate, morning and evening'. Numerous German cities suffered serious depopulation as a result of the Thirty Years War. Not that warfare was universally destructive. Although Antwerp and Ghent were mauled by Spanish armies, Amsterdam and Leiden benefited from the influx of refugees from the Southern Netherlands. During the 1590s, Paris and Rouen suffered badly from warfare, but Honfleur, Le Havre, and La Rochelle enjoyed the profits of privateering. In the eighteenth century, state investment boosted a number of garrison and naval towns.

II

Turning to urbanization trends, the evidence is much more abundant than for the Middle Ages, as early modern states and cities became concerned with recording population and other data. True, the demographic material is scrappy and difficult to interpret, and we know more about the bigger towns than the myriad smaller ones. Many of the individual population figures that follow can only be speculative. Nonetheless, everything suggests that the urban recovery of the long sixteenth century affected all parts of the continent. In the Mediterranean, signs at the end of the Middle Ages that Italian cities were losing some of their dynamism should not be overstressed. Northern Italy still hosted the largest cluster of European cities having over 40,000 inhabitants, and Venice (100,000 inhabitants in 1500) had become the dominant European hub for inter-continental trade, its commerce in Oriental spices, silks, and other luxury goods complemented by its overland commerce to southern Germany and the Low Countries. As one observer wrote in 1526: 'In the greatest numbers they [merchants] come to Venice from all countries, because with its easy access to the sea it is like a common market for the whole world'. And, when its commercial ascendancy waned, Venice's textile industries flourished, while its elites turned to the exploitation of the mainland territory, the *terra ferma*. Though less successful economically, Florence, Milan, Bologna, Padua, Pavia, and Verona all increased their populations during the sixteenth century as a result of heavy immigration from the countryside. Despite being sacked by imperial troops in the 1520s, Rome had doubled its size by 1600, as successive Popes rebuilt the city as a Counter-Reformation pilgrimage centre and the Court capital of the papal territories. Further south, Naples prospered under Spanish rule as an administrative and commercial metropole, its 275,000 inhabitants making it one of largest cities in Europe.

Spanish cities, likewise, experienced general expansion for much of the sixteenth century. Endowed after 1503 with the *Casa de Contratacion*, controlling trade with the Spanish Indies, Seville was transformed from a regional port into a thriving international entrepot; its population soared from about 55,000 in 1534 to 135,000 in 1600, and a frantic construction boom swept the city. Under the stimulus of the Indies trade, the whole area experienced intense urbanization: nearly 40 per cent of the towns in the Guadalquivir Valley had over 10,000 inhabitants. Further north, in the Castilian *meseta*, we find another strong network of large and medium-sized towns exercising a range of specialist functions: Valladolid, the ancient seat of Castilian government; Madrid, after 1560 the new imperial capital; Burgos, Toledo, and Medina del Campo, heavily engaged in long-distance commerce; Salamanca, famous for its university and leather trade; Cuenca, Segovia, and Zamora well known as industrial towns. In Catalonia, Barcelona failed to maintain its medieval success as an international port, since the city lacked access to Spanish colonial trade, but still the population increased substantially, due to modest industrial growth and heavy immigration.

Further east, urban expansion was significant, in spite of growing political instability and military inroads by the Ottoman Turks. In the Balkans, the Ottoman occupation probably had less disastrous effects than was once thought. Evidence for forty towns suggests widespread population increase due to heavy migration from the countryside. Different levels of town can be identified from small open towns, to those with strongholds, and major fortified centres. In Serbia, the older larger towns became political and economic centres of Turkish power; in Bosnia, the city of Sarajevo benefited from new construction and trade with Istanbul and Dubrovnik.

Before the close of the sixteenth century, however, the expansive era for Mediterranean cities was grinding to a halt. The Ottoman advance disrupted Levantine trade, while plague epidemics, the problems of agrarian productivity, and growing fiscal burdens caused by wars, all took their toll. Venice's golden age was becoming tarnished by 1600 as the Turkish threat provoked a crisis in business confidence and Dutch and English merchants, not content with opening new sea routes to the Far East, seized a growing share of Mediterranean trade; meanwhile, North European manufactures undercut and outflanked Venetian industry. Urban malaise permeated the major cities of northern Italy. Bologna, Pavia, and Mantua went into long-term economic and demographic decline, while Milan ran into serious difficulties in the early seventeenth century, as the city's silk and textile industries suffered from foreign and rural competition, and the elite classes shifted their focus from urban business to rural investment.

Urban decline was even more extensive in Spain, its onset heralded by
the terrible plague outbreaks and subsistence crises of the 1590s. Seville's
contraction was precipitous, its population sliding by a half during the
seventeenth century, partly due to the loss of its trade monopoly to
Cadiz in the 1650s. Elsewhere, in Andalusia, the urban decline was more
limited. But, in Castile, only Madrid, sustained by the growth of the
Court and government, continued to expand (reaching 150,000 or so in
the 1620s), whereas Sevogia, Toledo, Medina del Campo, and industrial
centres like Cuenca were badly affected. To some extent, Madrid drained
trades, merchants, and population from provincial centres, but they also
suffered from the collapse of the textile industry (due to Dutch and English
competition), and from the growing crisis in the agricultural sector.

In Western Europe, the urbanization trend after 1500 was more sustained,
despite the problems caused by warfare. Energized by their traffic to the
Mediterranean world, the cities of the Southern Netherlands led the urban
recovery in the early sixteenth century. With over 90,000 inhabitants,
Antwerp became a great beehive of European trade, eclipsing its old rival
Bruges. One Venetian ambassador called Antwerp the 'leading commercial
centre in the world'. As well as trading with Italy (overland), Germany,
and England, it started to engage, via the Portugese, in colonial commerce
to Asia. Improving on Italian banking methods, it became the principal
source of loans for the German Emperor, the English Crown, and other
rulers. Its large community of foreign traders and artisans made it creative
in many economic areas, developing, for instance, as the leading art market
in Western Europe. But Antwerp was closely integrated into a dynamic
network of towns in Flanders and Brabant. Though Bruges was losing
its old brilliance, Ghent and Brussels were expanding, the latter as a
Court capital, and a growing number of medium-sized towns did well
through the growth of specialist trades: thus, tapestries at Oudenaarde
(where the population doubled in the first half of the sixteenth century to
9,000), brewing at Menen, and linen at Kortrijk, Aalst, Eeklo, and Tielt.
Growth also extended into the towns of the Northern Netherlands which
steadily enlarged their share of Baltic commerce, so that Amsterdam, whose
population rose from 12,000 to 27,000 in the years 1500–1560, eclipsed
Lübeck, the old kingpin of the Hanseatic trade.

The Netherlands Revolt, from the 1560s, had serious urban consequences, including disruption to trade, military levies, disorder, and
destruction. Whilst Antwerp was worst affected, many of its inhabitants

fleeing to the Northern Netherlands, other towns in the south under Spanish control also suffered, at least in the short term. Prime beneficiaries were the cities of the new Dutch Republic, where the flow of merchants and skilled workers from the south brought new capital, commercial connections, and industrial know-how. Amsterdam's population jumped to 105,000 in 1622, the city using its entrenched position in the Baltic trade as a springboard for entry into Mediterranean commerce, while it steadily enlarged its role in the colonial trades with Asia and America. Mercantile success enabled it to take over the mantle of Antwerp as the principal financial and banking centre in Western Europe (see Chapter 8). At the same time, Amsterdam's rise was underpinned by its close integration into a network of specialist cities in the provinces of Holland and Zealand: the so-called Randstad. Here, Leiden (over 40,000 inhabitants in the 1620s) emerged as the leading textile centre for the New Draperies; Haarlem became well known for its linen; Gouda for pipe-making; and Delft as an artistic centre (seven firms in 1616; twenty-seven in 1661), and producer of ceramics. Affluent, and socially and culturally dynamic, Dutch cities took the lead in seventeenth-century Europe, the urbanization rate attaining a remarkably high 42 per cent by the 1670s, probably the highest level in Europe. However, the towns of the Southern Netherlands also bounced back in the early part of the century. Thus, Antwerp enjoyed a second burst of prosperity as a nexus of luxury production for the Spanish Empire, famous for its furniture-making, printing, diamond-cutting, and painters such as Rubens and Van Dyck.

Like their counterparts in the Low Countries, French cities enjoyed widespread revival in the early sixteenth century. As the capital of ambitious Renaissance kings, Paris may have reached about 250,000 people by about 1550, while the second biggest city, Rouen, may have had 75,000, and Lyon, with its important silk industry, printing trade, and commerce stretching into the Mediterranean as well as Northern Europe, counted nearly 60,000 inhabitants. The demographic upturn also lifted provincial capitals like Toulouse and Dijon (a textile as well as administrative town), and smaller clothing and fair towns such as Millau and Romans. However, the outbreak of the French religious wars from the 1560s unleashed a deluge of difficulties for many towns: disrupted trade, the influx of refugees from the countryside, heavy taxation, and military assault. Sharp falls in population occurred. At Lyon, one of the cockpits of conflict, the number of inhabitants may have slumped by a half; at Orléans, it fell from 47,000 to about 37,000, and similar decline affected many other provincial towns. Yet the restoration of royal government under Henry IV, at the end of the century, launched an urban revival. Paris increased to about 450,000 inhabitants in 1650; Lyon expanded markedly (to about 67,000), as did other cities like Amiens and Nantes.

Elsewhere in Western Europe, sustained urban development is evident into the early seventeenth century. Across the Channel, London chalked up a spectacular rise as a European and (after 1600) colonial port city and as the capital of an increasingly powerful English state: its population leaped from a modest 50,000 inhabitants at the start of the Tudor period to about 400,000 by the time of the English Civil War. But expansion was common among English provincial towns as well, stimulated by political stability, the expansion of domestic and overseas trade, and the growth of urban services. The upper reaches of the urban hierarchy showed considerable strength as emerging provincial capitals like Norwich, Exeter, and Bristol increased their populations by 20–35 per cent during the sixteenth century; middle-sized county towns like Gloucester and Leicester also grew. At the lower end of the urban order, fortunes were more variable. In East Anglia, for instance, we find a mixture of declining and expansive small towns. One basic problem was that the foundation of new market centres (or revival of old ones) generated intense competition between relatively unspecialized small towns, often only a few kilometres apart, which too often stifled growth.

In Germany, urban expansion continued, more or less, into the early seventeenth century, though again with local variations. Without a national capital and with few really large cities, growth was focused on a cadre of medium-size regional centres, mostly in the south and north-west; around them extended largely autonomous urban networks. In the south, the population of Augsburg more than doubled during the sixteenth century (to 48,000) as the city basked in the success of its fustian cloth industry, its output sold to well-dressed customers in Italy and Spain, while wealthy merchants like the Fugger and Welser families diversified from textiles into mining and banking. At the cultural crossroads between Mediterranean and Atlantic Europe, Augsburg developed as a flourishing artistic and cultural city whose painters, sculptors, and architects delineated in the public and private townscape their own distinctive versions of Italian Mannerism. With about 40,000 people crowded inside the city walls and another 20,000 more in its wider territory, Nuremberg was especially buoyant in the first half of the sixteenth century, its progress supported by its advanced metal crafts (making scientific instruments, clocks, gold and silverware), its important trading companies, its location on the important overland route from Venice, and its cultural and artistic fame, though war and Italian competition caused more difficulties in the second half of the century. Further north, Rhineland cities like Cologne and Mainz prospered, as did cities to the east such as Magdeburg and Wroclaw. Northern ports like Hamburg and Emden also did well: Hamburg raced ahead of Lübeck in northern trade, while Emden's expansion owed much to Dutch refugees fleeing warfare in the Low Countries.

Whether or not German urban growth was already slowing by the early seventeenth century, there can be no doubt that the Thirty Years War had a devastating effect from the 1630s, as Swedish, imperial, and other armies besieged, occupied, and laid waste cities and towns across the empire. Those in Brandenburg, Mecklenburg, the Rhineland, and the south were worst affected. Augsburg's population fell by over a half; at Nördlingen, between 1633 and 1636, the ranks of citizen households were reduced by a third. The proportion of taxpayers at Mainz declined by more than a half in the years 1629–50, while at Trier the population contracted by 45 per cent. Small towns suffered badly. Swamped by refugees from its hinterland, fleeing Swedish and Catholic forces, the small Hesse town of Ortenburg had half its population wiped out by plague in 1635. Only a small number of towns escaped. Strasbourg and Mulhouse were protected by their walls, and Hamburg's population rose from about 40,000 in 1600 to 75,000 in 1650, as the well-fortified city stayed out of the war, refugees poured in, and both sides relied on it as a financial exchange point.

Turning to outer Northern Europe, the sixteenth-century picture was again one of urban expansion, though with distinctive features. While the Hanseatic League decayed in the face of hostility from national rulers and competition from Dutch merchants, most of the bigger port towns of the region like Bergen, Turku, and Dundee prospered. Those ports which doubled as governmental centres, like Stockholm, Copenhagen, and Dublin, advanced at varying rates. Copenhagen's population increased fourfold between 1500 and 1600, though Stockholm, which became the capital of the new Swedish kingdom (including Finland) in the 1530s, saw more modest growth to 15,000 inhabitants (or less) in 1629. By 1640, Dublin may have had about 30,000 people, making it one of the biggest cities in the British Isles.

Helped by population growth and increased agrarian trade, small towns
also developed. Particularly striking in this part of Europe was the foundation of many new market or micro-towns with a few hundred inhabitants.
In Norway, the number of towns doubled, while, in the Swedish kingdom,
forty-five new towns were established between the 1580s and 1650s; in
Finland, for instance, towns were established at Oulu (1605) and Tornio
(1621), on the site of existing merchant camps, in order to control and
tax the profitable Lapland trade. Nearly 300 new Scottish burghs were
founded, mostly before 1650; and, in Ireland, the English Crown founded
or refounded a series of market towns in its settlement of Munster and
Ulster. However, many of the small towns in the region had a precarious
existence—often under the thumb of seigneurial lords. Royal policy in
Sweden after 1614 sought to confine overseas and long-distance trade to
a number of staple port towns, excluding small inland towns from trade
and so causing their stagnation or decline. In Ireland, military and political upheavals in the 1640s and 1650s had terrible consequences for small
towns like Drogheda, Wexford, and New Ross which were laid waste by
English forces.

In Eastern Europe, many lesser Hungarian towns vanished during Ottoman rule (after the 1520s), but considerable continuity is visible in the
case of the main cities, the ancient capital of Buda keeping its primacy. In
the Polish-Lithuanian kingdom, around 400 new seigneurial towns were
founded during the second half of the sixteenth century to exploit agricultural commercialization, as Polish grain fed the hungry urban populations
of Western and Mediterranean Europe; Gdansk, the principal export port
in this traffic, enjoyed a boom, attracting a flock of foreign merchants, and
its population rose to around 50,000. In the lands of the Bohemian Crown
there was a particularly strong surge of urbanization before the Thirty
Years War. Eastward, Czar Ivan's advance against the Tartars re-opened
trade routes to the Black Sea and beyond and led to the founding of new
commercial and frontier towns—both by the state and by secular and
monastic lords. Starting from about ninety-six Russian cities in the early
sixteenth century, the figure had risen to 170 at its close. Although the
Time of Troubles (1598–1613) adversely affected some Russian cities, by
the 1640s we find an upsurge of new towns; in the south, at least, most
of the townspeople (as in the city of Tambov founded about 1636) were
soldiers rather than traders or artisans. Overall, the Russian urbanization
rate hovered at about 2 per cent of the national population in mid-century.

After a phase of urban consolidation and extension, from the mid-seventeenth century the picture in much of Eastern Europe was bleak, especially in areas blighted by the Thirty Years War. Wroclaw, in Silesia, lost 40 per cent of its inhabitants, while in and around Prague half the houses were abandoned and the city's population fell from about 47,000 in 1610 to 27,000 about 1650. Bohemian towns did not recover from the destruction for several decades. Likewise, Warsaw was ransacked by the Swedish army in 1655–6 and 60 per cent of its buildings destroyed, and other Polish cities like Cracow or Jaworów suffered no less badly.

In sum, the sixteenth century saw a widespread urban recovery across Europe from the contraction of the late Middle Ages, but after 1600 the tide of expansion began to ebb, albeit with regional differences in timing and scale, and with capital cities and Atlantic ports often bucking the trend. Even so, by the end of the century urban decline or stagnation was common across the continent.

III

The first to be affected by the demographic downturn, Mediterranean cities showed a striking failure to bounce back. In Italy, most of the major urban centres like Milan, Genoa, Florence, and Venice were in the doldrums from the seventeenth century. One of the few bright spots was Naples which steadily recovered from the devastating plague of 1656 to reach perhaps 215,000 inhabitants at the start of the eighteenth century. Recovering its status as the capital of an independent kingdom in 1734, the city became the showpiece of a reforming monarchy. In southern Italy, many market towns were stagnant or in decline, but in the north a number gained from the migration of industry from the big centres. Small towns were often rebuilt and acquired a retailing and professional sector.

In Catalonia, the spread of the textile industry to the small towns and countryside contributed to the revival of Barcelona towards the end of the seventeenth century; the city also benefited from attempts to reorient commerce towards the colonial trades and later on from the establishment of a calico printing industry. Elsewhere in Spain, the scenario was bleak. After the urban crisis of the early seventeenth century, the urban trajectory remained downward, the biggest cities being worst affected: even Madrid lost population in the early eighteenth century. In contrast, the Portugese port cities of Lisbon and Oporto did well from Brazilian and European trade, state protectionism, and infrastructure improvement, while some smaller towns acquired silk and cloth manufactures.

In Western Europe, urban decline had a growing effect from the mid-seventeenth century, though once again there were variations between countries. In the Dutch Republic, the golden era of Dutch cities faded around the end of the century (see Figure 7.1) as urban manufactures suffered growing foreign competition, wars led to heavy taxation and trade disruption, and capital started to move away from urban business to landholding and finance. A principal victim was Leiden, where textile production slumped by 40 per cent and where the population fell from 60,000 in 1670 to 37,000 in 1749. Competing successfully with Amsterdam in the colonial trades, Rotterdam was one of the few bright spots, while the administrative capital, The Hague, also notched up modest growth. However, the Dutch urbanization rate drifted down from 42 per cent in 1672 to 39 per cent in 1750.

In the Southern Netherlands, repeated French invasions, particularly during the war of 1689–97, caused serious economic reverses and urban decline. The situation was aggravated by de-industrialization in the bigger

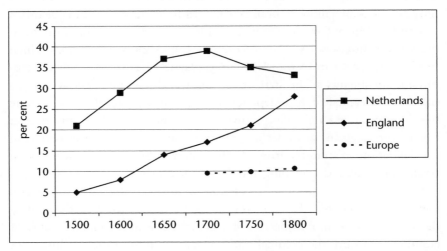

Fig. 7.1 Urbanization in England, the Netherlands, and Europe 1500–1800.
Source: Adapted from E. A. Wrigley, 'Urban growth and agricultural change: England and the Continent in the early modern period' in P. Borsay (ed.), *The Eighteenth-Century Town* (London, 1990), pp. 55–69. Towns above 10,000 inhabitants

cities as production was hit by foreign protectionism and competition from cheaper rural industry. At Antwerp, textile employment fell by three-quarters between 1650 and 1738, and the population went down during the early eighteenth century from 70,000 to 46,000. Meanwhile, Brussels dipped from 78,000 to 60,000 inhabitants, and smaller towns like Lier and Diest also contracted.

In the French kingdom, Paris continued on an upward path, its economy helped by swelling government activity, the influx of nobility, and the city's success as an innovative service centre; its population rose from 450,000 in 1650 to 570,000 a century later. Elsewhere, however, many cities stagnated or declined, among them Orléans, Tours, Angers, Dijon, and Reims, as well as numerous small towns. There were exceptions: Atlantic ports like Bordeaux and Nantes flourished, as did Marseille, increasingly successful in Mediterranean trade. But, generally, the French urban trend seems to have turned down in the period before 1750.

Across the Rhine, the crisis of the Thirty Years War had a profound and lasting effect, aggravated by general demographic and agrarian recession, and, in the border areas, by Louis XIV's military campaigns. Many old imperial cities, such as Nördlingen, Nuremberg, Cologne, and Erfurt stood still economically. On the other hand, residential towns took advantage of growing princely support, including the promotion of new industries. Capital of Brandenburg-Prussia, Berlin saw its population quadruple between 1670 and 1720, in part due to an influx of foreign workers and refugees. Even small princely towns, like Weilberg in Hesse, had an important accession of population after 1650, and were often rebuilt in the new classical style. However, in much of Germany, as in France, the scenario into the early eighteenth century was coloured by urban stagnation.

The one relatively dynamic urban area of Western Europe was England (see Figure 7.1). London continued its earlier spectacular advance, reaching around 600,000 in 1700 and possibly 750,000 by 1750, as economic growth was driven by accelerating inland trade and the city's role as a great European and colonial port; also influential was the accretion of government functions, the influx of wealthy landowners, and the proliferation of services from coffee-houses to concert-managers. The great majority of English provincial towns prospered too. Combining commercial, industrial, and service activity, regional capitals like Norwich and Bristol doubled or trebled their populations between the mid-seventeenth and mid-eighteenth centuries. Maidstone, Gloucester, and other medium-sized county towns were likewise advancing, aided by a specialist industry or services (many became fashionable meeting places for local landowners). At the bottom of the urban hierarchy, smaller towns also performed well: by 1750, many of the established ones displayed comfortable affluence, their main streets refurbished with elegant classical-style brick or stone buildings. Most striking, in the early eighteenth century, was the upsurge of new-style specialist centres. One group were manufacturing towns like Birmingham, Sheffield, or Manchester. Another cluster were new Atlantic ports, led by Liverpool. Finally, a coterie of leisure towns, mainly inland spas, began to put in a smart appearance, among them Tunbridge Wells, Scarborough, and, not least, Bath, with 6–8,000 inhabitants in 1750. If England still trailed other countries in its urbanization rate, it was catching up fast both in the scale and diversity of its urban development. According to E. A. Wrigley, 57 per cent of net urban growth in Europe in the first half of the eighteenth century was concentrated in England. Fundamental to this urban transformation was rising agrarian productivity, improved incomes and rising consumption, burgeoning industrial production, and a commercial revolution which involved extensive transport improvements and the opening up of Atlantic trade. These issues will be discussed in more detail in Chapter 8.

In Northern Europe, growth between 1650 and 1750 was largely confined to a few major cities, mostly capitals. In the Nordic countries, Copenhagen expanded briskly, reaching 80,000 in 1750, but Stockholm grew only modestly from about 57,000 in 1698 to perhaps 63,000 a half-century later. Many other urban centres fared less well. The Great Northern War and its associated outbreaks of disease and famine had a dire effect on Finnish and Estonian towns, while the average population size of Denmark's market towns crept up by only 10 per cent between 1672 and 1769. In the British Isles, the English urban dynamic began to spill over into Scotland and Ireland. By 1750, Edinburgh's population and economy—boosted by the Union with England in 1707—was growing substantially, and Glasgow was starting to take off as a great Atlantic entrepot. Progress among the smaller Scottish towns was slower, a number taking decades to recover from the demographic crisis of the 1690s. In Ireland, the rise of Dublin as a colonial capital city and Atlantic port was remarkable, doubling its population in the fifty years after 1700 to 129,000, but the ports of Cork, Limerick, and Belfast also prospered, albeit on a lesser scale. Smaller towns had mixed fortunes in the late seventeenth century, those in Ulster suffering from William III's military campaigns; but, by the 1730s, market towns in the north were growing from the linen trade, and bigger small towns elsewhere won new commercial and social functions. Even so, the aggregate urbanization rate for outer Northern Europe remained low.

In Eastern Europe, the picture was broadly similar, with only a few cities making any running. Founded in 1703 by Peter the Great on a swamp by the Neva River, and constructed largely by slave labour, St Petersburg grew prodigiously from one or two thousand people to about 95,000 in 1750, as the Court, government officials, and nobility of an aggrandizing imperial Russia took up residence there. Other capital cities expanded too. Warsaw recovered quite quickly from the Thirty Years War, mainly because of the influx of landowners who turned it into a residential town of magnate palaces and centre of the Enlightenment. In the same way, Prague, the second capital of the Austrian emperors, revived from about 40,000 in 1698 to 59,000 in 1750. But otherwise the picture was gloomy. Russian towns suffered from the development of rural industries and fairs by the nobility. Badly affected by wars, most Polish towns stagnated or declined into the mid-eighteenth century, some smaller places becoming ghost communities. After the Ottoman retreat and extension of Austrian rule, Hungarian towns began to revive, but from a low base. As in Northern Europe, urban levels in the region stayed depressed.

IV

Just as the period 1650–1750 was marked by widespread urban stagnation across Europe (except for England), so the second half of the eighteenth century can be seen as an era of urban revival, though streaked with significant regional variations. Western Europe dominated the picture and, once again, English cities proved the most dynamic, powered by a continuing sharp rise in gross domestic product GDP (see Figure 7.1).

What is striking about English urbanization is both the pace of the advance and the fact that most sectors of the urban network participated in the trend. London housed nearly a million inhabitants by the start of the nineteenth century, seizing the role of the leading global as well as European metropolis. However, as in the preceding period, traditional provincial capitals such as Norwich and Bristol put in a relatively strong performance, as did many county towns and market centres, particularly those in the industrializing districts of the Midlands and north. No less striking, the more specialist industrial centres enjoyed rapid take-off, industrial and commercial towns like Manchester, Birmingham, and Liverpool claiming more than 60,000 inhabitants by 1801, ahead of all the old provincial centres. Leisure towns also multiplied, with spa towns joined by the first seaside towns such as Weymouth and Brighton, mainly in southern England. A small company of military towns likewise emerged during the period.

Elsewhere in Western Europe urban expansion was less comprehensive but significant nonetheless. The strongest urban development occurred in the Southern Netherlands. From the mid-eighteenth century, encouraged by the Austrian administration and cheap wages, the textile industries of Brussels, Mechelen, Lier, Antwerp, and Ghent showed a new dynamism, contributing to significant urban revival; Brussels (75,000 in 1784) benefited from its greater role as a government centre, including the building of a new official quarter with parks and squares. Though Antwerp's harbour declined, Ostend grew strongly as a transit port—aided by dock investment and canal and road improvements. Small towns prospered too, as in Brabant, helped by transport investment and the expansion of the domestic market. Already, by the turn of the century, we see the development of new industrial-urban areas in Verviers and Liège, where the arrival of the English technician and entrepreneur William Cockerill acted as a catalyst in the introduction of new mechanized textile and later iron production; and in the Mons-Charleroi area, increasingly important for coalmining and then metal production. Another type of specialist urban centre was also becoming more important by 1800—the leisure town. Though Spa in the west had been one of the first European spa towns, it was only in the later eighteenth century that it consolidated its role; by then it had 2–3,000 inhabitants, tree-lined walks, and over 1,200 beds for tourists who included the high nobility.

Across the border, in France, the trend was again one of renewed urbanization, at least until the political upheavals of the 1790s. Paris further consolidated its economic primacy, notably in commerce, finance, and the service sector, its population rising to about 660,000 on the eve of the Revolution, but the provincial cities made a better showing too. Regional capitals like Lyon, Rouen, and Toulouse grew by between 10 and 20 per cent; and many medium-rank cities and small towns recovered. Improvements in transport and agriculture, the advance of domestic trade, and industrial specialization all contributed. Industrial expansion was especially important in the Lyon-Grenoble area which saw the development of silk, textile, and leather manufactures, exporting to Russia and America, and in the north in the villages and small towns around Lille and Rouen. As in the previous period, the Atlantic ports flourished: Bordeaux nearly doubled its population in the late eighteenth century, while Le Havre and Nantes (succoured by sugar and slavery) also increased in size.

In Germany, the old imperial cities remained largely becalmed. Nuremberg, Cologne, Ulm, and Erfurt all slipped down the urban rankings, though Augsburg battled to develop new cotton and tobacco industries, and Leipzig prospered because of its international fairs, juristic importance, and burgeoning book trade. Imperial cities in the south-west did worst. Towns in Swabia, Franconia, and Bavaria, which had contained 24 per cent of the country's urban population in 1600, housed only 10 per cent by 1800. Small imperial towns, many of them so-called home towns, were particularly prone to economic backwardness. In contrast, the residential cities and towns under princely control fared much better, buoyed up by greater governmental (including military) activity, the growth of the service sector, and princely policies aimed at economic modernization. The population of Berlin, capital of the increasingly militarized Prussian state, marched from 102,000 to 150,000 between 1750 and 1800; and Dresden under the electors of Saxony grew steadily during the eighteenth century. In the Rhineland, administrative capitals like Mannheim, Düsseldorf, and Mainz eclipsed their urban competitors. But princely towns did not have a monopoly of growth. Ports like Hamburg, Bremen, and Szczecin enjoyed quickening success, Hamburg attaining 100,000 inhabitants in the later eighteenth century, its economy fuelled by burgeoning European and Atlantic commerce. In the Austrian Empire, Enlightenment Vienna grew by 37 per cent to about 240,000 in 1800, and other Austrian towns like Linz and Graz similarly progressed.

The major exception to urban revival in Western Europe in the late eighteenth century was the Dutch Republic (see Figure 7.1) where the stagnation evident by 1700 turned into full-blown decline, as major cities in Holland and Zeeland suffered losses of population. As one Dutch writer observed in 1783, 'to anyone who feels the slightest sympathy for his fatherland, it is impossible to walk dry-eyed through the inner cities' of the Republic. How do we explain this urban failure? It seems likely that competition from rural industry and foreign manufactures, high wages, and alternative investment opportunities in agriculture, all played their part, as well as problems of transport and energy resources. Among the principal urban centres, only the governmental centre of The Hague and the Atlantic port cities of Amsterdam and Rotterdam escaped decline.

In outer Northern Europe expansion remained selective. While Stockholm stagnated, Copenhagen further enhanced its dominance of the Danish urban network, reaching about 100,000 by 1800. Denmark's small towns slumbered until the end of the eighteenth century, their economic prospects cramped by rural competition, though in Norway (also under Danish rule) port towns like Trondheim and Bergen prospered. In Sweden, there was a modest increase in the size and occupational diversity of medium- to smaller-size centres, but most of the country's provincial towns remained rooted in the countryside, and with their farms and orchards wore a distinctly rural aspect. Apart from the capital, only Gothenburg enjoyed important international trade. In the British Isles, the ripple effect of English urbanization and economic growth became ever more powerful. Edinburgh blossomed as a leading cultural and social nexus of the Enlightenment, as well as an administrative capital. In the west of Scotland, Glasgow's rise as a great Atlantic port stimulated an upsurge of processing industries in the area, along with manufacturing in small towns across the central Lowlands. Elsewhere, many established towns like Perth, Dundee, and Montrose acquired growing social and service activities, while their urban landscape was remodelled and improved. By 1800, Scottish urbanization was starting to close the gap with England's, the western Lowlands enjoying some of the highest growth in Britain after the north-west of England, and in consequence Scotland became incorporated into the West European city-network. In Ireland, too, expansion became more general, though the urbanization rate lagged well behind that in Britain. Celebrating its status as 'Hibernia's grand metropolis', Dublin's population soared to 182,000 in 1800, making it one of the top ten European cities, but Cork, Newry, and Belfast all had over 20,000 inhabitants by that time. In Ulster, many smaller towns thrived as centres of the linen trade, and across Ireland landowners spent heavily on the improvement and rebuilding of small market towns.

Turning to Eastern Europe, the capital cities still made the running. As a Court and imperial city, St Petersburg more than doubled its size in the late eighteenth century to about 220,000. Prague, fashionable as an Enlightenment Court city, with extensive neoclassical-style rebuilding, increased its population to 76,000. The Hungarian dual city of Buda-pest failed to gain real governmental functions until the last years of the century, but its markets attracted many domestic and foreign merchants, and in 1798 Pest was dubbed 'the emergent London of Hungary'; by then the population of the dual-city counted about 50,000. In the last phase of Poland's independence before final partition, Warsaw's population soared from 24,000 in 1754 to over 100,000 in 1792 as the city's trade and industry flourished and intellectual life sparkled. Otherwise, expansion across the region was more sluggish, constrained by the growth of serfdom, falling agricultural productivity, and diminished gross domestic product. In Russia, the number of towns increased and some, like Astrakhan at the mouth of the Volga River, burgeoned as commercial and administrative hubs, but the urbanization rate probably stayed around 5 per cent in the later eighteenth century. Hungary's medium and small towns, including those in the Hungarian Plain, gained from improvements in agriculture and the increase of inland trade in the Habsburg Empire: a town like Eger grew from 7,200 in the 1720s to over 17,000 in 1789. But the total urban population at the start of the nineteenth century was only about 10—14 per cent.

Across the Mediterranean world the picture was highly variable. In the Ottoman Balkans, there may have been some limited growth of towns, especially ports like Izmir and Salonika. In southern Italy, Naples continued its relentless rise, exceeding 400,000 people at the end of the eighteenth century, growth fuelled by its near monopoly of the political, financial, and consumer power of the Neapolitan kingdom. In the North, the demographic and economic pendulum began to swing back towards the bigger centres. Florence benefited from the revival of its silk industry, and Vicenza from ceramics, while in the Lombard Plain around Milan the city's merchants were engaged in the diffusion of industrial production to the villages.

In Spain, the earlier growth of Barcelona and the other Catalan towns accelerated, as textile and cotton manufacture surged; urban centres in Valencia and Murcia also prospered. Madrid's population rose sharply to 168,000 as the city was swamped by rural poor, pushed on to the road by the failures of the agrarian sector and attracted by the high spenders at Court. Other Castilian centres such as Toledo and Segovia apparently sank in inertia, though cities in the south such as Cadiz and Malaga, as well as smaller agro-towns in the region, took advantage of the expansion of Atlantic trade and produced agricultural exports for the colonies. However, the urbanization rate of the Mediterranean region was broadly static.

V

From this survey of urban trends during the early modern period several general conclusions can be deduced. Firstly, as will be evident from Table 7.1, after the seventeenth century a decisive change took place in the dynamics of European urbanization. Mediterranean cities, long at the forefront of urban growth and creativity, were increasingly relegated to the slow lane. Instead, urban networks in Western Europe, led by those of the Dutch Republic and then of England, took the pole position, not just in terms of urbanization but, as we shall see in the next chapters, in respect of economic, social, and cultural innovation. During the later eighteenth century, cities in the Southern Netherlands, France, and Germany were starting to follow the same path, albeit more selectively. In comparison, urban networks in Eastern and outer Northern Europe progressed more slowly. By 1800, as Figure 7.2 shows, the major European cities are found not only in the Mediterranean but in Western Europe, with a handful too in Eastern and outer Northern Europe.

A second conclusion is that growth in the European urban hierarchy was selective. Among the thousands of small towns, the sixteenth century was a time of recovery after the late medieval contraction. Many new towns were founded, particularly in Eastern and Northern Europe, and

Table 7.1. European urbanization 1500–1800

	1500: mean %	1500: median %	1700: mean %	1700: median %	1800: mean %	1800: median %
Mediterranean	16.7	16.7	18.5	19.4	17.0	17.4
Western Europe	14.7	9.0	20.6	20.7	21.3	17.3
Outer Northern Europe	2.1	2.1	4.7	4.7	8.1	8.1
Eastern Europe	4.8	5.1	4.5	4.6	5.5	4.9

Source: Adapted from P. Bairoch et al., *La Population des Villes Européennes de 800 à 1850* (Geneva, 1988). Towns over 5,000 inhabitants

others re-established. But the small towns which did best were those, as in the Low Countries, which acquired specialist craft or marketing functions. But not all small towns benefited, and some, as in England, suffered from excessive competition. Demographic recession from the seventeenth into the early eighteenth century advantaged some small towns as industry moved away from the bigger cities, and the last part of the period also saw broader advances. Small towns acquired a dynamic role in the spread of new rural industries, so-called proto-industrialization, serving as sources of capital, as production, marketing, and distribution centres. Indeed, in eighteenth-century Europe, particularly in England, the Low Countries, and Catalonia, proto-industrialization might be termed small-town industrialization. Eclipsed by the rise of the great ports, smaller havens turned increasingly to coastal trade, and (in England at least) started to develop as seaside resorts. More generally, they took on agricultural processing and specialist trade functions (as in Spain, northern Italy, and Hungary where there was a significant growth of agrarian towns on the Hungarian Plain); while some of the bigger ones started to develop as fashionable sociable centres (particularly notable in much of Western Europe). But many small or micro-towns bumped along throughout the period, just about keeping their heads above water. In the Nordic countries, for instance, small towns retained a strongly rural flavour under the domination of local landowners.

As we have seen, major and middle-rank provincial cities often had an even rougher passage. Though experiencing some expansion in the sixteenth century, they were badly affected by warfare, disrupted trade, state fiscal exactions, and rural and small-town competition. Populations stagnated or declined sharply in the seventeenth century, and for many places recovery only started during the eighteenth century, with English provincial towns leading the way and those elsewhere only starting to catch up in the second half of the century.

Of the traditional multi-functional or spinal cities in the period, the most dynamic were capital cities—as is evident from their major presence in the European ranking of leading cities (see Table 7.2 and Figure 7.2). Long-established capital cities, like London and Paris, had their importance magnified by the rise of more integrated and powerful European states. In addition, a wave of new capital cities was established in the early modern period: Stockholm in the 1530s, Madrid in the 1560s, Vienna in the 1620s (for the Austrian lands and Bohemia), Warsaw by the early

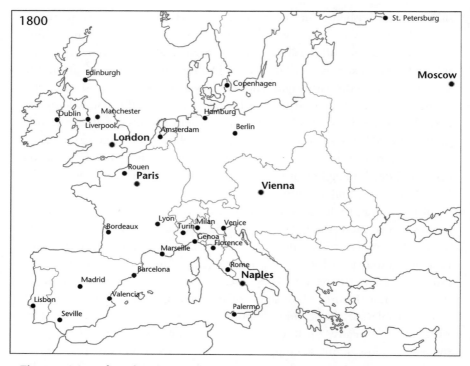

Fig. 7.2 Map of Leading European Cities about 1800. Cities in bold with over 250 000 inhabitants.
Population data adapted from Bairoch et al., *La Population des Villes Européennes de 800 à 1850* (Geneva, 1988). Basemap reproduced from *www.euratlas.com*, ©2003 Christos Nussli

seventeenth century, St Petersburg and Berlin soon after 1700. A parallel growth of secondary capitals also occurred, such as Dublin, Edinburgh, Buda, and Prague. Lavish Renaissance-style Courts, now largely fixed in the capital, along with the growing central bureaucracies and agencies needed to raise taxes, wage wars, and control the population, supplied a powerful economic momentum. Already, in the 1620s, Madrid had over 2,000 royal and city officials and, by the 1750s, the figure had jumped to 5,000, while in seventeenth-century France over a tenth of the kingdom's office-holders resided in Paris. By this time, an important component of metropolitan personnel were soldiers. At Berlin, for instance, military families constituted a quarter of the city's population, and money was lavished on military infrastructure.

Table 7.2. Leading European cities about 1800

London	950
Paris	550
Naples	430
Moscow	300
Vienna	250
St Petersburg	220
Amsterdam	220
Dublin	200
Lisbon	195
Berlin	170
Madrid	170
Rome	150
Palermo	140
Venice	140
Milan	135
Hamburg	130
Lyon	110
Copenhagen	100
Marseille	100
Barcelona	100
Bordeaux	95
Seville	95
Genoa	90
Manchester	85
Edinburgh	85
Liverpool	85
Turin	80
Florence	80
Rouen	80
Valencia	80

Source: Adapted from P. Bairoch et al, *La Population des Villes Européennes de 800 à 1850* (Geneva, 1988)

State power and patronage, ever more channelled through capitals, attracted large clusters of wealthy landowners from the provinces. In Queen Anne's London, about 4,000 landed families and their servants lived in the capital, financed heavily by rural rents. In Stockholm, sessions of Parliament attracted upwards of a thousand nobles who met, socialized, and debated in fashionable taverns and coffee-houses. Official and elite demand gave a strong stimulus to the housing market, industry, retailing, and the service sector, notably professional services and leisure activities. Increasingly remodelled in neoclassical style, the central spaces of capital cities became the luminous exhibition halls of the Enlightenment, as fashionable cultural life—from music-making to the theatre—came under metropolitan sway. High levels of consumption and economic activity created an enormous inflow of ordinary people from the countryside, including many beggars and poor. The result was that capital cities in this period became highly polarized worlds—cities, as Rousseau observed, of 'the most sumptuous wealth and the most deplorable misery'. Capital cities were the forcing ground for a new kind of social segregation, social balkanization, in urban society. Environmentally, they became notorious for their pollution (London already in 'a constant fog... [that] wraps it up entirely'). Anatomized in a torrent of sermons, plays, novels, periodicals, and pamphlets, capital cities became famous for a new sense of depersonalized and commodified relations, and for a new attitude to time. With the proliferation of clocks and personal watches, there was a growing stress on punctuality, while the pressure of business and growth of leisure activities led to a new schedule for meals and sociability: breakfast and lunch arrived, dinner migrated from midday to early evening, and fashionable entertainments were held no longer during the day but from evening to dawn—indeed, capital cities saw the first conquest of night. No less striking was the new velocity of movement, and metropolitan anonymity. In Paris, it was said 'one does not walk, one runs... [and] no one pays any attention to anyone else'.

Predictive of many aspects of modern urbanization, these protean megacities, competing explicitly with one another from the late seventeenth century over population size, public improvements, civility, and fashion, generated strong reactions. Mercier described Paris as 'flourishing but at the expense of the whole nation', and similar complaints were voiced about London, Naples, Madrid, and other capital cities. In reality, however, the impact of the growth of capital cities on their hinterlands was highly variable. Where there were weak national or regional economies, as in the case of Madrid or Naples, large metropolitan centres may have aggravated structural deficiencies; where economies were stronger, the impact, as in the case of Paris or London, seems to have been more benign, stimulating agrarian and sometimes industrial production, as well as commercial integration in the hinterland.

Other dynamic urban centres were often (as we know) specialist cities, including the Atlantic port cities (see Table 7.2 and Figure 7.2). By the eighteenth century, the great Mediterranean port cities, so important in the medieval era, were largely stagnant or in decline (Marseille and Barcelona the obvious exceptions), their share of European shipping reduced from 25 per cent in 1600 to 15 per cent in 1780. In contrast, we see a band of successful ports down the West European seaboard from Glasgow to Lisbon, which were prospering from the colonial trades to America and Asia. Two principal categories can be identified. First, those cities like London or Lisbon that combined port activity with a major administrative function: these enjoyed fast-track expansion. The second larger category comprised specialist centres, often situated like Le Havre, Bordeaux, or Liverpool in more distant locations that were good for shipping. Usually, they united Atlantic commerce with coastal and regional trade, and by the eighteenth century frequently spawned related industries: armaments at Le Havre, sugar-processing at Bristol, Nantes, and Bordeaux, and cottons in the Rouen area. Specialist port cities often shared distinctive features: they attracted important ethnic or religious minorities; their elites were relatively open; they invested heavily in port infrastructure (at Liverpool the dock area was extended from 3.5 acres in 1715 to 28.0 in 1796); and they were energetically engaged in international and national networking. By 1800, more than half of the most dynamic cities in Europe were Atlantic ports.

During the last decades of the period, specialist industrial centres were multiplying in Western Europe, most visibly in Britain. Only a few at this time were completely new towns, most had developed from small market centres like Verviers, Manchester, or Sheffield. Often they had a close, symbiotic link with the countryside. Frequently they supported cheap, lower-quality output in the nearby villages which was marketed through the town, while the urban settlement itself straggled with ribbon-type development into the countryside. As we shall see in Chapter 8, most production was still workshop- rather than factory-based, and increases in output derived from technical improvements and sub-division of processes rather than the introduction of expensive new technology. Even so, growing specialization is evident, as urban manufactures became involved in the finishing of hinterland products or the assembly of rural-made components. Larger manufacturing centres like Birmingham or Manchester moved steadily into trade and distribution: such towns rarely had more than half their workforce engaged in specialist manufacturing. Already, by the start of the nineteenth century, urban industrial regions were developing in Britain (for example, the West Midlands, and West Yorkshire), Belgium (around Liège), and France (around Lille and Lyon); often these complexes were anchored in mineral-rich areas. Chains of innovation operated, as entrepreneurs, new techniques, and skilled workers moved from one urban centre to another, while the bigger towns began to develop complementary rather than competing functions.

Other types of specialist town emerging by 1800 were resort towns and military towns. In the case of watering places where visitors bathed or drank the water, England led the way with its dozen or so spa towns by 1800. Apart from Bath, which by 1800 had about 30,000 inhabitants and housed a genteel retirement clientele, most were very small. Expansion was even more limited on the continent, with barely a handful of spa towns in Germany (for instance, Baden-Baden and Bad Doberan), Austria (Ems and Karslbad), France (Luchon and Plombières-les-Bains), the Low Countries (Spa), Spain (Trillo), and Italy (Porretta and Bagni di Pisa—both with few visitors.) Visitor activity was highly seasonal, usually peaking in the summer months; the rest of the time communities slumbered. Dependent heavily on royal or aristocratic patronage and the marketing of medical practitioners, the early ones (like Bath or Tunbridge) often had close links to metropolitan society and metropolitan entrepreneurs. But by 1800 there was a trend towards more remote locations, attracting fashionable visitors who were influenced by Romantic visions of the picturesque.

Similar influences, along with a new romantic vision of the sea and a vogue for cold water bathing, also stimulated the development of seaside resorts, often decayed ports, the first in England (for instance, Margate, Weymouth, and Brighton), followed by a trickle in Western Europe—Ostend, Boulogne, and Bad Doberan (doubling as a spa). Places for cultural tourism also started to appear, joining older pilgrimage venues like Santiago and Rome. Venice, Florence, and Naples attracted large numbers of smart elite visitors from Northern and Western Europe after 1700, while Stratford-upon-Avon launched its fame as Shakespeare's birthplace in the 1760s. Here, the foundations were laid for urban tourism, one of the most potent features of European city development in the modern and contemporary period.

Military towns formed another significant group. Frontier towns (for instance, bastides) had existed since the Middle Ages, but the changing nature of warfare in the early modern era led to a massive expansion of garrisons, fortifications, and barracks. Some places became major fortresses, like Maastricht (18,000 inhabitants, including 5,000 troops and their families) and Perpignan (11,000), though many were a lot smaller. On the Atlantic seaboard, important naval ports sprang up, mainly from the mid-seventeenth century, among them Chatham and Portsmouth, Lorient and Brest (whose 2,000 inhabitants in 1664 had risen to 30,000 by 1750). Other naval and dockyard towns included Toulon in the Mediterranean and Kronshtadt in the Baltic. All these places depended heavily on state finance and were essentially company towns. All tended to grow rapidly in time of war (Portsmouth's dockyard workforce quadrupled in the later eighteenth century), and to slump during periods of peace. Relations with local municipalities were rarely easy, with disputes over military privileges and demands, and the endemic problem of disorderly troops.

Finally, attention needs to be focused on another new development of the early modern period: European towns outside Europe. With its large-scale imperial expansion under the Conquistadores, Spain led the way. From the start of its exploration and invasion of Latin America, towns were established as instruments of royal political and economic control: for instance, at Panama (1514) and Veracruz (1519). By the 1630s, Spanish America had 330 towns. These included major ports but also inland towns for administration, acculturation, and exploitative purposes. Existing pre-Columbian settlements (like Mexico City and Cuenca) were taken over and new settlements founded. Spanish rule imposed a standard gridiron town plan, focused around a central plaza, probably reflecting Renaissance planning theories. Other colonial impositions included Spanish municipal institutions, with strong royal supervision, and the various agencies of the Counter-Reformation Church. Substantial numbers of colonists cemented Spanish rule. By comparison, Spanish cities in the Philippines were less markedly European (with fewer colonists), as were Portugese settlements on the coasts of Asia, Africa, and Brazil.

Despite de-urbanization in Spain during the seventeenth and eighteenth centuries, the period saw a further consolidation of the urban network in Spanish America with 600 more towns added. However, during this period the main impetus for extra-European expansion came from Western Europe, as the English, French, and Dutch all established colonies with settler populations in the Caribbean and North America, plus some smaller settlements in Asia and Africa. Reflecting commercial priorities, the most important towns were ports: New Amsterdam (later English New York), with about 1,500 inhabitants in 1660; Boston (17,000 in 1740); Montreal (8,000 in 1750); Philadelphia (26,000 in 1769); New Orleans (8,000 in 1800).

Despite expanding migration to British America, inland towns remained very small and dispersed, and urbanization rates low—5 per cent before the Revolution and 6.1 per cent around 1800. Nonetheless, the North American colonial towns displayed distinct features. Often they were laid out in gridiron patterns (for instance, Williamsburg or Montreal); they had municipal institutions; and acquired some of the trappings of the Enlightenment city, including neoclassical public buildings, theatres, assemblies, concerts, promenades, coffee-houses, and, in anglophone communities, a variety of clubs and societies. Even the European-controlled towns in Asia took on some of the image of the improved European city by the late eighteenth century. Thus, at Calcutta with 200,000 inhabitants by 1800 (only 3 per cent white), the European town had a town improvement commission and was rebuilt with classical-style edifices, while its social life boasted race-meetings, clubs, theatres, and other accoutrements of British urbanity.

VI

Given the growing range and number of specialist urban centres, the consolidation and greater integration of the European urban network headed by primate centres, and the general upturn in urban growth and development in the late eighteenth century, it looked as though the foundations had been laid for the creation of an urbanized Europe. But the foundations proved precarious and the period ended in crisis. During the 1790s, the French Revolution and the subsequent political upheavals and wars caused major disturbance to cities and towns across much of Europe. In France, it led to a reduction in the overall urbanization level by 1–2 per cent, with some of the biggest centres like Lyon damaged by military action and others affected by the disruption of trade, the crowds of refugees from elsewhere, and drastic reforms of the country's administrative structure. Caen lost thousands of inhabitants in the early 1790s, many of them servants, as the nobility withdrew from the town, and places like Strasbourg and Nancy also saw depopulation. The demographic plight of small towns may have been worse, with some like Meulan near Paris losing a quarter of their inhabitants and not recovering for many decades. At the same time, a number of France's new departmental cities gained in population.

Outside France, the revolutionary occupation of the Rhineland badly disrupted trade, led to the imposition of heavy taxes, and an exodus of the elite classes; in consequence, towns suffered large-scale population loss—up to 30 per cent in some cases. In the Low Countries, the picture was broadly similar, while in Italy Napoleon's invasion swept aside the autonomous city-states of Venice and Genoa, and upended most of the princely states. Here, the gain from political reform and modernization was soon outweighed by heavy military levies and urban disruption. Warfare rippled out to afflict Spanish, Russian, Nordic, and Irish towns—even colonial cities outside Europe. Only the British urban network was not badly affected by the wave of upheaval.

European cities in the early modern era achieved significant advances but suffered recurrent urban crises, some short-term, others longer term, some affecting one or two cities, and others affecting the main urban regions. We have already seen how communities faced a litany of economic, social, cultural, and political problems and changes. In the following chapters, we need to examine how towns, their leaders, and inhabitants coped with these challenges.

8

Economy 1500–1800

The early modern period saw a long term maturing and consolidation of the European urban economy in a traditional world still largely dominated until the eighteenth century by agriculture and the rural sector. There was an expansion of institutional regulation of the urban economy (largely engineered by the state). Building on late medieval developments, urban services multiplied, and internationalization had a mounting effect on trade, production, and consumption. By the last part of the period, manufacturing advances in scale, production methods, and regional concentration—with the rise of specialist towns—were starting to have an impact, especially in Western Europe. As a result of the spread of new market towns in Northern and Eastern Europe, urban economic activity expanded horizontally. It also grew vertically, as developments in retailing and services filtered down from bigger cities to a growing range of towns. On the other hand, as we saw in the previous chapter, there were major fluctuations in the pattern of urban growth, linked to population volatility, disease, warfare, and above all agrarian factors. The European urbanization of the sixteenth century was driven by demographic increase, with relatively limited improvement in urban trade and manufacturing, and went into reverse in much of Europe during the next century as demographic growth waned, agricultural output stagnated, and widening European wars disrupted economic activity. Only in the last part of the period did urban economic growth start to provide a potent engine for urbanization.

In the following pages, we look first at the changing economic pattern of urban–rural relations, and then at the impact of the state and regulation on the urban economy, while further sections focus on industry, trade, and the service sector.

I

In his *Wealth of Nations*, published in 1776, Adam Smith asserted that despite the growth of commerce and manufacture, 'every town draws its whole subsistence and all the materials of its industry from the country'. As in the Middle Ages, the rural sector supplied the urban economy not simply with food and raw materials, but with migrant labour (discussed in Chapter 9), investment flows, and demand. However, pace Smith, the balance of exchange between town and countryside started to shift during the eighteenth century as cities and towns, led by those in Western Europe, began to free themselves from the constraints and problems of rural supply and demand, and the dynamics of the urban economy had an accelerating impact on the agrarian sector.

In the sixteenth century, the agricultural sector was often as important within towns as beyond, taking over empty spaces left by population decay after the Black Death. Paris had large fields under cultivation within its walls, just as in Castile gardens, orchards, pastures, and arable fields were part of the urbanized area, and towns had large numbers of resident peasants and labourers. Many medium and smaller centres retained this agrarian dimension into the eighteenth century and after. At Wildberg, in the Black Forest region, a third of the town depended on farming their own land, and Geneva's city lands supplied a quarter of its cereal needs. Agriculture remained a vital pillar of the urban economy in Eastern and Northern Europe throughout the period. At the Hungarian towns of Esztergom and Sopron, most of the merchants and townspeople were engaged in farming, including wine-growing; and the latter was also common in Balkan cities.

Yet, as population pressure mounted over the sixteenth century, urban farm land, particularly in bigger cities, was built over or developed, and townspeople had to look further afield for supplies. In theory, towns with up to 50,000 inhabitants (the great majority of European cities) could be provisioned by local hinterlands in a radius of 45 kilometres, but this depended on good water transport and abundant harvests. Rising demand, and recurrent harvest shortages during the sixteenth century and later, forced cities to try and enlarge their provisioning areas, often in the process competing against one another. Some moves in this direction had already occurred in the medieval era, but the policy became more general after 1500. During the bad harvest years of the 1590s, London's insatiable appetite for grain drained much of south-east England and triggered localized food shortages in country towns. Paris developed an elaborate system of food provisioning, covering much of northern France, while Lyon was busy extending its supply zone to include Burgundy and the Mediterranean. Urban demand was an essential factor in the rise of the international grain trade between Baltic ports like Gdansk and Atlantic and Mediterranean cities. The late medieval pan-European cattle trades also expanded with urbanization, herds of oxen being driven south from Denmark, Germany, and the Northern Netherlands to the famous cattle fair at Lier near Antwerp, while great livestock fairs at Cracow and Lvov in Poland sold animals for consumption in German cities.

If food provisioning provided a vital stimulus to urban commerce during the sixteenth century, with merchants and dealers profiting handsomely, problems of food supply and high prices acted as an important constraint on urban living standards and demand. Recurrent subsistence crises in sixteenth-century cities reached a crescendo in the 1590s. After 1600, Dutch and English cities managed to provision their inhabitants quite effectively, but elsewhere food supply continued to provoke severe crises for European cities, as in the 1690s, and 1740; in some Mediterranean cities famine crises persisted until the start of the nineteenth century.

Imports of timber, for heating, industrial use, and construction, were also crucial for the urban economy. According to one estimate, a town of 10,000 inhabitants needed up to fifty carts of fuel per day: Cracow in the 1770s received 3,700 cartloads a year. In Western Europe, disafforestation compelled ever-widening supply areas. Great rafts of timber were floated down the Seine to Paris from the Morvan, while Dutch cities relied on imported wood from Sweden, pushing up prices in Stockholm. More and more, however, West European cities turned to other energy sources to supply industrial and domestic demand. Shipments of coal from Newcastle, mostly to London, rose to over 500,000 tons by 1660, and in the 1720s it was estimated that the coal trade earned Newcastle £250,000 a year. Towns in the Southern Netherlands likewise turned to coal, while in the north the Dutch exploited their peat reserves. Timber shortages in West European cities accelerated the shift towards building in brick and stone.

Food supply and energy costs were two key variables in urban economic development, but so was rural demand. Rural impoverishment in the sixteenth century, and again in some areas during the eighteenth century, depressed popular demand and precipitated a tidal surge of poor migrants into cities. But it was not all bad news. Rising agricultural prices benefited substantial farmers who became important purchasers of urban goods and services. Another element in the economic relationship between town and countryside involved investment flows. Since the Middle Ages, wealthy townsmen had regularly bought up country estates to gain social status and secure their food supply. During the sixteenth century, rural investment was spurred on by rising agricultural rents, but even when these slackened urban investment in land remained strong. In the Dutch Republic, Diderick van Velthuysen, from one of the leading families of Utrecht, bought himself the noble estate of Heemstede in the late seventeenth century, exemplifying a general trend among urban patricians—indeed a large part of Dutch capital was invested in property (and bonds), as commercial prospects became less rosy. In Venice, too, investment in landownership was encouraged by the declining profitability of overseas trade: by 1600, the Venetian patriciate owned about 11 per cent of the *terra ferma*'s cultivated land which produced one third of the city's grain imports. Not that all urban investment was in property. Town merchants and manufacturers put capital into rural industry and this trend became more pronounced in the eighteenth century, as we shall see below.

Reverse flows of capital—from countryside to town—also took place, via the presence and growing expenditure of landowners in the urban world, their wealth towering over that of most townsmen. Earlier, we noted the significant impact of the nobility moving into Mediterranean cities in the Middle Ages. In the seventeenth and eighteenth centuries, this landed influx became widespread across Europe, most striking in the case of capital cities. Paris, London, Madrid, and other state capitals were packed out with landowners spending prodigiously on conspicuous consumption and employing many townsmen. Busy renovating her Parisian home, Princess Kinsky had over a hundred tradesmen working on the mansion, including painters and guilders, sculptors, masons, cabinet-makers, upholsterers, and gardeners. Regional cities likewise hosted sizeable contingents of landowners, often attracted by parliaments or courts. In 1639, a quarter of the Catalan nobility may have been resident in Barcelona, and in the next century regional towns like Abbéville and Alençon in France, or Chester and Shrewsbury in England, had scores of landed residents. East European cities followed suit, places like Wroclaw having a growing array of aristocratic palaces. Even smaller towns might host a coterie of minor landowners and rentiers (not least wealthy widows), who patronized shops, lawyers, and leisure facilities. At Ludlow on the Welsh borders, for instance, gentlemen and professional folk comprised nearly 10 per cent of householders in the 1760s.

II

Economic relations between town and countryside were progressively regulated after 1500. Already, in the late Middle Ages, market rules had become elaborate as part of the growth of institutional controls in towns. Now, as food supplies became more unreliable, civic leaders sought to prevent the export of grain from the local area, and to stop speculation by merchants and other traders. In Spain, the Crown approved city granaries from the 1490s and Seville established one in 1505. The German city of Emden followed the trend in 1557; Milan in 1572; and by Elizabeth's reign London had a whole complex of grain warehouses. In crisis years of the 1580s, Burgos supplied a third of its citizenry with bread from its own store, while Coventry's cornstock served up to 40 per cent of the city's inhabitants in the late 1590s. Together with the registration of private grain stocks, measures to stop farmers hoarding, and controls on the export of cereals, urban granaries discouraged profiteering and panic buying, and so helped smooth market operations. Bread prices and bakers were equally supervised. After 1700 such controls were largely abandoned in Britain, though they survived longer elsewhere in urban Europe.

Governments frequently interfered in myriad aspects of town economic life. In Eastern Europe, states prevented merchants from trading in the countryside, while permitting nobles to engage in commerce and promote rural industries. In Sweden, the Crown banned inland towns from participating in overseas traffic. In Western Europe, governments often promoted the establishment of new urban industries by granting monopolies or privileges. Keen to employ foreign masters and artisans, Louis XIV's minister, Colbert, set up the manufacture of fine cloth at Abbéville and Caen, silk stockings at Lyon, woollen stockings at Paris, Poitiers, and Auxerre, and lace-making at Alençon. During the eighteenth century, states like Prussia sought to promote urban manufacturing as a central economic goal, often through the import of skilled workers and new technology from abroad. Likewise, many governments from the mid-seventeenth century introduced navigation acts and other protectionist measures to advantage their merchants and trade.

For interventionist rulers in the early modern period, the city was where the state and the economy interfaced. As we noted above, the growth of central government, its courts and bureaucracies, was especially beneficial for capital cities, but could also boost regional administrative towns. Military expenditure was lavished on garrison towns, particularly those on frontiers. Thus Perpignan, bulwark against Spain, received roughly four times more royal investment than it paid in taxes.

Too often, however, urban economies suffered from the relentless and exorbitant fiscal levies of states. Heavy state taxation to fund ever more costly wars was a prime cause of urban indebtedness in the seventeenth century, while the wars themselves often did serious damage to urban economies, as noted in Chapter 7. Economic life also suffered from state policy on religion, such as the official persecution of religious minorities. Thus, in seventeenth-century France, many Protestant Huguenots, including leading merchants and skilled masters, were driven into exile. Numbers at Metz and Caen fell by 40 per cent, even before the final mass expulsion by Louis XIV after 1685. By then, more tolerant states like Prussia and England were eager to attract religious refugees to their cities to promote new manufacturing specialisms. (Somewhat earlier, but for similar reasons, Ottoman rulers had encouraged Jews fleeing Iberian persecution to settle in Balkan cities).

Government policy was an important influence in the changing role of guilds in urban economic regulation. Although trade and craft guilds had become institutionalized in the later Middle Ages, their numbers and powers multiplied during the sixteenth and seventeenth centuries as states sought to use them to raise revenue and to police economic and social activity in towns. At Cracow, the tally of guilds doubled during the sixteenth century, while the Parisian number increased from sixty before 1673, to 129 in 1691. London got twenty-seven new livery companies in the early seventeenth century, and both Dutch and Catalonian towns acquired extra guilds too. In Vienna, many new guilds received their privileges from the Emperor, while Peter the Great introduced guilds into Russian towns—albeit with minor success.

As in the Middle Ages, guilds exercised a variety of economic functions, regulating the labour market through the admission of apprentices and new guild members, defending guild members from competition by outsiders, prosecuting illicit traders, and controlling the scale and quality of output.

Despite attempts by states to impose greater uniformity, the functioning of guilds was highly localized. As one Dutch guild declared, 'each town has its own laws and ordinances, … rooted in its specific context'. In some places they operated as a broadly united force within the political system: in others they acted more on their own, and fought hard with other guilds over status and privileges; frequently, the grouping of trades in a guild was politically motivated, arbitrary, and artificial. As well as having political functions, guilds might be important centres for elite or burgher socializing and solidarity. For these and other reasons, one must be wary of overstating their economic importance or of expecting them to have coherent or effective economic strategies. As cities expanded, there was often a growing army of illicit traders and workers beyond guild control (suburban jurisdictions like the Parisian Faubourg St Antoine, or the western districts of London were heavily populated by independent craftsmen and journeymen). Moreover, many new, larger-scale industries operated outside guilds—exemplified by Amsterdam's sugar-refining, soap-boiling and diamond-cutting industries; and the same was true for new service trades. By the eighteenth century, guilds often controlled a minor share of the urban economy. For example, at Saragossa and Toulouse guild members comprised only 15 per cent and 20–25 per cent respectively of local businessmen. In most English towns they were fading fast after the 1720s.

Thus, claims in the eighteenth century (and later) that guilds were necessarily protectionist and a deterrent to trade must be treated with more than a pinch of salt. In expanding towns guilds could be flexible, open to activity by outsiders and women, taking on illicit workers as subcontractors. Sometimes, as at Lyon, they could be the focus for trade and technological innovation. In declining towns like the smaller German imperial cities, guilds had only a limited responsibility for decline, compared to changes in trade patterns and the rise of urban rivals. But, if guilds were less crucial for economic development, in many towns they were an essential buttress of the socioeconomic order, particularly for respectable masters. Subject to municipal control, they were pillars of the local civic community. This helps to explain why efforts by eighteenth-century governments, imbued with laissez-faire ideas, to abolish guilds provoked local resistance. In France, Turgot's attempt to reform corporations in 1776–8 led to divisions within local elites. The suppression of guilds in French-occupied Europe during the Revolutionary era was often short-lived and the institution soon made a limited comeback at the local level.

III

Certainly, guilds were of limited help in coping with the structural difficulties besetting urban manufacturing during the sixteenth and seventeenth centuries. One problem related to rural industries that had spread in the later Middle Ages, particularly in the textile sector. Cheap labour in the countryside, sourced by population increase, made it difficult for urban craftsmen to compete, whatever the efforts of the guilds. As a result, production tended to migrate from the city. The problem was widespread in Germany, from north to south, and was equally pressing in Lombardy where low-cost rural and small-town manufacturing outflanked the more expensive textile manufacture of cities like Milan, Cremona, and Como, and urban merchants moved to trade in rural products. In Eastern Europe, rural industry, often owned by the nobility, benefited from tax exemptions: in Brandenburg, for example, the beer trade was forced to move from towns for this reason.

Urban industry fought back by diversifying into more specialist and fashionable forms of product. As we noted before, in the fifteenth and sixteenth centuries a number of old clothing towns in the Southern Netherlands turned to tapestry manufacture and other new trades. At Vicenza, silk production expanded, while in England old textile cities like Norwich shifted to the making of cheaper and lighter new draperies. From the late sixteenth century, urban textile manufacturers suffered from another threat—growing international rivalry. Clothing in Spanish cities like Toledo and Cordoba collapsed owing to competition from Dutch cities like Leiden and English West Country clothing towns.

One bright spot was the construction industry as housing demand revived during the sixteenth century, and there was a growing volume of public works, including town halls, hospitals, and military buildings. On the other hand, demand for basic urban wares such as shoes, tools, or clothing, produced by a multitude of small masters and lesser artisans, suffered from the deterioration in lower-class incomes in town and countryside. Here, the fragmentation of production and lack of specialization meant that too many craftsmen were competing with one another in the same limited market.

Yet, by the second half of the seventeenth century, there were the first signs, especially in Western Europe, of advances that would provide a platform for later industrial expansion. One was the multiplication of new trades producing luxury or fashionable consumer goods. In the Dutch Republic Delft, Amsterdam and other cities developed as veritable art studios, aided by an influx of Flemish refugees; paintings, produced in their thousands, with multiple copies of similar scenes (for instance winter landscapes, or rural festivities), were sold to middling as well as wealthier patrons. Whilst large amounts of porcelain were imported from Asia in the early eighteenth century, discovery of the method of using kaolin to make hard-paste ceramics led to a rapid growth of European output, first at Meissen, then at Worcester, and later at Limoges. Falling prices for ceramics from the mid-eighteenth century facilitated increasing sales to the middle-class market. Silk manufacture boomed in a number of cities: Lyon became a leading producer, while the majority of workers at Naples were employed in the trade. Textiles diversified widely with the growth of calico printing in Barcelona, Geneva, and London, as well as German and French cities. Stocking manufacture was another variant, large-scale output springing up in Midland towns like Leicester, Nottingham, and Loughborough.

The rise of the printing industry in the eighteenth century was also important, with the growth of more standardized and specialist production for a wide range of urban consumers. State controls tended to concentrate most production in a limited range of major cities such as Frankfurt-am-Main, Leipzig, Amsterdam, London, Turin, and Paris. Still, French provincial cities like Lyon and Rouen supported a dozen or more workshops in the Enlightenment era, while Hungarian towns had numerous printing presses before 1800.

Among the most important new consumer products were alcoholic drinks and processed foods. As we saw earlier, large-scale beer production, using an infusion of hops, got under way in the late Middle Ages, and, by 1600, wholesale brewers had emerged in many West and North European cities. Growing competition, both national and international, encouraged economic specialization. In the Southern Netherlands, Leuven and Diest became leading producers, and by the 1740s London's industry was dominated by a dozen firms producing over 40 per cent of the capital's strong beer in large integrated plants. From the later seventeenth century, other types of alcoholic drink, mainly distilled spirits, were produced and traded on a growing scale. In England, primary distilling was focused in a small number of towns (for instance, London and Leeds), though with extensive distribution to smaller towns and the countryside. In Poland, an export trade in vodka developed to Bohemia and the Ottoman

Empire, channelled through cities like Cracow. With rising consumption of sugar (and tobacco), imported from the Americas, refining became big business, particularly around the ports. Catering for a growing sweet tooth, patisseries and sweet manufacturers multiplied, as, for instance, in early eighteenth-century Saragossa in northern Spain.

Construction expanded ever more in the Enlightenment city. After 1700, civic improvement, including new public buildings, bridges, and streets, along with fashionable elite mansions and housing for the middling and artisan classes (over 80,000 new houses were put up in eighteenth-century London) gave employment to an army of small builders, artisans, and building labourers, as well as to the new professions of architects and surveyors. Such developments were particularly visible in European capital cities, regional capitals in Western Europe, and residential towns in Germany and Italy. London's expansion led to significant changes in the building industry, including increased standardization of building methods and the rise of contracting firms. Here, and in other English cities, speculative redevelopment began to sweep away many smaller, often wooden, houses and to replace them with back-to-back terraces for the lower classes.

Before the French Revolution, one can see not only the growth of new specialist industries in towns but also other structural changes—especially in Western Europe. First was the greater integration of urban and rural industry as cheaper output in the countryside complemented more upmarket production in town, both kinds of output being orchestrated and marketed by urban manufacturers and merchants. At Leicester, in the 1670s, a group of stocking-makers claimed to employ two thousand workers in the town and in nearby villages. Rejecting attempts to restrict the trade to townspeople, the masters declared 'it is not the curious making of a few stockings but the general making of many that is most for the public good', for that sets people on work and supplies stockings for all sorts of buyers. In Switzerland, merchants at Lucerne and other towns were involved in the development of rural textiles and watch-making. In northern France, Rouen became the hub for the clothing industry in its hinterland which increasingly went over to cotton, with Rouen itself controlling the finishing stages of production. Arguably, such developments created a new type of dispersed, de-centred urbanization.

A second development was the advent of networks of complementary rather than competing industrial centres. We have already observed, in Chapter 7, the emergence during the early seventeenth century of the so-called Randstad of industrial and commercial towns in the western provinces of the Dutch Republic. But this kind of urban network was more common after 1700, for instance, in the East Midlands (where Leicester, Nottingham, Derby, and Coventry all acquired different industrial specialisms), and in the industrial region around Lyon. A third, sometimes overlapping development, was the emergence of new industrial zones often linked to mineral and energy resources. Zones of this type in the English Black Country or the Liège-Verviers district of the Southern Netherlands linked up rural sites, industrializing small towns, and larger cities, which, as well as being engaged in manufacturing, served as distribution, marketing, and financial nodes for the area.

Fourth, product innovation often involved process innovation. A number of new industries, such as those making cutlery or chinaware, sought to imitate luxury products but used new techniques to cut costs and sell more cheaply to wider markets. In many industries, particularly textiles, there was a growing avalanche of individually small-scale but incrementally significant production and hardware advances. No less vital was the greater sub-division of manufacturing processes, enabling them to be carried out by unskilled workers, often by women and children.

Fifth, there was a clear shift in some industries—ranging from brewing and ceramics to textiles—towards larger units of production. Matthew Boulton employed over 600 workers at his works in Soho, Birmingham, making steam engines. At Augsburg, one of the calico mills employed 350 workers, while in Barcelona some large cotton factories had up to 150 employees. Augury of the manufacturing future, the first large purpose-built cotton-spinning factory using steam power was opened in Manchester in 1782, and soon after cotton mills began to proliferate at Manchester, Stockport, and elsewhere in the vicinity. But this precocious diffusion of innovation was exceptional. Attempts to introduce new technology in the Valencia silk industry failed due to worker resistance. In Britain, too, there was opposition to the spread of steam-power, even in its Birmingham birthplace. Here, and elsewhere, industrial production remained heavily workshop-based. However, within the workshop sector a two-tier system was evolving, as we discover in the Lyon silk industry, where a limited number of merchant manufacturers dominated and controlled the output of a large number of small masters.

Finally, the most radical manufacturing changes before about 1800 occurred in British cities and towns, with urban communities in the

Southern Netherlands, Germany, and other parts of Western Europe following behind. In the remaining European regions, apart from a few exceptions, industrial transformation had hardly begun. In Sweden, for instance, industries like linen-making remained, as in the past, heavily rural-based, with merchants and traders from small towns going out into the countryside to collect cloth for sale at fairs.

IV

Turning from industry to marketing, the urban role in local trade was reinforced during the sixteenth and seventeenth centuries by the creation of many new market towns, particularly in Eastern and Northern Europe (see Chapter 7). This was paralleled by the revival of older markets that had fallen into disuse during the late Middle Ages. Expanding market activity was driven heavily by agrarian trade during the sixteenth century, as demographic demand grew. Thus, villagers came from a score of nearby settlements to Penafiel, by the Douro river in Castile, 'to the markets that are held in the town ... to buy ... the provisions ... that they need'. By 1600, there are indications in the Low Countries and England of market specialization in particular commodities. As villagers poured in from the countryside to buy and sell wares, pressure mounted on the marketplace and complaints were voiced about its congestion. One tendency was for trading to shift from the open market to nearby premises, including drinking-houses. By the early eighteenth century, we discover the first signs in England of the decline of markets as the primary space for local commercial dealing in towns, though elsewhere they showed greater vitality.

International fairs which had dominated medieval long-distance trade attracting merchants and customers from wide areas may have lost their economic significance somewhat earlier. The great fairs at Lyon, Medina del Campo, and Antwerp suffered during the late sixteenth century from military disruption and the decline of the Mediterranean trade routes. Likewise, in Western Europe, regional fairs appear to have diminished in importance after 1700 as the inconvenience of outdoor trading deterred wealthier traders, who preferred to do business indoors in drinking-houses or exchanges. At the same time, more specialist fairs including horse and saffron fairs may have developed, and other general fairs like the Stourbridge fair outside Cambridge or the St Denis fair in Paris turned into crowded funfairs. On the other hand, in Northern and Eastern Europe, town fairs retained their importance into the nineteenth century. In Sweden, most fairs still took place in the winter because it was easier to move goods by sledge over the snow and ice. Leipzig's three great fairs remained pivotal for trade and financial dealing between Eastern and Western Europe and the 10,000 foreign visitors a year, many from eastern areas, found 'an indescribable wealth of goods... on offer'. In Russia the number of fairs may have quadrupled between 1675 and 1775.

Yet, after 1700, the writing was on the wall, as both markets and fairs faced the challenge of specialist retail shops that sold luxury and new consumer wares. As we saw in Chapter 3, luxury shops (along with more traditional shops-cum-workshops) had operated in larger cities since the Middle Ages, but their numbers and visibility grew strongly from the late sixteenth century. At Paris, fashion shops clustered around the Palais de Justice, whilst in London the New Exchange, which opened in the Strand in 1609, housed two floors of retail space, selling a cornucopia of luxury wares from silks to feathers, and ceramics to drugs. In Antwerp, fashion shops appeared for the first time in the 1660s, and forty years later the city had about sixty premises *à la mode* that sold smart clothing and haberdashery. By the 1750s, London had one shop for every thirty inhabitants, and twenty years later Antwerp had one for every sixteen. Booksellers proliferated: in the Dutch Republic forty-one towns had a bookstore and Amsterdam over 120.

Retailing was boosted not just by the defects of traditional marketing and the rising incomes of the better off, but also by the growing rejection of the old religious and moral rhetoric against luxury, by the new availability of fashionable consumer goods (often designed specifically for the urban market), and by the influx of wealthy landowners and their families to cities. If earlier fashion shops (as in Paris) were often cramped and dark, well before 1800 they were elaborately designed and furnished. Shop interiors were well lit, had large counters, and were lavishly equipped with mirrors and gilt wood and mahogany fittings, while glass windows (instead of wooden shutters) facilitated shop displays and window shopping. Selling practices were increasingly codified (with the spread of fixed prices), and staff polite and welcoming—not least for the growing number of female shoppers. Shopkeepers (a sizeable number of them women) counselled customers on their choice of purchases, and so implicitly on their social image. Shops engaged in heavy advertising, to promote sales of the latest fashions, and their premises were frequently located close to theatres, assembly rooms, and other sites of public sociability, thereby integrating them into the smart *cursus* of urban leisure and entertainment.

More basic food, clothes, and corner-shops likewise multiplied. Food shops doubled in Venice in the seventeenth and eighteenth centuries, while the Dutch town of Maastricht had 613 retailers by the 1730s, including fifty coffee dealers and sixty-one selling tea. In the second half of the eighteenth century, English county towns and lesser market centres contained numerous fixed shops that retailed food, clothing, furniture, books, ironmongery, and other wares. In Catalonia, we find urban retail shops run by small companies linked to cloth producers. We know less about retailing developments elsewhere in Europe: more research needs to be done. But for the present, at least, it looks as though the shopping revolution began in West European cities.

Retail developments were a vital part of the process by which domestic and international trade became integrated and focused on early modern towns. As we noted above, the old trade from the Levant to the ports of northern Italy, and so overland into North-Western Europe, had been eclipsed by the early seventeenth century with the ascent of the Asian and American trades, which contributed to the stagnation of many Mediterranean cities and the rise of specialist Atlantic port cities. This was not the only change. Whereas the Levantine trade was a high-profit and relatively low-volume commerce (the Venetian fleet in the fifteenth and sixteenth centuries counted only 15–20,000 tons of shipping), the American and Asian trades were both very profitable and involved a relatively large volume of goods. European shipping probably trebled in tonnage between 1670 and 1780 (to 3.4 million), the lion's share trading out of British ports. At Liverpool, the tonnage of shipping entering the port rose thirtyfold during the eighteenth century to 450,000 tons. Although luxury goods such as Asian textiles, chinaware, and spices were prominent in long-distance commerce, imports also covered large quantities of much cheaper consumer commodities such as tobacco, coffee, tea, and sugar (tea consumption rose sharply in English towns at the end of the eighteenth century, while per capita sugar consumption at Paris reached 5.3 kilos a year in the 1790s). After processing at refineries near the ports, these products reached customers via a joined-up chain of internal trade, its links including wholesalers as well as retailers. If the early colonial trades were largely import led, by the second half of the eighteenth century urban trading networks supplied merchants at the ports with mounting quantities of manufactured goods for export, often the output of nascent industrial districts.

While the great Atlantic ports and their merchants were the main protagonists in the growth of long-distance, extra-European trade, medium-sized ports (aided by infrastructure improvement) took advantage of the expansion of the European re-export, transit, and carrying trades. Colonial and intra-European trades were frequently hinged together. Growing Portuguese traffic with Brazil in the eighteenth century was supplied in part by English exports of manufactured goods shipped to Lisbon and Oporto from Bristol and West Country ports, as well as from London. In return, Portuguese wines were imported into English ports to lubricate London and provincial taverns, and the rest was paid for by Brazilian gold. In the same way, Birmingham workshops produced guns, toys, and other metal products for North American markets, using in part iron imported from Sweden. Stockholm merchants may have used the surplus from this trade to cover the commercial deficit on growing imports (especially of grain) from other Baltic countries. Baltic ports and shipping advanced strongly at this time: at Stockholm, the number of merchant houses rose to over a hundred in the late eighteenth century.

Expansion in overseas trade should not make us forget the growing scale of internal trade. Major improvements in river navigation, canals, and inter-urban roads played their part here. In the Austrian Netherlands, the government invested in the navigation of the Demer, Dijle, and Grote Nete; gave approval for the city of Leuven to make a canal to the Rupel; and constructed over 500 kilometres of new paved roads in the Duchy of Brabant, often on the initiative of local authorities. As inland trade burgeoned, wholesale merchants acquired a pivotal role—at least in some regions. Before the French Revolution, larger shopkeepers at Maidstone in Kent were doubling as wholesalers, selling at a discount to small retailers in the town's hinterland. Metropolitan wholesalers and their itinerant salesmen also infiltrated provincial trade.

V

Merchants and retailers formed only part of the expanding service sector in European towns. While the first breakthrough in the provision of urban services happened in the later Middle Ages (see Chapter 3), it was during the seventeenth and eighteenth centuries that the real take-off occurred. One important category comprised professional services. As in the past, the clergy remained an influential professional group, not least in Counter-Reformation cities: thus, clergy comprised 2 per cent of the population of Leon in the 1590s and 3 per cent at Grenoble during the early eighteenth century. The economic power of religious institutions was equally significant. Nonetheless, the main growth in professional services involved lawyers and medical practitioners. Although lawyers and notaries were already numerous in medieval towns, especially in the Mediterranean world, their growing presence after the Renaissance was encouraged by the rise of the state and the new complexity of municipal government, along with increased litigation. Lawyers appeared as leading figures in German imperial cities from the sixteenth century, as did notaries in Mediterranean cities like Lucca and Seville. In Georgian London, the number of lawyers probably stabilized around 10,000 but their wealth and influence advanced inexorably.

Medical practitioners—ranging from graduate practitioners to apothecaries and herbalists—also proliferated from the sixteenth century, reflecting heightened public concern over health and the greater ability of patients to pay for consultations. The city of Groningen in the Dutch Republic had fourteen physicians during the sixteenth century and fifty-three in the next. Further south, Toulouse in the late eighteenth century supported 100 medical men (plus one or two dentists) for a population of about 53,000, while Saragossa had eighty-eight for 44,000. If metropolitan physicians made hay financially, even provincial medical men like Esprit Calvet of Avignon or Claver Morris of Wells could be comfortably well off. The spread of new urban infirmaries during the eighteenth century gave important employment and status to physicians and surgeons, though many townspeople patronized a legion of quacks and patent medicine sellers as well.

After the Reformation, educational services continued to develop, as we shall see in Chapter 10. The result was a growing number of teachers of all kinds. Enlightenment Paris, for instance, had many hundreds of Church, lay and commercial schoolteachers. By 1800, the older professions were joined by a host of new ones, catering for rising elite and middle-class demand and the needs of the urban economy. Among them were architects, surveyors, engineers, publishers and journalists, dentists, stockbrokers, and bankers.

As in the earlier period, international banking and finance was restricted to a select circle of European cities, mostly great commercial metropoles.

In the sixteenth century, Antwerp had taken over from the Italian cities and Bruges as the leading European financial centre, its south German and other financiers heavily involved in discounting bills of exchange, lending to foreign rulers, and helping to finance overseas trade and mining. When Antwerp's commercial primacy was eclipsed by Amsterdam, the Dutch city hosted a growing community of foreign merchant bankers, including Jews and French Huguenots. With its Wisselbank or public bank (founded in 1609 on the Venetian model), Amsterdam became the leading European centre for exchange and deposit banking as well as foreign lending, while its Bourse (built in 1608) buttressed the city's vigorous stock market. Despite commercial recession after 1680, Amsterdam's financial significance continued up to the French Revolution, particularly as a capital market, but by then London was in the ascendant as the main European centre for commodity trading, insurance, and share dealing, such business carried on by numerous bankers, stockbrokers, and other specialist dealers. After 1700, Paris emerged as another leading financial centre: its banking houses increased from fifty-one in 1721 to over seventy in 1780.

Nor were financial services confined to specialist bankers and brokers. In Louis XVI's Paris, notaries were vital in the mobilization of credit for a great variety of purposes—buying the public debt, purchasing government offices, financing construction work and family settlements. Across the Channel, country banks were founded in many English provincial towns by attorneys, local merchants, and entrepreneurs and were prominent in local deposit banking.

Finally, attention must be paid to entertainment and leisure services. Pivotal here were drinking-houses, whether spacious and respectable au-berges, inns, and taverns, or smaller, popular alehouse houses or cabarets. These premises not only offered drink, refreshment, and sometimes lodging, but also a place to do business, to enjoy neighbourly interaction, to sing and listen to music. Already important in the late Middle Ages, their numbers swelled after 1500, inflated in part by increased demand from itinerant traders and migrants, in part by the desperate need of poor townspeople for income, and in part by the relative profitability of the business. At Shrewsbury, on the English border with Wales, the incidence of drinking-houses more than trebled between the 1560s and 1620s, well ahead of the rate of population increase. Antwerp in 1584 had 376 public houses or one for every thirty-two houses. The biggest cities had the highest density of houses. In some parts of London before the Civil War we find one licensed drinking house for every sixteen houses. A visitor to Lyon in 1664 claimed that in almost every house one found a cabaret, while Moscow at this time swarmed with drinking-houses. As we shall discover below, civic leaders in the sixteenth and seventeenth centuries were highly nervous of the danger of drinking-houses for public order and morality. On the other hand they recognized their extensive commercial function and the way they provided subsistence for many lesser townspeople.

By the eighteenth century, the number of urban drinking-houses was starting to stabilize, with fewer illicit houses. This was due in part to increased state and municipal regulation but also to the growing power of brewers and other wholesale drink suppliers in the trade, who preferred to supply only substantial outlets. With reduced competition, the trade became more prosperous and respectable. Around French towns like Paris and Reims fashionable taverns or *ginguettes* attracted streams of middling folk enjoying an outing. In English towns, landlords became leading cultural entrepreneurs, promoting a wide-range of new leisure activities to draw customers to their houses (see Chapter 10). Improved drinking-houses were fewer on the ground outside Western Europe, however. A procession of French and English visitors denounced the inns and other drinking premises of Mediterranean and Northern cities as squalid and detestable.

By 1700, public drinking premises faced competition from new types of victualling establishments. Coffee-houses spread to London from the Ottoman Empire in the 1650s and quickly won fashionable kudos. Paris had a cafe by the 1670s, Venice by 1683, and Vienna two years later. The fashion soon percolated down to provincial towns. The imperial city of Augsburg had eight premises by the 1720s, while Antwerpers could visit a cluster of coffee- and chocolate-houses around the Exchange. But the numbers were never very great: Paris had 300 cafés in 1714 and 1,800 before the French Revolution. Londoners could choose from 500 or so coffee-houses about 1700, but over the next century their ranks declined due to the relentless competition of public drinking-houses. Cheaper spirit-houses also spread, appealing to the less well off. Their growth was particularly important in Eastern Europe. In Russian cities, spirit-shops became a government monopoly and state revenues were heavily dependent on *kabaki* selling vodka.

In the late eighteenth century, two more players in the service sector arrived: hotels and restaurants. Though hotels of some kind existed earlier in continental cities, modern-style hotels reserved for the wealthier classes only appear from the last decades of the eighteenth century, as fashionable visitors and tourists sought to escape from the noise and crowds of old-style inns. No less important, the first restaurants opened in Paris in the 1760s, and by 1804 the city boasted five or six hundred.

Finally, the Enlightenment city set the stage for the flowering of new-style leisure activities in the eighteenth century—from public music-making and theatre to pleasure gardens and spectator sports. As we will see in Chapter 10, the development was particularly widespread in English towns but it also had some effect in bigger West European cities as well. A number of places sought to promote such activities as a way of attracting business to the town. At York, under Queen Anne, the council noted that the establishment of an annual horse-race 'may be of advantage and profit to the … city', while a subsidy to the music society a few decades later was justified on the grounds that it brought 'company to the city who spend money and advance trade'. Whereas official patronage was more important in continental cities, in Britain the new activities tended to be run on a commercial or voluntary basis, and this trend began to spread abroad by the end of the period. As well as attracting the free-spending elite to town, Enlightenment leisure generated a bevy of specialist jobs: theatre managers, star actors, stage designers, concert promoters, music teachers, and professional musicians.

VI

By the late eighteenth century, much of the template for a modern urban economy had been sketched: an increasingly sophisticated marketing and distribution system with the growing importance of retail shops; industrial specialization, product innovation, industrial districts, and even the first factories; the rise of large-scale intercontinental trade; and the explosive growth of the service sector. Yet many of these advances were partial, selective, and heavily focused on Western Europe, with England leading the way. Elsewhere, in other European regions, much of the urban economy remained resolutely traditional, only marginally affected by change.

Even in Western Europe, serious problems persisted in the urban economy. Though the threat from harvest failures was starting to abate, economic crises caused by war or trade disruption continued to recur, indeed they may have been accentuated by greater internationalization.

Critically, the growth of manufacturing and other sectors was rarely able to provide sufficient employment for poorer townspeople and the tens of thousands of destitute migrants who tramped to town. Economic advances in the late eighteenth century coincided with a deteriorating social situation for many townspeople. At the very end of the period, as we noted in Chapter 7, the French Revolution and its aftermath proved highly disruptive to urban economies. Heavy taxation and levies, military campaigns, the restructuring of national and local administration, and the flight of refugees, especially of elites from French-occupied cities, triggered economic instability. In the next chapter, we need to examine the social implications of these and other economic changes in the early modern city.

9

Social Life 1500–1800

Living in the parish of St Michael, Cornhill, in the heart of London as the young servant of a wealthy fishmonger John Bathurst, Robert Smith was infected with the smallpox virus towards the middle of May 1655, probably after talking with a sick neighbour or selling fish to a customer. Not immediately affected, he carried on work but ten days later he showed the classic symptoms of fever, backache, and vomiting, and soon after tiny red spots spread over his body. The spots speedily turned into large pus-filled blisters that split the skin horizontally, causing horrible pain and loss of speech. Death followed soon after, probably from a heart attack or shock, and Robert Smith was buried in St Michael's Church on 28 May. Smallpox was rampant in European cities by the seventeenth and eighteenth centuries. At Amsterdam and Rotterdam, epidemic outbreaks happened about every three years and inflated urban mortality rates by up to 50 per cent. In Georgian London, smallpox was the principal cause of death among those under the age of twenty.

If smallpox was one of the chief urban killers in the second half of this period, up to the 1660s the most catastrophic mortality in European cities was unleashed by recurrent outbreaks of bubonic plague, which (unlike in the late Middle Ages) were heavily concentrated in urban settings. London had seven major epidemics between 1563 and 1665, with mortality rates as high as 24 per cent. At Moscow, the outbreak of 1654 may have killed up to 80 per cent of the inhabitants. The great plague of 1630 nearly halved Milan's population, and at Pavia the losses were about 40 per cent. As we argued before, severe epidemics from the late sixteenth century helped tip the Mediterranean region's larger cities into longer-term decline. Though plague largely disappeared from Europe in the 1660s, with only isolated returns (as in Baltic towns in 1711, and Marseille in 1720–2), cities remained lethal for their inhabitants until the end of the period. Here, smallpox was supported by a deadly chorus of other epidemic diseases such as measles, typhoid, dysentery, and similar waterborne infections. Infants and young children were at particular risk. In early eighteenth-century London, the infant mortality rate ran at over 350 per 1,000 births. Also highly vulnerable were young apprentices, servants, and other newcomers to town, people like Robert Smith, who lacked the necessary immunity to urban diseases. In this way, immigration clearly contributed to high urban mortality rates, though it was hardly the essential precondition, as Allan Sharlin once argued.

For much of the early modern era, high mortality rates exceeded natural population increase in the main cities. During the sixteenth and early seventeenth centuries, we find years of natural surplus (birth exceeding burials) offset by massive plague mortality. Effects of epidemic disease were aggravated by recurrent subsistence crises, particularly serious in the 1590s and 1690s when the problems of harvest failure were compounded by wars. In England, during the last years of Elizabeth's reign, deaths from famine occurred from Kendal and Penrith in the north to Barnstaple and Exeter in the south-west. A century later, equally urban subsistence crises affected France, Scotland, and the Southern Netherlands. At Beauvais, in northern France, the biggest parish of St Etienne saw burials rise eleven times, as prices soared during the harvest crisis of 1693–4 and disease followed in the footsteps of famine.

Demographic deficits may have been aggravated by relatively low fertility rates. In part, this reflected the high levels of impoverishment in towns, but by the eighteenth century other factors operated, including higher rates of celibacy and the growing adoption of some kind of contraception, probably abstinence or *coitus interruptus*, by the better-off classes, as has been documented at Geneva and Rouen and among the London Quakers. Demographic deficits were recurrent in major Enlightenment cities like Stockholm, Bordeaux, and Mainz, while Hamburg enjoyed only eight years of population surplus between 1767 and 1790 and its cumulative deficit neared 5,000. In smaller towns, natural increase was more common due to a lower incidence of epidemics but, even so, marked variations existed between towns, and those expanding were prone to greater mortality. Only at the close of the period does the situation start to improve in a minority of towns as mortality rates responded to the decline of subsistence crises, increasing treatment (inoculation, later vaccination) against smallpox, and environmental advances, such as cleaner water supplies, at least for the better off. But in many towns, particularly in Northern, Eastern and Mediterranean Europe, demographic deficits persisted into the nineteenth century.

In the rest of this chapter, we examine the role of migration; the changing shape of the social hierarchy in the sixteenth and seventeenth centuries; the growth of poverty and other social problems in this period, and how communities tried to cope; later sections focus on the eighteenth century and look at the new wave of social pressures and the urban response, as well as at wider social trends (including the status of women).

I

Given high mortality rates, most European cities and towns depended in this period, as earlier, on high rates of immigration to maintain or increase their populations. London's voracious growth meant that about a million people migrated to the capital between 1550 and 1750—roughly 9,000 a year in the late seventeenth century. Hamburg noted that its increased size was due to the 'great flood of foreigners' coming to the city, and the situation was similar in French provincial cities. At Bordeaux, the number of immigrants at marriage rose by over 160 per cent between the 1730s and 1780s. Urban immigration was vital for small towns as well as larger ones, and all urban regions had a similar experience. Immigration was particularly dynamic during economic booms or after the end of a plague outbreak. At the height of Amsterdam's commercial success, in the early 1640s, only a quarter of bridegrooms marrying for the first time were born in the city.

Heavy inflows of outsiders were imperative because the turnover rate was so high. Many migrants came only on a seasonal or temporary basis, returning home soon afterwards. In 1650, Amsterdam officials complained that countrymen travelled to the city only during the winter time—when village work was slack—with the aim of getting poor relief there. Masons from the Limousin worked in Paris or Bordeaux for a few months every year to supplement their rural incomes. Out-migrants from cities included young women who had earned enough from service for a marriage dowry, and artisans who had acquired skills to help them set up in business in the country. If the urban economy contracted badly, there might be a large exodus, as we find in Castilian towns like Segovia and Toledo in the early part of the seventeenth century, or Geneva in the latter part; this often triggered stagnation or falls in the urban population.

Migration from the countryside continued to be the most important category of mobility. As in earlier times, towns offered greater chances of betterment: more job opportunities, higher wages, charitable support, and more personal freedom away from seigneurial or village controls. But during the sixteenth and seventeenth centuries, and again in the late eighteenth century, rural migration was propelled by push or subsistence factors, such as overpopulation, unemployment, land shortages, and agrarian crisis in the countryside. In the later 1580s, it was rumoured that as many as 4,000 peasants had entered Rome on a single night in desperate search for food. In 1629, a Bergamo doctor described how famine-stricken peasants had poured into that town 'most of them blackened [by the sun], parched, emaciated, weakened and in a poor state'. Conventionally, most rural immigrants travelled relatively short distances from nearby villages and were familiar with their destination town, but in crisis times poor subsistence movers journeyed from much further afield, sometimes in family groups. Poor migrants tramping to London before the Civil War included not only contingents from south-east England, but others from the western counties, the north, Ireland and Wales. Migration to Madrid in the seventeenth century involved large-scale movement by poor villagers and labourers from across northern and north-western Spain.

Warfare was another cause of long-distance movement, especially during the sixteenth and seventeenth centuries. Refugees poured into Dutch cities from the military conflict in the Southern Netherlands and later from Germany during the Thirty Years War; into Swiss cities from the French Civil Wars; into English east coast towns and north German cities after the Netherlands Revolt. Ethnic movement was also boosted by state religious policies. The French Crown's onslaught on its Protestant subjects in the seventeenth century ended in the creation of large Huguenot communities in London, Berlin, and Amsterdam.

Ethnic diversity was one of the most distinctive features of dynamic European cities in the early modern era, as it had been during the Middle Ages. When James Howell visited Amsterdam, in 1619, he wrote that he lodged in 'a Frenchman's house who is one of the deacons of our English Brownists' [sectarian] church here; it is not far from the synagogue of the Jews who have a free and open exercise of their religion here'. Tolerant religious policies and a relatively open economy meant that the city was awash with Jews from Portugal and Eastern Europe, German Protestants, French Huguenots, and English dissenters, just as Hamburg's permissive regime attracted sizeable numbers of Italian Catholics and Dutch Calvinists, as well as Jews and French Protestants. Minorities brought commercial expertise and innovations (for instance, new chemical technology and production to Amsterdam) and underpinned urban prosperity. As before, it was not just the great ports that hosted minorities. Jews were numerous and well integrated in Polish, Lithuanian, and Balkan towns, and by the eighteenth century London and Berlin had sizeable ethnic groups. The African slave trade meant that blacks were an increasingly common sight: Georgian London had around 5,000. By contrast, in the Mediterranean region the older tolerance of foreigners, already under pressure in Spanish cities in the fifteenth century, collapsed after 1600. Converted Jews and Muslims were expelled from Spanish cities and there was a steady exodus of Jews and other minorities from Italian cities. One of the few exceptions was the free port of Trieste which in the eighteenth century hosted a rapidly expanding Jewish community together with Protestant, Greek Orthodox, and Armenian minorities: in this period, it became one of the leading Mediterranean ports and financial centres.

Three other types of migration acquired heightened significance in the early modern era. The first was inter-urban movement involving artisans. Already widespread in Mediterranean cities before 1500, it seems to have become more organized in Western Europe from the sixteenth century as urban trade and industry developed (by the 1690s, 6,000 stone masons travelled annually to Paris from the Haute-Marche for construction work). In France and Germany, we find a steady growth of *compagnonnages* for migrant journeymen, and by 1650 the artisan *tour de France* was established, as journeymen moved around the country in search of work. In British towns, the spread of trade benefit clubs from the later seventeenth century had a similar function, enabling unemployed craftsmen to move from one place to another to get a job. Across Europe, diaries and autobiographies of skilled workers underline the centrality of mobility in their lives.

The second type of migration has already been mentioned in previous chapters: that by landowners, taking up residence in town, often for several months of the year. As well as pressure by states to involve landowners in Court and administrative activity, usually urban-based, after 1700 rural life was progressively seen and criticized in fashionable literature as backward and boring, compared to the smart leisure and entertainment pursuits on offer in urban society. Another attraction was the new improved housing being constructed for the elite classes in larger cities, while more professional estate-management enabled expensive urban tastes to be funded by a steady flow of rural rents. Particularly important was the way that the landed classes frequently brought their wives (and families) with them.

Women—not just upper-class ladies but servant girls, the wives of rural migrants, as well as widows—comprised a third category of migrants, one about which too little is known. Arguably, some cities had more significant flows of female migrants (at specific times) than others: in other words, the gender bias reflected both external pressures and the changing structure of economic demand in towns. For late seventeenth-century England, research has revealed a decisive shift towards female-dominated movement to London and other towns in eastern England, probably due to a growing labour market for female domestics and workers in new services like retailing. In contrast, ports and industrial town, with their strong appetite for male labour, attracted a high proportion of male movers.

A culture of mobility permeated urban society in this period, marked by the diverse types of migration and the heavy turnover rate. Even those who settled in early modern towns proved highly mobile. At Cuenca, in Spain, one in ten of the inhabitants changed residence in the town every year. In the Southwark area of south London only a quarter of householders stayed in the same house for ten years, the rest moving elsewhere in the district or beyond. Mobility among domestic servants and journeymen was notoriously high.

Large-scale migration served both to replenish and reinforce the existing social order and social hierarchy, but also caused social strains. Migrants from prosperous backgrounds, whether landed, professional, or mercantile, were needed to bring new capital and contacts to the urban elite class. Fundamental here was the fact that most elite families rarely lasted more than two or three generations, due to heavy mortality, financial problems, or movement back to the countryside. By contrast, poorer newcomers endlessly replenished the reservoirs of urban labourers and destitute. For much of the early modern period, as in the past, physical migration afforded only meagre opportunities for social mobility. It was no coincidence that the legend of Dick Whittington, a poor immigrant who became mayor of medieval London, was first recorded in city folklore at the end of the sixteenth century when there was a huge inrush of newcomers to the capital.

II

During the sixteenth and early seventeenth centuries the cascade of poor migrants into towns may have accentuated the trend towards greater polarization of the social hierarchy that was already visible in late medieval towns. Urban elites grew significantly wealthier, benefiting from the expansion of trade and rising property prices. At Genoa the taxable wealth of the noble patrician class rose by 80 per cent between 1575 and 1624, while north of the Alps at Augsburg the number of rich citizens nearly doubled in the sixteenth century and 8 per cent of taxpayers controlled 86 per cent of taxable property. Upper-class households lavished money on improved housing, furnishings, tapestries, silver plate, and books. At Canterbury, wealthier distributive traders spent twice as much on luxury furnishing as building craftsmen in the late sixteenth century, but four times as much in the early seventeenth.

Middle-rank craftsmen and traders faced considerable difficulty. Their position stagnated in many towns and only did better in expanding centres such as Amsterdam. Suffering competition from illicit traders in town and rural masters, they also faced sharp fluctuations in demand for basic goods and services due to harvest failures, trade depression, and war. In consequence, they enjoyed scant improvements in their lifestyle and were vulnerable to financial ruin. Indicative of this trend, at the medium-sized town of Coesfeld in Westphalia the lowest category of taxpayers (day workers and servants) rose from 29 per cent in 1580 to 39 per cent in 1594, while the next tax class of small independent craftsmen fell from 39 to 24 per cent. In several Kentish towns during the crisis years of the 1590s those recorded as needing relief included middle-sized households headed by respectable craftsmen like glaziers, masons, and bakers, some of whom had previously paid poor taxes themselves.

At the bottom of the social order, petty craftsmen and journeymen, labourers and their families, many of them newcomers to town, suffered a widespread deterioration in real incomes and living conditions, as a result of rising food and housing costs, low wages and recurrent unemployment and underemployment. Yet increased social polarization was not mirrored in greater social segregation. Though poor newcomers might drift initially to hovels and cheap rents in outer areas, and magnates and merchants preferred an inner-city location, near the levers of power, the abiding picture remained one of a mixed use of urban space. In sixteenth-century Paris and Rome, for example, aristocratic and merchant houses were encircled by those of artisans and lesser residents. As population pressure grew, landlords exploited the market to crowd more and more people into cellars, courts, and back alleys in the centres of European towns.

Conventional marginal groups such as women, the elderly, and young people also experienced a deterioration in their status. True, wives (and widows) of merchants and other members of the urban elite continued to enjoy a recognized social position. Able to move around in public places, they were increasingly literate, often owned books and had a hand in furnishing their homes with consumer goods. However, the indications are that (except in a few towns like Lyon) such women were no longer able to engage in trade and business on their own account and were now largely excluded from guilds and confraternities—in line with the widespread stress on their legal incapacity. If the wives of respectable traders might help their husbands with business and have a respected role in neighbourly networks, poorer women were forced into semi-licit trades, such as street-vending and drink-trading (selling alcohol out of their kitchens), as well as fetching water, working as prostitutes, and washing laundry. The elderly, too, were expected to work—to supplement the support of relations and neighbours, and any official handouts. Elderly women, many of them widows, had to foster bastards, nurse plague victims, and embalm bodies. Aged in his eighties and 'very infirm', a Ludlow man had nothing to support him 'but what [he] gets by carrying rags'.

Sons of wealthier townsmen or countrymen had opportunities via schooling, apprenticeship, and marriage, to enter the guilds and the es-tablished urban community. Those from lesser backgrounds fared much less well. In London, 40 per cent of those apprenticed never finished their terms. Badly exploited in poor trades, living crowded huggermugger in their masters' houses, many drifted from apprenticeship into unemploy-ment, vagrancy, and petty crime. Others became permanent journeymen, unable to afford to set up in their own business. As the proportion of young people in the urban population increased—perhaps up to half were aged under twenty—they came under attack from preachers and civic authorities concerned at the threat to public order. In 1601, Arthur Dent denounced the 'many lazy losels and luskish youths both in towns and villages which do nothing all the day long but walk the streets, sit upon the stalls and frequent taverns and alehouses'. Guild controls over apprentice and journeymen were strengthened and runaway servants targeted by civic officials. To some extent, young men could find mutual support in formal and informal age groups, often linked to neighbourhood and craft institutions like alehouses, abbeys of misrule, and journeymen clubs. But for many young people urban life was precarious and destitution never far away.

III

During the second half of the sixteenth century, poverty often seemed out of control in European cities. Though the total number of destitute (rather than those relieved) is difficult to assess, in some English towns in the 1590s the figure probably hovered around 70 per cent of the population. Augsburg's poor doubled in the early seventeenth century, with the result that over half the households there were impoverished. Core groups of poor—widows, the elderly, the sick, and orphaned children—were joined not just by labourers, the semi-skilled and crowds of rural incomers, women, and teenagers, but in crisis years by better-off families. As well as the long-term social deterioration, repeated short-term social crises erupted. Harvest failures, as in the 1590s, led to soaring food prices, the reduction of non-food demand, and a tidal wall of impoverishment. Plague likewise had acute social as well as demographic implications. The famous Toulouse physician and astrologer Oger Ferrier counselled: 'Three words against the plague …. flee quickly, go far and don't hurry back'. Many prosperous citizens followed this advice, closed up their houses, fled town, and left their workers and their families to fend for themselves. Social life was further hit by quarantine blockades and market closures, spawning food shortages, large-scale deprivation, and social discontent. Plague could lead to rioting and disorder as when crowds of women burnt down pest houses at Salisbury in 1627 and Colchester in 1631 for fear they would spread contagion.

Civic leaders were increasingly concerned with the problems of public disorder associated with the upsurge of urban destitution and other social crises. In Naples, in 1585, a crowd lynched and ritually dismembered a magistrate during a riot over the price of bread. In France, we hear that 'complaint, protest and resistance were part of everyday life' in seventeenth-century cities. Between 1580 and 1700, major civic conflicts flared up in over a score of German cities, including Aachen, Cologne, Frankfurt, Hamburg, and Lübeck. However, most of the serious popular disturbances in European towns in the sixteenth and early seventeenth centuries were triggered by political, fiscal, or military issues, even if social distress seeped into the picture. Often magistrates turned a blind eye to protests against outsiders—tax officials or grain traders—provided the agitation did not go out of control and turn on civic officials: but then there might be harsh retaliation including executions. Broadly speaking, popular attacks on the urban upper class were relatively few and specific—usually involving only a few individuals.

In fact, much of the disorder in towns that so worried magistrates involved small-time crime—petty theft and robberies. Reports of organized criminal gangs crop up in major cities like London, and there were outbreaks of banditry in and around Italian cities during the economic crisis at the end of the sixteenth century: between 1594 and 1595, for instance, forty-six Veronese artisans were tried in Padua for banding together and 'declaring themselves publicly as hired killers willing to serve anyone with their weapons'. However, if there was a more general surge of crime in crisis years, probably the great majority of offences were opportunistic acts by individuals, 'through want and necessity'. In comparison to the medieval town where violence was widespread, serious crime such as homicide was in long-term decline after the Renaissance, as a result of increasing institutional controls. In bigger cities, like Amsterdam and Stockholm, homicide rates fell sharply from the sixteenth to eighteenth centuries. But the problem of crime is always as much about perceptions as about realities and the ruling classes of European cities saw disorder, along with the tidal waves of subsistence migration and destitution, threatening to overwhelm their communities in the sixteenth and early seventeenth centuries.

IV

How did communities cope with the mounting social problems? Almost certainly, traditional mechanisms of social organization inherited from the medieval town came under great strain. In the case of mobility, the family, that basic unit of urban social life, continued to provide important help for kinsmen arriving from the local countryside. But, with the spread of longer-distance movement, many poor migrants had no relations in town.

Beset by poverty and unemployment, lower-class households were small in size (below average) and often headed by a single parent. Partners were forced to separate and go off in search of work; frequently, they never married. Thus, Katherine Knight of the English port of Hythe said she lived apart from her family 'for want of means …. each making shift for their own employment'. Rising rents meant that poor families had to live in a cellar or shed or share a room with other people, while single labourers often slept on the street. Lacking resources, many lower-class families could give little support to relations and others in need. When, for instance, Herman Verbeecq, an Amsterdam artisan, lost his job in the 1650s and his wife was about to give birth, his wife's sister was unwilling to help them out.

By comparison, the family world of the urban upper classes was further consolidated in this period. As we noted earlier, growing wealth was associated with improvements to elite housing, while the number of household members including servants probably increased; a typical patrician household might have as many as twenty members, compared to the three or so in the case of a poor labouring family. As in the past, marriage was a vital instrument in the integration of prosperous outsiders into the urban elite and for extending networks of kin, friendship, and trust that were so important for trade and business. In Spanish cities, like Santander or Cartagena, elites pursued patterns of commercial endogamy that encouraged marriages with similar groups in other trading cities.

Elite concerns about the integrity of family life and the subordination of individual members were increasingly articulated through the secular regulation of adultery, bigamy, and incest and by the adoption of new forms of religious discipline. At Zürich, the reformer Zwingli and the city council established a marriage court in 1525 in charge of divorce and other marital cases, an innovation copied by other cities in Germany and Switzerland. Parallel moral courts were established, leading to the progressive criminalization of non-marital sexuality.

Neighbourhood networks, sustained by the proximity of rich and poorer inhabitants, continued to have a major social function in European cities. As in the past they had a dual function, both regulatory and supportive. Neighbours monitored and mediated in disputes, kept an eye on everything to do with family relations (the behaviour of married partners, lodgers, and the like), as well as giving help (loans, money, comfort) to the needy. In the sixteenth century, however, neighbourly mutuality came under pressure from the high levels of urban mobility and the tidal influx of poor and beggars. The Amsterdamer Herman Verbeecq, though desperate for help, was scornful of his neighbours whom he called 'foreigners'. Neighbourly charity may have become limited to the local core poor, widows, the sick, and the like. In the 1560s, a Canterbury widow, Mother Bassocke, 'of extreme necessity goes from door to door begging with her pot in her hand for drink with also a basket for her meat', but poor beggars encountered growing hostility from respectable householders. On the other hand, neighbourly centres like alehouses and cabarets assumed a greater role, providing a stopover place for newcomers to town, offering a warm refuge for local men to gather by the fire, and selling them drink on credit.

In general, the social discipline function of the neighbourhood became more explicit. Following late medieval trends, neighbourhood structures were more and more formalized and integrated into communal control, focused around well-established families. In Low Country towns, neighbourhood bodies had elaborate rules and regulations, officers and meetings: at Haarlem, for instance, they attended funerals, held annual banquets, kept a treasury, and undertook a great range of social control activities. Neighbourhood figures like midwives reported on clandestine births and the paternity of bastards. In English towns, neighbourhood worthies formed the caucus of parish vestries, supervising relief to the local needy, and local worthies denounced and prosecuted poorer folk for going to alehouses on Sundays or participating in traditional popular entertainments.

At the community level, the response to mounting social problems was strongly institutionalized. Almost always, intervention combined repression with palliative measures. Fundamental was the widespread recognition and implementation of the earlier distinction between the deserving poor—widows, the elderly, the sick, and orphans, together with respectable families that had fallen on hard times—and the undeserving or godless poor, predominantly itinerants and able-bodied labourers. A high priority now was the attack on poor immigrants. At Zamora, in northern Spain, the council in 1531 ordered all peasants to leave the city on pain of 100 lashes, and successive efforts were made to expel incomers. In subsequent decades, especially times of harvest failure, frantic campaigns were launched by cities and towns across Europe, from Madrid to Stockholm, to exclude or eject newcomers, often through the appointment of special officials. Migrants frequently turned to begging, and draconian measures were introduced to restrict the practice to the deserving poor.

As migrants and poor people drifted into crime, fierce measures were deployed to deal with offenders. In 1595, a provost-marshal was appointed in London, with a force of thirty cavalry, to implement martial law against the disorderly; in Italian cities, the authorities encouraged secret denunciations of offenders and introduced new punishments of exile, the galleys, and death. At Perugia and other cities executions of criminals increased substantially in the last part of the sixteenth century. With the growth of prostitution among poor women, the late medieval toleration of organized brothels was abandoned and prostitutes widely prosecuted.

To deal with food shortages, many cities, as we saw, adopted the model of municipal granaries, already introduced in the fifteenth century. Cities also extended the late medieval practice of establishing specialist institutions to deal with social problems. Municipal orphanages were created, or enlarged, to deal with the problem of abandoned or parentless children. Monti di Pietà, which provided cheap loans to the poor, had appeared in some Italian cities in the fifteenth century, but spread now to Rome, Naples, Brescia, and Padua.

However, the main thrust of the urban response to mounting social problems was directed at the erection of centralized relief agencies. Already found in some Mediterranean cities during the fifteenth century, such institutions spread rapidly across Europe after 1500. Influencing this development was not just the mounting scale of social problems, but the new ambitions of civic governments, as well as growing state involvement. Centralized agencies appeared at Nuremburg in 1522, Strasbourg in 1523, and Mons and Ypres in 1525. The policy spread quickly from one place to another. When Lille magistrates established a central hospital in 1527, it was quickly copied at Valenciennes, and in 1531 Emperor Charles V ordered that the innovation be introduced in other Netherland towns. Similar institutions were widely adopted in Italian cities, while an Aumone-Générale was established at Lyon in 1534 and imitated elsewhere in France. Influential humanist writers like Juan Luis Vives promoted the idea and it was adopted in Catholic and Protestants cities alike.

Among religious confessions the principal difference was in the relationship between the centralized institutions and other relief bodies. In Catholic cities relief also came from confraternities, often reorganized or newly founded, and from new religious orders and foundations, inspired by the Counter-Reformation, such as the Ursulines, Clerks Regular of Somascha, Capuchins, and Theatines. In Protestant Europe, central hospitals in towns tended to be complemented by relief from religious congregations or in some countries by outdoor relief. At Emden, in northern Germany, the central Gasthaus (which incorporated a hospital, school, and orphanage) provided indoor relief, while outdoor relief was administered by deacons of the Protestant consistory. In Dutch cities, like Zwolle, the majority of poor received outdoor relief. In England, legislation from the 1530s put the main stress on outdoor parish relief. Cities like London, Norwich, Southampton, and Plymouth had hospitals-cum-workhouses but they never played the central role found in continental cities.

The overall proportion of poor relieved in European cities varied from 11 per cent at Warwick in the 1580s and the same figure at Vitré in 1597, to 16 per cent in Toledo in 1573 and 25 per cent at Trier in 1623. But almost always relief was selective, mainly aiding the resident, deserving poor. Relief (which now frequently involved the interrogation and inspection of the needy) was regularly combined with moral and religious disciplining. Authorities in both Protestant and Catholic cities placed growing emphasis on church attendance, sobriety, sexual continence, and marital fidelity among the poor.

Undeniably, formal intervention was an important part of the urban response to mounting social problems in the sixteenth and seventeenth centuries, but it would be wrong to exaggerate its effectiveness. It worked best when it was able to coopt wider burgher interest. In dealing with major social problems, it contained them, without dealing with structural issues, though, to be fair, many of these were probably beyond the capacity of early modern municipalities or states. The outcome was clear from the high urban mortality figures: urban deprivation often ended in vertical mobility to the grave.

V

The urban demographic downturn in the seventeenth century may have reduced the effect of long-term social problems, though epidemic disease, military conflict, and harvest failure produced recurrent urban mortality crises, as we noted earlier. When urbanization revived during the eighteenth century, social pressure mounted once more, but the urban response may have been more effective, though varying between countries. Fundamental to the new difficulties was the growing rural crisis: renewed population increase in the countryside, combined with agrarian change, however limited, provoked a terrible upsurge of landless and unemployed, ending in a tide of pauper movement to town, particularly high during bad harvests. In 1764, 40,000 poor flooded into Naples where they were described as 'so haggard and thin that they hardly appeared human'. In the 1790s, revolutionary upheavals in France accentuated the movement to town, with recent immigrants comprising up to 40 per cent of the population at Bayeux.

Though the urban economy was probably starting to generate more employment, the modest improvements in real wages after 1700 were reversed by sharply rising food prices in the latter part of the eighteenth century. Poverty levels climbed in many European cities. At Hamburg, the number of listed poor was about 10 per cent in 1787, and two decades later the figure had risen to 32 per cent in some parts of the city. At Lyon, during the great crisis of the late 1780s, about 20,000 people were being relieved, and at Montpellier 40 per cent of the population needed aid. Mortality crises recurred: as at Berlin in 1740, 1758, 1763, 1772, and 1798. Food riots multiplied and there were sporadic major disturbances, often in capital cities: for example, at Stockholm in 1743, 1789, 1793, and 1799. Complaints spread of rising crime rates. Large numbers of poor women, frequently from the countryside, were forced into prostitution as part of a strategy for survival: Paris may have had about 10–15,000 prostitutes, and they also thronged the streets of Amsterdam and London. Female pauperization contributed to the explosion of illegitimate births in the later eighteenth century, rising fivefold in some towns: numbers of abandoned children increased in desperate tandem. Social pressures were especially acute in the expanding suburbs. At the end of the eighteenth century, the Parisian Faubourg St Marcel hosted many marginal groups: new migrants and the indigent (a third of the residents required relief), illicit workers, prostitutes, and petty criminals.

How did European cities respond to the renewed wave of social problems? On the one hand, through a continuity of policy and institutions. Vagrants and beggars were harassed and punished, especially in crisis years—in Russian cities, begging was criminalized under Catherine the Great. Prostitutes were rounded up: in Paris, for example, an inspector of police was appointed in 1747 to control their activity. Centralized relief agencies, that had been created earlier, functioned up to the 1790s, though they often encountered mounting financial problems. In Italy, religious organizations like the Casa Santa dell'Annunziata and Casa Santa di San Giacomo, two of the main relief agencies in Naples, were denounced for their failures and abuses.

On the other hand, new trends emerged in institutional arrangements. Firstly, there was a growing secularization of poor relief as the old Church-based agencies lost their influence. Secondly, punitive treatment of the poor gave way to a more utilitarian attitude, with a stress on training for the discipline of labour. Thirdly, social problems came to be regarded more as managerial, bureaucratic issues, rather than as a direct threat to the urban social order. Finally, there was a new plurality of specialist organizations to deal with different categories of poor. Frequently, they were run or supported by the professional and business classes and had a commercial or voluntary function. At Paris, the Société Philanthropique (1780) assisted widows, the elderly, and blind, while London had a large array of voluntary societies dispensing aid to those in prison for debt, the sick poor, the vagrant poor, the blind, and prostitutes.

Other voluntary mechanisms provided aid for migrant and skilled workers coming to town. In London, Bristol, and Glasgow regional and ethnic societies assisted newcomers and their families. In Paris, networks of migrant traders such as water-carriers from the Auvergne or Savoyard chimney sweeps helped their countrymen to find work. Though traditional journeymen confraternities and *compagnonnages* still offered assistance for artisans, mutual aid societies multiplied during the eighteenth century, sometimes doubling as trade clubs. In the 1730s, we hear of benefit clubs 'very numerous' in London 'for the relief and mutual support of the poorer sort of artisans'. Similar clubs appeared at Paris and Toulouse and in Dutch cities by the 1780s.

From the perspective of poorer townspeople themselves, there is evidence for the emergence in this period of a mixed strategy of subsistence, by which they could more systematically exploit a variety of options to sustain themselves through all but the worst times. Here, official relief was only part of the picture. People in need often combined it with doles from charity organizations, with help from relatives and neighbours, money from clubs, begging and temporary work (including prostitution), or loans from publicans and pawnbrokers, to make ends meet.

In sum, urban social problems may have come rather more under control in the late eighteenth century, notably in West European cities. In the Mediterranean region, problems of poverty could still overwhelm urban centres, and in Russia poverty and child abandonment were endemic in the major cities. But, generally speaking, the massive pauper mortality of earlier centuries abated. Despite elite complaints, urban crime rates seem to have kept in line with urbanization rates, surges in offences occurring mostly at the end of wars when troops were disbanded (see Chapter 11).

VI

Such advances, greatest in Western Europe, were the result not only of more complex institutional and voluntary arrangements, but of other economic and social developments. As noted in Chapter 8, the growth of manufacturing specialisms, together with the expansion of trade, the tertiary sector, and domestic service created more diversity and resilience in the urban economy, and provided greater job opportunities, including female employment (thus helping family incomes). Where they occurred, long-term improvements in living standards for the middling and artisan classes helped reinforce the ability of the family and household to act as a buffer against social problems, for instance, in smoothing the passage of kinsmen to town. How far there was any reinforcement of neighbourliness is debatable. In principle, growing social segregation may have made poor neighbourhoods more sympathetic to supporting inhabitants and newcomers in difficulty. Poorer suburbs offered a terrain for growing social solidarity among the lower orders expressed in festivals, songs, strikes, and political movements. On the other hand, with few rich residents, such areas may have lacked the resources to aid poorer people financially.

Also acting as a buttress against the return of social catastrophe on the earlier scale, was the progressive transformation of the urban social hierarchy. At the top of the social ladder the old commercial elites were enlarged by the inflow of landowners, who brought not only wealth, consumer expenditure, and employment but also new ideas of civil and social policy. Likewise, the growing number and range of professional men in European cities served as a bridge between the old mercantile and new landed elite, as well having links to the rising middling classes—manufacturers, prosperous retailers, and the like. Before 1800, there are the first signs of an urban bourgeoisie—more numerous, and generally better off than earlier middling groups, and displaying greater social and cultural confidence.

This was especially evident in the most dynamic metropolitan towns. At Paris, it has been estimated that bourgeois households numbered about 25,000 before the Revolution; in late Georgian London, tax records suggest 27,000 households belonged to the middle classes. Middling groups enjoyed growing economic leverage: at Toulouse, for instance, the 12–16 per cent of the population classed as bourgeois controlled 45 per cent of the capital available for dowries. Growing social status was exemplified by the way they developed networks across the community, often through new-style societies, and revealed a growing appetite for smart leisure activities—emulating their social superiors. At Montpellier, a local commentator praised the cultural blurring of elite and middling ranks: 'today there are no more differences in the way they run their households, give dinner parties and dress'.

New bourgeois social ambitions were reflected in their domestic lifestyle. Research on probate inventories has shown the rapid accumulation of consumer goods, often less expensive versions of luxury products. In Paris, individual beds, bed curtains (green was a favourite colour), clocks, and secular pictures increasingly decorated middle-class homes, but the development was not limited to capitals. In a Scottish town like Dundee over half of wealthier households had mahogany furniture, chinaware, clocks, looking glasses, and featherbeds, just as in the eastern Baltic ceramic tea-sets, silver pots, and jugs, German and other porcelain, and books graced the houses of Estonian townsmen. Fashionable furnishings and consumer wares demarcated the different rooms of wealthier houses, as gender segregation and new notions of privacy and domestic leisure created more specialist spaces—boudoirs, libraries, salons, dining-rooms, and the like. In this domesticated private world, wealthier families like that of the Lyon lawyer Laurent Degas could relax, read, and play chess or music together.

As we have noted, greater social segregation was appearing before 1800 with the advent of bourgeois residential areas in major West European cities—marked by improved housing, street improvement, better policing, and control of the poor. By contrast, the lower orders were crowded into poorer districts, without street improvement, often on the urban periphery in squalid tenements and courts without the faintest notions of privacy or decency. Yet it is premature to speak of class formation in this period. If the bourgeoisie in major metropolitan cities were by 1800 starting to assert their social power, power that would reach its climax in the late nineteenth century, in many towns the social hierarchy remained much more traditional with the landed and commercial elites in charge and the middling ranks divided.

Among the lower orders, greater social fragmentation was taking place. Small masters and skilled workers were increasing in numbers. Organized through trade and benefit clubs, as well as traditional bodies, they probably enjoyed some improvement in living standards, at least until the last years of the century. They even picked up some of the fruits of the new consumerism, their houses boasting chinaware, rush-chairs, clocks, and books. By contrast, as we know, the position for unskilled labourers and migrant poor was more precarious, often deteriorating in many European cities.

Especially notable in the eighteenth century was the selective advance in the social status of hitherto marginal groups. Wives and daughters of the elite were better educated and became involved in a whirl of smart leisure and social activities. In London and Paris, fashionable women organized social and intellectual salons; in Edinburgh, a group of women established a literary club. Concerts, the theatre, assemblies, along with visiting and private entertainments attracted many upper-class women, who also enjoyed shopping trips as an urban pursuit. Wealthier bourgeois women participated in some of these activities, as they became less active in their husbands' business life. Mrs Thrale, the socialite wife of a London brewer, hosted so many fashionable dinner parties that even she was forced to complain 'tis a ruin'. Private entertainment, including music-making, was only one way in which better-off women entrenched their position in the home. The spread of private spaces reserved for women, their increasing importance in choosing furniture and other household items, the feminization of domestic service, and the growing emphasis on cleanliness all tended to enhance their household status.

The status of lower-class women was more problematic. Greater job opportunities in towns, the decline of the guilds, and improved literacy may have led to enhanced social standing for some groups. At Paris, Mercier praised the role of artisans' wives who 'work in concert with their husbands and are consequently in a good position .... the soul of the shop'. In English towns, female benefit societies, which recruited mainly the wives of artisans, multiplied in the late eighteenth century. However, the situation for the vast majority of poorer women in towns almost certainly got worse, as testified by the rapid increase of illegitimate children.

For young people there was a similar selective change in status. Offspring of the elite and bourgeoisie may have benefited from consumerism and rising educational opportunities. However, for the lower classes, the decline of the guilds weakened the formal status of apprenticeship, and the spread of new industries meant that many young people entered into backbreaking, exhausting work at an early age. As we shall see, ethnic and religious minorities were increasingly tolerated in eighteenth-century cities, particularly in Western Europe. But one can detect an immigrant hierarchy. In London, Sephardic Jews came to dominate the stock market, but poorer minorities such as the Ashkenazi Jews or Irish in English towns suffered discrimination and harassment.

Arguably, greater affluence, social coherence and stability helped buttress, to some extent, the eighteenth-century urban response to renewed social pressures in Western Europe. Outside this region, slower economic improvement was followed by more limited changes in the social structure. Landowners flocked to the bigger Spanish cities but the clergy still outnumbered the small number of lay professionals, and commercial groups were slow to revive. In the Mediterranean, as in much of Northern and Eastern Europe (outside the capital cities), it is likely that urban society remained heavily polarized and traditional, but more research needs to be done.

Across Europe, the French Revolution and the subsequent wars caused not only widespread economic disruption but also social upheaval. As we know, refugees poured into the cities from the countryside, and the landed elites fled. Urban poor-relief institutions were reformed in French-controlled cities and the Church and clergy lost what remained of their power. Poverty levels increased and there was a surge of bourgeois anxiety about the social intentions of the lower classes. After two centuries of recurrent social crises, the transforming processes of the eighteenth century proved as partial and flawed as the economic transformation of cities. In the next two chapters, we turn to look at the cultural and political developments in European cities from the Reformation to the French Revolution.

10

Culture and Landscape
1500–1800

On the eve of the Reformation, the iconic image of the European city, portrayed in early maps and landscapes, on civic seals, and as the backcloth in religious paintings or patrician portraits, was that of a Christian community defined by its town walls and gates, and embellished with a spiky coronet of church spires. This urban representation followed a tradition dating back to the early Middle Ages. Three centuries later, conventional images started to be those of an open Enlightenment city, patterned with parks and boulevards (replacing demolished town walls), while its churches were rivalled in splendour by theatres and opera houses, and by the classical-styled mansions of the urban elite. As this metamorphosis illustrates, the early modern period witnessed abiding changes in the cultural identity and landscape of many European cities and towns. In part, these changes were shaped by the major demographic fluctuations, economic developments, and social processes discussed in previous chapters. Political forces, including the rise of states, also had a powerful impact.

Initially, as we will see in the following sections, many European cities sought to respond to the new pressures of the sixteenth century by asserting their cultural voice and lineaments of identity in a broadly traditional way, drawing on those late medieval developments in building, religion, education, and ceremonial. The Protestant reform movement, launched by Luther's attack on the Papacy and Church abuses at Wittenberg in 1517, at first enabled urban communities to proclaim their own religious image, whether Lutheran, Calvinist, or Catholic. Increasingly, however, cities became trapped by national and international religious movements and conflict. Only in the later part of the period do we see cities once again taking the initiative to re-establish their cultural integrity and identity within the broad framework of the Enlightenment movement.

I

Town walls were not merely civic icons. They continued to be rebuilt and extended during the sixteenth century to answer the military threat posed by armies equipped with powerful artillery, and also to enclose expanding urban populations. Naples and other Italian cities had their walls reinforced in the early sixteenth century, while Antwerp's fortifications were extended in 1542, as the urban population sprawled outside the old city boundaries. With the onset of savage religious warfare in the 1560s, many French cities struggled to upgrade their walls, employing architect-engineers to install the new principles of Italian fortification. At the start of the Dutch Revolt, a dozen Netherlands towns had been turned into artillery fortresses and the walls of eighteen more had been partially rebuilt in the Italian style.

Church building generally came to a halt in Protestant cities after the Reformation (though there was a good deal of internal remodelling) and numerous religious houses, confraternity halls, and parish churches were demolished or converted for secular purposes. York, for example, lost sixteen churches after 1547. By contrast, the Catholic Counter-Reformation led to a wave of religious and related building from the late sixteenth century, with old churches rebuilt and new classical-style and baroque edifices raised. In Orthodox Russia, too, a surge of church construction took place under the Romanovs: by the 1620s a town like Vologda (5—6,000 inhabitants) had sixty churches, including a cathedral as well as three monasteries.

At the same time, European towns of all denominations saw a major growth of new secular buildings, often to house their urban magistracies. In England, over 130 town halls were built, renovated or converted from other uses during the period 1500 to 1640. Among the most splendid European town halls erected at this time were the Renaissance-style building at Gdansk, built by Netherland masters at the end of the sixteenth century and with a dazzling interior of painted and sculpted decoration; and the palatial town hall of Amsterdam, designed by Jacob van Campen in an Italianate baroque style, its ornate motifs celebrating the end of the Thirty Years War.

II

The Reformation (like the subsequent Counter-Reformation) was an urban-based movement in which cities often played decisive roles in the early stages of religious change. Urban reformation was as much the product of economic, social, and political currents on the ground as of theological influences. Religious upheaval sucked in a wide variety of extraneous pressures and demands, some general but others highly specific to a community. Among the pressures for reform within cities were long-standing grievances over Church privileges, for instance, over markets and court jurisdiction, and resentment at Church wealth and abuses. On the other hand, everything indicates (as we saw in Chapter 5) that many European towns before the Reformation experienced intense religious fervour and voluntary activity among the laity at the parish level. Medieval heresy did not have a large following among European townsmen, nor did it have a major impact on the early progress of the Reformation. More influential were humanist ideas of social and cultural reform, spreading from Renaissance Italy by the early decades of the sixteenth century. Such ideas gained a sizeable following among the elite and professional classes of West European cities, for instance, at Nuremberg and other south German cities; at Strasbourg in the Rhineland; and in Low Country cities such as Antwerp, where the leading humanist writer Erasmus influenced a small circle of magistrates, clergy, and businessmen. Urban humanism often chimed with a concern for communal reform, drawing on and reformulating Italian notions of civic republicanism. It was through these humanist groups and networks that Luther's ideas moved like wildfire between German cities and thence to other European centres.

By the 1520s, growing sections of the urban elite in European cities were promoting Protestant reform. Thus, at Zwickau, the city authorities invited Luther to preach (in 1522), supported reformist preachers, and three years later expelled the Franciscan friars. Sometimes reform initiatives involved an attempt by one elite group to replace another; in other places, reform action was taken (as at Strasbourg) by well-established patrician families. Religious reform was sometimes part of an attempt to consolidate and renew the civic community through the acquisition of Church resources and control of ecclesiastical space. At a number of cities (for instance, at Geneva in 1537), the Reformation was adopted by the renewal of the communal oath by the citizenry. Church property was often seized for urban purposes, such as for poor relief or education: at Marburg, in Germany, the Protestant university moved into a former friary as did the city's Latin School at Gdansk. Ecclesiastical franchises were abolished or restricted. But control over urban space was also extended vertically—down to the level of the household. In Protestant cities we find a stress on sexual discipline and moral order based on the pious, educated household.

If elite action was often decisive for letting Protestant activists out of the bag, in a number of towns popular reformist movements also developed, as at Augsburg and Wittenberg. In the 1520s and 1530s, evangelical Anabaptists gained support at Zürich and Strasbourg and, most dramatically and exceptionally, at Münster millenarian Anabaptists took control of the city council and maintained their theocratic power by violent means, until their suppression by the bishop and an imperial army. In the Low Countries, during the 1560s, iconoclastic activity, though led by preachers, mobilized the lower classes who were suffering from trade and industrial recession. But, in general, ruling groups reacted strongly against popular movements, either trying to head them off with concessions, or engaging in heavy-handed repression.

Maintaining civic control over religious policy was difficult for various reasons. Pressure came from bands of religious refugees moving between cities. Emden, after the 1550s, experienced an influx of English and then Dutch and French refugees who agitated for reform in the city. Also influential at Emden was the role of the local ruler, the Protestant Countess of East Friesland, who expelled the Franciscan friars. In many European cities, local nobles or rulers were crucial from an early stage in setting the religious agenda. At Leipzig, the ruling council was pressured by Duke George of Saxony to prevent the spread of Lutheran ideas. In England and Sweden, local urban support for reform was often limited and the kings' support for Protestant innovations proved crucial. In France, Protestant advances in the early sixteenth century were opposed by a strong royal government but a succession of weak rulers from the 1560s opened the door to a medley of groups, including civic magistrates and preachers as well as provincial nobles, to promote (or oppose) Protestant reform for their own purposes. The outcome was a series of religious wars that engulfed much of the kingdom, including many cities. Smaller provincial towns were especially vulnerable to the religious demands of local nobility, but with the breakdown of royal government even Paris was taken over by the

Catholic League in the years 1588–94 and came under the militant urban leadership of the Sixteen.

As the Reformation progressed, European cities became either Protestant, frequently with a Catholic minority (sometimes tolerated, as in Amsterdam, more often persecuted as at Strasbourg); or Catholic (with persecuted minorities); or confessional cohabiters, having either de facto or legally established equality between Catholics and Protestants (this was mainly the case in German cities). Protestant cities often had their own uneasy internal balance between Calvinist and Lutheran congregations. Though there was a wide diversity of religious experience, many of these arrangements were a recipe for internal conflict or external pressure. At Augsburg, where Catholics and Protestants shared municipal power after 1548, religious cohabitation suffered repeated attack from the Catholic Church and, during the Thirty Years War, from Swedish and imperial rulers.

In the Low Countries, Germany, France, and the Mediterranean states, Catholic rulers, supported by the Counter-Reformation Papacy, generally acted firmly to prevent or reverse the urban reception of Protestantism. At the same time, there was often strong communal support for the Catholic Church. At Toulouse, threatened in the 1560s by a Calvinist advance in the region, citizens rallied to the Catholic cause, believing that its rejection was tantamount to the overthrow of the city's identity and traditions. In northern England, a number of towns in traditionalist areas displayed a similar reluctance to adopt state-sponsored Protestant innovation.

Catholic rulers (like their Protestant colleagues) deployed powerful weapons to force recalcitrant towns to fall into line on religious policy. Battling to suppress the Dutch Revolt, Spanish concessions at the Treaty of Arras were followed by the banishment of Protestant activists and brutal repression of others at Antwerp, Lille, and elsewhere, leading to widespread acceptance of the Catholic restoration. The Protestant city of La Rochelle was besieged and bombarded by Louis XIII and a large part of its remaining Protestant population expelled after its capitulation in 1628. The Inquisition was used in Mediterranean cities against heretics and religious minorities. However, in the long run, the success of the Counter-Reformation in cities owed a good deal to its appeal to urban needs—in some ways mirroring the attractions of Protestantism. After the Council of Trent, the Catholic Church stressed the need for: a reformed, educated clergy; reorganized ecclesiastical institutions (medieval confraternities and religious orders were often replaced by new bodies, more directly under official control); and moral and sexual regulations that had the effect of supporting urban controls over an unstable social order.

After the Reformation, religion remained a central pillar of cultural life and identity in both Catholic and Protestant cities, despite periods of internal tension and recurrent conflict with external forces. Indeed, the role of urban religion was often reinforced, as we have noted, by the enlistment of the different confessions in magisterial campaigns against mounting social problems. Urban rituals and ceremonies—so vital since the Middle Ages for articulating communal identity and order, and for promoting urban visibility in the wider world—were likewise adapted to underpin the social and political regime. In Protestant cities, many late medieval ceremonies were swept aside after the Reformation. Thus, at Chester, on the border with Wales, Shrovetide festivities were reformed as early as 1540, and the Whitsun religious plays were finally suppressed in the 1570s. Other rituals were reorganized in line with the growth of civic oligarchy and in response to concerns over public order. The sheriff's breakfast was now restricted to members of the ruling elite, while Chester's traditional procession of the Christmas watch became responsible for arresting vagabonds, criminals, and drunkards. From 1610, St George's Day, once the time when the city's Whitsun plays were proclaimed, was turned over to horse-races, in order to attract landowners to town and so boost the urban economy. Here we can recognize (as in the late Middle Ages) the significant tourist function of urban ceremony.

In Catholic cities, too, there was a significant reshaping of ritual activity. Unlike in Protestant Europe, religious processions multiplied in Catholic cities—a middle-rank community might have a dozen or more in the seventeenth century; but now they were more closely controlled by local elites and popular festivities were largely suppressed. At Rome, the Popes sought to remodel the ritual landscape by the creation of new streets and the installation of obelisks and columns in central spaces, while traditional communal rituals were phased out and new ceremonies emphasized the Papal Court. In Barcelona, ceremonies became heavily identified with the ruling class.

III

Influenced by late medieval and humanist ideas, both Protestant reformers and Catholics highlighted the contribution of education to spiritual life and the social and moral order. After the Reformation, new educational institutions were established at Strasbourg, including an elementary school for each parish, two Latin schools, a library, and a medical lecture course. In Catholic Europe, Jesuit colleges were established at Cologne in 1544, Vienna in 1552, and Worms in 1557, with many others elsewhere. At Barcelona, the Jesuit Collegi de Cordelles became crucial to the education of the local ruling class, eclipsing the old university. New universities were also established in the struggle between the confessions. The Lutheran Count of Hesse-Darmstadt established Giessen University in 1607 in opposition to the Calvinist one at nearby Marburg, while the Swedish kings founded Protestant universities at Tarttu (1632), Turku (1640), and Greifswald (1656) as they sought to consolidate control over their Baltic dominions. At the lower end of the teaching spectrum, confessional rivalry likewise played its part in the establishment of elementary schools. In seventeenth-century Metz, the Protestant congregation had a vast network of petty schools with bursaries for poor children to attend. In Italy, Schools of Christian Doctrine approved by the Council of Trent reached large numbers of children on Sundays and holidays—as many as 12,000 in Milan and 6,000 in Venice.

Although the religious stimulus to educational expansion was significant, so too was the growth of trade and the service sector. As part of this picture, we see a proliferation of vernacular schools. Italian cities were still in the forefront into the sixteenth century, with an increasing number of communal grammar schools. But vernacular schools also spread into the cities of southern Germany, the Low Countries, England, and Sweden. Though the majority of pupils were boys, in the Dutch Republic large numbers of girls were taught as well.

Expanded schooling led to a rising tide of educational skill. In late sixteenth-century Dijon, 46 per cent of craftsmen were still illiterate, but fifty years later this had fallen to 32 per cent. In Rouen, a little later, only 34 per cent of men could not read or write (though the figure was 59 per cent for women). At Amsterdam, about 70 per cent of bridegrooms could sign their names by the end of the seventeenth century. A growing proportion of townspeople owned or had access to books. At Canterbury, in the 1560s, about one in twelve of better-off townsmen owned a book, but this figure had risen to nearly a half before the English Civil War. At Rouen, up to two thirds of the Protestant citizens in the seventeenth century owned a printed work, though the figure was lower among Catholics. Many of the publications found in households were religious books like the Bible, but increasingly literary, travel, political, and popular works penetrated the home, as a result of the enormous expansion of the printing industry, especially in Western Europe. Though state censorship put a brake on the output of dissident religious and political works during the sixteenth and seventeenth centuries, and tended to centralize production in capital cities, still there was a huge growth of titles and editions. In the 1660s, the London chapbook publisher Charles Tias had about 90,000 books in stock.

Recent work has emphasized the continuing interaction between the printed book and older oral traditions, but there seems little doubt that literacy, schooling, and the new media world steadily divided urban and rural cultural worlds. By the seventeenth century, urban and rural dialects started to diverge, the latter regarded by the metropolitan classes as archaic and backward. This period may also have seen the advent of a distinctive language for capital cities such as 'cockney' in London.

New trends are also evident in urban artistic output. If sixteenth-century art produced in Italian or Netherlands cities continued to include a high proportion of religious works, by the next century there was a widening typology of output and new sites of production, notably in the Dutch Republic and England. Particularly striking was the urbanization of art. Whilst in earlier times, representations of the city had often appeared only as a backdrop to religious art, now the saints depart and the city in all its guises takes the front of stage. Around 1600 portraits of town magistrates are found not just in the main cities but in smaller provincial towns. In the Low Countries, collective portraits of the civic militia and other bodies became fashionable. For the first time, ordinary townsmen and women, including the elderly, those from ethnic minorities, street traders, and the poor start, started to figure commonly as artistic subjects. Some Dutch artists specialized in domestic interiors, and here interior and townscape painting developed hand in hand. The depiction of the townscape took a growing variety of forms—panoramic landscapes, birdseye views, maps, and detailed street or house scenes. Eager to promote their image, cities commissioned paintings of their communities. Engraved views of cities, sometimes plagiarized from earlier works, were published in series like Braun and Hohenberg's monumental six-volume *Civitaties Orbis Terrarum* (1572–1617). However stereotyped, images of leading European cities could be compared and contrasted for the first time. The explosion of fairly cheap engraved prints from the sixteenth century made all these urban images—landscapes, views, portraits and also maps—available to a wider audience: some even hung on alehouse or cabaret walls.

If sixteenth-century town maps were still impressionistic in the medieval mode, by the seventeenth century a new generation of cartographers led by those in Amsterdam had introduced mathematical clarity and precision to the representation of urban space. Maps were commissioned by Swiss, English, and Portugese cities to define their territory, particularly when this was questioned by outsiders. Warfare also spawned a multiplicity of accurate urban plans, particularly of fortifications. As major cities grew in size, a market sprang up for maps giving a detailed street plan, often as a guide to visitors. Restoration London saw a spate of them: thirty-one were published between 1660 and 1690; while Parisians had a choice of forty printed maps in the years after 1700.

By the mid-seventeenth century, urban cultural life was at the crossroads. Urban identity up till then was still strongly defined by religion and public buildings. Despite the growth of urban education and literacy, there were continuing connections with the popular cultural world of the countryside, reinforced by the tidal wave of poorer immigrants. For all the denunciations of preachers and efforts to control them by civic authorities, traditional plays, country dances, songs, music, and rituals were still performed in town streets or in neighbourhood drinking-houses. At Seville, on Sundays, ritual battles took place between city gangs beside the city gates, watched by hundreds of spectators on the town walls, cheering their favourites. Similarly, the famous Venetian battles of fists erupted on feast days and Sundays on neighbourhood bridges between the popular Castellani and Nicolotti factions, many of the fighters recent arrivals to the city. Witchcraft beliefs and allegations, though less widespread than in the countryside, impacted on towns or districts of towns, with sporadic panics or witch hunts at Loudun, Trier, Würzburg, Bamberg, and elsewhere. Many of those tried in cities were either supposed witches from the countryside or rural immigrants. Urban witchcraft cases were often clustered in small market towns with their strong agrarian overtones. At the same time, charges of urban witchcraft may have had their own special features, such as stronger political undercurrents and a greater stress on collective possession, supposedly by demons.

If traditional cultural ideas and identity were already being challenged in the seventeenth century by the growing power of the state and nobility, by secularization and by political and social polarization, it was from the turn of the century that the most crucial changes started to occur as cities and towns led by those in Western Europe sought to establish a new cultural role and image in an increasingly integrated national and international scene, one in which fashion, pluralism, and improvement became key motifs. Capital cities led the way in these developments, but they were steadily diffused through the urban network, and by the end of the period provincial towns were, in their turn, influencing metropolitan activity.

IV

Four main developments can be identified in the second half of the period: the erosion of traditional cultural activities; the further growth of education; the rise of new leisure activities; and the transformation of urban space. Religion remained a powerful force in urban cultural life, but in Western Europe it was displaced from its dominant centrality on the urban cultural stage. Already, from the later sixteenth century, a number of cities, as in the Dutch Republic, practised de facto toleration of religious minorities for commercial purposes. By the eighteenth century, the argument for toleration and religious pluralism was widely asserted in European cities. In German residential cities like Berlin or Mainz rulers encouraged a mixture of religious faiths—Catholics, Lutherans, Calvinists, and Jews. At Hamburg, increasing toleration of Catholics and Jews arrived as the city sought to compete with other places pursuing liberal policies. In Switzerland, confessional constraints were relaxed at Berne in 1724 and Zürich in 1737, while, in Sweden, religious minorities were accorded toleration by law in 1782. Catholic states saw a similar if later trend. In France, Austria, and southern Italy, the expulsion of the Jesuits after mid-century, and the papal suppression of the order in 1773, highlighted the shift to a more secular regime. Toleration Acts were passed in Austria in 1781 and France in 1787, and religious houses were closed down by the Austrian Emperor Joseph II the same decade. In Paris, popular belief in miracles, still widespread earlier in the century, faded in the second half, while the proportion of religious works decreased in book collections.

   This is not to underplay the continuing power of religion in urban cultural life. Measures in favour of toleration were opposed in a number of German cities. In British towns, Methodist and other revivalist movements swept through many centres of rapid urbanization. Into the eighteenth century, in Catholic countries from Hungary to Spain, grand baroque and neoclassical churches were raised in cities, and new or rebuilt religious edifices made an impressive sight in Protestant metropoles like London and Berlin. Into the early twentieth century, religious belief remained one of the most important cultural commitments of the great majority of European town dwellers. However, the Church was increasingly only one strand in urban cultural life and had to compete with secular competitors, including new leisure entertainments. Already, about 1700, we hear that Toulouse's town elite was showing less interest in religious devotion and more concern for metropolitan manners and fashions.

In the same way, traditional ceremonial was in evident decline. At Turin, older communal rituals disappeared while, in Hamburg, new state festivities replaced old communal ceremonies. London's rustic May Day rituals metamorphosed into a festival for soot-caked, town chimney sweeps, and the capital's streets were crowded with new processions organized by the freemasons and other voluntary associations. Popular entertainments like street football were progressively shunned by the urban respectable classes as unfashionable and backward.

V

Urban education became more dynamic and secularized. Religious schools lost momentum and a growing range of new, better-organized elementary and commercial schools offered literacy and business training to an expanding share of the population, including women. From the late seventeenth century, French towns were always more literate than the countryside and high metropolitan literacy rates (90 per cent for Parisian men) spread to smaller towns: at Meulan, in northern France, male illiteracy fell from 29 per cent around 1700 to 15 per cent near the end of the century. By the later eighteenth century, the great majority of men in Europe's larger cities were literate—90 per cent in Madrid, 94 per cent of owner occupiers in Berlin; though, at the end of the period, rapid urban growth in some places, particularly industrializing towns, may have started to depress literacy rates. Women remained markedly less literate (64 per cent illiterate in Madrid, 36 per cent in Amsterdam), but the female illiteracy trend was downward: at Meulan it fell from 50 per cent to 22 per cent during the eighteenth century.

Book reading and the ownership of books soared, especially among better-off townspeople. Half the Parisians leaving inventories in the late eighteenth century owned books, and a quarter of them had substantial collections. It was not just the number but range of books that was striking. Religious works were eclipsed by a kaleidoscope of political, philosophical, travel, historical, and literary works, including novels. By the mid-eighteenth century, Estonian townspeople owned histories, novels, books on mathematics, geography, and commerce, the majority in German but others in French, English, and Swedish.

New-style town histories, which had first appeared in the sixteenth century (for instance, Corrozet on Paris, Stow on London), were published now for many towns both large and small, often highlighting not just urban origins but recent developments, including new public buildings, and population and economic advances. In England, eight histories of this type came off the press in the years 1701 to 1720, mainly written for members of the local elite, but over fifty were published in the last two decades of the eighteenth century, the majority targeting a middle-class readership.

As state censorship became less effective in many Enlightenment countries (and collapsed in England), radical works could be bought from a growing number of booksellers. Namur, in the Southern Netherlands, had a dozen bookshops which stocked works on the English Revolution, corruption at the French court, pornography, and much else. Book consumption was encouraged by the spread of book clubs, literary circle, cabinets de lectures, and libraries—many of them set up by booksellers—and by the rise of the newspaper press which provided advertising and the oxygen of publicity for the world of print.

Though manuscript newsletters and short-lived printed newspapers had appeared in Dutch, German, and other cities before the mid-seventeenth century, over the next 150 years most of the principal urban centres from Stockholm and Copenhagen, to Madrid and Lisbon, acquired journals reporting a potpourri of political news, domestic and foreign, battles, fashion, and sociable activity. Before 1700, Germany had over 200 papers, while Parisian newspapers circulated through the country, their columns retailing news (of variable accuracy) from the capital and abroad, helping turn provincial towns away from old-style cultural localism. By the 1780s, English readers could choose from over a dozen London newspapers and fifty or so published by provincial printers, who, like those at York and Leeds, tailored their national coverage to local audiences.

VI

The press played a powerful role in the broadcasting of the latest metropolitan and international ideas, and contributed heavily to the rise of new leisure and entertainment activities. No less important, were those developments in the drink trade discussed in Chapter 8, including the enhanced respectability and size of older-type drinking-houses and the proliferation of new kinds like coffee-houses and cafés. In British cities, and to a lesser extent elsewhere, drinking-houses served as important venues for the new leisure activities, just as their landlords became leading cultural entrepreneurs.

In the 1670s, the first commercial concerts in England were held at an East London alehouse, promoted by the publican John Bannister, and by the 1730s public music-making was a flourishing leisure attraction in the British capital, performed at subscription and benefit concerts, scores of music societies, and the opera. In West European cities, a similar trend is apparent, albeit with a stronger Court or institutional influence. Paris hosted Le Concert Spirituel from 1725, concerts being performed in a large hall in the Tuileries Palace, with several hundred people in the audience. At Brussels, the Court of the Austrian governor-general served as the focus of much musical activity, but a growing array of musical events was held by the late eighteenth century. In Germany public concerts developed from those of music societies, such as at Leipzig (after 1743) where the orchestra acquired a fine new concert hall in 1781 and took its name, the Gewandhaus. Here, and at Berlin, music lovers could choose from competing concert series before the end of the period. In Vienna, imperial and aristocratic patronage remained crucial for musicians, but by the 1780s more commercial concerts had arrived. At St Petersburg, noble-sponsored concerts were held from the 1740s, while musical life was increasingly lively and varied in the main Hungarian towns.

Invented at Venice in the 1630s, opera remained one of the most prestigious musical art forms in the eighteenth century and many of the metropolitan cities had an opera house, including Münich (1654), Brussels (1700), Dresden (1719), Warsaw (1725, rebuilt 1748), Berlin (1742), and Prague (1783, where Mozart's *Don Giovanni* was first performed). Leading Enlightenment cities competed with one another internationally in musical fame and status.

Public music-making quickly spread to provincial cities. By the 1730s and 1740s, many English country towns had music clubs and concerts, and a few might even have a temporary opera house, as at Chester in 1741 where a city hospital was fitted out for performances of Italian operas. In France, concerts were organized by the academies at Bordeaux, Lyon, Marseille, and elsewhere. At Montpellier, all the top-rank families belonged to the Academie de Musique and members paid an annual subscription to attend operas, concerts, and chamber music in a civic concert hall. Music became a virtuoso part of the urban cultural scene, accompanied by the rise of professional musicians, music publishers, concert promoters, star performers, and famous composers like Mozart and Haydn who went on international tours of European cities. More and more, public music-making overlapped with private musical life, as the growth of sheet music and the greater availability of early pianos encouraged performances at home, often by female members of elite and middle-class families.

No less significant were the developments in art and the theatre. By the eighteenth century, a major restructuring of the fine arts had taken place, marked by a proliferation of artistic societies, training academies, public exhibitions, art dealers, foreign imports, and the growing output of print manufacturers: the commercialization of the art market, already starting earlier, came of age. In the case of the theatre, earlier itinerant troupes of players and makeshift stages in inns, town halls, and open spaces gave way to purpose-built playhouses and more or less resident companies of actors. Eighteenth-century Paris had six *théatres de boulevard* and Venice seven (plus lesser venues). Other cities followed suit: Hamburg had a permanent theatre after 1765; Strasbourg had both French and German theatres; and Toulouse's Théatre du Capitole (1740) offered the latest plays, ballet, and opera for the elite. In England, even smaller country towns had purpose-built playhouses in the late Georgian era. Appealing to a growing audience, theatres became more spacious and equipped with extended stages and better lighting. The rebuilding of London theatres at Covent Garden and Drury Lane in the last part of the eighteenth century created auditoria seating audiences of over 3,000. Theatres became worlds in which the latest fashions in dress, language, morals, and manners were displayed (and debated) not just on stage but in the amphitheatre, where spectators came as much to be seen as to see, and where wider political and social networking and discourse could take place.

Outdoor activities likewise flowered. From the seventeenth century, many West European cities had tree-lined walks, usually on the outskirts of towns, where the local elite could promenade, meet, and converse. The neglect of such walks in Italian cities was criticized by a French visitor in the 1730s, who wrote 'none of them have public walks which can compare with those in our smallest towns'. The symbolic acquisition of a cultivated version of nature by the city at a time of rising urban densities was also exemplified in the spread of commercial pleasure gardens after 1700, intermingling elaborate walks and green vistas (like those of a country house) with music, refreshment, and illuminations. Redesigned in the 1730s and 1740s, London's Spring Gardens (later Vauxhall) and Ranelagh attracted up to 10,000 visitors at some events. Similar facilities were found in Paris, the towns of Ghent, Spa, and Brussels in the Southern Netherlands, and St Petersburg, but not apparently in German cities. Municipal parks were mainly a later phenomenon, but in capital cities like London and Stockholm royal parks such as Hyde Park and Djurgården were open to public access and provided a variety of entertainments.

Spectators played an important part in the growth of sport as an organized, commercial, and urban leisure activity, though here the main development was concentrated on England. Already, by the 1730s, cricket matches were played before large crowds at Blackheath on the outskirts of London, as cricket moved from being a regional, largely rural game to a national, urban sport. By the 1790s, the game was supervised by the London-based Marylebone cricket club. Probably the most successful sport was horse-racing, which started in towns during the sixteenth century, but really took off in the late seventeenth. Around 1770, England had eighty-nine race courses, almost all of them in or close to large or small towns (for instance, York and Ludlow), with nearly 300 race days a year. Archery similarly evolved as a fashionable organized sport, with a dozen or more clubs across the country, and annual tournaments at Blackheath. While all three sports had royal or aristocratic patronage, they attracted large audiences of spectators from a wide social spectrum. Primarily urban-based, they had an important commercial aspect—often promoted by drink traders and involving heavy gambling; and they were increasingly regulated by clubs and societies.

By comparison, organized commercial sport was much slower to gain a foothold in continental cities (as we shall see in Chapter 15, the main take-off here was in the later nineteenth century), probably because of the continuing prevalence and patronage of traditional communal games and sports. Joseph Baretti noted in the 1760s the absence in Italy of English-style sports and the prevalence of traditional ones like *pallone* (handball), climbing trees for prizes, and horse races without riders. At Toulouse, in 1765, a horse-race meeting was arranged by an Englishman and drew large crowds, but the idea failed to take off. However, by this time the older game of *boules* was run on an organized basis by urban societies in Western France—at Laval, Nantes, and elsewhere.

Clubs and societies served as a focus for many of the new kinds of secular cultural activity. Though, as we know, voluntary bodies such as religious confraternities and guilds had flourished since the late Middle Ages and continued to function on a declining basis into the eighteenth century, what was new in the Enlightenment era was the increasingly diverse, urban, and secular nature of associational life. British cities led the way. During the eighteenth century, about 12,000 clubs and societies met in English towns, and London may have had over 3,000 societies by 1800, its members recruited from the elite, middle classes, and skilled workers. Society membership was predominantly male. Over a hundred different types are encountered from sporting, musical, and theatrical clubs to benefit, bird-fancying, book, debating, gambling, horticultural, improvement, literary, political, scientific, and social clubs. The most successful in organizational and recruitment terms was freemasonry. The Masonic order was established in London in 1717 with four metropolitan lodges, and by 1800 there were over 400 in English and Welsh towns.

A small number of private learned academies or literary circles had existed in Mediterranean cities, often with noble patronage since the fifteenth century, but, from the seventeenth, continental rulers promoted the foundation of state academies, often with official funding and with courtiers and bureaucrats as members. By the early eighteenth century, state academies of this type functioned in capital cities like Paris (several after the 1630s), St Petersburg (1724), Stockholm (1739), and Copenhagen (1742), but also in regional centres such as Toulouse, Uppsala, Bordeaux, Barcelona, Bologna, and Messina. Some of the smaller academies had a voluntary dimension, and by the second half of the century clubs and societies started to proliferate in continental cities, particularly in Western Europe. In France, the most dynamic type were Masonic lodges, inspired initially by the English movement: over 800 were established in the years 1732–93, though many were short-lived. Other societies in France included learned and literary societies, philanthropic and agricultural ones, medical societies, sport and social clubs, and, from the 1780s especially, mutual aid and political societies. In Germany, the incidence varied between cities and princely states, but a variety of large and smaller towns hosted language and scientific societies, Masonic, student, and debating clubs, and patriotic improvement societies. Mainz, under an enlightened elector, boasted Masonic, Rosicrucian, and Illuminati lodges, a noble club, and an important Reading Club equipped with its own reading and society rooms. In Dutch cities, too, there was a growing range of societies, though still limited by comparison to England. Elsewhere in Europe, clubs and societies were fewer and more localized, mostly concentrated in the bigger centres like Dublin, Edinburgh, St Petersburg, and Stockholm.

Public music-making, theatre, pleasure gardens, sport, and societies comprised only the more formalized elements of the new enlightened cultural world of the eighteenth century. No less vital and influential, were informal activities including balls and private dinners, literary salons, scientific lectures, and social visiting. As we saw in Chapter 8, fashionable shopping was an important component of urban leisure activities in bigger cities, retail outlets often situated in streets close to theatres and concert halls.

Underpinning these developments was the spread and reception of Enlightenment notions of civility and politeness, rationality and improvement; the growing ascendancy of capital and residential cities; the influx to town of landowners and the growing affluence of the middle classes and, to a lesser extent, of skilled workers; the expansion of the service sector and the emergence of new professional groups and cultural entrepreneurs; the erosion of the cultural hegemony of religion; and changes in the urban landscape.

VII

Crucial in terms of landscape was the transformation of the central areas of towns, in order to make a fashionable social space for enlightened cultural activity, an infrastructure of pleasure. Major changes here included the introduction of street lighting (already, in the 1720s, a Swiss visitor to London praised the way that 'most of the streets are wonderfully well lighted'), alongside street widening and paving, and the provision of drainage and pedestrian walkways. Particularly emblematic of the new cultural image of the European city was the slow but inexorable demolition of old town walls and gates—since the early medieval era umbilically linked to notions of civic identity. Now, with the obsolescence of ancient fortifications against national armies, the growing sprawl of towns outside the walls, and, above all, new complex concepts of urban autonomy in a progressively international cultural world, the circuit of town walls was no longer seen as a defence of a city's cultural identity but rather as an obstacle to cultural progress. Thus, at Paris and elsewhere, the old fortifications were converted into boulevards.

Such changes were only part of the new design of urban space in central districts. Though Italian Renaissance cities led the way, by the early eighteenth century Baroque or neo-Palladian architecture was widely adopted in Western Europe. New public buildings in brick or stone were erected—theatres, opera-houses, hospitals, and barracks, as well as churches. In addition, a wave of smart mansions, terrace houses, and apartment buildings arrived for resident landowners, merchants, and the wealthier middling classes, often interspersed with private parks or gardens. In London, terraced squares strode out westwards from Westminster towards Mayfair. In 1698, Paris was described as a 'new city within this 40 years.... most of the great hostels are built or re-edified...'; and, by the 1750s, smart purpose-built apartment blocks had started to appear. In newer urban districts a more open grid pattern became the norm, instead of the maze of crowded narrow streets typical of the older city. At Lisbon, after the earthquake of 1755, the Baixa district was laid out in a rectangular pattern with a hierarchy of streets and drainage system that aimed to make the city safe, airy, and enlightened. Of Berlin, Mme de Stael declared in the 1780s, its 'streets are very wide, perfectly aligned, the houses beautiful and the ensemble regular'.

Greater urban order was induced by the inscription of street names on street walls (in Paris from the 1720s) and house numbering, along with the removal of the myriad shop signs that had festooned and obstructed public spaces. Meanwhile, we find a greater division between public and private space—the advent for instance of iron-railings, steps, and porticoes separating house and street—and a greater concern for cleanliness, starting with Dutch cities in the seventeenth century with their polished doors, cleaned windows, white walls, and scrubbed floors (cleaning equipment figured prominently in Dutch domestic paintings), and spreading to English towns during the eighteenth century.

While the big metropolitan centres led the way in this transformation of the urban landscape, regional and residential towns in Western Europe often followed suit. Early spa or seaside towns were also quick to construct new buildings in the classical style, and in English smaller towns like Stamford and Lichfield had widened, lit and, paved streets, together with new town halls, chapels and trade halls before the end of the period.

Elsewhere, changes were much slower to arrive. Small imperial cities in Germany or French market towns remained rooted in their traditional landscape, which became a kind of protective defence against the outside world. In Hungary and other parts of Eastern Europe, urban housing remained small-scale even in town centres and overcrowding widespread. Apart from some elite edifices in stone, Moscow housing, according to the traveller Adam Olearius, was 'built of pine and spruce logs... The roofs are shingled and then covered with birch bark or sod. For this reason they often have great fires'. In Northern Europe, too, log-housing dominated towns and houses often lacked proper foundations.

Even in the improved cities and towns of Western Europe, the transformation was only partial and selective. While the better-off classes paraded in their finery through the new cultural districts, the poorer classes crowded into what remained of old city cores or in unimproved peripheral suburbs, where the lack of waste disposal led to contaminated water, and high mortality. Here squalid shanty towns sprang up, often constructed in wood. When new housing was erected by speculators, it took the form of cheaply built tenements, back-to back terraces, and courts—the future slums of the nineteenth century.

Moreover, even the fashionable, enlightened community was faced with the growing problem of endemic environmental pollution. Despite the new interest in domestic cleanliness, emblematic of the future, residents, rich and poor, had to put up with the pervasive stench of the European city. Visitors to the urban world sensed its distinctiveness through the nose. While the medieval and Renaissance town had smelled primarily of animal and human excrement, inescapable on the streets, in the Enlightenment city those odours, particularly pungent in summer, were overlaid by the noxious fumes of domestic hearths, often now coal-burning, and growing industrial production. In the case of major cities like London pollution was smelt from many kilometres away, and blackened public buildings and monuments from the seventeenth century.

To sum up, the rise of an enlightened cultural world, with all its limits, was primarily a West European phenomenon. As English cultural dynamism began to affect the British Isles, many of the innovations in music-making, associational life, theatre, and the built environment began to spread to the main Scottish and Irish towns, but the advance was later. In the Nordic countries, Stockholm and Copenhagen acquired new-style theatres, concert series, and urban infrastructure, but elsewhere developments were much more limited. In Eastern Europe, the principal changes were displayed in capitals like St Petersburg and Warsaw. In the Mediterranean, Naples under Charles of Bourbon might claim to be a new, improved Enlightenment city (one foreign visitor wrote that it had the 'look of Paris or London'), and elsewhere in Italy we discover assemblies, academies, literary journals, theatres, opera, and public music-making, but in many cities cultural life was constrained by state censorship, the power of the Church, and general conservatism.

The urban cultural transformation of the eighteenth century was principally directed at the elite and bourgeois classes, providing them with new avenues for social integration, social networking, and class formation. Many lower-class townspeople, often recent immigrants from the countryside, still retained their loyalty to more traditional entertainments and festivities—music and dancing, fairs, folk street games like football and work rituals, such as St Monday, usually spliced with heavy drinking. At this social level, popular belief in witchcraft continued into the nineteenth century. At the same time, there are indications in English towns that the new fashionable entertainments such as sports and clubs, promoted by commercial entrepreneurs like drink traders, were filtering down to skilled workers and small traders. From the 1780s, magistrates took growing action against traditional games and entertainments on the grounds of maintaining public morality and order.

VIII

This chapter has argued that developments in urban cultural life in the early modern period were paradoxical. During the sixteenth century, the distinctive cultural autonomy of towns, the ability to shape their own cultural agenda, often came under pressure from the Reformation and confessionalization, from the rise of states and other external forces. By the eighteenth century, religion and those other traditional markers of urban cultural identity were steadily eclipsed by a host of new secular, often commercial cultural developments, often with metropolitan and international overtones. On the other hand, cities increasingly manipulated new cultural activities, along with the reconstruction of the urban landscape, to assert their own cultural reputation and promote their economies. As one observer commented, as 'cities become more beautiful and more heavily ornamented, they are also perceived as more distinct and attract more people … to visit them'. Enlightenment cities came to dominate the production and consumption of new cultural ideas, fashions, and venues. Yet already, before 1800, we see the first serious undercurrent of anti-urbanism, as metropolitan cities like London or Paris were condemned as centres of vice and dissipation, as cancers sucking the lifeblood of national and provincial life, as the sinks of national political corruption.

In the 1790s, the French Revolution unleashed a series of radical changes, promoting but sometimes contradicting preceding trends, including the confiscation of religious property, the de-Christianization campaign after 1793–4, and the ban on voluntary associations in 1793. Culture and governance, as we have seen in this chapter, constantly interact, and in the next chapter we turn to examine the political and governmental changes affecting European cities during the early modern era.

11
Governance 1500–1800

In November 1576, Henry III of France and his queen made a joyous entry into the city of Orléans. Outside the gates, seated in a ceremonial grandstand, draped with rich hangings, the king watched a march past by the city's militia, followed by 200 royal pages (dressed up in orange velvet jerkins with grey and green hats), snaking processions of aged professors and students, royal officials, and, finally, the mayor and aldermen in their coloured gowns, and other leading citizens. After various speeches of welcome, the mayor knelt down and presented the king with the keys of the town, but Henry signalled for him to rise and keep the keys, mounted his horse, and rode into the city to a salvo of guns from the city gates. The gates were decorated with 'painted and architectural ornaments', including banners of welcome ('All you citizens come to meet their king'), and the city's coat of arms and anagram (painted in gold letters)—'LA N'OSER [DO NOT DARE THERE]'. Streets were hung with tapestries and thronged with people, inhabitants hung out of their windows, and everyone was shouting 'Vive le roy'. Several hundred poor children from Orléans' Aumone-Générale perched on a tall scaffold outside their hospital to cry loyal greetings. Afterwards, the king went to the cathedral to hear a Te Deum and then passed through a highly decorated archway to his lodging, while the queen made her own entry under a rich canopy, preceded by pages carrying flaming torches and companies of trumpeters playing antiphonal fanfares. Two days later, after other events including high Mass, the royal party left for the States-General at Blois.

Royal or princely entries of this type, usually at the start of reigns or on royal marriages, were a regular feature of political and ceremonial life in European cities from the late Middle Ages up to the seventeenth century. Incorporating tableaux vivants, ceremonial architecture, and exotic personages (sometimes American Indians or Turks), combining images of war and religion, and precisely choreographed—the gestures, spatial arrangements, music and colours, the banners all having powerful symbolism—these increasingly elaborate and expensive events, manifested civic identity and pride in urban institutions, highlighted the power of the urban ruling elite, and, above all, celebrated the power of rulers over cities, a power which, as we shall see, grew markedly from the sixteenth century as states became more centralized, bureaucratic, and militarized. In contrast to the Middle Ages when European cities enjoyed a significant if variable level of autonomy, with some places enjoying extensive freedom, the early modern era saw a general diminution in the local independence of urban communities.

Indicative of the new ascendancy of states was the decline of many of the medieval city leagues. In Northern Europe, the Hanseatic League fell to pieces due to pressure from the English kings and other rulers, the Spanish Conquest of the Southern Netherlands, and the large-scale commercial disruption caused by the Thirty Years War: the final meeting was held in the 1660s. In the Holy Roman Empire, leagues of cities continued to be formed into the seventeenth century, but mainly on a temporary basis and most, like that of the Alsatian cities, suffered eclipse. The only one to thrive was the confederation of Swiss towns which absorbed the rural nobility and peasant cantons and, despite internal religious conflicts in the sixteenth century, won international recognition as an independent state at the Treaty of Westphalia in 1648. After the Dutch Revolt, the major cities of the Northern Netherlands, led by Amsterdam, established an urban-dominated republic, but one in which the ruling stadtholder family, the House of Orange, sought repeatedly (as in 1650 and 1672) to seize control over the cities.

The rise of nation-states was not entirely bad news for cities. As we noted above, capital cities benefited economically from the expansion of governmental and juristic functions located there, and some provincial towns (not least military towns) also profited from state investment. Yet there can be little question that across Europe the balance of political power swung in this period fundamentally and definitively away from cities, and this shift was also associated with changes in urban administration and civic rule.

This chapter looks in turn at the expansion of urban government; the growth and consolidation of oligarchic rule; and the nature and reasons for the decline of urban autonomy. It also examines moves for the reorganization of urban government during the eighteenth century.

I

As we saw in Chapter 6, urban governance had made considerable strides before the end of the Middle Ages. In some respects developments after 1500 built on earlier achievements, but changes of direction are also clear, in part driven by the pressure of events, particularly the upsurge of social problems that threatened urban communities in the sixteenth and early seventeenth centuries. Many cities, from the 1520s, introduced new measures and often centralized agencies to deal with the poor and migrant destitute (see Chapter 9). Public granaries, price controls, plague outbreaks, and relief schemes all increasingly concerned town authorities, as did policies to deal with begging, crime, and street disorder spawned by the influx of needy.

Economic problems associated with industrial competition from the countryside and elsewhere, and trade disruption due to war, likewise posed many challenges to civic government, though most of the administrative responses such as trade restrictions or work-stocks for the unemployed were short-term and ineffectual. At the same time, there was increased regulation and supervision of the trade guilds not only for economic reasons, but as part of an attempt to bring them under greater magisterial control. In Dijon, for instance, we see the town council battling to strengthen its power over the trade guilds by trying to widen entry to guild office. In English towns, magistrates passed numerous ordinances regulating the activity of the guilds, their members, their apprentices, and journeymen.

Environmental difficulties spawned by rapid urbanization and housing shortages, and the recurrent outbreaks of epidemics, all stimulated town authorities to greater activity, often extending policies initiated in the later Middle Ages. Numerous cities made efforts to improve the quality and quantity of their water supply, especially for the better-off classes. Councils took over earlier ecclesiastical systems or constructed new infrastructure. In London, £300,000 was spent on bringing water to the city, facilities including water-wheels on the Thames (with supplies piped to houses), and the New River Company which transported spring water from the countryside north of the city to the households of the better off. At Gdansk, the city employed Italian and Dutch engineers to improve the water supply, and a large water tower was built. However, in many European towns the outcome was relatively small. With towns overcrowded and congested,

attempts were made to control sanitation practices, to clear waste rubbish
and obstructions from the streets and marketplaces, to maintain roads, and
to deal with the industrial pollution and stench that was strongly identified
with disease. Again, such policies seem to have had only limited impact,
partly because of the accelerating scale of the problems and also because
of the opposition of vested interests as well as ordinary people, who
resented the way traditional practices were being criminalized. As we noted
above, the Reformation boosted municipal activity. In Protestant cities,
magistrates promoted and financed preachers, schools, and the reformation
of manners, including sexual behaviour, as they endeavoured to erect
godly commonwealths. In addition, ecclesiastical franchises and a good
deal of Church land and property were brought under civic control by
town authorities, extending the area of urban political space. In Counter-
Reformation cities, changes were less drastic, but here too there was an
extension of elite influence in religious life, for instance, over confraternities.

Everywhere, communities encountered growing problems of jurisdictional conflict. In cities, where new universities were established or older
ones expanded, recurrent conflict occurred between town and gown—over
jurisdiction, economy activity, university processions, ceremonies, and
much else. Student disturbances at the Swedish-controlled cities of Turku,
Uppsala, and Tartu provoked serious tension with municipal and state
authorities. In France, municipalities clashed with Parlements and royal
courts, and in England town councils waged expensive legal battles with
county magistrates and landowners.

Politically, town councils became heavily engaged in relations with
central government and its ever-increasing demands. To defend municipal
interests, bigger cities like Lyon had agents or deputations at Court for
months at a time to lobby for them, as well as sending parliamentary representation. In the Holy Roman Empire, imperial diets involved prolonged
attendance, often far from home, by delegations from imperial cities. Back
in their own communities, urban leaders spent a growing amount of time
enforcing a flood of state laws and decrees, and, above all, raising money
and troops for military action by rulers who frequently ignored civic privileges and exemptions from state demands. In France, the urban military
construction following the outbreak of civil war in the 1560s inflicted
heavy financial burdens on cities.

All this expanded urban activity necessitated a further increase of municipal officials, following the trend established before 1500. New officials

multiplied for dealing with the poor, for instance, as did the number of lawyers holding civic office. Many of the new urban officials were amateurs or poorly paid, combined their posts with other work, and got money through fees, abuse, and corruption. As noted above, municipal structures may have been reinforced by the incorporation of neighbourhood and guild bodies into civic administration. Nonetheless, the picture of municipal government in this period is one of relative failure and ineffectiveness. Arguably, councils were trying to do too much and the social, environmental, and other problems they experienced were beyond their capacity to handle. Undoubtedly, the financial situation contributed to their predicament. Many communities, whether imperial cities or French or English towns, suffered mounting financial pressures during the sixteenth and seventeenth centuries as higher civic expenditure, accentuated by price inflation and state fiscal, military, and other demands, collided with the sluggish increase of traditional civic revenues. Large financial deficits became a widespread problem in European cities. Town councils often had to borrow, frequently from magistrates. At s'-Hertogenbosch, in the early sixteenth century, the town, needing to pay imperial levies, sold annuities for almost 388,000 guilders, many of the key lenders drawn from urban officials. At Gloucester, the convention was established by the 1570s that the four incoming civic stewards (treasurers) lent the town sufficient money to cover the current deficit; but there were recurrent crises when incoming stewards refused to pay. Numerous French towns nearly went bankrupt in the last decades of the sixteenth century.

II

The financial difficulties of towns and the need to get rich councillors to bail out city administration from their own pockets was one of the factors contributing to the further consolidation of civic oligarchy across Europe in the early modern period. As we know, select rule was already common in the late medieval city, but it became more institutionalized and powerful after 1500. In Venice, the Council of Ten enlarged its authority by setting up a series of new magistracies during the sixteenth century to deal with economic and other problems. Across Europe, municipal elections became less frequent and less important, as in late sixteenth-century Paris where the majority of civic offices changed hands through resignation and cooption.

In Dutch cities, oligarchic power was concentrated in the hands of an elite minority, while in English towns cooption to the bench became widespread and elected offices like that of mayor rotated among the same persons. Frequently, the number of leading magistrates contracted: at Lyon, the powerful consulate was reduced to five members after 1595. In Italy, where the closure of the patriciate had already begun at Venice in the thirteenth century, the practice spread to other cities, such as Naples (after 1553). In Polish towns, magisterial office tended to become hereditary, and elsewhere family networks also grew in influence.

Meantime, civic leadership, its wealth and expertise, was strengthened by an accession of outsiders, often bonded to the patrician class through marriage. At Amsterdam, one sixth of the ruling group were immigrants, some from Dutch cities, others from France, Germany, and the Southern Netherlands. In seventeenth-century Venice, there was an accession of landowners from the *terra ferma* to the ruling class, and individual gentry gained seats on English town councils in the late seventeenth century. No less important, was the greater role (already visible in Mediterranean cities in the late Middle Ages) of professional men, notably jurists. At Barcelona, a growing number of lawyers moved into civic government in the sixteenth and seventeenth centuries, and the same trend is evident at Lübeck, Leipzig, and other European cities.

What other factors contributed to the consolidation of oligarchic leadership? One was the growing volume and pressure of urban administration that often required rapid decision-making by a small group of city rulers. A second factor was the mounting economic and social polarization in cities which meant that only a limited group of citizens were able to afford the time and expense of civic politics. Third, states preferred to deal with a small caucus of civic leaders whom they could rely on to carry out government orders. Increasingly, states intervened to regulate the size of the ruling group or to nominate its members. At Ghent and Utrecht, Emperor Charles V seized complete control of the election of magistrates, while at Vienna imperial action ensured that a tiny civic group monopolized high office. At La Rochelle, in 1535, the French king converted the elected mayor into a nominated official and curtailed the position of other officials. In turn, central governments acted to shore up the authority of oligarchic rulers, when they encountered communal opposition. Loyal patricians might be rewarded by being incorporated into the state patronage system: thus, in France, experienced magistrates were recruited by the state into royal service, while the sale of offices (venality) after 1604 accorded civic officials political security in return for tax payments to the Crown.

Closed patriciates did not necessarily mean that the ruling class was politically out of touch. As in earlier times, patricians often had clientage networks that extended across the community. Careful politicians sought to canvas communal support as well as royal favour, to be city fathers as well as royal agents. Rituals of civic voting, debate, and decision-making might help secure wider burgher recognition for municipal leadership. In smaller towns, like some of the lesser imperial cities in Germany, town leaders were well known and close to ordinary inhabitants: thus, at the town of Rottweil, south of Stuttgart, the 130 town offices were shared out among just 800 citizen households. Nonetheless, in many places the trend towards civic oligarchy was demarcated on the ground. Town leaders tended to move their gatherings away from traditional civic spaces, preferring instead new, more secluded venues. In Gdansk, the common burghers were excluded from the new Renaissance-style town hall, while at Leicester the city's guildhall had a special chamber or mayor's parlour from the 1630s set aside for meetings of the aldermanic bench, the inner ruling circle.

Growth of oligarchy provoked tension and conflict. At La Rochelle, Hamburg, Strasbourg, Cologne, Gloucester, and elsewhere protests exploded over allegations that magistrates were feathering their own nests, through nepotism, selling contracts, and taking bribes. Corruption was structural to pre-modern urban governance where, as we know, officials were poorly, if ever, paid, and magisterial abuse can be seen as a form of compensation for the growing burdens of civic office-holding, but it fuelled widespread opposition to oligarchic power. In Venice, in the 1580s, there was a strong reaction to the encroaching power of the Council of Ten. In Dutch cities, agitation by citizens, sometimes lasting several weeks, attempted to open up urban government and to strengthen the representative character of the civic militias. In Germany, urban revolts against oligarchic power could last much longer. In English towns, resentment over oligarchic dominance spilled over during the English Revolution and led to the expulsion of some town leaders and the limited reform of civic government in London and several provincial cities.

III

One of the basic problems of civic politicians during the sixteenth and
seventeenth centuries was that, while their power and authority within local
communities was enhanced, their relative position in the wider political
universe was steadily eroded by the decline of urban autonomy through
the widespread interference of the state and landowners. As well as seeking
to control town councils, rulers intervened to regulate trade guilds. Under
the Medici, Florentine guilds were reduced to state agencies, while Charles
V sought to deprive the guilds in imperial towns of their political roles. In
France, there were recurrent royal attempts to remodel (and later suppress)
guilds.

Municipal policy was steadily overshadowed by state agendas. Urban
manufacturing was a key government concern. As we saw in Chapter 8,
the sector might benefit from the creation of state monopolies or by schemes
to attract foreign workers. But state intervention could also have disastrous
consequences. The Spanish Crown's liberalization (1548–58) of the home
market to textile imports (while banning exports) contributed to the crisis of
woollen manufactures in Cordoba, Seville, and elsewhere. In social policy,
too, states intervened aggressively, either through national legislation or
through direct action. At Paris, where the Crown established the royal
lieutenancy of police in the 1660s, the new officials were ordered to take
measures against offenders, ignoring traditional urban jurisdictions: by 1700,
there was growing royal surveillance of Parisian servants, apprentices, and
vagabonds. In Turin, the ducal superintendent of police acquired similar
extensive power at the expense of the municipality.

During the early stages of the Reformation, as we saw in Chapter 10,
cities often tried to use religious changes as a way of enhancing urban
authority, but within a generation their room to manoeuvre was constrained
by state policies which aimed to impose religious conformity. Though
cities in Germany, France, and the Netherlands played an important part
in opposition to government religious policies, the consequent civil wars
often led to military attack. Even when the religious autonomy of cities
was recognized by rulers, as in the Holy Roman Empire by the Peace
of Augsburg or in the case of French Protestant cities by Henry IV's
Edict of Nantes, state recognition and protection proved incomplete and
ineffectual. In south German cities, like Augsburg, Protestant minorities

came under mounting attack from the state and Catholic Church, while in France Henry IV's successors harassed Protestant cities, stripped them of their privileges, and penalized their Protestant inhabitants.

Even when they were not attacking cities, European rulers imposed great fiscal and other pressures on urban communities. In France, military levies on towns tipped many into financial crisis. In Spain, the Crown's desperate need to finance a multiplicity of international wars led to royal attempts to blackmail cities like Cordoba, Toledo, and Seville into paying heavy fines or surrendering large parts of their jurisdiction over smaller towns. Between 1653 and 1679, the Spanish government extorted 17 million ducats from Madrid to be paid by new taxes, and eventually the city toppled into an indebtedness which lasted through the eighteenth century.

Yet, if there was a general erosion of urban autonomy, its nature and extent varied markedly across Europe. Civic decline was probably most marked in those Mediterranean cities that had enjoyed the greatest independence during the medieval era. Following a trend visible earlier, more and more Italian cities fell under seigneurial or foreign control and civic privileges were ignored. At Rome, the city authorities were marginalized by the families of the Popes, the papal nobility, and the religious orders: urban public space was redesigned as a theatre for papal and noble power. The political decline of Spanish cities was almost as precipitous. Already, by the late fifteenth century, Ferdinand and Isabella had begun a systematic remodelling of civic magistracies in Castile and Aragon, and this process continued. At Barcelona, and elsewhere, citizen councillors became overshadowed by royal nominees. In Andalusian towns, effective authority was no longer in the hands of the city council but of the royal *procurador mayor*. As already noted, cities were saddled with heavy taxes and other levies. After the failure of the rising of the *Communeros* in the 1520s, urban resistance to royal policy occurred only sporadically in Spain. The most serious outburst came in Catalonia where urban and rural opposition united after 1640 to deal a body blow to royal centralizing measures in that province.

In Western Europe, the picture was more mixed. In France and England, where civic autonomy had not been strong in the Middle Ages, there was a steady accretion of royal control during the sixteenth and seventeenth centuries. French towns experienced growing fiscal and other pressure under Henry II, and during the civil wars urban communities across the kingdom suffered from repeated government exactions. Concerned to re-establish national unity after the end of the wars, Henry IV returned to the medieval policy of recognizing urban privileges, particularly of strategic towns, but subsequent kings cancelled privileges, purged town councils, sold civic offices, and introduced extensive government controls. In England, a wave of charters by Tudor governments increased the number of royal boroughs and tightened central controls, often via oligarchic magistracies. Internal conflicts within boroughs before 1640 triggered appeals to the Privy Council and Court politicians for help, whose intervention served to reinforce central authority. During the English Revolution and after the Restoration of Charles II, large-scale purges of political and religious dissidents took place and corporations were remodelled in order to influence parliamentary elections: in the 1680s, this sometimes spawned two rival councils battling for power. After the Glorious Revolution of 1688, however, government intervention in municipal government tended to decline, though party conflict between Whigs and Tories led to widespread ministerial meddling in boroughs at election times.

In the Northern Netherlands, the Dutch revolt against Spain secured the extensive privileges of the major cities and towns, particularly in the western provinces, in return for their becoming the leading financiers of the Dutch Republic (Amsterdam paid a quarter of all Dutch taxes). As already noted, repeated attempts were made by the stadtholders to create a more centralist regime, particularly during times of war, but Dutch cities continued to exercise a large measure of local autonomy, as well as enjoying an influential position in the provincial estates. Negotiation and rivalry between cities and provinces gave the regents of even smaller urban centres considerable room for political and financial manoeuvre in the political regime of the Dutch republic until its collapse in the 1790s.

In Germany, the imperial cities faced mounting challenges to their late medieval autonomy. In the south, smaller cities were drawn into becoming Habsburg clients, providing troops and funds for imperial wars. In 1552, the Emperor Charles V imposed new constitutions on numerous imperial cities of the region, curtailing popular participation. Divisions within imperial cities between oligarchs and citizens led to growing imperial intervention as emperors tried to extend their control over the cities. During the Thirty Years War, German cities, imperial and otherwise, faced heavy taxes and other levies from the Emperor and princes. In general, however, the Treaty of Westphalia in 1648 enabled many imperial towns to hang on to their privileges, while the declining power of the Habsburgs outside their own territories diminished, though it did not obviate the threat to civic autonomy (for example, internal conflict at Frankfurt after 1705 led to extensive imperial interference). Even so, the relative political autonomy of the imperial cities was bought at a heavy price, including marginalization from the emerging and dynamic princely states which deployed mercantilist policies to promote the economies of their own towns. Residential towns from Prussian Berlin to archiepiscopal Mainz and Bavarian Münich enjoyed few privileges: their civic officials and policies were largely determined by their rulers. But princely patronage provided important infrastructure investment and other economic and cultural dividends.

In Northern and Eastern Europe, the generally exiguous level of urban autonomy observed before 1500 continued through the early modern period. Not only did the Swedish Crown strictly regulate urban trading rights, but, in the early seventeenth century, it promulgated radical plans for the remodelling of towns like Kalmar, Jönköping, and Stockholm; in the last town, the government established the position of governor to carry out royal policies over the heads of the city council. Having earlier supported its cities against the Hanseatic League, the Danish Crown introduced bureaucratic measures against them. Old civic bodies were replaced by 'magistrat' boards whose members were appointed by the king (though more informal representative bodies also sprang up). In Poland, the political position of towns likewise deteriorated. Many of the new urban centres that were founded were under seigneurial control, town merchants were excluded from foreign trade, burghers were forbidden to buy land, and even leading cities like Gdansk or Warsaw had little say in the Polish Diet. In the Bohemian lands the royal free cities retained significant autonomy, but across Russia, as we saw earlier, the growth of the urban network was closely linked to the expanding power and territorial ambitions of the imperial government. Three sets of state regulations in 1649, 1721, and 1785 created administrative frameworks for cities, and most of the main urban centres had state administrative and military functions. Urban autonomy was minimal and it is not clear that Russian urban leaders understood the concept.

In the sixteenth century, and much of the seventeenth, state policies towards cities were largely driven by a desire to control national political space and to fund wars against other rulers. Rulers rarely showed much understanding of urban interests, despite all the lobbying by towns. Policies were intrusive, disruptive, and burdensome, and benefits for cities, when they occurred, were mainly incidental. Taking together the failures of expanded municipal government, the financial problems, the tension and conflict caused by the growth of oligarchy and state interference, the abiding impression is that urban governance stumbled from one crisis to another in the post-Reformation era.

IV

Even before 1700, however, more positive signs may be detected. Vital here was the changed relationship with states. Competition between European states and the growing influence of progressive, Enlightenment ideas led to the introduction of policies that sought to improve national economies in which cities were now regarded as valuable players. Frequently, a new measure of cooperation is visible between urban and government authorities, and state intervention had less disruptive, more benign effects. In terms of infrastructure, there was growing state finance or sanction for transport improvements between cities. In France, the wave of government road building from the mid-eighteenth century benefited the principal administrative towns, but also the main havens. In the Southern Netherlands, ports like Ostend, as well as major and smaller inland towns, likewise gained from the transport improvements of the Austrian regime. In addition, states promoted economic modernization, including the abolition of guilds and trade tariffs, and gave support for the renewal of the urban infrastructure.

In general terms, the eighteenth century marked an advance in the quality of urban government and services. This was particularly noticeable in the bigger cities of Western Europe that were benefiting from economic growth. Improvement to the urban infrastructure and built environment was widespread—not just where the state was involved. Together with demolition of old fortifications, new public buildings were constructed by municipalities, including those for leisure or philanthropic activities such as opera houses and hospitals. In the Breton towns, in western France, new public works included thirty squares and bridges, fourteen public fountains, ten *hotels de villes* and assorted market halls, prisons and the like; some were paid for by private investors; others by the local authorities. In twelve towns in the West Riding of Yorkshire, total expenditure on public buildings rose from £2,800 in 1700–9 to £52,300 in the 1770s and over £93,000 two decades later. As well as new public buildings, streets were paved, pedestrian pavements laid down, and street lighting installed in central districts of towns. Though urban improvement was particularly striking in Western Europe, it was also found elsewhere. In Warsaw, a street commission operated after 1742 to pave streets, lay drains, and build footbridges, and from the next decade Dublin had the Wide Street Commissioners who undertook similar improvements.

Environmental improvements included attempts to reduce stench by moving cemeteries and markets to the urban periphery, though the increasing domestic and industrial use of coal spewed out new choking clouds of air pollution. The arrival of new pumps enabled better provision of piped water in respectable areas. At Brussels, the Court district of the city was supplied by a private company from the later eighteenth century; Georgian London had a medley of competing water companies; and Paris planned a central agency under the city council to provide water. However, in water supply, as in other fields of urban improvement, the better-off urban areas and their inhabitants gained most. Supplies to London's smart West End ran at 70 per cent more than to the poorer East End.

Urban improvement was encouraged by a growing awareness of its economic value—as a way of attracting the affluent classes to town. No less significant was the growing trend for public comparison between urban centres. International competition between the leading capital cities is explicit from the late seventeenth century, and within a generation or so old-fashioned urban infrastructure was disparaged and ridiculed in the press, travel guides, and so on. In the 1760s, one English newspaper exclaimed that 'every city almost of the kingdom displays a taste of improvement, Exeter alone bears an exception' and needs renewal. This is not to exaggerate the extent of urban improvement. As West European visitors were not slow to point out, many cities in the Mediterranean and Northern and Eastern Europe remained unimproved, with filthy, narrow streets, and animals wandering around. Even in remodelled cities, urban improvement was often concentrated in the fashionable central districts of cities, not in the poorer outskirts or suburbs.

What about other urban advances? As we saw in Chapter 9, there was no major reform of poor-relief structures during the eighteenth century, but some attempt was made at rationalization. Relief became more professional, secular, and specialist, with the creation of institutions to deal, for example, with prostitution and the mentally ill. Nevertheless, they were often overwhelmed by the surging influx of rural destitute in the last decades of the century. More successful, if on a selective basis, were attempts to improve policing, especially in the central districts of big cities. In the French capital, for instance, the number of crimes tried at the Chatelet remained relatively stable between 1755 and 1785. Policing became better organized through more regular, semi-professional forces. In Paris, the *commissaries de police* acquired more men, money, and equipment, and from the 1770s became more centralized and professional. In 1742, the Berlin police were reorganized, and in English cities new watch commissions and police courts may have had an impact. At the same time, greater surveillance in central districts probably displaced some criminality and disorder to the suburbs.

Such improvements may have been facilitated by the enhanced professionalism of civic administration. Town clerks, for example, had considerably greater authority, autonomy, and administrative experience than in the past. In policing, as in other fields, new posts were created and there was a trend towards salaried officials. On the other hand, administrative expansion was not accompanied by any major changes in municipal political structures. Civic oligarchy remained the norm, indeed may have become more accentuated. In Dutch cities, the ruling elite shrank after the end of the seventeenth century, while German and Swiss cities were still ruled by narrow caucuses. In the English borough of Gloucester, the aldermanic bench consolidated its political ascendancy, and it is likely that many other English towns followed a similar trend. Popular resentment against *ancien régime* politics was fed by the growth of the press and pamphleteering, and by seditious songs and gossip in taverns and squares. Unrest simmered against oligarchic rule, as in the Dutch Republic in 1748 and the 1780s, when the discrediting of the ruling elites by war led to the mobilization of burgher militias and other citizen groups demanding reform. But up to the 1790s (and later in some countries) old-fashioned civic oligarchy remained in charge in most European cities.

If civic oligarchy remained the norm, there was some liberalization of other urban controls. After 1700, confessional restrictions on citizenship and trade were progressively relaxed, and magistrates showed a declining interest in ecclesiastical affairs. In West European cities especially, trade guilds and corporations, often closely integrated with civic government, were either abolished or lost their dominance, sometimes through state action, as in France, or because they were bypassed by new trades and businesses outside their control. Manufacturing and commercial activity was often organized through new bodies such as Chambers of Commerce: at Lille, the Chamber of Commerce (established in 1715) advocated greater trade liberalization than the magistracy. In some Spanish cities, private companies were established to promote economic investment, training, and industry. At Huy, in the Southern Netherlands, commercial companies supported textile production as well as other urban improvement.

Such new commercial bodies were part of a broadening of urban governance in the bigger cities, pioneered in Western Europe. Improvement societies were founded in English, Dutch, and German cities to debate and advocate urban economic and social reform. At Hamburg, the second Patriotic Society, inspired by the London Society of Arts, put forward various schemes for poor relief and educational improvement in the city, a number of which were adopted. In England, Parliament sanctioned several hundred quasi-voluntary improvement commissions, the members often including a broad circle of better-off townspeople, to implement infrastructure improvements for streets and pavements, lighting, bridges, hospitals, docks, and much else.

Improvement organizations were only part of a wider proliferation of voluntary associations in European cities during the eighteenth century, as we saw in Chapter 10. Although these had diverse cultural, leisure, political, and social objectives, they shared one key political function. They created a new political space for the elites in cities to meet and network in ways outside the traditional arena of municipal institutions, and so served to integrate different upper- and middle-class groups, including better-off immigrants, into the urban political process. In Dutch cities, societies were an important focus for opposition to the old civic oligarchy in 1787. During the early stages of the French Revolution they mobilized both reformist and radical opinion in French and other European cities.

Yet the underlying problems of *ancien régime* cities remained. The relationship of municipalities to the state or local rulers was often problematic and tense, particularly in continental Europe. Instead of interfering in individual communities, eighteenth-century governments tended to impose policies on towns as a bloc, for instance, in the suppression of guilds or in the reform of magistracies. In Britain, the transformation of the functioning of the state after the Glorious Revolution may have given urban leaders greater room to operate, but this was exceptional. Another weakness was the continuing problem of urban finances. In French cities, such as Strasbourg or Valenciennes, financial deficits owed much to royal fiscal demands; in Dutch cities, urban finances were petrified by political resistance to increases in consumption taxes. Even in English towns, buoyed up by economic success, where urban revenues rose strongly and town finances were run with greater professionalism, everything ended in tears: the high cost of urban improvement led to mounting corporate indebtednesss and charges of corruption and profligacy. More research needs to be done on cities in other European regions to identify possible trends in urban governance there. However, even in Western Europe, the modest advances in municipal administration were often thrown into the air after 1789.

In France, the Revolution, with its phases of constitutional reform, radical upheaval, Terror, Directory, and Napoleonic dictatorship, imposed massive political changes on French cities. Abolition of venality opened civic office to the bourgeoisie, who increasingly replaced the old municipal oligarchies. The same groups consolidated their power in towns by purchasing Church property after the suppression of religious houses in 1790. Political mobilization through clubs contributed to mounting conflict. While some cities such as Paris and Marseille moved towards political extremism, others, like Lyon, resisted heavy taxation and military levies through popular risings that were brutally suppressed. After the terrible siege of Lyon in 1793 by revolutionary forces, a proposal was actually made to change the city's name. Even cities away from the main upheavals experienced decisive changes of political function, with the imposition of a new hierarchy of territorial units and administrative centres in 1790. After 1800, Napoleon enforced strict central controls over cities through the new prefectoral system.

Revolutionary changes likewise affected cities in countries attacked or occupied by French armies. In the Southern Netherlands, annexed to France after 1795, heavy war levies and the suppression of monasteries triggered popular opposition in towns, though the urban bourgeoisie benefited from greater civic power, the sale of Church lands, and commercial access to French markets. In Dutch cities, the urban radicals suppressed in the 1780s welcomed the French invaders, but the institutional reforms of 1798 not only abolished urban guilds but also led to a loss of civic autonomy. Municipal finances collapsed under the weight of French taxes, and town rulers faced mounting social and financial problems. In the cities of the Rhineland, the French occupation after 1795 brought civic reform but also heavy taxation and the flight of the landed elite from towns. The old

Italian city-state system was upended by the French military advance, and even such cities as Milan, where the bourgeoisie welcomed the Napoleonic armies, suffered heavy taxation and depredations.

Outside the spreading French Empire, continental states responded to the French threat by a variety of changes. In Bavaria, state control over magistracies was increased and old imperial cities like Nuremberg were brought under royal control. In Prussia, the government under von Stein gave cities limited self-government (1808). Only in England were there no obvious institutional reforms during the revolutionary era.

V

How, then, do we evaluate the overall performance of early modern cities whose development has been outlined in Chapters 6—11? As we have stressed, urban communities in this period faced a concatenation of difficulties and oscillating fortunes. The rapid European-wide recovery in urbanization levels during the sixteenth century was relatively short-lived, and was succeeded by a strong downturn during the seventeenth century (earlier in some regions than others), that was only reversed by renewed expansion up to the 1790s, strongest in Western Europe. Urbanization is never a guarantee of economic growth, and, during the sixteenth and seventeenth centuries, many urban centres faced mounting industrial competition—from other towns and from producers in the countryside—while trade was depressed and disrupted by harvest crises, plague outbreaks, and ever more extensive warfare. Poverty and related social problems were endemic, with surges of immiseration during the sixteenth century and later eighteenth century, as agrarian problems unleashed a torrent of subsistence migration from countryside to town. Again, the Reformation and subsequent confessional conflict challenged the traditional cultural identity of towns, just as the aggrandisement of states and rulers diminished civic political autonomy.

On the other hand, as the pattern of international trade changed with the growth of Asian and American commerce, the European urban order realigned itself away from the Mediterranean to the Atlantic, and we see the ascent of Western Europe as the leading urban region, its dynamism ensuring its dominance of the European urban world into the twentieth century. Along with the strong urban growth in Western Europe, the period saw the completion of the network of smaller towns in Northern and Eastern Europe, from Ireland and Scotland to Scandinavia and Russia, and the emergence of fast-track urban communities—capital cities, and more specialist Atlantic ports, industrial towns, and military and resort centres. In addition, as we saw in Chapter 7, European colonization and trade spawned hundreds of colonial cities and towns outside Europe, notably in the Americas.

By the eighteenth century, the urban economy was acquiring a more modern profile with the spread of specialist workshop industries and limited new technology in English Midland and northern towns and in localized urban regions of the Southern Netherlands, France, Germany, and Spain. No less crucial for the future was the expansion of the service sector. Of vital significance here was the growth of modern-style retailing, the advent of the press, and the new kaleidoscope of successful professional groups.

Underpinning the success of the more dynamic urban centres was explicit and recognized competition and emulation, promoted by elite tourism, newspapers and other media, improved communications, industrial spies, and state intervention. Capital cities were locked into competitive exchange (English fashions and clubs in Paris, Parisian fashions in London), but even provincial towns began to watch and note each other's achievements. Spas and other resort towns were pioneers of urban marketing, but middle-rank towns were increasingly competitive on the cultural front. At the end of the period Richard Phillips, a Leicester man, compared and ranked the urban attributes of Leicester and the nearby towns of Nottingham and Derby for their manners, literature, music, politics, and so on. Competition and emulation could be reconciled through the development of regional networks with complementary functions between towns: for example, the Randstad towns in Holland during the seventeenth century and the networks of industrial and service towns in the West Midlands and Yorkshire in the Georgian period. As inter-urban transport and communication improved, the foundations were being laid for the linked-up national and cross-border networking of the nineteenth century and after.

If poverty was endemic in European cities in this period, migration remained structural to urban life. Migrants more than offset urban population deficits or fuelled population growth. They served to renew and invigorate the elite classes and their wider networking, as well as to transfer innovation and expertise. As we have seen, the most dynamic European cities in this era—ports like Amsterdam and capitals like London and

Berlin—welcomed high inflows of immigrants, particularly ethnic and religious minorities. Female migration was also of growing significance for Enlightenment cities. Wives, daughters, and widows of the landed and affluent classes took up urban residence and played a vital part in stimulating the consumer market, retailing, and new leisure activities. Ordinary female migrants, crucial for the growing female surplus in many towns, also had a vital innovative effect in manufacturing (reducing costs, providing more flexible labour), in shopping, and in domestic service (contributing to the feminization of the household). Though urban society remained traditional in many respects, before 1800 we can see the first emergence of two developments crucial for the nineteenth-century city: the advent of a bourgeois or middle class in some leading centres like London and Paris, and the onset of residential segregation.

Though the Reformation generated confessional division, by the eighteenth century a more rational, secular cultural vision was being pioneered by metropolitan cities which was starting to infiltrate provincial society, at least in Western Europe. Urban cultural identity was being reconfigured in new ways, incorporating a complicated mosaic of markers from the older religiosity and education to leisure and entertainment, new senses of time and space, and a new ordering of the landscape.

Arguably, the innovative and dynamic trends in early modern European towns lacked synchronization. There are clearer signs of economic and cultural innovation and change than of social or political transformation. As we noted in this chapter, before the 1790s only a modest improvement occurred in the political and administrative structures of European cities. Some institutional reforms took place under French influence at the end of the period, but these were partially reversed after the Napoleonic defeat in 1815. In sum, despite some achievements, the early modern city left a large legacy of problems, among them issues of poverty and social order, of municipal government, and the relationship of cities and the state. As a result, many communities were in a weak position to confront the massive challenges thrown up by accelerating urbanization during the nineteenth century.

PART
III

12

Urban Trends 1800–2000

The last part of this book examines the period from the early nineteenth century to the late twentieth century when, step by step, Europe became an urban continent. After the Second World War the majority of the European population, in some countries the great majority of the population, was living in towns rather than villages, and conurbations became increasingly numerous. In 1990, according to one estimate, Europe had 225 cities with over 200,000 inhabitants and forty of its cities counted more than a million people. Urban production and demand came to dominate European economy activity, while urban priorities transformed political agendas and Europe's cultural life was urbanized. In some countries the rural category disappeared from statistical records.

Urban ascendancy in the modern era was not achieved without cost. City expansion in the decades after 1800 was accompanied by economic crises, alongside sharp deteriorations in the living standards, environmental conditions, and health of a large part of the population, and over the longer term there was mounting social segregation. Tension occurred with powerful nation-states over their increased regulation and control of cities and towns. While nineteenth-century citizens were proud of the growing extent and panoramic monumentality of their communities, admiring them from cathedral spires, from balloons, from architectural extravaganza like the Eiffel Tower, and on the ground in commercial panoramas and displays at international exhibitions, urban cultural identity came under pressure and anti-urbanism flared at times, particularly in the early twentieth century. Rivalry between cities intensified, especially towards the end of our period, a development that has been attributed to globalization. Some of these problems were hardly new to European cities and towns, and indeed may be seen as structural to them, but they were undoubtedly heightened by the large-scale urbanization of the modern era.

Yet, as in earlier times, such challenges to the European city stimulated creativity across a whole spectrum of activities, as urban centres became leading laboratories for innovation in technology, finance, social policy, public services, governance, the creation of designed green space, and mass culture.

From the springboard of eighteenth-century developments, West European towns leapt into the lead in creativity and growth after 1800, but, as we shall see, before the First World War other regions, first Northern Europe and later the Mediterranean and Eastern Europe, began to catch up in rates of urbanization. At the same time, differential growth marked out different types of community. Large cities, especially capital cities, grew strongly up to the 1960s; by contrast, regional centres and small market towns did relatively less well, though their fortunes partially revived during the late twentieth century. While Europe saw the continuity and resilience of its traditional multi-functional towns, the nineteenth and twentieth centuries were remarkable for the advance of more specialist urban communities: industrial cities, ports engaged in large-scale international trade, leisure towns, including seaside resorts, and military towns. While towns of this type had already existed before 1800, mainly in Britain, the numbers, range and geographical distribution increased markedly during the nineteenth and early twentieth centuries; however, as we will see, many specialist towns encountered economic decline from the 1970s. The dynamism of the European urban network, especially in the late nineteenth and early twentieth centuries, also spilled outside Europe with the rise of colonial and neo-colonial towns from the Americas to Asia and Australasia.

This chapter starts by outlining the broad trends in European urbanization between about 1800 and 2000, focusing in particular on the crucial regional developments across the continent and indicating the main engines of growth. Here, the concern is to escape from the conventional preoccupation with Western Europe. The second part of the chapter examines the performance of different types of urban community, seeking to identify the urban winners and losers. With this overall picture sketched, the next chapters (13—16) will investigate in detail the economic, social, and cultural, as well as political forces, which shaped the creation of the modern and contemporary European city.

I

European urbanization in the modern and contemporary period occurred in three broad phases: the first up to about 1870, a time of accelerating but still limited urban growth; the second from the 1870s until the 1960s, an era of general expansion; the last from the 1960s until the end of the century, a period of some urbanization but also selective de-urbanization. In the early nineteenth century, urban growth was mainly concentrated in Western Europe where it was led by cities and towns in Britain and Belgium, which had already enjoyed significant expansion before 1800. England remained the key player, its urban order probably reinforced rather than disrupted by the French revolutionary wars. Here, urban growth was energized by the development of large-scale textile and iron industries (increasingly propelled by steam power), by a profusion of specialist, often workshop-type manufactures, by the rapid expansion of overseas commerce and the service sector, and by the spread of railways. Political stability after the 1830s may also have contributed to growth. As in the previous century, the urban dynamic was broadly based. London remained the world's largest city, its population soaring from about 1 million in 1801 to 2.7 million in 1851 and 3.9 million in 1871. However, there was a raft of successful old and new regional centres, including Newcastle, Manchester, and Birmingham, which served as marketing, financial, and service hubs for industrializing regions. No less important, specialist towns advanced in number and size: manufacturing centres, including older towns like Sheffield and Leeds, and completely new towns like Middlesbrough and Merthyr Tydvil; major international ports such as Liverpool and Hull; and seaside towns like Brighton and Blackpool (now outdoing the old inland spas). Steadily integrated into the British (and West European) urban network, Scottish urbanization accelerated, under the dual leadership of the port and industrial centre of Glasgow and the administrative capital of Edinburgh. Under their stimulus, smaller industrial and commercial towns flourished across the central lowlands. By mid-century, about 53 per cent of the British population was living in towns, and the figure surpassed 61 per cent two decades later.

Across the North Sea, the upheavals of the Napoleonic era and Dutch rule 1815–30 retarded but did not halt Belgian urbanization. Progressively, the industrial areas of the late eighteenth century centred on Verviers-Liège and Mons-Charleroi, which were linked, via the new railways, into an urban system incorporating Brussels, the national capital after 1830 (251,000 inhabitants by 1850–1), and Antwerp, now focused on port activity. Belgian urbanization benefited from a flood of peasant labour from the countryside and from British investment and entrepreneurs; also influential were the kingdom's laissez-faire policies, and the trading opportunities offered by an expanding German economy.

Elsewhere, urban growth remained more patchy and localized. In the early nineteenth century, German urbanization was still highly variable according to regions. If the Congress of Vienna in 1815 led to the consolidation of states and takeover of many of the old imperial cities and the Zollverein after 1834 encouraged greater economic integration, the dividends for towns were often mixed. In the south, lack of agricultural and institutional reform contributed to extensive urban malaise, though Nuremberg revived as a metal manufacturing centre. In the Rhineland, towns had gained from French and subsequent Prussian reforms and agrarian improvement; even so, industrial development was still heavily workshop-based with strong links to the countryside. Across Germany and Austria, capital and residential cities grew (Vienna nearly doubled its population during the early nineteenth century to about 476,000 in 1860), but middle-size and smaller towns remained predominant.

In France, Paris was boosted by state consolidation under Napoleon and further political and economic centralization under his successors: the capital's population recovered fairly quickly from its demographic downturn in the 1790s, and reached a million by 1850. By comparison, provincial centres like Bordeaux or Nantes increased more slowly, and some provincial towns (deprived of their administrative functions as a result of the French Revolution) fared badly. The backward state of agriculture and recurrent political instability were powerful constraints on growth. Urban industrial expansion remained scattered, though important nodes thickened around Lille and Rouen (mostly textiles) in the north, and at Mulhouse in Alsace (cotton and machine manufacture), while in the Lyon and St Etienne region the major textile industries were joined from the 1830s and 1840s by mining, chemical, and metal production. Michelet described the industrial area of Rive-de-Gier near St Etienne, emerging from the countryside: 'agriculture gradually disappears. Scrub covers the mountains. Black and smoking factories emitting the thick and stinking coal fumes'. In Western

Europe, only Dutch cities remained resolutely in the doldrums—held back by ineffectual government, poor railway communications, high labour costs, and the competing investment attractions of the agricultural sector.

In the Mediterranean world, urban growth was flat and urban networks retained strong traditional features, despite, or perhaps because of, the heritage of large cities in parts of Italy and Spain. Institutional and agrarian conservatism were major obstacles to advance. During the early nineteenth century, expansion was confined to a few areas. In northern Italy, proto-industrialization provided the basis for manufacturing growth in the Genoa, Turin, and Milan triangle, but elsewhere most industrial activity was tied to old-style urban crafts. Apart from Barcelona, the principal cities in Iberia, including Madrid and Lisbon, grew only modestly. Barcelona benefited from the buoyancy of the Catalan textile towns, helped now by modern machinery imported from Britain. Further east, the disintegration of the Ottoman Empire led to the formation of new Balkan states and the renaissance of some cities: thus, from the 1830s, Athens developed not only as the Bavarian-styled capital of a new Greek state but as a classical heritage site, though its population still counted only 41,000 in 1861.

The picture was not dissimilar in outer Northern Europe, where just a few pockets of urban industrial expansion can be found during the early nineteenth century. Ireland experienced a ripple effect from Britain as Ulster's linen towns and Belfast flourished, their development closely associated with Scottish urbanization. Sweden's industry remained heavily localized in the countryside and most of the main urban centres were situated on the coast. Stockholm, like the Irish capital Dublin, grew only torpidly at this time, and the Swedish urbanization rate stagnated at around 10 per cent. Under Russian control (after 1809), Finland's towns were slow to develop: the new capital Helsinki had only 21,000 inhabitants in 1850. The situation was similar in Norway (ruled by the Swedish Crown until 1905), where Christiana (the later Oslo) had no more than 28,000 people at mid-century, and most of the other towns (except for Bergen and Trondheim) recorded barely a few hundred residents.

Largely under oppressive Russian or Austrian sway after 1815, Eastern Europe remained overwhelmingly rural in character. Russian trade and manufacturing (including well over half of factories) stayed heavily embedded in the countryside, and migration to town was obstructed by serfdom (not abolished until 1861). Uncertainty about the status of towns makes it difficult to assess growth rates before the 1860s, but urbanization was probably stagnant at 7–9 per cent, with most increases concentrated in bigger cities like Moscow, Odessa, and St Petersburg. Badly hit by the Napoleonic siege in 1812, Moscow recovered to over 400,000 inhabitants by mid-century, flourishing mainly as a merchant centre; Odessa, founded in 1794, grew rapidly as a cosmopolitan commercial city and free port (after 1819) on the Black Sea; and St Petersburg, the government and imperial Court capital, was said to grow 'not by the year but by the hour', her population soaring to 487,000 in the 1850s. In Poland, growth was equally selective. Warsaw's population quadrupled between 1810 and 1870, approaching 300,000; but other cultural and commercial centres like Cracow and Gdansk grew more slowly, none exceeding 100,000 inhabitants by 1870.

Outside Britain, Belgium, and localized areas of Western Europe the pace of urban development in the early nineteenth century was tardy (compare Tables 7.1 and 12.1). What were the constraints on urban growth? Clearly, the French revolutionary era generated major economic and political instability and short-term de-urbanization in some countries. Moreover, the defeat of Napoleon and the new international order created at Vienna in 1815 was no panacea. The following decades saw recurrent political instability in France and the Low Countries, and political reaction in Austria. As we shall see in later chapters, institutional reform—abolition of guilds and internal trade barriers, and municipal restructuring—was delayed, especially outside Western Europe. Old urban elites often kept or recovered power, adapting slowly to change, and landowners retained a powerful voice in national governments to the detriment of city interests. Partly for that reason, rural industry remained a strong competitor to urban development. Linked to this was the widespread lack of agricultural improvement across most of the continent, constraining output, and keeping a large part of the population on the land. Lastly, progress was delayed by the slow dissemination of new industrial technology from Britain, inhibited by government controls until the 1840s, and by economic conservatism in many European countries. In a number of key respects the early nineteenth-century city belonged more to the urban world of the eighteenth century than to the modern era.

Even so, by the 1850s a growing proportion of Europe's population resided in towns (see Table 12.1): an average of 25 per cent in Western Europe, and between 8 and 17 per cent in other regions. Where new steamships sailed and trains chugged (shortening average journey times by

to 424,000 in 1891. The city's horizon became thick with smokestacks and factories, blast furnaces, and gas works, most belonging to new large enterprises. Despite its failure to attract modern industry, Rome grew rapidly as the national capital after 1870, its size increasing to half a million in 1911 and 1.2 million under Mussolini. By contrast, many towns in southern Italy slumbered up to the Second World War.

Spanish cities experienced a similar selective advance. Thus, in the north, the Basque towns consolidated their importance as new iron, steel, and shipbuilding industries developed (Bilbao gained 3,000 new firms between 1900 and 1930), while Catalan towns, led by Barcelona, moved away from the old established textile and cotton industries towards engineering, cement, and electrical production; in both areas, industry was helped by the arrival of hydro-electric power in the 1880s. Madrid likewise expanded its population from 332,000 in 1870 to 834,000 sixty years later. Elsewhere, as in the south, the towns were becalmed: the city of Seville, for instance, under the thumb of landowners, had no banks and little industry, and its population of 148,000 continued to crowd together inside the old city walls. Dynamic centres like Madrid and Barcelona suffered badly from the bombardment and repression of the Spanish Civil War during the 1930s. In Portugal, the urban order stagnated into the early twentieth century and most towns remained small: only Lisbon grew fast.

In the eastern Mediterranean, urbanization was equally desultory. Though Athens was extensively rebuilt and staged the Olympic Games in 1896, its population stood at just 125,000 about this time, though it grew faster after the First World War when Greek refugees poured in from Turkey. As Ottoman power steadily collapsed in the late nineteenth century, new states and capitals were created like Sofia and Bucharest, which sought to emulate West European models, but other Balkan cities were more sleepy. During the inter-war period, urbanization advanced at a snail's pace. Greek urbanization stood at 32 per cent by 1940, but in Bulgaria the comparable figure was only 22 per cent. Across the Mediterranean, the same litany of factors limiting urbanization can be found, and among them was a striking lack of modernization in the agrarian sector; low educational standards; recurrent political instability; oppressive but often ineffectual central government; the conservatism of local elites; and the late arrival of large-scale industrialization.

Patchy development was equally evident in Eastern Europe—the least urbanized urban region in 1910 (see Table 12.1 and Figure 12.1). In Russia, liberal reforms in the 1860s, the railway revolution, and the massive stimulus it gave to urban industry and commerce, all generated substantial urban growth. Most spectacular was the rise of St Petersburg to 2.2 million in 1914, its economy no longer driven by the Court and government but by manufacturing and financial expansion: a tenth of the population was employed in industry, many working in large factories. However, Moscow retained its influence as the leading commercial and manufacturing hub in European Russia, buttressed by important economic development in its hinterland. In the Ukraine, Kiev more than trebled its size in the late nineteenth century, its large multi-ethnic population employed in many industries, including the food-processing sector, and services. More moderate expansion occurred in smaller communities. Overall, the population of Russian cities (including those outside Europe) rose nearly threefold between 1870 and 1910.

In spite of Russian repression, Poland saw the rapid growth of Warsaw (with giant factories by 1914), the development of major industrial centres like Lodz, and the revival of ancient cultural cities like Cracow, vital for Polish national identity; even so, in 1918, only 24 per cent of the population lived in towns. In pre-war Latvia, Riga became a leading port of the Russian Empire; its population rose fivefold, and the city celebrated its prosperity and cosmopolitanism in a rich tapestry of art nouveau buildings. In Hungary, the unification of Buda and Pest in 1873 was the prelude to rapid large-scale building, industrial and commercial development, and a shower of new leisure services (including many coffee-houses). As one of the capitals of the Austro-Hungarian Empire, and as the largest port on the Danube, the city's prosperity was accompanied by important demographic expansion: its 880,000 inhabitants in 1910 made it the eighth biggest city in Europe. Outside Budapest, however, Hungarian towns made less progress, held back by the lack of agricultural advance. In the Czech lands, industrialization took off as iron and steel production, engineering, and mining promoted the development of new industrial towns, while Prague had 183,000 inhabitants in 1890. The urbanization rate in the Hungarian-controlled part of the empire reached 20.4 per cent in 1910.

The collapse of the Austrian and Russian Empires and the creation of new states in the region after the First World War opened the door to further change. In Russia, the Communist Revolution initially led to de-urbanization of about 30 per cent in the years 1917–20, followed by a political vogue for anti-urbanism; but, by the 1930s, Stalin was strongly promoting cities as engines of economic modernization and industrialization. Moscow, the new Soviet capital, quickly recovered from its losses after the Revolution and grew from 1 million in 1920 to 4.2 million in 1939. Though losing its capital status, St Peterburg/Leningrad increased its population from 1.1 million in 1923, and 3.1 million in 1939, while Kiev's population quadrupled. Urban growth was augmented by massive rural depopulation as a result of brutal agrarian reform. In newly independent Poland, Warsaw's inhabitants increased to 1.3 million in 1940–1, but overall urban growth in the country, affected by industrial depression, notched up only a few extra percentage points. In the new smaller-scale Hungary, urbanization reached 36.3 per cent in 1930. Across Eastern Europe, the Second World War had a devastating effect on cities and towns. In Russia, 1,700 towns were damaged, and some were levelled. St Petersburg/Leningrad's population fell by three-quarters due to the German siege. As elsewhere, however, post-war recovery was surprisingly rapid.

In the late nineteenth and early twentieth centuries, European cities and towns marched broadly in the same urbanizing direction, though in Western and Northern Europe at a faster pace than elsewhere. In some ways, this was a golden age for European cities. As will be seen in Chapters 13–16, industrial growth, dynamism, and versatility were matched by an expansive service sector; urban living standards began to improve for the majority of town dwellers, and social problems, so acute before 1900, began to be contained. The cultural influence of cities was increasingly multifaceted and the urban landscape was frequently redesigned. Not least, city governments began to function more effectively, offering a much wider range of services to all their citizenry.

III

The post-war era was characterized by renewed urban growth across Europe, as is suggested by Table 12.2, based on the comparable work of Moriconi-Ebrard (the data-sets are not directly compatible with those in Table 12.1 and sometimes vary from national estimates):

In Western Europe, the advance was more limited because of the maturity of the urban order. The fastest growth occurred in France, its urbanization rate still lagging after the war. Whereas 56 per cent of the

Table 12.2. European urbanization 1950−1990

	1950: mean %	1950: median %	1990: mean %	1990: median %
Mediterranean	30.0	21.4	55.6	56.0
Western Europe	66.2	71.5	72.0	72.2
Outer Northern Europe	36.9	36.8	51.6	55.2
Eastern Europe	30.7	33.0	59.0	60.7

Source: F. Moriconi-Ebrard, Geopolis: pour comparer les villes du monde. (Paris, 1994)

French population lived in towns in 1954, the figure had risen to 70 per cent only fourteen years later. The urban advance here and elsewhere reflected the historically high levels of growth in European gross national product (per capita), according to Paul Bairoch running at 4.5 per cent per annum in the period 1950−73 (against an annual rate of only 0.9 per cent 1913−1950). Keynesian economics, trade liberalization (promoted by the first steps towards European integration), rising living standards, agrarian reform, and immigration (including increased non-European mobility) all contributed to the post-war urban advance.

However, by the 1970s, large clouds were on the horizon. Many of the famous flagship cities were most affected. Metropolitan centres like London, Brussels, and Paris suffered from galloping suburbanization and decentralization. Behind this exodus lay increased personal mobility (due to the motor car), rising living standards, changing attitudes to family life and nature, as well as improved job opportunities away from older city areas. Problems of the major West European cities were compounded by the mounting crisis in urban manufacturing, which will be discussed in Chapter 13. Manufacturing decline was not confined to the metropolitan cities but affected a wide swathe of towns. Worst hit were the specialist industrial cities, a high proportion located in Western Europe, which had been so dynamic in the nineteenth century. Meantime, most port towns, particularly those on the Atlantic coast, were badly affected by restructuring and modernization in the shipping industry.

If many specialist industrial and port towns suffered long-term economic problems, most other West European centres managed to recover or at least stabilise their fortunes by the 1990s. Here, public services and the relative buoyancy and flexibility of the private service and financial sector helped cushion urban economies and enabled them to diversify. As usual, the capital cities showed the greatest capacity to bounce back, but the growth of the service sector also provided a boost for a wide range of traditional provincial towns too (discussed below). Nonetheless, economic transformation contributed to mounting social problems in large West European cities (see Chapter 14). Arguably, the long-established primacy of West European cities started to unravel in the late twentieth century.

By comparison, the evolving city system of Northern Europe achieved more momentum. With up to 74 per cent of the Nordic population, according to some estimates, resident in urban areas by 1970−6, the figure had reached up to 81 per cent in 2000. Although the major Nordic cities of Stockholm, Helsinki, and Oslo suffered from a reduction of inhabitants in the 1970s and 1980s due to decentralization, this trend was reversed by 2001; only Copenhagen experienced a long-term fall of population. Whereas some older manufacturing industries, such as textiles, fell into difficulty, restructuring took place in others, such as the paper and metal industries, and a rash of new technology industries appeared (see Chapter 13). Without the many old specialist industrial centres of Western Europe, the region escaped large-scale urban dislocation during the 1970s and 1980s, and urban economies adapted flexibly to new opportunities, including the rapid growth of the service sector. In the Nordic countries the state played a significant role in urban growth, through the promotion of new industrial sites, heavy investment in education and infrastructure, and policies for increased municipal autonomy. In consequence, in Finland and Sweden not only the capitals but also major provincial cities (Tampere, Jyväskylä, Malmö, Gothenburg) flourished at the end of the period, and even some smaller towns. In Ireland, the old industrial towns of the north declined badly, affected by political conflict as well as international competition, but Dublin and the towns of the Irish Republic enjoyed rapid development from about 1980, stimulated by European Union support for agrarian reform and infrastructure improvement, and by the spread of high technology industry. Dublin's population grew from 852,000 in 1971 to 1.1 million twenty-five years later, and the Irish urbanization rate jumped from 46 per cent in 1960 to 57 per cent in 1990. Regional growth forecasts in 2006 ranked six cities from outer Northern Europe among the twenty leading European centres (Dublin, Stockholm, and Helsinki in the top eight).

In Eastern Europe, the Soviet occupation of much of the region after the Second World War led to sustained urbanization through state promotion of heavy industry and the creation of new industrial and planned cities, where up to 60 per cent of the populations worked in a single sector. Communist Hungary had eleven Socialist cities of this type, while in Ceausescu's Romania villages were suppressed to furnish completely new industrial towns. In Russia, the urbanization rate reached 51 per cent in 1961 and growth was particularly strong during the 1960s and 1970s. Moscow's population leapt from 3.2 million in 1945 to 8.9 million in 1987, with much of the increase the result of immigration. By 1970, more than half the Polish, Czech, and Hungarian populations were town dwellers, and here and in other Eastern bloc countries urbanization continued up to 1990, by which time the average urbanization rate for the region stood at about 59 per cent (see Table 12.2).

After the Soviet collapse in 1989–90, Russian cities experienced some temporary fall of population (St Petersburg lost half a million residents 1991–2001), but elsewhere in Eastern Europe policies of political and economic liberalization tended to promote urban growth with the expansion of the service sector and tourism in capitals such as Warsaw and Prague. In the Baltic region, cities like Tallinn and Riga enjoyed important redevelopment and renewed prosperity. Worst affected were the planned industrial towns which ran into crisis due to the end of the Communist command economy and fierce international competition: thus, Tatabánya and Ózd in Hungary suffered a serious loss of inhabitants during the 1990s. In general, though, the economic prognosis for the major cities of Eastern Europe was positive at the start of the twenty-first century: Russian cities recovered their demographic losses and centres like Warsaw, Prague, and Budapest were forecast to perform well in terms of production and employment growth.

Like Eastern Europe, much of the Mediterranean region enjoyed a burst of urbanization during the late twentieth century (see Table 12.2). The upturn was particularly dynamic during the 1960s. Spanish cities like Valladolid, Saragossa, and Madrid grew rapidly at this time. Portugese growth accelerated, too, though Lisbon remained the most vigorous centre. In Italy, the Milan-Turin-Genoa region continued to serve as the main engine of expansion, attracting many workers from the south. In Greece, the majority of the population resided in towns by 1971, while in Communist Bulgaria the urbanization rate trebled to 65 per cent about this time. Urbanization was supported in part by large-scale agricultural modernization (increasingly financed in non-Communist countries by the European

Union), which released a swarm of rural migrants to cities. Thus, Spain in the 1960s and 1970s witnessed a mass exodus of peasants from the Granada region (and elsewhere) to the shanty towns of Barcelona and Valencia to work in industry. Large-scale factory-based industries flourished in parts of northern Italy, and in some of the major Spanish cities, but much of the manufacturing structure of the Mediterranean remained small-scale, many family businesses employing only a handful of workers.

Hence, the Mediterranean urban order largely bypassed the heavy manufacturing phase of urbanization that had been so important in Western Europe: it thus escaped some of the worst ravages of de-industrialization in the 1970s. Here, the exception was the Communist Balkans where an attempt to follow the Soviet model of urban industrialization led to a sharp increase in the number of cities, many of them industrial centres with over 100,000 inhabitants; as elsewhere this had disastrous consequences during the 1980s and 1990s. However, across the Mediterranean region, urban economies generally benefited from an expansive service sector, helped by the growth of the state and the new importance of the Mediterranean coast as a holiday destination. In addition, cities promoted themselves through new museums, theatres, art galleries, and international sports events. Once again, capital cities displayed powerful momentum: Rome grew rapidly up to the 1980s, many of its 3 million inhabitants resident in the sprawling, chaotic penumbra, while Belgrade's population reached over a million in 1981.

By the close of the twentieth century, Mediterranean urbanization was running out of steam. Agrarian reform had largely run its course and migration from the countryside declined. State financial cutbacks dampened the growth of administrative services; environmental pollution was growing; horrendous political conflict in the Balkans led to damage to cities, economic disruption, and a massive decline of tourism in the area (though this was partially displaced to the towns of the Western Mediterranean). Many major cities in the region suffered stagnation or loss of population in the 1990s.

Two broad points are clear so far from this survey of urban trends. Firstly, European urbanization, as in previous centuries, was marked by strong regional variations, but by the late twentieth century the lagging regions had mostly caught up, with urban growth rates in Eastern and Mediterranean Europe particularly strong up to the 1980s. The map of leading European cities in 2000 (see Figure 12.2) shows a wide regional

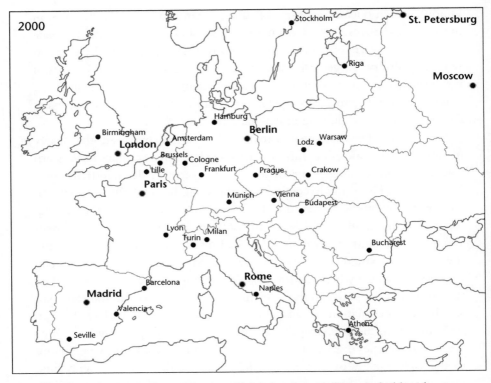

Fig. 12.2 Map of Leading European Cities about 2000. Cities in bold with over two million inhabitants.

distribution. Secondly, some types of urban community fared better than others. In the final part of this chapter, we shall focus directly on the winners and losers, taking firstly the more traditional, multi-functional towns, and then focusing on the growing range of specialist communities.

IV

Heading the traditional urban hierarchy in much of Europe were, of course, capital cities: some like Paris and London important since the Middle Ages, others like Madrid, St Petersburg, Vienna, and Stockholm developing essentially in the early modern period. Numbers grew substantially in the modern era with the consecration of Rome and Berlin as capitals of unified states, the foundation of Athens, Belgrade, Bucharest, and Sofia as the state capitals of new Balkan countries after the Ottoman collapse, and a last surge of new national capitals (often previously secondary capitals) after the First World War, among them Dublin, Helsinki, the Baltic capitals, Prague, Budapest, and Warsaw. In 1917, St Petersburg was replaced by Moscow as the Russian capital.

In the early nineteenth century only a few of these primate centres, notably London, Paris, and Brussels, enjoyed large-scale growth and construction; otherwise expansion tended to be modest. The biggest city in the world, London by the 1830s already had the crowds ('people apparently without end'), the pollution (poisonous 'peasouper' fogs), and the sense of anomie (men, animals, and machines appearing 'like streams of living atoms reeling to a fro') that one associates with the modern mega-city, but most metropoles in this period retained strongly traditional features: crowded central districts with unhealthy narrow streets; constricting military defences; limited social segregation and modest infrastructure improvement.

The incarnation of capital cities as modern metropolises, equipped with the institutions of the nation state, diversified economies, a cavalcade of cultural activity, and a grand, monumental landscape, was achieved during the late nineteenth century and start of the twentieth. Whilst London's sanitation improvements in the 1840s established a model for other capitals, it was Haussmann's redesign of central Paris in the 1850s and 1860s, opening up the grand boulevards, turning the central districts over to bourgeois apartment blocks, hotels, government offices, and department stores, forcing poorer inhabitants and industry to decamp to the suburbs, that influenced the rebuilding of most European capitals by 1900. As nation-states increasingly competed with one another, so did their capitals, whether in architecture, technical services (fierce rivalry flared at the end of the nineteenth century to become the leading electrified 'City of Light'), or economic development. As already noted, populations soared: five European capitals had more than 2 million inhabitants by 1914. No less striking was their spatial extension. London, with its penumbra of villa suburbs, covered 1,792 sq. kilometres by 1914, but many others such as Paris, Brussels, St Petersburg, Stockholm, Copenhagen, and Berlin boasted their own sprawling suburban districts. After the First World War, Paris had 2.9 million residents plus another 1.5 million on the outskirts who lived mostly in shanty-towns. Right across Europe, irrespective of region, capital cities became the kingpins of the urban order.

Metropolitan expansion was boosted not just by the increase of state functions and bureaucracies, but by economic diversification. Of Paris, Paul Valery wrote: 'much more than a political capital and an industrial centre, [it is] a port of first importance and a great market, an artificial paradise and a sanctuary of culture'. Many capitals were great overseas ports and flourished on the explosive growth of European and global trade. Frequently, they were the leading manufacturing centres in their countries: Berlin had Siemenstadt and Charlottenburg; northern Paris housed many car, aviation, and chemical industries, employing thousands of workers; St Petersburg had a ring of large factories. Meantime, a multiplicity of department stores and retail shops catered for the metropolitan bourgeoisie (see Chapter 13). Again, in both the performing and visual arts the national metropolis was the cradle of innovation, commonly linked to state patronage and the commercial sector. Capitals reinforced their position as national transport hubs, shiny steel rails converging on their railway termini, while after the First World War the first international airports opened in their vicinity. Capitals became leading tourist destinations, their images heavily publicized in the new media, including films. To refresh, entertain, and lodge the crowds of visitors, restaurants, cafés, and hotels sprang up in every boulevard.

The massive expansion of national capitals was not unproblematic. Suffering serious social problems, beset by tensions with government, they provoked growing anti-urban sentiment before and after the First World War. Nonetheless, the great age of the capital cities continued, more or less, into the late twentieth century, buoyed up by the apparently inexorable rise of the state and their economic importance. In Soviet bloc countries, Communist centralization privileged capital cities like Moscow and Warsaw at the expense of provincial centres.

From the 1970s, decentralization, state regional policies, and the general crisis in European manufacturing (and in many cases the decline of port employment) posed major challenges, particularly to capital cities in Western Europe. Yet, as we have noted, capitals demonstrated a striking ability to recover, aided by their dominance of national and international business and transport networks. The upturn in world banking and finance since the 1980s consolidated their business primacy. In the 1990s, 100 per cent of Spanish company headquarters were based in Madrid; 85 per cent of British ones in London; and 90 per cent of French ones in Paris. Moscow was the focus for 80 per cent of direct foreign investment in Russia.

Sixteen of Europe's capitals were represented in the top hundred of the world's richest cities in 2005. Tourism has continued to flourish (in 2001 capital cities comprised 60 per cent of the top twenty tourist destinations in Europe), stimulating a massive development of hotel, catering, and cleaning services. Heavily backed by national governments, metropolitan authorities have marketed their attractions as business, cultural, and leisure centres in often aggressive ways, including redevelopment projects (Dublin's Temple Bar district), cultural *grand projets* (the Tate Modern, the Gare D'Orsay Museum), and international cultural and sporting events.

Generally, the durability and continued influence of European capital cities into the contemporary era has been striking (see Figure 12.2). Rather exceptional was Berlin, which lost its national status after the division of Germany in 1945, and struggled to recover its metropolitan power after reunification in 1991, but even here the city enjoyed growing success at the end of our period. Indeed, primate cities have been the most successful of the traditional spinal hierarchy of European urban centres.

V

By comparison, regional cities, often presiding since the Middle Ages over extensive hinterlands and networks of smaller towns, have enjoyed mixed fortunes. In the nineteenth century, those ancient centres which boasted important specialist industries, such as Newcastle, Lyon, Lille, Milan, and Barcelona expanded strongly, flourishing as commercial, cultural, and political centres in economically vibrant regions. The great majority of regional centres did less well, however, stagnating or growing fairly slowly, constrained by a lack of industrial momentum and by limited agrarian improvement in their hinterlands. In Britain, ancient regional cities like Norwich or Exeter went into relative decline, though the first was recovering before 1900; French cities such as Bordeaux and Toulouse failed to capitalize on their earlier importance; and in Germany former residential cities and imperial cities, without a new manufacturing function, turned into backwaters: thus, the Westphalian city of Münster was marginalized from industrial growth in the region and its ranking fell sharply. Regional centres in the Mediterranean and Eastern Europe often suffered similar problems, though in the Nordic countries a number of middle-rank cities like Gothenburg, Malmö, and Tampere developed new industrial specialisms.

During the twentieth century, however, improved communications, enlarged state expenditure, growing agrarian reform, the spread of new industries, and reformed municipal government revived the fortunes of many of these regional cities. In England, the renaissance of places like Norwich, Exeter, York, Maidstone, and Colchester was already starting in the inter-war era and became notable in the late twentieth century. In the Netherlands, the city of Groningen posted success after 1945 as a city of services, about eight in ten its of labour force being employed in public services, education, and retailing; across the German border, Münster enjoyed similar prosperity in the last decades of the twentieth century. In Finland, smaller regional centres like Jyväskylä and Oulu did well (Oulu's population climbed from 78,000 in 1965 to 121,000 in 2000); here, new industries were attracted or supported by educational and scientific agencies, often linked to universities. Clearly, state funding has played a part in boosting the wider administrative and service functions of many regional towns, but, equally important, energetic councils have sought to revive their regional cultural role, through new or revamped museums and art galleries, local radio stations, music festivals, and the like.

As we know, much less research has been done on Europe's thousands of small market towns, many of them dating back to the high Middle Ages. Nonetheless, we can speculate that the great majority grew relatively slowly for much of the nineteenth century, held back by the decline of traditional crafts, by dependence on landowners and a slow moving agrarian sector, and by belated advances in infrastructure and communications (many railways bypassed small towns). Decline was by no means universal, however. A significant minority flourished as manufacturing centres. In the Ruhr, for instance, small towns like Essen and Dortmund were caught up in the nineteenth-century industrial tsunami and surged as major urban centres with populations of over 200,000 by 1910. Another group of small towns developed as transport centres, mainly for the new railways. Other small communities acquired a leisure function as spas and seaside towns, frequently through the initiative of a local landowner—for instance, the Duke of Devonshire at Eastbourne. All in all, however, there can be little doubt that the proportion of the urban population living in small towns fell steadily during the nineteenth and early twentieth centuries. In Britain, the share of the population living in small towns slipped from 16 per cent in 1851 to 9 per cent in 1901 and just over 6 per cent in 1951. Nearly half the French urban population still lived in towns of less than 10,000 in 1831; but by 1911 the figure had slumped to 20 per cent. In the Mediterranean region the downward spiral was less dramatic. In Spain, the small-town share of the total population slid from 50 per cent in 1900 to 40 per cent in 1960.

During the late twentieth century, the picture changed again, though once more with mixed dividends for small towns. Some took advantage of the decentralization of metropolitan centres noted earlier. This was notable around London, Stockholm, Madrid, and Rome. In eastern France, out-migration from Strasbourg had a similar effect on some smaller communities in the region. In some areas, there was a spread of new technology industries to small towns. Another beneficiary group consists of those well-preserved small towns and ports which developed as destinations for seaside holidays or cultural tourism—among the latter, the heavily renovated town of Carcassonne in southern France, the book town of Hay-on-Wye, on the Welsh border, and the various UNESCO World Heritage site towns like Rauma in Finland. In contrast, small towns in more peripheral areas have regularly undergone depopulation as a result of out-migration, ageing populations, and the steady attrition of their urban functions, including the loss of industries, shops, and other businesses. Frequently, only their basic administrative functions serve as a safety net keeping up their urban identity.

VI

Broadly speaking, the traditional urban order maintained its coherence and resilience through the modern era and generated, in the case of capital cities and at least some of the regional centres and smaller towns, vital sources of urban dynamism or renewal. Nonetheless, as we know, one of the most striking urban developments of this period was the rise of more specialist urban centres, primarily manufacturing towns, great port towns, military and leisure towns. Three preliminary points can be made. First, some of these towns were completely new centres, but the majority had started as traditional small market or port towns. Second, these specialist centres, though sharing a dependence on a particular sector were rarely specialist *tout court*. Many diversified into other sectors, needing basic trades and services to sustain their expanding populations. Nonetheless, in many industrial towns manufacturing engaged 50 per cent or more of the workforce, substantially higher than in traditional towns, and with a greater concentration in one or two sectors. Third, specialist towns tended to create networks of complementary towns: whether regional industrial networks as in the West Midlands, the Ruhr, or Pas de Calais, underpinned by access to energy and mineral resources, a mobile labour supply, and shared transport and financial links; port towns linked by trade and merchant networking; or resort towns, as on the south-west coast of France, offering a finely-tuned array of services for an increasingly sophisticated tourist market.

In the case of manufacturing towns, high growth was driven by heavy immigration, which in the early nineteenth century often spawned terrible living conditions, as provision of services and infrastructure ran far behind demand. The situation was especially difficult in completely new towns like Merthyr Tydfil in South Wales which by the 1830s had turned rapidly from a village 'into a crowded and filthy manufacturing town', blighted by exceptionally high mortality rates, and where effective town government was lacking for decades after the town's explosive expansion. Roubaix was another new town, originally a craft village, whose many textile mills attracted a population of 100,000 and generated massive social and environmental problems. A second type of new industrial centre grew out of old small and medium-size towns. Thus, the episcopal city of Limoges developed as a national and international centre for the ceramics industry with a score or more of factories. Here, too, urban services lagged well behind rapid population growth: many streets were left unpaved, and poor quality housing bred high mortality. Bochum was another old-style country town that grew rapidly from mining, iron, and steel. Two thirds of residents were migrants and almost 80 per cent of the population was engaged in the industrial sector in the 1880s. A third category of specialist industrial centre comprised company towns, which grew up under one dominant employer who frequently furnished services, institutions, and housing as a way of controlling the workforce. Examples were Le Creusot in Burgundy, where the Schneider dynasty fabricated an iron and steel town with model houses and sanitation; the town of Crewe, established (in 1843) by a British railway company, where over two thirds of household heads in the 1880s worked for the railway; and Eindhoven, in the Netherlands, where the Philips family took over the town after 1891 and ran much of its economic and civic life. Finally, as we noted above, a spate of new state planned industrial towns were created in Communist countries after the Second World War to meet Russian economic needs, such as Sillamäe in Estonia, set up in Estonia in 1946 to exploit the shale oil industry, or Stuchka, in Latvia (founded 1960), serving a new hydro-electric power plant.

The vulnerability of such towns was already evident from early on, cyclical commercial crises through the nineteenth century spawning waves of unemployment and social deprivation. Industrial towns like Middlesbrough, Sunderland, and the Ruhr towns (such as Oberhausen) suffered equally badly during the Great Depression, and from the 1970s many manufacturing centres like Sheffield, Roubaix, or Duisburg experienced a catastrophic decline of their core industries resulting in high and persistent levels of unemployment. Scarred by industrial pollution, specialist communities found it difficult to adapt and acquire new service functions, not least because they faced strong competition from well-established, multi-functional towns.

Overseas port cities pursued a not dissimilar trajectory of rapid growth succeeded by sharp decline in the later twentieth century. Already, before 1800, Asian and Atlantic commerce was heavily concentrated in a limited number of great ports. A number doubled as capital cities but the rest, including Glasgow, Liverpool, Hamburg, Rotterdam, Le Havre, Bilbao, and Marseille, were specialist cargo and liner ports, usually in excellent maritime locations, though often semi-detached from the main urban network. During the nineteenth century, port activity soared, driven by the rapid expansion of colonial and global trade (including rising exports of European manufactures and imports of raw materials and later foodstuffs), and the steamship revolution. At Liverpool, the volume of registered shipping using the port rose four to five times between 1858 and 1914, while Bremen's merchant fleet increased fortyfold during the nineteenth century; by 1909, 84 per cent of its tonnage was steam-powered. Great ports benefited from large-scale infrastructure investment, and the development of processing and refining industries (Bremen was important for tobacco and coffee processing) and shipbuilding (for instance, at Glasgow, Lübeck, Hamburg, and Le Havre). If the great ports did best, middle-rank and smaller ports also profited from the general expansion and specialization of European and coastal trade (see Chapter 13).

Alongside strong demographic growth came high levels of mortality (due to seaborne epidemics) and heavy immigration, often involving ethnic minorities. At Glasgow in 1851 nearly one in five of the city's population was Irish, and ports like Marseille and Genoa received immigrants from all over the Mediterranean. Too often, municipal politics were conservative and parsimonious, and (as in the case of industrial towns) urban services were slow to catch up with the demographic explosion: there were major housing shortages and acute social problems. Widespread poverty was caused not only by cyclical trade slumps but also by the high incidence of seasonal and casual employment.

By 1900, a number of the leading ports had acquired not only some manufactures but also service activities such as insurance. For all these efforts at diversification, however, the majority remained heavily dependent on shipping and their economies had a narrow employment base. In the 1930s, many suffered badly from the Great Depression. Unemployment at Liverpool, for instance, jumped to 28 per cent in 1932. Most of the major ports were badly damaged during the Second World War: thus, Hamburg lost almost half its housing stock due to bombing in July 1943. Recovery after the war proved short-lived. From the 1960s, mechanization started to have a major impact on port employment and over the next decades containerization accelerated the process. At Liverpool, the registered dock labour force fell from 23,000 in 1963 to just 2,000 a couple of decades later. In addition, international shipping companies tended to concentrate their activities in a small number of global ports—mega-hubs with advanced facilities. In many countries, specialist non-urban harbours grew in importance, often dealing in a particular trade such as car imports. As a result, most European port cities stagnated in the later twentieth century. Even those like Rotterdam and Antwerp that grew, saw their docks and facilities moving downstream, away from the city. From Sunderland and Belfast to Palermo and Malaga, port cities comprised the largest group of declining cities in late twentieth century Europe, notable for their high levels of unemployment. In France, half the ten major cities with the worst rates of economic growth in the 1980s were ports. Attempts to resuscitate the leading port cities through the development of cultural services (such as the Merseyside Maritime Museum at Liverpool or Bilbao's Guggenheim Museum), had some success, but numerous middle-rank and smaller ports were subject to acute problems of employment and redevelopment, albeit with exceptions: thus, Calais benefited from heavy investment in port facilities to enjoy strong growth in its cross-Channel and European traffic.

Leisure towns were always much smaller than industrial cities or major port centres. A few, including spas and seaside towns, had already emerged before 1800, mainly in England, but the main take-off was from the 1830s and 1840s and at the end of the century the continent had hundreds of spa towns. A significant proportion were located in less developed areas with their scenic views, cheap labour, and limited economic alternatives: thus, Austro-Hungary had thirty-three resorts in 1910, compared to twenty-four in Germany, seventy in France, four in Italy, and twenty in Switzerland. Offering medical treatment and polite sociability, spa town development was irrigated by rising bourgeois prosperity and the arrival of the railways (often doubling visitor numbers in a few years). Also influential was the growing impact of the medical profession, municipal and private investment, and tourist publicity. Spas figured widely in the novels of Fyodor Dostoevsky, Emile Zola, and Thomas Mann, usually portrayed as special, even fantastical worlds, but also important was the idea of the spa as a place to return to nature. Scenic views in the south Tyrol, for instance, led to the emergence of Meran as a health resort from the 1830s, patronized by nobles and royalty as well as the fashionable bourgeoisie. But, in the years before the First World War, the spas became less select as trainloads of plain middle-class families debouched, not so enamoured of fancy water treatments and more keen on climate, recreation, and respectability (Meran's visitors surged from 7,500 in 1883 to 40,000 in 1913).

If spa resorts increasingly flourished in less developed parts of Central and Eastern Europe, initially, the main tide of seaside resorts lapped Western Europe, where steamships, railways, and trams brought troops of visitors from the capital cities or industrial towns to promenade, to enjoy the clean, unpolluted air, to dip perhaps in the chill Atlantic or Baltic waters, and to marvel at the romantic image of sea and shore. As with the spa towns, there was heavy marketing from the nineteenth century by towns and railway companies, joined later by hotels, holiday companies, and state tourist offices. Belle of the North Atlantic resorts, Brighton doubled in size after 1851, reaching 131,000 in 1911, while Ostend trebled its population to 45,000 in the decades before the First World War.

Further south, seaside towns surfaced rather later. From the 1840s, San Sebastian and Santander in northern Spain attracted royal and noble patrons as well as the fashionable bourgeoisie, while over the French border Biarritz, favoured by Queen Victoria and Napoleon III, watched its population grow markedly in the last third of the century, housed in ever more fanciful villas. But, as late as 1893, a survey of over 400 European seaside towns located more than 80 per cent in Western Europe. By the First World War, though, Mediterranean resorts were advancing at a fast pace. Among the leaders, Nice had 66,000 residents in 1881 but more than twice that number in 1911, and 242,000 in 1936. Though established as a resort in the 1840s, Rimini still had only 19,000 visitors in 1922, but 75,000 during the high summer of the 1930s. By then, resorts were spreading to the Adriatic coast (for instance, Dubrovnik). After the Second World War, middle-class and mass tourism fuelled a boom in seaside facilities along the Mediterranean shore, from the Costa Blanca to the Greek islands and Black Sea, many of them situated in and around decayed port towns, grafted on to existing urban hierarchies without supplanting them.

Though leisure resorts often derived from older small towns, they displayed distinctive features: seasonality of business—limited to three months a year; the high mobility of visitors and workers; initial fashionable patronage, but later wider social access; the overwhelming dominance of the service sector (largely small businesses); more relaxed social behaviour; and the architecture of pleasure—from piers to promenades, from funfairs to nightclubs.

Like other specialist towns, however, many leisure towns suffered from their over-dependence on one sector and were vulnerable to changes in leisure markets, competition with other centres, and environmental problems. Spa towns in the twentieth century came to depend on the sick and elderly rather than the sociable, and too often stagnated. Seaside towns in North-West Europe had their heyday in the years after the Second World War when affluent workers and their families crowded there for their summer holidays. From the 1970s, their populations waned, as they lost out to cheaper and warmer holiday destinations in Southern Europe. At the end of our period, Mediterranean seaside towns faced growing competition from beach resorts outside Europe. Those on the Black Sea that had catered for Soviet tourists crashed badly after the collapse of the Communist regime in 1990.

A last category of specialist towns consisted of military towns, probably between thirty and forty in modern Europe. One group was that of naval and dockyard towns, among them Plymouth, Portsmouth, and Chatham in England, Brest and Toulon in France, and Kronshtadt near St Petersburg, the largest naval base in the Baltic. Another group was that of barrack towns, such as Aldershot in England or Koblenz in Germany. Military towns made big strides in number and size during the nineteenth century, particularly in the decades leading up to the First World War. Brest's population coasted from 66,000 in the 1860s to 90,000 in 1911, while that of Aldershot marched from 17,000 to 35,000 during the same period. But such communities were always highly dependent on state military expenditure and their labour force fell back sharply in peacetime. After the loss of empires in the late twentieth century, and the end of the Cold War in 1990, most have stagnated or declined, at best turning into heritage sites. Brest and St-Nazaire figured among French towns with the worst employment record, while Kronshtadt appeared derelict and depressed in 2001.

VII

To complete this survey of the different types of urban community, it is important to remember the many thousands of European-style towns outside Europe—colonial and neo-colonial cities. Though a large part of the colonial towns founded, mainly in the Americas, during the first wave of European imperial expansion (see Chapter 7) had been liberated by independence movements against Britain and Spain in the decades before and after 1800, the second great wave of European colonial expansion during the nineteenth century in Africa, Asia, and Australasia produced new generations of Europeanized towns abroad. Given the parallel surge of European urbanization at this time, it is hardly surprising that cities became, more than ever, vital instruments both of European economic and political hegemony and intra-European rivalry. Several different types are recognizable. One was the settler town. Unlike in the earlier period, when many of the new cities were populated by large contingents of European colonists, in the nineteenth century settler towns were mostly limited to French North Africa, parts of South Africa, Canada, and Australasia, with cities like Melbourne, Sydney, and Auckland.

Elsewhere, in Asia and much of Africa, most colonial cities, some ancient centres brought under colonial rule or new cities like Singapore (1819) and Hong Kong (1842), had only small cadres of expatriate officials, soldiers, and merchants (rarely more than 3–7 per cent of the total inhabitants). Populations of French Saigon or Dutch Batavia soared in the late nineteenth century. In British India there was a similar expansion of port cities like Bombay and Calcutta, heavily integrated into imperial trade, as well as the creation of administrative centres, and even resort towns—hill towns like Simla—for the European elite.

A third category of community were neo-colonial cities, as in the independent republics of Latin America, like Buenos Aires (178,000 in

1869 and 1.5 million in 1914), Santiago de Chile and San José (Costa Rica), which continued to rely on European investment, immigrants, and cultural inputs. Reflecting the economic, political, and cultural dynamic of European cities during the late nineteenth century, colonial and neo-colonial towns were influenced, more or less, by West European models of town planning, infrastructure improvement, public buildings and parks, suburbanization (particularly in Australia with the splendid Victorian suburbs of Melbourne), social segregation (reinforced by race), and cultural style. The exchange was not one sided. Just as colonial and neo-colonial cities contributed, through trade, investment opportunities, and demand to European economic development, so the imperial world shaped the monuments, landscape, and cultural ideas of European cities, through architecture, the media, imperial exhibitions, and other events. However, by the Second World War, if not before, the heyday of the European colonial city was on the wane as imperial power began to fade, nationalist movements mobilized, and alternative political and cultural forces (principally American) began to assert their influence. At the close of the twentieth century, former colonial and neo-colonial centres, especially in Asia, had often turned into roaring urban tigers, mega-cities competing against the European urban system.

VIII

To conclude, the European urban order saw dramatic changes between 1800 and 2000. In the nineteenth and early twentieth centuries accelerating urbanization across continent, moving from Western Europe to Northern Europe and progressively to other regions, was accompanied by the apparently inexorable ascent of capital cities, the selective prosperity of traditional provincial centres, and an upsurge of new more specialist towns. The later twentieth century witnessed equally drastic upheavals within the urban network, as cities in Western Europe in particular suffered growing demographic and other problems, and serious challenges confronted metropolitan cities and specialist urban communities. The complex economic, political, and other factors which influenced these developments will be explored in detail below.

At the same time, modern European cities demonstrated growing durability, affluence, and effectiveness. In the two centuries after 1800 they overcame many of the terrible natural and other threats that had dogged their fortunes in earlier times. Among the natural threats only earthquakes continued to create havoc into the late twentieth century (as at Skopje in 1963 which destroyed most of the city). As we will see in Chapter 14, epidemic disease persisted, particularly in poorer urban regions, until the First World War, but thereafter improvements in public health, water supply, and medical care led to the containment of the problem. Another major natural threat, fire, had largely disappeared by the late nineteenth century as a destroyer of towns, due to advances in construction and planning (for instance, firebreaks in wooden Nordic towns), fire services, and fire insurance. The last great fires afflicting European cities were associated with bombing during the Second World War. True, warfare, particularly during the two world wars, created major crises for cities, involving high mortality, physical destruction, difficulties of food supply, and the like. Nevertheless, the recovery periods were relatively rapid, unlike in previous times. During the Second World War, planning for the reconstruction of cities and even some rebuilding was under way before the end of hostilities. Again, following the Balkan wars of the 1990s, devastation hit many urban centres but the revival was swift: Sarajevo's population nearly halved from 529,000 in 1991 to 300,000 five years later, but by 2006 stood at 602,000.

As well as these ancient challenges, European cities in the modern and contemporary era faced many other problems—economic, social, cultural, and political—linked to mass urbanization, high levels of immigration, the growth of the international economy, the rise of states and central governments, and much else. In the next chapters, we will investigate how the urban order managed to respond to these challenges, and try to evaluate the achievements of the European city at the end of the twentieth century.

13
Economy 1800–2000

The two centuries after 1800 saw the urbanizing of the European
economy. Agriculture lost its primacy and urban economic life moved
from its earlier dependency on the countryside to a new world increasingly
shaped by national and international forces. Though the relationship of
cities and globalization has become a controversial issue in recent years,
the international impact on cities was long-term and dynamic for much of
the modern period (as it had been on a more limited basis since the high
Middle Ages). Internationalization played a vital role in the rise of urban
manufacturing during the nineteenth and twentieth centuries, and in the
industrial crisis in European cities after the 1970s. In the same way, the
development of the service sector in European cities, which some scholars
have seen as a key part of the current globalization process, must be viewed
as a long-term development. As we saw in Chapter 3, the first take-off in
urban services took place in the fifteenth century in response to the late
medieval recession, and during the nineteenth century the growth of the
service sector was umbilically linked to industrialization and the expansion
of state and municipal power.

In this chapter, we shall argue for the composite nature of urban
economic growth, concerned with the factors propelling innovation and
change, but also with the contribution of more traditional sectors, and their
interaction. After a section exploring the old-style links with the rural economy, the analysis turns to examine the expansion of urban manufacturing,
stressing the impact not just of large-scale factory production—highly visible and striking to contemporaries—but of the continuing importance of
more traditional workshop output, a type of organization which provided
a key to the growth of advanced technology manufacturing in the later
twentieth century, at a time when large-scale industry largely disintegrated
in European cities. The same narrative of continuity and change informs

the subsequent discussion of the tertiary sector, as traditional services were transformed and new ones multiplied. The chapter concludes with a brief discussion of the contribution of municipal policy to urban economic development.

I

As regards to the urban relationship with agriculture, local and regional food supply was still relatively important everywhere in the early nineteenth century. Smaller towns retained a substantial agricultural sector, including small farms, cowsheds, piggeries, orchards, and (in southern Europe) vineyards within the walls or limits. Animals were widely kept even in major European cities until the First World War. As well as the myriad horses that powered all kinds of transport, cities like Liverpool and Bradford had thousands of cows producing milk for urban consumers. Around 1900, Swedish cities opened municipal pig-farms, the animals being fed from the garbage collection. Local agricultural trade remained vital in the nineteenth century: at Verdun in Northern France, for instance, agricultural products comprised 90 per cent of the taxed goods brought into the town. In the Mediterranean region, this business stayed important well into the twentieth century, with peasants selling their produce directly to townspeople or at market, even in big cities like Seville or Belgrade. Around 1900, 80 per cent of workers in Moscow factories were owners or part owners of rural land, and during the 1990s nearly half the ordinary residents of Russian cities coped with the economic crisis by getting extra income from some form of agriculture.

As late as the 1840s and 1850s, harvest failures triggered food shortages in French and Flemish cities, as well as unleashing a flood of desperate peasants into Irish, British, and Belgian towns. However, the gradual commercialization and modernization of European farming, the spread of railways to move domestic products cheaply, and, after the 1870s, the new availability of cereals and other foodstuffs from outside Europe transformed the link between town and hinterland, and released more villagers to work in towns. Trains steaming to Manchester from the 1840s brought wagon loads of fruit and vegetables from across England, as well as livestock from Scotland. Imports of refrigerated meat from the Southern Hemisphere triggered the decline of London's abattoirs after 1900, while fresh food from the English Home Counties was replaced in London's shops by branded, processed foods, often from abroad.

Landowners remained important figures in European towns (especially regional cities) after 1800, continuing to divert rural rents there to fund urban expenditure; but their numbers and impact steadily diminished (though less so in Eastern Europe), as rural residence became more fashionable and comfortable, while the power of other groups in the urban economy grew disproportionately. A similar trend may have occurred in the reverse direction, with regard to urban investment in agriculture. Though less is known, falling agrarian prices, rents and property values, along with the rapid opening up of opportunities in the urban economy led to a slow unwinding of investments by wealthier townspeople in the countryside, though purchases of rural property by ordinary inhabitants, often immigrants repatriating funds to their home villages, continued into the late twentieth century in Mediterranean Europe.

II

The long-standing, symbiotic relationship of towns with rural industry— supplying capital, sharing work and processes, marketing rural output—survived into the first part of the nineteenth century. In industrializing regions in Western Europe, such as the East Midlands or the St Quentin-Valenciennes area, a substantial proportion of manufacturing output stayed rural-based up to the 1860s and 1870s, despite mounting competition from urban factories and workshops. In effect, a complementary system operated as cheaper village production (subsidized by pauperization) supplemented mechanized urban manufacturing, the combined output marketed by town merchants. Elsewhere, in Northern and Eastern Europe, industry remained largely rural-centred with more tenuous links to towns. Thus, in Sweden and Russia many factories in the mid-nineteenth century were situated in the countryside. By 1900, however, rural industry was generally eclipsed by urban production, thereby accelerating the rural population drift to town.

Initially, urban manufacturing kept many traditional features, even in the most dynamic areas. In a number of industries, seasonality of employment meant that workers could go summer harvesting in the adjoining countryside. Units of production were often small. Frequently, new technology was slow to be introduced because of the high costs and state controls on its export from Britain. Only after the 1840s was there increasing industrial concentration and the growth of larger units of production, due to the greater availability of new technology, the spread of railways, and (on the continent) greater state intervention. However, workshop or domestic production remained the norm in many industries up to the 1870s and later. In the East Midlands, hosiery continued to be produced both in urban workshops and domestically. At Basel, entrepreneurs introduced the steam engine in 1837, and ten years later over two thousand were employed in the city's silk industries; yet 10,000 workers were still employed in domestic production, mainly in the nearby countryside. Even in Manchester, the capital of cotton mills, large firms operated cheek by jowl with a multitude of very small firms.

Early adoption of steam-powered mechanization and factory production was limited to a few industries. Iron was one. From the 1820s, Liège introduced the Cort puddling process from England, and around 1830 the foundry at Seraing employed 2,000 people—one of the largest units on the continent. Cotton was another early start, steam-driven, large-scale industry. Manchester by 1821 had sixty-six cotton mills, employing nearly 52,000 hands (twice the number in 1811). In Catalonian towns, the import of English machinery launched a tenfold increase of cotton output, while firms at Mulhouse in Alsace installed large steam-powered mills to catch up with the British. Steadily, mechanization spread into other industries such as paper and glass-making (both modernized in Belgium by the 1830s and 1840s), and beer brewing (Münich breweries had steam engines on the English model from the 1840s). 'Walking among the high chimneys and the howl of [steam]engines' at Wroclaw, one writer averred, 'it feels as if one were in some factory town in England'.

One important constraint on industrial expansion was institutional. Despite moves to suppress guilds in a number of countries during the Napoleonic period, many continued to survive in some form, and as competition increased they became more ossified and restrictive. Journeyman *compagnonnages* were still common in French towns in 1848. New attempts to suppress guilds were made after the 1848 revolutions but some hung on: those at Nuremberg were only closed down in 1868. Even without the backing of traditional institutions, conservative merchants, masters, and workers obstructed change. Thus, Dutch producers clung desperately to their old industrial techniques during the first half of the nineteenth century, despite growing Belgian competition. In Rhineland cities, such as Cologne, elite conservatism meant an unwillingness to invest in innovation and new technology, an attitude that only modified after 1840 with the arrival of new businessmen in the elite class.

By the 1860s, however, major changes were clearly under way. The rapid expansion of the railways (financed by the private sector in Britain and often the state elsewhere) served as a powerful stimulus to iron and steel production and consolidation, as well as to commercial integration. After 1842, the British Parliament allowed the export of machinery and various British entrepreneurs set up plants in continental cities. Thus, Isaac Holden moved to France from the West Riding in 1849, bringing new wool-combing technology, and opened up factories at St Denis and Reims. State policy increasingly swept aside old institutional constraints. In Germany, the Zollverein after 1834 promoted trade integration, and tolls and excise barriers between city and countryside were finally removed during the 1860s; in Sweden, full freedom to trade was implemented the same decade, as was the reform of commercial laws and abolition of serfdom and guilds in Russia. The spate of free trade treaties in the 1860s (such as the Anglo-French treaty of 1860) helped international integration too. Urban elites became less conservative. At Mönchengladbach, for instance, local entrepreneurs set up a spinning works using capital accumulated from the earlier domestic system, and by the 1860s it had a workforce of over a thousand. Meantime, workforces became more stable and better organized, seeking less to resist innovation than to modify its impact and share in its benefits through greater union organization and strikes.

During the late nineteenth century, urban industrial production took off. At Holden's worsted spinning factory at Croix, near Roubaix, output increased thirtyfold in the half-century up to the 1890s. Fuchsine dye production at the Badische factory at Ludwigshafen soared over a hundred times between 1871 and 1902, making the factory the biggest producer in Germany. Factories became widespread in many industries, generated by the spread of steam power and (after about 1900) by electricity, which enabled continuous production as well as reduced costs. In the Limoges porcelain industry, the number of steam engines doubled in the last years of the nineteenth century, while the factory workforce nearly trebled in size. At Warsaw, the corps of factory workers rose almost six times between 1879 and 1914. Early factories were often

small and retained traditional workshop elements of production. But
the trend was towards larger-scale units. About 1896, 37 per cent of
Swedish factories employed above 200 workers, and some years later over
a third of Basel workers laboured in factories with more than a hundred
employees.

Firms grew markedly in size and by 1900 a shift was taking place away
from family firms. In the towns around Lille and in the Ruhr, small
businesses fell sharply in importance. At Strasbourg, the number of brewing
firms declined from seventy-one to six in the late nineteenth century, while
Warsaw's metal industry came to be dominated by just three great firms.
Similarly, Milan after the turn of the century witnessed the consolidation
of large enterprises, and in many places the power of large companies was
reinforced by the spread of cartels.

Factory production was only part of the picture, however. What we see
is a dual manufacturing structure developing, as workshop output (and the
family firm) held on to its position in specialist trades, niche industries,
and the low cost sector. At St Etienne, the new bicycle industry was split
between a small number of large firms, employing hundreds of workers, and
several dozen small enterprises having only a handful. In industries under
pressure from factory production, small employers frequently resorted to
female and other forms of cheap labour to stay competitive. At Toulouse,
most manufacturing units employed less than ten persons, but a substantial
increase of output occurred, as in the hat industry, through an upsurge in the
number of firms, the adoption of small-scale innovations, the targeting of
overseas markets, and, not least, the feminization of the workforce (by 1911,
90 per cent were women, compared to 14 per cent in 1821). Groningen's
large firms with their better wages and conditions employed mostly local
inhabitants, while newcomers to town had to work in lower-paid, more
insecure, artisanal jobs.

Probably the most traditional and fragmented industry was the construction sector. Work boomed in the late nineteenth century, due to the
growth of private housing and large-scale commercial and public works.
The rebuilding of Paris under Napoleon III engaged at its peak a fifth
of the metropolitan labour force. In greater Berlin, the number of building workers nearly doubled between 1880 and 1910, but the number of
firms rose at about the same rate: throughout the period they employed
on average only about fifteen workers. Fragmentation was not the only

problem: the constraints of the land market and the emergence of building cycles of boom and slump further contributed to instability in the industry.

III

The strength of urban industry by the First World War was in its capacity to diversify. There was a growing move into engineering, the electrical, and chemical industries, optics and car and aircraft production, the latter boosted by the war. In Leeds, the declining textile trades gave way to new employment in engineering and ready-to-wear clothing, while Coventry turned to car and bicycle manufacture when its silk and watch-making sectors declined. After the war, consumer industries proliferated, linked to the spread of electricity and improved living standards. New manufacturing capacity sprang up in old and new centres. In the 1930s, for instance, fifty US firms set up factories in West London, a number of them producing vacuum cleaners and other domestic appliances. At the same time, new firms flourished in smaller provincial towns—thus, car manufacture at Oxford and Luton. The Great Depression and subsequent wave of protectionism caused a crisis in staple urban industries like textiles, iron and steel, and shipbuilding, though some rationalization, modernization, and diversification had begun before 1939.

After the Second World War, the rapid economic recovery involved the resurgence of urban manufacturing capacity across Europe. Older urban industries like textiles, shipbuilding, and iron and steel expanded to meet replacement demand, along with new energy-intensive sectors, including cars, consumer durables, electronics, and chemicals. At Birmingham, for instance, the car industry saw high levels of capital investment and large-scale construction of new, highly mechanized factories (paid for and let out by the council), together with rising manufacturing productivity. In cities across Europe, the building industry boomed due to post-war reconstruction and massive housing programmes, growth fuelled by the introduction of new industrialized building techniques (one Soviet housing agency proclaimed 'Here We Assemble Homes Like Others Assemble Cars!').

However, by the 1970s and 1980s, large-scale manufacturing had run into severe difficulties due to the higher costs and reduced domestic demand caused by the oil crises, mounting international competition, poor

labour productivity, and limited investment in new technology. The sharp
reduction in Europe's share of world trade in manufactures had a huge
impact in the large metropolitan centres and industrial cities. London's
manufacturing labour force fell from 1.5 million at the start of the 1960s,
to 600,000 in 1985, just as half a million industrial jobs disappeared in the
Paris basin over the two or three decades after 1974. Metropolitan cities
were affected across Europe from Brussels to Rome and Vienna, though
one or two of the Mediterranean cities like Athens and Lisbon bucked the
trend (see Table 13.1).

In old-established industrial towns, especially in Western Europe, the
crisis in large-scale, so-called Fordist manufacturing was acute, often
starting in the 1960s. In the Valenciennes and Sambre region, on the
French–Belgian border, the 1960s and 1970s saw the restructuring and
rundown of the iron and steel, coal and textile industries, and a rapid
growth of urban unemployment. Birmingham's manufacturing sector contracted by 13.3 per cent in the 1960s; engineering, electrical goods, vehicles,
and textiles all suffered—heralding much greater declines in subsequent

Table 13.1. Changes in economic structure (%) in large metropolitan regions in
Europe, 1980 and 1990

Cities	Manufactur. Industries		Total secondary		Commerce, hotels, restaurants		Banking, insurance, market services		Total tertiary	
	1980	1990	1980	1990	1980	1990	1980	1990	1980	1990
Greater London	18.8	12.1	24.3	18.2	15.2	12.1	35.0	48.6	75.6	81.8
Greater Paris	24.2	19.7	30.0	23.6	16.3	14.9	33.9	42.7	70.0	76.4
Brussels-Capital Region	13.2	11.8	19.0	16.3	21.8	18.9	28.8	37.2	81.0	83.7
Randstad Holland	20.1	17.6	26.5	22.6	16.4	17.1	28.9	36.8	70.9	74.2
Rome	14.7	9.6	21.5	13.8	14.2	16.8	25.1	34.7	76.3	85.3
Madrid	21.4	18.1	26.9	24.6	19.8	20.5	30.1	31.9	72.6	75.1
Vienna	25.7	21.3	33.3	27.1	21.2	18.3	20.4	32.5	66.6	72.6
Scandinavian capitals	18.1	15.4	24.3	21.5	17.6	14.0	24.3	33.1	74.8	77.8
Lisbon	20.0	24.1	26.5	30.1	24.9	23.8	19.7	21.0	70.3	66.2
Athens	21.5	21.7	28.3	27.0	19.0	17.0	20.8	19.7	70.1	70.9

Source: Adapted from C. Elmhorn, Brussels: A Reflexive World City (Stockholm, 2001), p. 146. Based
on changes in value added percentage (value added refers to the additional value created at a particular
stage of production or economic activity)

years. In the Manchester area, total manufacturing employment fell by more than a third in the years 1951–76.

Industrial contraction was not universal in European towns at this time. In some of the Ruhr towns decline was delayed by active state intervention, modernization, and the development of new engineering specialisms. In northern Italy, the Nordic countries, France, and Germany new consumer, engineering, and high-technology industries (often associated with science parks) grew up in the 1980s and 1990s, usually in towns away from the old industrial centres. Often, there was a new emphasis on decentralized or smaller unit production with flexible workforces. Post-Fordist production thus inherited some of the features of the earlier workshop system. In Alsace, many of the old textile factories disappeared, but new biotech and environmental firms emerged at Strasbourg and Colmar, boosted by heavy foreign investment, cross-border linkages and government subsidies. Developments in outer Northern Europe were particularly significant as a number of towns (in conjunction with the state and private sector) promoted the development of new advanced industries linked to health care, and information and communication technologies (ICT). Swedish towns, affected by a decline in the 1960s and 1970s, saw industrial employment recover in the 1980s. At Oulu, in northern Finland, the growth of innovative clusters of industries in electronics, telecommunications, and software was facilitated by close links with the local university (including the creation of a nearby technology park in 1982) and by state industrial policy that targeted small companies. At the end of the twentieth century, key new industries, including ICT, were still concentrated in urban areas, but new technology enabled a more polycentric structure in which smaller places like Oulu or Cork in Ireland could compete in the global knowledge market. In consequence, towns in the Northern region of Europe have become leaders in the adoption of ICT, frequently outdistancing Western Europe.

Nonetheless, the general collapse of old export industries in European towns, with many of the specialist industrial cities of Western Europe particularly affected, was a decisive watershed in European urban history with important social and other repercussions. Thereafter much of the volume of urban manufacturing employment in European towns was sustained by basic sectors such as construction and the food and drink industries. Here, there was often large-scale consolidation through the formation of national and international corporations.

IV

Dramatic decline in the large-scale manufacturing sector in European cities after the 1970s was counter-balanced in part by a surge of the service sector which helped, to some extent, to stabilize urban economies (see Table 13.1). Already, in 1978, 45 per cent of the labour force in German cities comprised white-collar workers, against 42 per cent in industrial occupations. Exceptions (and those still suffering high unemployment in the 1990s) were the specialist industrial centres, particularly in heavy sectors such as iron and steel or coalmining, where environmental contamination and the nature of the labour force (mostly male blue-collar workers) made it more difficult to transform the local economy through the expansion of services.

As we know, the tertiary sector was already important in European towns by 1800, and there was an almost inexorable rise from the 1860s and 1870s. In London, in the seventy years up to 1911, two thirds of all new jobs created were in services and transportation, and a comparable growth is found in Paris. If the trend was most marked in metropolitan centres, something similar occurred across the urban economy. Thus, Basel's service sector, including commerce and transportation, advanced from 28 per cent of the active population in 1870 to 40 per cent in 1910. What we see is that major traditional services like domestic service, commerce and distribution, the drink and entertainment trades, the media, and professions generally expanded or were transformed, while new or hitherto minor sectors, such as transport, utilities, clerical work, and public service, grew strongly. Particularly striking was the rise of the banking and finance sector. In urban services, as in manufacturing, there was a powerful interaction of continuity and change.

Employment-wise, domestic service remained one of the largest tertiary occupations in the nineteenth-century city. With the growth of bourgeois housing and domesticity, there was an almost insatiable demand for servants. In Britain, the number rose from 1.2 million in 1851 to over 2 million before the end of the century. Workers were mainly women, often young country girls seeking their first job in town and having limited access to manufacturing work. After the First World War, however, numbers diminished sharply as middle-class households mechanized and old household chores such as laundry, cleaning, or baking disappeared, and services were bought in from specialist outside suppliers.

By contrast, commerce and distribution generally went from strength to strength. Ever since the Middle Ages overseas trade had been one of the economic foundations of the European city, and the nineteenth century saw a rapid growth of commerce with the Americas and Asia—often with those colonial ports and cities noted in Chapter 12: thus, world trade grew at an annual rate of 4.8 per cent between 1860 and 1890. In the last decades, this included a growing volume of food supplies and oil carried by new refrigerated ships and tankers. International trade was heavily concentrated in the great ports that invested heavily in dockyard infrastructure. In Britain, the four leading port cities controlled 60 per cent of all shipping. Concentration of this type was encouraged by consolidation in the shipping industry: by 1905, seven German shipping lines owned nearly two thirds of national tonnage.

Yet global trade should not divert our attention from the mounting importance of intra-European commerce, stimulated by tariff liberalization, industrialization, and modernization spreading across the continent. Even in Britain, the leading global trader, almost half of all the shipping in British ports before 1914 came from Europe. Expanding European and coastal commerce gave wide opportunities for second-rank ports to develop. Thus, Malmö in Sweden prospered as a corn export centre, and smaller British ports like Aberdeen, Plymouth, Sunderland, and Bristol profited from buoyant coastal business. Calais did well from cross-Channel traffic after the arrival of the railways in the 1860s, while new port works from the 1870s boosted its European and international import trade. In the twentieth century, Europe's overseas commerce continued to grow strongly, but a growing share fell under non-European control, and, as we noted in Chapter 12, the number of successful European ports (and port employment) declined sharply at the end of the period.

As for distribution, traditional markets and fairs continued to have some distributive role into the late nineteenth century, even in more advanced urban areas. In the Forez area of France, including St Etienne, the number of fairs doubled and markets quadrupled during the nineteenth century, because of the great volume of local trade. In Russia, the establishment of a fair at Nizhnii Novgorod in 1817 gave a tremendous boost to the town, drawing up to 2 million visitors there in the 1860s. Indeed, the incidence of fairs rose strongly across the Russian Empire into the late nineteenth century particularly in the most expansive districts, until the arrival of the railways finally terminated their role. However, by 1900, the sun had set over the old distributive system, and Europe's markets were steadily reduced to selling a small range of fresh products, whilst ancient fairs had largely degenerated into funfairs.

Specialist wholesale merchants, already present before 1800, became ever more important in the bigger towns as they built up extensive networks of agents and retail clients. Wholesale warehouses developed in Paris during the 1830s and 1840s and were often located near railway stations. Later in the century, Moscow was the biggest wholesale centre in Russia, sending supplies to traders in the south and east of the country, but even smaller provincial towns by this time hosted a cluster of wholesale merchants, who provisioned town and countryside.

What about retailing? As we saw in Chapter 8, modern-style shops were already quite numerous in West European cities by the eighteenth century, but both luxury outlets and corner stores multiplied rapidly after 1800. In Britain, the number of shops rose by over 300 per cent in the first half of the nineteenth century, well ahead of the rate of urbanization, but the pace of growth fell back in the later nineteenth century as the market became saturated and retail consolidation started to occur. Elsewhere, the advance was equally rapid, if somewhat later. Shops in Vienna trebled in number between 1870 and 1902, while the increase in the Parisian suburbs was eightfold over roughly the same period. Smaller provincial towns saw a surge too; in Swedish country towns retail outlets often doubled in number during the late nineteenth century.

Luxury retailers proliferated especially in the great cities. Already, in the 1820s, London's Regent Street had become a fashionable shopping parade with its glass shop fronts, shop blinds, pedestrian pavements, and street lighting. Luxury outlets occupied fashionable arcades or *passages* with glazed roofs and gas lighting where affluent customers could be cosseted from inclement weather and protected from beggars. Paris, in the 1820s, had over a hundred *passages* and others opened in London, Brussels, Milan, and French and British provincial cities Another variant on the same theme was the bazaar: London had fifteen bazaars, among them Soho bazaar, established in 1816, where more than two hundred traders sold in multi-level galleries.

All this was a prelude to the arrival of the department store in the mid-nineteenth century. Central Paris under Haussmann offered the perfect home, and Le Bon Marché opened its first shop there in 1852, before moving to purpose-built premises in 1869; the world's largest department store, it employed 4,500 staff by 1906. Paris soon boasted an array of department stores, and most major cities (including Moscow) followed suit. Arguably the grandest, London's Selfridge store, opened in 1909 in a new steel-framed building (one of the first of its type in Europe), which had eight floors, 100 departments and 1,400 employees. By 1895, German towns claimed 120 department stores, and within a couple of decades four times that figure.

Department stores pioneered a spectrum of modern retailing methods: large, brightly lit glass windows; elaborate window dressing and interior design; electric sign advertising (after 1900), along with artistic posters, billboards, and media 'events'; heavily promoted 'sales'; and, for those tired of shopping—tea rooms, tinkling music, and talkative hairdressers. Large bevies of women staff catered for the flux of female customers. By the First World War, department stores were the stars of the retail trade, their success the product not just of entrepreneurial flair but of bourgeois affluence, the enhanced social autonomy of middle-class women, and quickening travel from the suburbs.

The rise of small stores catering for the urban lower classes was no less striking, with a great variety of different types. Paris, in 1848, possessed a hundred stores selling ready-to-wear clothes, and by the end of the century several thousand. A similar trend appeared in Germany and other European cities. Many small shops were set up by migrants in poor neighbourhoods, starting up with credit from wholesalers. Poorer women ran part-time corner shops to supplement family incomes, and in the early nineteenth century some small shopkeepers doubled as traditional street traders. London may have had as many as 45,000 itinerant traders in the 1850s. In Russian cities, street trading continued into the early twentieth century, but elsewhere police action increasingly drove them off the main streets, confining them to poorer neighbourhoods.

By the end of the nineteenth century, the retail trade was transformed in other ways, such as the rapid spread of chain stores with multiple outlets. Multiple food stores first appeared in British towns during the 1850s, and by 1885, thirty-one firms had over ten shops; by 1910, the figure was 114. The retailing structure established by the First World War, combining department stores, chain stores, and independent retailers, continued until the late twentieth century. Department stores penetrated middle-rank towns and suburban areas, and by the Second World War had extended their appeal to the better-off working classes. Chain stores continued to spread, while independent shops survived either as luxury outlets or as small corner stores in poorer neighbourhoods, selling largely on credit.

Retailing was restructured in the late twentieth century with important implications for cities. Factors influencing this development included lower-class affluence; the growth of private cars; the redevelopment of town centres and demographic decentralization. The general trend away from manufacturing towards services also played its part. Chain stores massively consolidated their power in the retail business, particularly in food sales and basic commodities. Large-scale investment was channelled into purpose-built store complexes, combining several chain-store outlets. One of the first in Britain was the Whitgift Centre at Croydon in South London in the 1960s, and by 1994 the country had over 800 urban superstores and 62 hypermarkets (each having more than 5,000 square metres). Chain-store complexes of this type, appearing in many bigger European cities by the 1990s, not only seized a large share of retail trade but moved the focus of retailing to the outskirts of towns and adopted the style of North American shopping malls with their standardized, privatized, and socially controlled space. One common result was the decline of more traditional department stores and independent retailers in town centres. In small French towns, the number of specialist shops fell by about 20 per cent between 1979 and 1993, and the picture was increasingly widespread in European cities by 2000.

Shops were not the only important retail activity in modern cities, of course. Another traditional component of the urban tertiary sector was the drink trade and entertainment sector. During the nineteenth century, drink outlets proliferated, some of them doubling as shops. While the upper and bourgeois classes tended to move away from public drinking, poor men flooding into towns turned to drinking-houses for refreshment, lodging, sociability, and support. In France, the number of *debits de boissons* rose by a third in the two decades after 1880 (with 40,000 in Paris), while the incidence of mainly urban premises trebled in Switzerland before 1900. Growth was particularly strong in industrial towns. At Bochum, it was said 'taverns existed ... like sand at the seaside'.

Echoing early modern denunciations, bourgeois criticism was trenchant. Traugott Siegfried decried how 'the public houses replaces the church, drowns the school and strangles the private house'. After 1900, measures were taken by state and town authorities to curb the number of popular drink outlets. London's public houses declined from 7,800 in 1900 to 5,900 in 1915 and 4,900 in 1938. Norway adopted prohibition during the 1910s, as did Russia, followed by Finland in 1921. The drink trade suffered not just from greater official regulation. Rising lower-class living standards generated a widening popular appetite for new types of leisure entertainment—from organized sports and dance halls to cinemas (see Chapter 15).

Equally crucial, drinking premises lost ground to more specialist catering businesses. Restaurants and chop houses appear in Paris and London from the later eighteenth century, and a hundred years later restaurant chains had arrived, such as the Duval restaurants in Paris which employed 1,200 staff. Across the Channel, Lyons' first teashop opened in 1894, and by the 1920s the company ran 250 premises in high streets up and down the country. Cafés became brightly lit, fashionable, and ornate: Budapest had several hundred by 1900, while Paris's café-concerts became intoxicating attractions for foreign tourists and the suburban bourgeoisie. Serving both businessmen and tourists were hotels—growing in number, scale, and luxury. At Vienna, a number of elite hotels were opened on the Ringstrasse in the 1870s; in Amsterdam, they were a phenomenon of the 1880s; and, by 1900, Budapest had fifty or more.

During the twentieth century, the drink and entertainment business saw the growth of international chains, particularly after the 1950s, but much of the sector has remained fragmented which has enabled a flexible response to shifts in urban fashion and demand. Popular take-away outlets (such as British fish-and-chip shops) had already appeared around 1900, replacing itinerant traders, and numbers multiplied after the Second World War: for instance, snack bars (*klein-cafeteria*) in Dutch towns increased from under 200 in 1951 to over 3,200 a couple of decades later. From the 1970s and 1980s, changing attitudes towards alcohol (particularly among young women), heavy marketing by the drink industry, and official deregulation, powered an upsurge of bars, nightclubs, and other outlets, often seen as important for the revival of urban economies and employment. At Manchester, in 1989, the drink and entertainment trades were estimated to generate £350 million and employ 10,000 workers in the city and region.

Already, before the First World War, entertainment venues were a striking feature of big city streets. The Finnish writer Sigurd Frosterus wondered at London's Strand district where 'stretching in unbroken chains all along the pavements are theatres, restaurants and music-halls, a fantastic electric architecture'. Already significant before 1800, the arts made a growing contribution to the urban economy. As we will see in Chapter 15, there was a proliferation of music concerts and venues, while theatrical activity and employment likewise expanded: in French cities like Bordeaux and Marseille several hundred people worked in the city playhouses, and by the First World War Berlin had three opera houses and fifty theatres, plus music halls, employing an extensive labour force. In similar style, the growth of the art market supported a rising number of artists and dealers.

For publicity, entertainment industries depended heavily on the media sector, and here again we find significant innovations. From the late nineteenth century, the traditional publishing business was particularly buoyant. As one French writer exclaimed: 'Books rise, overflow, spread; it's an inundation'. In the 1920s, 19 per cent of all Berlin workers were employed in printing. The media sector was further boosted by the rise of the popular press from the 1880s (aided by a drastic fall in the price of paper), along with the growth of mass advertising: by the 1890s, several North American advertising agencies were established in London. During the inter-war era media activity diversified and work in radio, television, film, and show business took off, principally in and around the metropolitan centres. Before 1940, the BBC was employing almost 5,000 staff, mostly in London, while Rome during the 1960s had up to 6,000 people working in the film industry, plus many thousands more in television, music, and radio. In 2004, 8 per cent of Helsinki's labour force was employed in the media and related cultural business, including important music exports.

Influential in European towns since the Middle Ages, the professions had a mounting impact on the urban economy and contributed to the growth of what has been termed information-based human capital. If the churches and clergy had waning influence after the First World War (see Chapter 15), lawyers and legal firms retained a powerful presence at all levels of the urban order, and medical services expanded strongly, at least from the 1870s. During the first part of the century, the ratio of medical practitioners to population was stable or declined, but thereafter numbers increased substantially. Germany had 3.2 doctors per 10,000 inhabitants in

1876 and 4.8 by 1909; in England the comparable figures were 6.5 (1871)
and 7.1 (1911). Especially notable was the growth of town hospitals: in
England many voluntary hospitals were built from the 1860s. In Germany
the number of hospital facilities doubled in the last quarter of the century.
As well as doctors, nurses and auxiliaries increased strongly, along with
psychiatrists, dentists, medical quacks, and patent medicine suppliers. A
further great surge of medical services occurred during the late twentieth
century as a result of social welfare reforms.

Another long-established sector, education, expanded as a result of the
introduction of compulsory schooling in most European countries by 1900
and the development of the higher education sector. In Germany's big cities
per capita expenditure on schooling rose sixfold between 1890 and 1910,
a trend matched in England by local authority expenditure on schools. In
French and English provincial cities, a flurry of new urban universities and
linked scientific institutes sprang up in the decades before and after the
First World War, often with support from local councils and businessmen.
In Brussels, the wealthy entrepreneur Ernest Solvay founded a series of
research institutes linked to the Free University. At Vienna, the growth of
medical specialization and new institutes for chemistry and physics created
a *Mediziner-Viertel* in the city.

An even more extensive growth in schooling and universities, largely
state-funded, occurred after the Second World War. Both in capitalist
and Communist countries, education became a central pillar of the new
economy of late twentieth-century cities. St Petersburg/Leningrad, in the
1980s, claimed about 300 scientific institutes and 41 institutes of higher
learning, employing a fifth of the metropolitan workforce. The following
decade, French provincial cities shared at least twenty universities with
over 30,000 students each. The surge of student numbers was universal
across Europe (fourfold in Spain and Italy, sixfold in Finland 1946–80),
giving a vital stimulus to local urban economies. Thus, in 1994–5, Cardiff
University in south Wales created a total income of £97.2 million for the
city and £102.1 million in the region as a whole. Higher education has
also been critical in supplying labour for new industries and services. With
heavy state and municipal investment in the sector, Nordic cities gained a
highly educated workforce: in Helsinki, in 2000, a fifth of the population
(over fifteen years) possessed a university degree.

V

If the expansion of the tertiary sector owed much to the diversification or transformation of established services, still the nineteenth century saw the development of major new areas. One was the advance of utilities such as water, gas, and electricity. Gas and water companies spread during the early nineteenth century, but most were private companies and services were geared to better-off households. London had its first gas supply in 1814 and the main British cities soon after. Major cities in Western Europe followed suit (Brussels in 1819, Rotterdam and Berlin in 1826), and by mid-century those in the Northern and Mediterranean regions began to install gas supplies. Though starting in the Middle Ages, water supply remained very incomplete well into the nineteenth century: up to 1870, only 3 per cent of German towns had a central water supply and the great majority of European townspeople had no access to piped water. In the later part of the century, however, investment in urban utilities was ratcheted up. In Britain, investment in gas and water supply more than doubled between the 1850s and 1890s, while that in new electricity plant soared from £0.3 million in the 1880s to £5.2 million during 1911–20. Services reached a growing proportion of the urban population, including those in the poorer suburbs. Before the First World War, all Dutch towns had gas supplies and 93 per cent of Berlin homes enjoyed piped water. North European cities copied the West European model, but elsewhere services remained patchy. Russia, in 1913, had only 220 electricity stations, half the number in Sweden. In Western and Northern Europe, utilities were increasingly brought under municipal control (see Chapter 16), but in other regions foreign companies led the development of services up to the First World War.

Public transport experienced massive expansion in the later nineteenth century. In the earlier period, many communities were still compact enough for most journeys to be done on foot, but in the principal cities horse omnibuses arrived from the 1820s, and horse tramways from the 1860s (for example, Berlin 1865, Liverpool 1868). Around the turn of the century, many leading West European cities established municipal services, including new electric tram or underground systems, with the result that passenger numbers soared. About 1900, Berliners made 459 million trips on public transport (trams, buses and railway) or 185 a person per year; 400 million passengers travelled on the Paris metro system in 1914, and 761 million in 1937. Public use was heaviest in big cities, reflecting greater social and economic demand but also their capacity to fund services. Employment in the sector grew strongly. London Transport was set up in 1933 with 70,500 staff and by 1947 the figure stood at almost 97,000.

Public transport services continued to develop after the Second World War: in 1971, over a million people a day used public transport in Paris. From the interwar period, however, private-car traffic grew inexorably, especially in the bigger centres. In Stockholm, the number of cars quadrupled between 1918 and 1930, while Amsterdam's more than doubled in the years 1928–39. But the main growth came after the Second World War. Hamburg had 80,000 cars in 1938, but 430,000 thirty years later, with the trend accelerating thereafter. In the four biggest Dutch cities, car ownership jumped from about fifty per 1,000 inhabitants in 1960 to over 300 in 1980. The European car stock (outside the Soviet bloc) doubled between 1975 and 1995, and from the 1990s car ownership rose sharply in East European cities too. The growth of private transport had major economic and environmental implications, fuelling pollution and traffic congestion (by the 1970s, traffic speeds were down to walking speeds, especially in provincial cities like Exeter or Gothenburg), and boosting demand for car parks and garage services. In West Berlin, the number of garage businesses increased fourfold between 1951 and 1979.

As we shall see in detail in Chapter 16, the expansion of state and municipal government from the late nineteenth century covered a wide range of new areas—not only education, utilities, and transport but planning, public health, housing, green space, and cultural and leisure activities. One result was a massive inflation of municipal employment—after its relative insignificance in the early nineteenth century. Despite the financial upheavals of the inter-war era, civic expenditure on municipal staff and activities continued to rise, but the main take-off occurred after 1945, with municipal budgets sometimes increasing four or five times. In Soviet bloc cities, a similar expansion of administrative services and employment occurred. Even in the 1980s and 1990s, when state and local finances suffered greater problems, urban employment in this sector proved surprisingly resilient in most countries.

VI

The development of banking and financial services further exemplified the transformation of the tertiary economy. Though banking and related activities had been a high-value function of European towns since the thirteenth century, the number of urban players had been small, primarily confined to a changing cast-list of commercial metropoles, and the economic effects had been mostly confined to overseas trade and state lending. The nineteenth century saw a widening impact, as London and Paris replaced Amsterdam as leading international financial centres. London became the prime market for state loans, as well as settling bills of exchange; here, large merchants banks operated alongside numerous private firms involved in domestic banking. Paris attracted many foreign banks and financed a great deal of foreign and domestic trade. Frankfurt and Brussels also strengthened their financial standing in the first half of the century: Frankfurt hosted 117 banking houses by 1837. Railway construction, the growth of joint-stock banking, and the increase of trade boosted banking activity. London and Paris, for instance, were heavily involved in the export of capital and railway investment after the 1850s.

The late nineteenth century saw a number of crucial changes. Paris lost its leading position after 1870, but London and Brussels enhanced their international standing, while the new imperial capital Berlin replaced Frankfurt. Sustained by the burgeoning of world trade and capital flows, and by the new stability created by the spread of the gold standard, London enjoyed a glittering era as the home of many big banks and international companies, as an insurance market and as a stock exchange (its market capitalization more than that of New York and Paris combined). As a consequence, the working population of London's financial district doubled. Imperial Berlin likewise saw the rise of big banks and the stock market, while Brussels banks became heavily engaged in overseas investment. Generally, there was a shift into public joint-stock banking.

In the metropolitan centres, banks and insurance companies increasingly erected or took over grandiose premises on main streets—contributing to the emergence of central business districts. No less striking, specialist financial services moved down the urban hierarchy. Banks and insurance offices, frequently the branches of metropolitan firms, multiplied on the high streets of provincial towns as well. Western Europe was very much in the lead in these developments. Most Spanish cities had few banks before the twentieth century and those in Nordic cities tended to be small.

During the twentieth century, national and international banking firms entrenched their position in European cities, and similar trends are visible in the insurance and related industries (though, again, national variations are evident). Employment in the sector grew strongly. Already, by 1925, 100,000 Berliners, perhaps 5 per cent of the labour force, were working in banks and financial services. In terms of global finance, the rise of New York after the First World War overshadowed European centres, though London hung on to key international functions. From the 1950s, a substantial expansion in the domestic financial sector occurred in European towns (outside the Soviet bloc) as rising affluence, consumerism, and the housing boom stimulated both private savings and borrowing. At the international level, London began to reassert itself as a key financial player, joined by Zürich and, to a lesser extent, Frankfurt. Increased capital flows from the 1970s, deregulation of exchange controls, stock-market liberalization at Frankfurt, Paris, and London (1984–6), world trade expansion, and the advent of new financial instruments promoted banking and insurance company consolidation in the major centres. In 1996, London, Frankfurt, and Paris hosted three of the top seven world futures and options exchanges, while the capital turnover of the London Stock Exchange rose to £32.2 billion in 1996. By 2004, London employed 311,000 in its financial sector and Frankfurt 90,000. Foreign banks played a dramatic role in the new developments: London had over 100 in 1961, and more than 450 by 1987; by comparison, Stockholm had only twenty-six foreign banks in 2006. Alongside banks, company headquarters were strongly concentrated in metropolitan business districts.

Yet, for all the dynamism, wealth, and impact of banking and associated services, especially in a small number of late twentieth-century European cities like London and Paris enjoying global financial status, the sector's overall effect on the wider urban economy should not be overstated (see Table 13.1). In terms of general economic restructuring, more traditional urban services, including retailing and the drink and entertainment trades, were also important. Here, consumption has been driven not merely by local urban residents, affected by changing lifestyles, but by the expansion of the tourist market, which grew in the 1980s at 9.6 per cent per annum. In 1982, London had 20 million visitors—double that in 1962—and, of these, up to 8 million came from abroad. Vienna, in the early 1990s, had 7 million overnight tourists, accommodated in 340 hotels. Numbers continued to rise thereafter. One consequence of the growing segmentation and specialization of the tourist market (mass tourism complemented by cultural and business tourism) was that tourist revenues benefited a growing range of urban economies at the end of the period, including lively metropolitan cities like Dublin, Amsterdam, Manchester, and Barcelona; historic second-flight capitals like Edinburgh, Prague, and Helsinki; seaside and resort towns, and smaller historic communities. For instance, at Beziers, near the Franco-Spanish border, the city marketed its August *corrida* festival so successfully that in 2005 a million visitors crowded the town, generating millions of euros for the local economy.

VII

As the Beziers example illustrates, in the last decades of the twentieth century, city authorities across Europe were heavily engaged in the marketing of their tourist and other economic and cultural attractions, often in fierce competition with one another. In the case of resort towns, this kind of urban marketing dated back to the eighteenth century. Indeed, civic intervention in the urban economy has a long pedigree, as we discussed in earlier parts of this book. Though state reform and deregulation policies swept aside traditional civic guilds and other municipal controls in the early and mid-nineteenth centuries, in subsequent decades many city councils sought to promote urban growth and employment through infrastructure improvements, investment in local education and science, utilities, and public transport. Up to 1939, towns remained busy trying to attract new industries.

After the Second World War, direct municipal influence over the local urban economy was squeezed: by the impact of growing state intervention and centralization (in which city councils often served as little more than agents of state policy), and by the trend towards national and international economic consolidation and integration. Thus, the great manufacturing crisis of the 1970s and 1980s was so widespread and structural that the limited efforts of municipal authorities to reverse the collapse or moderate its effects proved fruitless. Only concerted action by state and local authorities, along with the trade unions and private sector, as in Germany, could have any effect and then only on a selective basis. Towards the end of the twentieth century, however, a growing number of municipal governments became more active again, supporting industrial and research innovation (see Chapter 16), and also promoting the national and international visibility of their cities as tourist, financial, and commercial centres. As well as advertising, heavy stress has been put on the construction of new conference and transport facilities (airports, tramways), and the staging of international sporting competitions or cultural spectacles. Such events have frequently generated considerable dividends for the local economy. Barcelona's Olympic Games brought 9,264 million US dollars in direct investment, while Helsinki's year as one of the European Cities of Culture in 2000 yielded about 67 million euros for national GDP. Cities have exploited such events not only to boost employment prospects but also to initiate large-scale urban renewal projects (Manchester's staging of the Commonwealth Games in 2002 helped the regeneration of a 1,120 hectare area of east Manchester).

VIII

In this chapter, we have argued that the strength of the European urban economy in the modern period was rooted in its composite, multi-stranded nature, combining both traditional and new sectors. While West European cities forged ahead in the creation of a dual system of large-scale factory-based and smaller workshop-type manufacturing during the nineteenth century, this process was paralleled by the massive remodelling of the service sector. Pivotal in Western Europe was the role not just of older established metropolitan and regional cities but of specialist industrial towns (and regions), Atlantic port cities, and leisure towns. Economic development in other urban regions lagged behind and only partially replicated West European trends, with large-scale industrialization and specialist industrial centres largely confined to the cities of Eastern Europe, especially under Soviet rule. Elsewhere, industrial expansion was smaller scale (without specialist manufacturing centres), but the relative growth of the service sector was even more pronounced.

In the late twentieth century, the great manufacturing crisis of the 1970s and 1980s, poorly recognized at the time, badly affected the urban economy. West European cities suffered most of all, and numerous specialist industrial towns found it difficult to adapt and move in new directions. The crisis of the great and lesser ports, discussed in Chapter 12, further affected this region. Up to a point, urban recovery in Western Europe was engineered through the articulation of new or expanded service activities. In the new competitive environment at the start of the twenty-first century, however, it is arguable that the urban economies of outer Northern Europe have done best, developing a wide range of advanced and high-technology industries, often based on decentralized, smaller-scale production in medium and smaller centres, as well as supporting new commercial and other services.

In this chapter, we have described the long-term economic achieve-ments—and setbacks—of European cities. Even in the expansive phases, there might be mixed social dividends, with the better-off classes prospering, while poorer residents faced acute problems of housing and social depriva-tion. The complex social implications of the economic transformation of European cities must be addressed in the next chapter.

14
Social Life 1800–2000

Caroline Luckhurst was the daughter of a middle-class family in late Victorian London. Her father was a prosperous railway official wearing a top hat on public occasions and residing in a spacious semi-detached villa in the leafy suburbs of Blackheath. A younger child, apparently disadvantaged in the family, Caroline moved out of the capital to the countryside, worked as a servant in a large house, and met there the youngest son of a small farmer. Much to her family's anger, they married, had several children, and fell into relative poverty. In the 1930s, the youngest child, Kathleen, moved to the local county town, first as a domestic servant in a large household, then as a shop assistant. Kay (once in town she shortened her name, taking that of a famous film star) fell in love with and wedded a young man, then living with his siblings in a tenement in a slum area of town. Both of them ambitious, if poorly schooled, after the Second World War they set up a corner shop, did quite well, bought a car and television and began to take holidays. When her first husband died suddenly, Kay married again—this time to an Irishman, one of the growing number of ethnic immigrants in booming, post-war Britain. Always keen on education, Kay used all the new opportunities of the Welfare State to benefit herself and her family; her only child went away to university, the first in the family, and her grandchildren likewise. In her old age at the end of the twentieth century, with her comfortably furnished bungalow and colourful garden, Kay had moved upwards and on her own terms, as a woman, into the suburban respectable classes.

The history of Kay and her family offers a small light—through one pane in a huge lattice window of stories—on the great complexity of social experience in the nineteenth and twentieth centuries. As in the urban economy, profound transformations occurred to many aspects of urban social life during the two centuries after 1800. Mobility became ever more complex, with the onset of large-scale, longer-distance, trans-national and later extra-European immigration, so that by 2000 many larger European cities and towns had become multi-cultural communities. In addition, European cities experienced: the rise of the bourgeoisie with its problems of cohesion and downward social mobility; the increasing prosperity, social mobility, and social status of the urban lower classes during the course of the twentieth century; and, not least, the new social standing and role of women like Kay, in the past normally pushed to the margins of urban life. These and many other social changes—from the extinction of urban mortality crises and the growth of social segregation to new attitudes to the young and elderly—contributed to a reconfiguration of the social order of European cities. All this had important implications for those key structures in urban society—the family, the neighbourhood, and the community. In the following sections we examine these issues in turn.

Change was often limited or localized in the first part of the nineteenth century. Real acceleration occurred in the climactic era of rapid urbaniza-tion and economic growth from the 1870s up to the Second World War. This was followed by the consolidation and amplification of many advances in the late twentieth century, albeit with some reverses towards the end of the period. Progress was spatially uneven too. As in patterns of urban and economic growth, cities and towns in Britain and Western Europe served as the forcing ground of social transformation, followed (with a time lag) by those in Northern Europe and elsewhere.

I

Urban social life at the start of the nineteenth century retained many traditional features and strong links to the countryside. It was not just that townspeople, often recent arrivals from villages, took part in farm work and wore peasant dress (sometimes, as in Moscow, until the end of the nineteenth century), but that in many urban communities the social structure remained dominated by traditional elites who kept close ties to the land. Though the French Revolution had given a powerful shock to such elites, the Allied triumph after 1815 often restored or reinforced their position—at least in the short term. In capital cities such as Vienna, Berlin, London, and St Petersburg aristocratic landowners enjoyed an important social presence. In St Petersburg, in 1843, the nobility comprised over

10 per cent of the population, while Hungarian nobles led the patrician class of Budapest until the 1880s. In provincial cities the pattern was more variable, but old-fashioned regional centres like Poitiers in south-west France, Seville, centre of the fertile Andalusian plain, or English country towns, still hosted influential groups of landed families, often with close ties to the Church. In Western Europe, by the mid-nineteenth century, such old-fashioned elites were increasingly overshadowed by new social classes, though they held on to their influence longer in Eastern and Mediterranean Europe.

Other aspects of the urban social structure after 1800 also retained traditional features, though modified by those new developments of the eighteenth century that we discussed in Chapter 9. If the bourgeoisie in metropolitan cities was starting to flex its social muscle, in many towns the social hierarchy remained much more traditional with the old commercial elites in charge and the middling ranks divided. Lower down the social scale, occupational distinctions were reflected still in dress (including colour of clothes), and skilled workers organized themselves where they could, through guilds and *compagnonnages*, as well as early unions or mutual clubs. Here, the main concern was, as ever, to protect their social status from the flood of unskilled and casual labourers, domestic servants, and the destitute, many of them pouring in from the countryside. As we shall see, urban destitution, rising since the late eighteenth century, was endemic in towns even in the more dynamic regions.

Despite some broadening of the social hierarchy in the Enlightenment city, urban communities into the early nineteenth century encompassed relatively small numbers of socially and politically privileged citizens or burghers—essentially better-off adult men—and large communities of those excluded from the established social order. Such underprivileged embraced not only the elderly and the sick, often impoverished, but large numbers of unskilled young men from poor backgrounds. If sons of the elite and middling classes did better through improved education and other opportunities, the majority of young people suffered a deteriorating position. The same was true for women, who still enjoyed few legal or political rights and limited economic opportunities. As we know, wealthier townswomen in the late eighteenth century organized sociable gatherings, took part in enlightened leisure and cultural activities, and joined together in religious and philanthropic activity. But circumstances for many lower-class women were very difficult from the late eighteenth century.

282   SOCIAL LIFE 1800—2000

II

Immigration continued to be one of the most necessary, dynamic, innovative, and disruptive forces in urban social life. Accelerating urbanization in the modern era was only made possible by a huge influx of immigrants. Paris had as many as 150,000 immigrants in the years 1856—66, and net migration to Rotterdam was running at 43,000 during the 1890s. Here and elsewhere, inflows oscillated widely from decade to decade, according to the state of the labour market and external factors such as the extent of rural hardship. Turnover rates stayed high: 40 per cent of single female migrants to the Belgian textile town of Verviers left within a year, 70 per cent after two years; at Düsseldorf, more than three-quarters of all immigrants departed inside twelve months. Nonetheless, between 60 and 90 per cent of urban growth across Europe during the nineteenth century derived from immigration.

As in earlier times, high inflows of newcomers were made imperative by the weak natural growth of population: at Moscow, the immigration rate was four times that of natural increase during the last decades of the nineteenth century. One critical factor was the high level of mortality, particularly among children. Asiatic cholera which swept (via Russia) through European cities in the 1830s, killing 2,200 in Vienna (1831), 20,000 in Paris (1832), and 3,365 in Stockholm (1834) returned sporadically until just before the First World War (10,000 died at Hamburg in 1892 and Naples had a serious outbreak in 1910—11). Typhus, tuberculosis, and smallpox (despite the advent of vaccination from the 1790s) also continued their ravages. Too often, the incidence of disease was heightened by environmental deterioration: overcrowded housing, polluted water supplies, and inadequate sanitation were all squalid bedfellows of rapid urban and industrial expansion. At the Belgian industrial city of Seraing, mortality rates climbed in the decades up to the 1870s and heavy infant mortality was a terrible scourge. Crude urban death rates in Germany rose from the 1830s, with mortality peaking in the 1860s and 1870s. At Moscow, where two thirds or more of all houses lacked water supply and mains sanitation, infant mortality remained at 300 per 1,000 until the 1890s, but the situation was not much better in West European cities. While urban mortality remained above rural levels, urban fertility rates were variable, in some communities lower than in the countryside, but in industrial towns often higher.

Overall, migration continued to dominate the pattern of urban growth during the nineteenth century (as in earlier times), but the pattern of movement changed. Traditionally, immigration was often short term and seasonal, contributing to the high turnover rates. Poorer migrants, many of them travelling on their own, came from the neighbouring countryside to escape agrarian downturns, the problems of rural industry, or to supplement rural incomes. Frequently, they planned to send money home and return to their villages as soon as they could: work in town was part of their strategy for rural survival. However, by the last decades of the nineteenth century, seasonal or short-term migration, particularly in Western Europe, was falling as a result of agrarian restructuring and the widespread collapse of rural industries: thus, movement to town became more permanent. No less vital, linked to the spread of the railways and the acceleration of urban growth, was the shift towards longer-distance movement. At Eindhoven, in the Netherlands, the share of local incomers fell from 80 per cent in the mid-nineteenth century to under 60 per cent after the First World War. On the Mediterranean coast, Provence ceased to be the main source of workers for Marseille's labour market, as a growing proportion of newcomers travelled from across France and Italy.

Urban labour markets had growing externalities, which were in great part defined and energized by migration. Foreign immigration became widespread in the decades before 1900. At Basel, Swiss migrants were outnumbered by Germans and Italians; 40 per cent of workers at the French textile town of Roubaix had come over the border from Belgium; and, in the Ruhr, industrial towns like Oberhausen and Bochum accepted growing numbers of migrants from the east, including many Poles. Not just industrial towns but capital cities and ports, already with significant ethnic populations in the early modern period, attracted a multiplicity of minorities. In 1911, 7 per cent of the Parisian population was foreign, while on the Black Sea Odessa's inhabitants included many French, Italians, Greeks, Germans, and Jews (34 per cent of the total by 1914).

Improvements in urban mortality towards the end of the nineteenth century reduced the indispensability of migration for urban growth, but did not obviate its importance. Standardized mortality rates fell—at Manchester and its environs from twenty-six per 1,000 in the 1870s to twenty-three in the 1890s—and there were similar declines in London, Berlin, Stockholm, and other European cities and towns, mainly through improvements in infant mortality. Basic here were environmental and hygienic advances, especially the provision of piped water supplies to poorer districts, the installation of sewage systems, and greater recognition of the need for cleanliness in the home (discussed below). For the first time since the Middle Ages, urban mortality rates fell below those of the countryside, while acute infectious diseases as the leading cause of death began to give way to the role of chronic and degenerative diseases. Even so, the consequent boost to natural population increase in towns was balanced by an almost simultaneous reduction in urban fertility rates. The explanation seems to have been the growing popular adoption of *coitus interruptus* as a form of birth control, this happening at a time when parents became aware that more of their children were surviving infancy. In addition, improved living standards led to changing parental aspirations for their children and a new perception of masculinity, where a large family came to be regarded as a sign of fecklessness rather than virility.

Yet, despite these radical changes in the demographic equation, migration remained a leading component of urban growth up to the Second World War, especially in East European and Mediterranean cities where improvements in urban mortality rates were slower to arrive (Russian cities experienced severe mortality crises in 1915–22 and 1929–34), and rural push factors retained their force. Three-quarters of all urban growth in Soviet cities between 1922 and 1940 stemmed from immigration and this influx continued after 1945, just as newcomers constituted the major part of Rome's population increase up to the 1960s. By contrast, in cities in Western Europe and Nordic countries like Sweden and Finland, natural increase came to predominate before the Second World War.

What was the social impact of this large-scale immigration? How well did newcomers adapt and exploit the opportunities for social mobility in the modern city? Undoubtedly, the high turnover of newcomers noted earlier reflected in part the difficulties many encountered on arrival in urban communities. As in the past, most movement to town was socially horizontal: rural labourers or peasants with few skills or resources mostly drifted into the massed ranks of the urban poor, while country girls found jobs in domestic service. Generally, the better-off and better-educated movers from the countryside had greater chances of advancement. Family, neighbourhood, churches, and clubs and societies played a vital mediating role in the reception of newcomers. Neighbourhoods, with their public houses, cafés, dances, and entertainments, brought together newcomers and residents. Village and regional organizations in towns rendered help and assistance in finding work and credit. By 1939, Paris had nearly 150 mutual societies for Auvergnats in the capital, just as cafés in Athens, identified with particular rural localities, acted as a nexus of support for new arrivals.

At the same time, migrant support mechanisms could function as a barrier to integration and social advancement. At Turin, certain types of close-knit family network whose members worked in the same trade proved less helpful in the integration process than ones that had a more open and diversified character. The wider urban context was equally important. Those cities, particularly the bigger ports, which had a long history of immigration were often the most welcoming, specific districts taking wave after wave of newcomers.

The same opportunities (and difficulties) of integration through clubs, churches, credit networks, and the like faced the escalating numbers of ethnic migrants from the end of the nineteenth century. Some, like the Finns in St Petersburg (24,000 in 1881) or Walloon Belgians in French textile towns, found it easier to integrate than others—for example, Irish Catholic arrivals in British Protestant towns, Poles in the Ruhr's indus-trial centres, or the small contingents of Chinese in ports like London, Rotterdam, and Hamburg. Violence against Irish and Chinese migrants was common, as were attacks on Jews in Vienna and other cities of the Austro-Hungarian Empire before 1914, attacks that foreshadowed their widespread harassment during the inter-war period and culmin-ated in the horrendous extermination of Jewish communities by the Nazis.

After the Second World War, when native, largely rural migration to European towns contracted (except in the Mediterranean region), large-scale ethnic migration took its place, initially from Southern Europe, and then by the 1960s from outside Europe, notably the Caribbean, Asia, Turkey, and North Africa. In many instances, companies recruited workers for booming post-war urban industries, though by the 1970s states were starting to restrict this type of movement. Foreign migrants frequently made homes in inner-city districts that were deserted by native residents moving to better housing and green space in the suburbs. In greater London, the total population declined from 7.5 million to 6.6 million between 1971 and 1981, while the non-native population (mostly of Asian and Afro-Caribbean origin) rose by 130,000 to 1.2 million.

Ethnic migrants in the twentieth-century city never formed the majority of the population, unlike their rural counterparts in the nineteenth and earlier centuries. Admittedly, in the last decades of our period, a number of West European cities acquired large first- and second-generation immigrant communities: at Amsterdam, almost half the population by 2000; at the Midland city of Leicester, over 90,000 New Commonwealth residents by 1991—more than a third of the population; again, nearly a third of Brussels' population in 1995 was of foreign nationality. However, such figures may overstate the urban proportion (because of the suburbanization of native residents), and in most European cities during the 1990s non-nationals comprised a much smaller share of the population: 16.8 per cent at Stockholm, 13.1 per cent in the Paris agglomeration, 10.2 per cent at Lyon, and about 9 per cent in Vienna. Though immigrant numbers continued to rise in the 1990s and after, the overall incidence in Europe has remained significantly lower than in North American cities.

As with earlier ethnic migration, tension erupted between the new minorities and some host communities in the late twentieth century. Race was less important than wider urban trends, not least the poverty and unemployment consequent upon the collapse of the manufacturing sector in which many immigrants worked. Aggravating the situation were poor housing conditions for minority groups both in inner-city areas and in the new social housing estates on the periphery (as in Paris) where they were settled. Moves towards community self-help through residential closeness, voluntary and religious activity, and other networking may have heightened the suspicion of native residents. Cutbacks in civic social services after the 1980s further aggravated the problems of integration. On the other hand, where municipalities actively designed and promoted policies to integrate minority groups they proved relatively successful (see Chapter 16).

Immigration remained vital for urban success throughout the period. The demographic impact continued into the late twentieth century when migrants, particularly ethnic newcomers, became ever more significant, due to the accelerating fall in fertility and population replacement rates. But migrants also brought new ideas and techniques, new contacts, and new urban strategies. In the early nineteenth century, an influx of migrants changed the character of Cologne's ruling elite and aided the city's upturn as a leading commercial and financial centre. At Antwerp, too, immigrants were heavily implicated in the city's revival as a great port. Culturally, it is impossible to think of the dazzling achievements of pre-1914 Vienna without recognizing the influential role of marginalized Jews—musicians, writers, and intellectuals, among them Mahler, Schoenberg, Freud, Adler, and Schnitzler. In the inter-war era, Russians, Jews, Americans, and other foreigners contributed largely to the image of Paris, part myth, part reality, as a vibrant artistic and intellectual cosmopolitan world, which excited admiration across the continent and beyond. To benefit most from immigrants, cities needed to be open to their reception into the urban mainstream.

III

Migration has been structural to the diversity and dynamism of the European city since the Middle Ages. However, many of the other social developments affecting the European city after 1800 were radically new. By the 1860s, the rise of the middle class or bourgeoisie (the term is used interchangeably) led to a fundamental reshaping of the urban social order. The new bourgeois ascendancy was driven by growing prosperity among the manufacturing, commercial, and professional classes, as a result of urban growth and industrial expansion. In Paris, for instance, the value of inherited property, largely owned by the middle classes, rose sixfold between 1847 and 1911. Other factors behind bourgeois success included their growing political influence due to parliamentary reform, and the relative economic eclipse of the old agrarian interests and landed elites.

The bourgeoisie were always a relatively small social group in nineteenth-century cities, ranging from 8 per cent of occupied males in big commercial and administrative cities to 1 or 2 per cent in industrial towns. Though the decline of the guilds ended many traditional divisions between middling groups, the bourgeoisie always exhibited fault lines and tensions, shaped by differences of wealth, by religious and political divisions, and by the nagging fear of social failure and downward mobility. So what gave the bourgeoisie its coherence and social force? Up to the mid-nineteenth century, it defined itself against those traditional elite groups, which it sought to replace; later on, it increasingly proclaimed its ascendancy over the emerging lower orders. No less important was the way it created over one or two generations a distinctive urban lifestyle which became an influential model for European society as a whole.

The nineteenth-century bourgeoisie had a profound sense of space and boundaries. In domestic life, their households put a growing stress on privacy. This was facilitated by the steady separation of business and private life and the increasing size of the home in which rooms were set aside for men (the library or study), women (the bedroom and salon), children, and servants (the latter with their own separate entry and staircase). Urbanization also had a growing impact on urban space, contributing to social zoning. In English cities, middle-class villas, often with walled gardens, multiplied on the fashionable, western edges of town, away from the pollution, poverty, and perceived disorder of urban centres, in the process creating segregated suburbs. One French visitor observed in 1855, 'The practice of London residents... living in the outskirts and using the town only for offices and shops for the transaction of business', but this trend was widespread elsewhere by the 1870s, whether in industrial centres like Wolverhampton and Leicester or smaller county towns like Maidstone.

In continental cities, the nascent bourgeoisie preferred to live in spacious purpose-built apartment blocks which were located either in redeveloped central districts (as in Paris) or on the edge of the old city (as in Vienna). However, even here, the villa model was popular among the well off by 1914, made aesthetically fashionable by the Garden City movement and financially astute by rising rents in city centres: Moscow, St Petersburg, Stockholm, and Berlin saw a wave of suburban villas after 1900, though they were less visible in Mediterranean cities. Internally, the domestic and gendered privacy pioneered by the English middle classes was gradually adopted by the continental bourgeoisie from the 1840s. And everywhere the bourgeois home became an elaborate showcase to consumerism, stuffed with heavy furniture (often in pseudo-antique style), pictures, plants, pianos, velvet curtains, and a clutter of decorative trappings—together denoting comfort, respectability, and status. A family's history and identity could be constructed through its furniture and decorations, items being inherited or received as nuptial gifts, while the ideal bourgeois home was self-contained, orderly, and clean (as far as the heavy furnishings allowed), kept so by a troop of domestic servants.

Bourgeois housing provided the backdrop for the celebration of the family—drawing on the eighteenth-century culture of sensibility but transforming it through romanticism into a new cult of domesticity. Private life was dominated by family sociability such as dinners, parties, and musical soirées in which women played an active part. In Swedish cities, as elsewhere, the middle-class celebration of birthdays, name days, and wedding anniversaries highlighted the lifecycle of the family. As levels of infant mortality subsided and forms of family planning were adopted by couples, expectations for children increased. Education was emphasized for both sexes, with learning at home followed (for boys) by grammar school and university; this not only opened the door to employment but demarcated the social separation from the unschooled lower classes. Following the example of the old patrician classes, the marriage of children was viewed as an indispensable tool for engineering family fortunes, just as intermarriage reinforced the dynastic, expansive character of the bourgeoisie, extending its networking across region and nation. Marital failure, as in the case of Caroline Luckhurst with whom we began this chapter, led to social de-recognition for the individuals concerned.

In counterpoint to a respectable private life, successful bourgeois men took a prominent part in urban public life (though their wives had a more limited role outside the home, at least until the last part of the century). As well as dominating municipal politics before the First World War, they were heavily involved in religion, and equally influential in established and dissenting churches and secularist movements. Though party politics and religion might divide middle-class groups, other public activities offered more of a common ground. As will be seen in Chapter 15, cultural activities such as concert-going and voluntary associations provided neutral, integrating arenas for the middle classes to gather, socialize and organize, while facilitating links between cities and fostering growing national identity.

The bourgeoisie constructed and occupied a re-styled public space in town centres that was demarcated by new town halls, art galleries, and libraries. They were also important sponsors and patrons of ornamental gardens and promenades which became an essential feature of municipal life in the last third of the nineteenth century and enabled them to parade in their finery. Before the First World War, interest in open-air leisure led to a new pursuit of competitive sports, often organized through middle-class clubs.

During the nineteenth century, the middle classes in European cities buttressed their own sense of identity through a consummate zeal to control, improve, and reform the lower classes. Rising bourgeois anxiety over crime and political disorder (for instance, the Chartist riots or 1848 risings) gave backing, at critical points, to repressive police measures by governments. Meantime, middle-class philanthropy combined poor relief with invasions of the privacy and family life of ordinary people that would have sparked fierce resistance if it had been perpetrated on the middle classes themselves. From the mid-nineteenth century, middle-class reformism included the health and hygiene movement, and schools, museums, and libraries to educate working-class minds.

No standard bourgeois or middle class obtained in European cities during the nineteenth century. Significant differences existed between countries and cities, and as usual the bigger centres in Western Europe were in the forefront of change. In some places the bourgeoisie was more closed or fragmented than in others, and the dominant occupational groups might also vary. Yet the rise of an essentially urban bourgeoisie that displayed shared values and concerns with work and achievement, with education and a rational cultural life, had a powerful influence on urban society across the board.

By the start of the twentieth century, the social ascendancy of this class was contested—by the spread of working-class politics, improved lower-class living standards, and a growing sense of working-class identity. Initially, the challenge may have reinforced bourgeois cohesion, but in the inter-war era the position of the urban middle class was weakened by economic crises (as in 1929–32), by universal suffrage, by the decline of church-going and other bourgeois cultural activities, and by the growth of mass entertainments such as the cinema, radio, and popular music which enfranchised all social groups. Social democracy, after the Second World War, gave the last rites to a distinctive urban bourgeois identity, if not to bourgeois networking and leverage.

IV

By contrast, the formation of an urban working class was always a more tenuous and localized phenomenon, and here living standards were undeniably crucial. In the first half of the nineteenth century, the social position of the mass of lower-class townspeople deteriorated, partly because of the decline of traditional trades, and the heavy influx of rural poor. In Belgium, it was said 'since 1846 ... bands of starving women and children have poured into the cities from the countryside'. Even workers in expanding sectors were adversely affected, as we saw in Chapter 13, by bad working conditions, recurrent trade slumps, and irregular employment. There were food shortages in towns, and food adulteration and contamination was widespread. Fundamental to the social deterioration was the failure of urban infrastructure to keep pace with urbanization. Housing deficits became acute. At the port of Antwerp, the number of private dwellings grew by 30 per cent, to accommodate a 200 per cent increase of population; in Amsterdam, the comparable figures were 5 per cent and 45 per cent. The consequences were high rents, overcrowding, and the spread of shanty-towns on the urban periphery. Over half of Antwerp's poorer households had less than six square metres per person, and two thirds of its slum houses, narrow and low, were occupied by more than one family. In many towns, workers crowded into cellars, single rooms, and blind courtyards, queuing for communal latrines. In Paris, significant numbers of poor householders had no means of heating or cooking. Housing shortages were exacerbated by constraints in the land market and urban reconstruction in central districts that evicted many poorer families from their homes (at least 76,000 Londoners were displaced by Victorian railway schemes).

Civic improvement was mainly designed to service the needs of the better off, and water supply and other utilities were rarely extended to poorer districts. Industrial pollution—damp, dust, and stench—pervaded lower-class neighbourhoods. Their streets and courts were filthy, strewn with sticky mud, festering offal and other waste. Poverty levels were hardly any better than in the early modern period. In the 1810s, the number of indigent in Liège approached a third of the population, and the same proportion needed relief at Ghent and Cologne three decades later. Poor beggars crowded the streets, and flocks of unemployed and poverty-stricken dossed down in London's parks; Rome had tens of thousands of homeless beggars. Social deterioration resulted in declining urban heights—the stunting of young men in big cities—and the high death rates noted earlier.

Inadequate poor relief meant that the lower classes were driven back on the customary mixed strategy of subsistence, including the support of kinsfolk and neighbourhood. Local drinking-houses, the traditional focus of popular male solidarity, places to get loans, information, and help, rose in number and drunkenness was endemic. Where possible, poorer women aided each other with small loans of food and utensils. However, neighbourliness provided only limited help against prolonged economic and social crises. Labourers had limited access to the mutual organizations and trade unions dominated by skilled artisans. Instead, they fell back on other traditional tactics, including begging, casual jobs, loans from pawnbrokers, and petty crime. Official crime rates and the number of offenders rose strongly in England in the early nineteenth century, though the statistics may exaggerate the trend. The crime situation was probably worst in the new industrial towns and major ports with their high turnover of workers, unstable employment, and weak policing.

As in the eighteenth century, skilled workers did better than the unskilled and labouring classes. Helped by family dynasties in particular trades, they enjoyed higher wages, more job security, better housing, and greater access to schooling, and they sought to preserve these advantages through exclusive trade unions, clubs, and similar bodies, through tramping between 'houses of call' to escape unemployment, and through strikes and political activity. Even so, their position varied between trades—worst in declining sectors. In general, artisans were becoming more dependent on larger firms and, like the unskilled, were badly affected by rising food prices and general trade slumps, such as in the late 1840s.

In the later part of the nineteenth century, some of these problems persisted or got worse, as a result of accelerating rates of industrial and urban growth and immigration. Although improvements in real wages occurred from the 1870s they were reversible. Workers were still badly affected by slumps (for instance, in the 1870s and in 1889–91) and the job insecurity caused by underemployment and seasonal layoffs. Thus, Parisian boilermakers had to leave home every summer to look for casual repair work in the French provinces as a result of factory closures in the capital. Nonetheless, after the turn of the century, more sustained advances in living standards occurred. In the Ruhr towns, for instance, real wages increased by a third. Industrial concentration and the growth of larger factories offered greater job security, albeit at the cost of more relentless and continuous work, often in dangerous and degrading conditions (factory gates shut against late arrivals, fines, heavy surveillance—in one Moscow factory the toilet was elevated on a platform so anyone using it could be checked by the foreman). On the other hand, working hours steadily declined. In German cities like Leipzig they fell by two or three hours a week in the years before 1900, a trend replicated in French, Swedish, and Russian cities before the First World War.

Although improvements took place in public welfare and educational provision (see Chapter 16), housing remained the worst problem confronting the urban lower classes into the early twentieth century. In the 1880s, about half of Milan's population was jammed into one- or two-room apartments. Tenement courts at Roubaix rose from 156 in 1891 to 1,524 by 1912, when they housed 157,000 people in squalid conditions, while in St Petersburg as many as 60,000 people lived in cellars. Lacking proper streets or sewerage, shanty-towns shot up around most larger cities from Stockholm and Moscow to Paris and Lisbon, the outcome of an amalgam of factors—cheap land and rents, increased public transport, and the decentralization of employment. For all the heated public debate and media campaigns over 'slums', only minimal official intervention took place in the private housing market before 1914, with very little provision of social housing.

Even so, a growing sense of working-class identity took shape in the decades before and after the First World War, mainly in the industrializing centres of Western and Northern Europe. Economically, it was stimulated by the growth of large-scale, mainly factory production, the decline of skill and wage differentials between skilled and unskilled workers, and the long-term improvement in real wages. Reductions in seasonal migration and mobility rates, alongside increased social segregation and urban zoning, may also have fostered a greater measure of social stability and cohesion among the lower classes. Politically, trade unions (no longer dominated by artisans) and leftist political parties sought to sharpen working-class consciousness and solidarity through clubs, strikes, and other forms of mobilization. In German cities, for example, the Social Democratic Party orchestrated a host of choral, theatrical, and educational societies to capture working-class support.

Arguably, one sign of improved working-class stability and living standards was the apparent reduction of crime levels during the period. At Middlesbrough, for instance, reported indictable offences fell by nearly two thirds between the 1870s and 1890s, while burglaries declined by a half, and serious crimes by 60 per cent. Generally, the period saw a relative decline in both property offences and crime against the person: in Stockholm, for instance, homicide rates reached their lowest level in the early twentieth century. The downturn was not universal: some industrial cities in the Ruhr with high levels of immigration suffered an explosion of crime in the 1890s. Nor was it all the time: economic crises and hardship led to sharp spurts of criminality. Nor was it simply a function of advances in living conditions. Improvements in policing and the greater integration of police into the urban community, which created more working-class acceptance, also played their part (see Chapter 16).

Working-class formation was often highly localized. Strongest in specialist industrial centres and ports, it was less cogent in more traditional urban communities or where the fragmented service sector was more dominant. Class consciousness often displayed a powerful sense of identification with and loyalty to place, expressed through local celebrations, processions, poems, and the like. At the neighbourhood level, working-class life increasingly flourished, helped by improved living standards and greater stability. Though neighbourly support remained an important resource for those down on their luck, working-class neighbourhoods became more assertive, proud of their identity. Popular male sociability was long associated with the drinking-house, but from the end of the nineteenth century alternative venues started to appear, such as cheap cafés. Meantime, we see a transition to a new range of leisure activities, including sports (particularly football, primarily a working-class game), music halls, dancing, working-men's associations, and occasional day trips to the sea or countryside.

Influential after the First World War was growing action by municipal authorities, often under socialist control, to provide services for the working classes. The housing problem was progressively contained by a massive growth of social housing (discussed in Chapter 16), and extensive working-class estates were created. After 1900, water supply, utilities, sewerage, and public transport were steadily extended to lower-class districts, making them fully viable. Cheap fares for workers enabled them to reside some way from their workplace, often on the urban periphery. Better wages led to an improved diet for many ordinary families and the purchase (often on credit) of basic consumer goods such as cheap furniture and linoleum. But the picture was not all rosy. Large pockets of destitution persisted, particularly in the old industrial towns and ports hit by the Great Depression. At Lille, where 15,000 people still lived in slum courts, unemployment soared in the 1930s, diets deteriorated, and meat became a luxury. At Rotterdam, a third of families asked for municipal relief in 1935. Slum housing—overcrowded, disease-ridden, humiliating—disfigured every European town before the Second World War.

As we saw in the vignette of Kay Luckhurst's life, living standards for ordinary townspeople only really took off on a sustained basis in the expansive decades after the Second World War. Income differentials between the middle and working classes were at last reduced. In Britain, townspeople saw average income per head rise by 1,300 per cent between 1951 and 1981, as against 500 per cent in the previous fifty years. In German cities, income levels more than doubled between the 1950s and 1970s, and workers enjoyed further reductions in the working week—falling from forty-eight hours in 1950 to under forty-two hours thirty years later. In France, the forty-hour week was established in 1957 and three-week and then four-week paid holidays followed. In Soviet cities, too, living standards rose markedly from the 1960s. Increased female employment contributed to larger family incomes, while ordinary people benefited from improved medical services and a massive programme of urban social housing in virtually all countries, alongside large-scale subsidies for private housing. Public expenditure on schooling and higher education also expanded quickly, opening up new opportunities for the hitherto disadvantaged lower classes.

The old boundaries between the social classes were eroded in other ways, not least through consumerism. Per capita consumption in French towns grew by 49 per cent in the 1950s and continued to increase thereafter. By the 1970s, many of Seville's inhabitants, whether from the middle or lower classes, owned the same consumer goods, including utensils and furniture, even if those from lower levels had to work harder or longer to achieve the same lifestyle. Car ownership raced ahead and gave ordinary urban residents, like their affluent counterparts, a new mobility for leisure and holidays: the car was a great social leveller. Many employees could now move house to the urban periphery in order to enjoy the same kind of privacy and green space that the bourgeoisie had made their own in the nineteenth century. In such ways, the working-class identity of the early twentieth century, strongly spatially defined, was eroded in many European cities.

Urban manufacturing's collapse, well under way by the 1970s, had wide-ranging social repercussions. Those effects were often aggravated by cutbacks in state and municipal welfare provision after 1980. Unemployment rose sharply, particularly in the old industrial towns and port cities: at Roubaix, it soared from 6.2 per cent in 1975 to 24.5 per cent in 1990; at Duisburg, it reached a similar figure. In such places, traditional working-class communities, dominated by male blue-collar workers, were largely upended. Urban poverty made a major reappearance even in more prosperous cities, with ethnic minorities as well as manual workers worst affected. At Frankfurt, in 1994, 20 per cent of the population was living below the poverty line, including many immigrants. In Eastern Europe, the decline of Communist welfare systems contributed to the widespread increase of those townspeople living below the poverty line in the 1990s.

As we noted in Chapter 13, European urban economies often responded to the crisis by developing tertiary activities that absorbed many unemployed. Here, the growing weakness of trade unions from the 1980s and the connivance of governments led to a widespread erosion of employment rights, including the spread of casual or contract work and in some countries an increase in working hours. In general, however, living standards for the majority of townspeople were preserved, by the continuing importance of public-sector employment, social transfers, and the contribution of female employment to family incomes.

Even so, at the end of the period we discover widespread indications of increased social differentiation, particularly in West European cities. Whether such differentiation should be seen, as Saskia Sassen and others have argued, as a necessary function of globalization—including the delocalization of industry and the growth of leading cities as financial centres—remains controversial. The causation appears highly complex, linked both to economic trends, including the growth of new technology and professionalization, but also to changes in welfare policy, family structure, and ethnicity. Social differentiation has proved less acute in North European cities where states have maintained a high level of welfare provision (for instance, subsidized housing and statutory benefits). By contrast, living standards in Russian cities witnessed a massive decline in the 1990s that was associated with the opening up to an international economy, rapidly rising unemployment, reduced consumption, and forced diversification into multiple jobs—from agriculture to street vending—to make ends meet.

V

Of all the social changes affecting European cities in the nineteenth and twentieth centuries, the transformation in the social status of women was one of the most crucial and influential. European urban and gender history up to the twentieth century was largely a male-scripted discourse. For much of the nineteenth century, as earlier, the institutional and legal position for women remained restrictive—in principle, marginalizing them from the public sphere. At the same time, legal variations operated between countries, and social realities were equally variable. For better-off women, the growing celebration of bourgeois family life elevated their status both in the home and beyond. Despite their lack of legal and political rights, they might enjoy participation in public life, through religious and charitable activity, attendance at concerts and plays, and shopping. Domesticity and diffidence were increasingly cast off. Joining a philanthropic society, one Uppsala woman confessed: 'a woman ought really to work in the shadows, but the spirit of the times demanded a sacrifice'. A minority of wealthy women (for instance in Antwerp or Moscow) were actively involved in business life.

By contrast, the social condition of many lower-class women in the nineteenth century got worse. The employment market tended to work against them, since manufacturing expansion in West European cities absorbed mostly male labour. One of the exceptions was that of textiles where large numbers of young women were employed, as in braid-making at St Chamond or cotton manufacture at Ghent. However, too many of the women flooding into town from the villages were forced into domestic service, petty trading (as street traders or running a drink shop), and prostitution, the latter catering for the large numbers of male immigrants. London in mid-century was said to have 24,000 prostitutes, Paris 34,000, and Berlin 15,000 (though the figures are highly problematic). Given low wages, recurrent unemployment, and high population turnover, it is hardly surprising that common-law marriages and illegitimacy were widespread. In the Paris area, 25 per cent of all babies were born to single mothers (mostly immigrants), and in the early nineteenth century half of them abandoned their babies. With or without children, women were often left on their own, deserted by a partner or bereaved by his premature death: at Verviers, for instance, a fifth of women aged fifty were already widows. In such a difficult world, women relied on kin and the support of the neighbourhood, above all the network of other mothers, though as we noted earlier such help was probably limited by the destitution and instability of poorer districts.

From the later nineteenth century, however, the status of women was probably on an improving, upward trend. Groups of middle-class women organized and mobilized through associations to reform their property rights (secured in Sweden in 1874, Britain in 1882, Germany in 1900, and France 1907), and to gain the suffrage: Finland was the first country to award female emancipation in 1905 and other countries conceded it before or soon after the First World War. By then, middle-class women were starting to enter the universities, local government, and the professions. They became active in shaping health campaigns and arguing the cause for urban green space. Improvements in working conditions for ordinary townswomen were slower to trickle through, and contradictory trends occurred. Female employment in manufacturing declined: in the Roubaix area the proportion of female textile workers fell from 36 per cent to 29 per cent between 1896 and 1904, while at Basel female employment in the silk industry contracted by a tenth in the years before 1900. Female domestic service also started to diminish after 1900, as bourgeois families bought in services and adopted labour-saving appliances. Even prostitution probably declined as police controls increased and male migration subsided. In some sectors, female employment developed: in retailing (department stores employed contingents of women shop assistants and many small corner stores were run by women), in schoolteaching, and in white-collar jobs in business and local government. But these opportunities were greatest in the major urban centres and mainly helped better-educated women.

At the Finnish town of Jyväskylä, women complained (in 1909) of the paucity of job openings for them, and this feeling was doubtless echoed in many other provincial towns. Lack of female work might have a damaging effect on family incomes. But lack of suitable work was not the only reason for the growing trend for more women to stay at home (69 per cent at Düsseldorf in 1907, 61 per cent at Dresden). Another was the increased rate of lower-class marriage, which was probably the outcome of lower levels of mobility and better real wages rather than increased elite and Church hectoring against common-law partnerships. Also influential was the growing public emphasis on the responsibility of women for family hygiene and health. In Paris, from the end of the nineteenth century, poor women were taught hygiene at clinics and their houses were inspected. Cleanliness, the result of hard female toil, more and more defined the territory of the home, not least through those polished steps and door knockers, cleaned pavement, and window sills that presented its external face to a critical neighbourhood.

For some lower-class women, the inter-war period marked a further improvement in their status, as a consequence of better family incomes, and the expansion of social housing, with maternity and other municipal services. Women began to take greater control over their lives through the knowledge and practice of contraception. They also had enhanced awareness of social and consumer opportunities through films and radio. For those married to better-off workers in employment during the 1930s, the house, with its meagre but growing array of consumer durables, had become a home and the married woman was its manager. But not everyone was so lucky. For many working-class families, particularly in traditional industries, the Great Depression caused misery and destitution, and the housewife found it desperately difficult to cope.

After the Second World War, however, came a renewed momentum for change, particularly from the 1960s. The domestic model of the townswoman was radically revised. In most countries, a growing proportion of active women entered the labour force, mainly the service sector. Rising female participation rates in higher education, now open to all social classes, facilitated the access of women into the professions and public and business life, though with continuing discrimination over salaries and promotion (in 1978, female wage rates in Britain were only 60 per cent of the male equivalent). Increased female employment collided with the older vision of the domestic private family. Further expansion of housing in the suburbs helped consolidate this vision, as did the spread of family-friendly consumer goods such as the sofa (and three-piece suite) and the television (at least initially). In part, the tension between female work and family life was reconciled by the growth of public and private transport, the spread of labour-saving appliances in the home, increased male participation in household chores, and better social services, including greater provision of nursery education.

In the last years of the twentieth century, female employment levels continued to rise, boosted by the post-industrial transition to an urban service economy; in 2005, activity rates were highest in the Nordic countries. Wage rates still lagged behind those of men, but the gap was narrowing. On the other hand, female identification with domestic married life waned markedly. From the 1970s, marriage declined sharply in most parts of Europe and common-law relations became more widespread; by the end of our period, entry into marriage often came after the creation of a family unit and not as the precondition for one. At the same time, divorce increased, roughly trebling in most North and West European countries between 1965 and 1985. By the 1990s, nearly half of all marriages in Nordic countries ended in divorce, and up to 40 per cent in Western Europe; by contrast, Mediterranean and East European rates were lower, though in Russia the incidence was high: at Tambov, for instance, 80 per cent of marriages ended in divorce within a few years. Most striking in the late twentieth-century city was the growing presence of women in public life—overturning the picture of exclusion and marginality that we have seen since the Middle Ages. Thus, the proportion of female members of Helsinki city council rose from under a third in 1961 to nearly a half by 2001.

VI

If the period saw a revolutionary breakthrough for urban women, what about those other minority groups such as the young and elderly who have recurred in this study? As in earlier periods, young people were marginalized in nineteenth-century urban society and sought mutual support and entertainment in neighbourhood games like street football, in drinking, and other pursuits which were denounced and harassed by the authorities. Well into the twentieth century, campaigns were launched against hooligans, *edelweisspirates* (in Nazi Germany), teddy boys and rockers in England, and *stiliagi* in Soviet Russia. But, already before 1900, the churches, middle-class reformers, and politicians, concerned at the urban social crisis and the large numbers of young migrants and other young people in cities, made greater efforts to help and integrate them: through expanded public education and medical services; through church missions, sport, camping, and other leisure activities; through involvement in civic festivals; and, from the end of the nineteenth century, through specific youth organizations like the British Boys' Brigade, Girls' Friendly Society and Scouts, or German Jugendwehr and Protestant boys' leagues. In the inter-war era various political parties sought to recruit youth support through the Socialist Guild of Youth, Hitler Youth, or the French right-wing Camelots du Roi.

The period after the Second World War witnessed an important advance in the social status of young people, as a result of improved educational opportunities, including access to universities (leading to large student populations in many university towns), higher incomes (real wages for adolescents rose 50 per cent in Britain 1938–58, twice the rate for adults), and the efflorescence of goods and services directed at young people.

Relaxation of family and neighbourly controls gave more social freedom to young people—exemplified by increased teenage pregnancies, drink consumption, and shopping. Since the 1980s, however, de-industrialization, suburbanization, unemployment (35 per cent of the 20–24 age group at Marseille in the 1990s), and new work practices have tightened the pressure on the urban young, challenging their improved social status. Once again, the authorities have tended to focus on the problems associated with young people, including crime, street disorder, and drug and alcohol abuse.

For the elderly, the twentieth century offered significant advances in social and economic status. In the pre-modern period, old people, particularly widows, comprised a significant contingent of the urban poor and this remained true through the nineteenth century. Though poor relief gave some limited aid, families and neighbours were often the main carers. The major change here came around the turn of the century due to the inauguration of state pensions. By the 1940s, 80 per cent of elderly Britons were in receipt of state benefits and subsequently this became universal. Improved living standards and medical services, especially after 1945, contributed to increased longevity. In the early modern period, the proportion of the population over sixty was less than 10 per cent; by 1985, it was 21 per cent and continuing to rise. The elderly also benefited from the post-war economic boom. In the 1980s, British pensioners enjoyed two thirds of average non-pensioner income; in Finland, in 2004, the comparable figure was about 70 per cent. All this encouraged greater mobility, higher consumption (including holidays), and more autonomy for older people. On the other hand, by 2000, rising costs of benefits and medical care for a growing elderly population generated mounting financial problems for state and municipal authorities. This, in turn, prompted the introduction of forms of health rationing and moves to raise retirement ages. Despite improvements in public support, relations and neighbours still continued to function as an essential resource for the advanced elderly at the end of our period.

VII

By the close of the twentieth century, the urban social order had experienced drastic change, a process that had eradicated many of the structures that we saw emerge during the medieval and early modern periods. Old elites had largely faded away by the second half of the nineteenth century. The earlier highly segmented social hierarchy had been eclipsed by the rise of an expansive bourgeoisie, by the later advent of a working class, and after the Second World War by the erosion of class boundaries.

Yet, if the old urban social hierarchy was replaced, the wealth pyramid in towns proved more persistent, flattening notably after the Second World War, but becoming more acute at other times, in the early nineteenth century and again at the end of the twentieth century. One of the most striking developments of the period, as we have seen, was the increase of social segregation, marked by the rise of middle-class villa estates and, after the First World War, the spread of distinct areas of social housing, in this way turning parts of suburbia proletarian. Such estates were particularly extensive in West European cities from Bradford to Lyon and Vienna. Not that the growth of proletarian suburbs was inevitable. As we shall see in Chapter 16, municipal policy could have a significant role in moderating social segregation both in the suburbs and inner-city areas.

For all the relative success in integrating migrants, women, young people, and many elderly into the urban community, despite the massive secular improvements in living standards for the bottom half of the urban population, despite increased opportunities in the post-war era for social mobility such as Kay Luckhurst and her family enjoyed, major communities of exclusion remained in 2000. Among them, one might identify unemployed manual workers, single-headed families (having considerably lower incomes than conventional households), isolated elderly, and disadvantaged ethnic minorities, often excluded from jobs in the regenerated urban economy (metropolitan expansion may suck in suburban workers leaving high city unemployment rates). Many of these groups have become concentrated together in specific areas of big cities—particularly in inner-city districts or isolated suburbs. New slums have been created of deprivation, poor housing, and high mortality (the indicators, as at Manchester, often several times worse than for better-off districts of the same city). Such problems were most marked at the end of our period in West European cities, and least visible in Nordic cities, where municipal policies on social integration had a more positive impact.

Social deterioration in new slum districts at the end of the twentieth century spawned a new fear of crime as a generalized urban experience. Public perceptions were fanned by an upturn in crime rates, especially for violent offences, problems of drug abuse and alcoholism, media exaggeration, civic retrenchment (leading to cutbacks in policing in some cities), and changes in the pattern of policing (for instance, more motorized patrolling and the growing role of security firms). Up to the late 1990s, only 28 per cent of mayors of large French cities believed that the crime situation in their communities was very worrying and 80 per cent blamed the media. But the situation on the ground, notably in the deprived areas of big centres, was clearly deteriorating at the time. In the St Denis area of Paris and the northern banlieues, beset by high levels of poverty, immigration, drug-trafficking, and unemployment, crime was running in some places at 200 offences a day; violent incidents on buses rose by a third in 1997. But major eruptions of crime and disorder from such areas into European city centres were relatively few. Even in cities experiencing major ethnic and social strains, municipal welfare policy and support for family and neighbourly action, as well as policing, could be effective in containing and ameliorating problems.

What, finally, about those structural units of urban society—family, neighbourhood, and community—so crucial for urban social life since the Middle Ages? The private family, as we have seen, experienced a cycle of rising social importance, as first the bourgeoisie and later the working classes invested it with demographic, moral, and cultural functions. In the later twentieth century, the family lost some of this wider significance, at least among native populations, through divorce, single-headed households, and female work outside the home. However, in some ethnic communities the family, including the extended grouping, retained a wide range of traditional responsibilities, not least as a bulwark against deprivation and a restraint on anti-social behaviour.

The neighbourhood, too, has seen important changes in its role in urban society. For the nineteenth century middle classes, the concept was transferred to the segregated space of apartment blocks or leafy suburbs with church-going, dinner parties, and systems of social control. For lower-class residents, the neighbourhood was consolidated, indeed may have enjoyed its heyday in the later nineteenth and early twentieth centuries, due to increased social segregation (often via social housing) and the reduced mobility and greater affluence of households: at this time, women continued to play a key role, as in the past, in defining and controlling norms of behaviour. But, in the later twentieth century, the functioning of many neighbourhoods was undermined by the decentralization of population (often to high-rise apartment blocks), the growth of motor traffic (making the street unsafe for children, street games, or neighbourly gosssip), and the rapid increase of female employment away from the home. In some places, municipal planning policy sought to revive the role of the neighbourhood, but with uncertain results. In the Dutch city of Groningen, a newly built neighbourhood had planned communal areas, but the residents did their best to privatize these spaces. By comparison, in ethnic districts of cities, the traditional functions of the neighbourhood—as a nexus for networking and mutual support, as a stage for street entertainment and celebration—often retained greater vibrancy.

Since the nineteenth century, notions of urban community have been challenged by massive spatial fragmentation, social change, internationalization, and the centralizing power of the state. As we shall see in the following chapters, during the late nineteenth century determined attempts were made by urban leaders to reinvigorate notions of community identity through wider political participation, municipal interventionism, and the remodelling of city centres; in the later twentieth, new efforts were made with the same objectives, often in conjunction with the commercial sector. For all the social upheavals of the modern era, European cities have retained a relatively high level of community identity, and here urban cultural institutions and the urban landscape, our next subject, have made a critical contribution.

15

Culture and Landscape
1800–2000

In Hjalmar Söderberg's novel *Doktor Glas* (1905), the Swedish doctor declares: 'Never have I felt happier and prouder to be from a city than when I returned from the countryside as a child one autumn evening and saw the lights glowing... Now I thought those poor devils back in the country will have to ... trudge about in the dark and the dirt'. During the modern period, European city culture, increasingly self-assured and multifaceted, wiped off the last traces of rural tradition, and European cultural life turned urban. Not only did metropolitan time, synchronized by the railways from the 1840s, become universal, but so too, albeit slowly, did the new pattern of meal times pioneered in European capitals during the eighteenth century (see Chapter 7). The world of towns largely effaced the distinctive cultural universe of the countryside, and even villagers identified themselves as coming from the local town. Urban cultural ideas, activities, and institutions were ever more powerful in national society. The advance was most striking in Western Europe, slower in other regions, but, by the close of the twentieth century, urban culture had become all pervasive, its impact facilitated by the decline of agrarian economies, communication changes, and the potency of the urban message.

Paradoxically, while cultural life in general became urbanized, the distinctive identity of the city itself was challenged by a great variety of forces. Internally, the city experienced a loss of its old physical coherence through spatial expansion and fragmentation, while the dominance of local elite figures as cultural power-brokers was overturned by social change after the First World War. Externally, the civic voice had to adapt to the growing impact of national and international influences, such as the spread of foreign films and the Modernist design movement. Yet there were important continuities too. One was the role of Christian religion, so critical in the medieval origins of European city identity, and still a significant ingredient in the matrix of urban cultural life, at least up to the Second World War. In the same way, much of the secular culture of the modern city—music-making, art, theatres, and museums—built on the heritage of the Enlightenment city which was discussed in Chapter 10.

In this chapter, we examine in turn religion and education; the growth of bourgeois secular culture and the remaking of popular cultural activity; the rise of so-called mass entertainments; the changing image of the city; and, finally, the shaping of the urban landscape, through the prism of private and public buildings and planning.

I

For many of Europe's townspeople, church-going and religious belief remained their most important cultural commitment into the early twentieth century. Church attendance was highest among the bourgeoisie, albeit with important differences between countries. For the middle classes, church attendance reinforced class identity and gave opportunities for social networking at the neighbourhood or community level. In Britain, many of the urban middle classes, particularly in the industrializing towns, belonged to Protestant sects. At Manchester, in 1851, 34 per cent of church-goers went to the city's thirty-two Anglican churches, while 42 per cent attended the eighty Nonconformist chapels. But the Church of England retained important support among urban elites and in old regional centres and country towns. In France, the bourgeoisie was mainly split between Catholics and Republican secularists, while in German cities church-going was still largely defined by the religious frontiers established in the seventeenth century, though Prussian liberals were increasingly critical of the Church on political grounds. In Italian and Iberian cities, the Catholic Church largely retained its powerful monopoly.

Church leaders in the nineteenth century were fearful of the threat posed to religion by rapid urbanization, high mobility, factory work, and pauperization, all apparently opening the doors to irreligion. In fact, urban attendance remained relatively high, often spurred on by denominational competition. For many ordinary townspeople, fresh from the countryside, religious affiliation offered not only continuity with their rural origins and values, but a set of symbols and connections which enabled them to gain a new identity and standing in an otherwise uncertain social world. The link between neighbourhood and church was strong. At French towns, like Lille, popular and neighbourhood fetes, both formal and informal, were numerous, among them the lamplighters' fete at the end of September when children went in processions through the streets singing and carrying candles. In the Rhineland, the Düsseldorf area had 2,000 religious processions a year, many of them linked to parish feasts and fairs. There was also widespread support for other forms of popular religiosity such as church burials and weddings.

Even so, by the later nineteenth century, the pressure on urban religion was mounting as church attendance figures waned. As early as 1869, only 3 per cent of Berlin Protestants attended services and by 1913 the rate was down to 1 per cent; in Stockholm, during the 1880s, only 10 per cent of adult men communicated. Elsewhere in European cities, the figures were higher but the trend was downward by 1900. Fundamental was the failure of many churches to remodel their traditional organization—number and distribution of churches and clergy—to face the challenge of rapidly expanding cities. In large centres like Berlin and Barcelona the deteriorating ratio of churches to population led to enormous parishes. Church building programmes were under way in Belgium and Britain by the 1840s, but came much later in German and French cities: in Russia, the acute shortage of church provision lasted until the Revolution.

By the later nineteenth century, churches suffered attacks from radical political parties, and mounting competition from new leisure attractions, including clubs, sports, and commercial entertainments. The churches fought back, sponsoring a dense mesh of music and youth organizations, sports clubs, and self-improvement groups. In Belgian cities, Catholics set up networks of working-men's clubs and other bodies from the 1880s, and, in France, the Catholic Church supported over 1,700 sports clubs, mostly in towns. Denominations competed with one another over provision. In the Netherlands, both Protestants and Catholics founded a wide variety of sport, gardening, singing, and youth clubs. Church activists adopted new commercial developments. Before the Revolution, for instance, St Petersburg preachers used magic lantern shows to proselytize, and in the inter-war period many churches copied elements of the new mass culture such as illustrated magazines, mass meetings, and services on the radio.

Nevertheless, during the early twentieth century, church participation was in steady decline. In Amsterdam, membership of the Dutch Reformed Church slumped by nearly a half between 1909 and 1930, and the proportion of those professing no religion more than trebled. Leading Spanish cities like Madrid and Barcelona, echoing to fierce republican attacks on the Catholic Church, watched participation at Mass fall as low as 7 per cent in some parishes. Across Britain, attendance at Sunday schools halved in the years 1910–56, though with variations between towns. The picture was not entirely gloomy. Even where church attendance slid, popular support for traditional religious rites and the local church remained active. Middle-class church-going held up better than among the lower classes, though even this was dipping in the inter-war era, due to alternative attractions: by 1939, religion was ceasing to be a key ingredient defining elite or bourgeois identity. In Soviet Russia, secularism was officially proclaimed, the Orthodox Church was harassed, churches demolished, and church membership declined to a small proportion of the urban population.

During the late twentieth century, a collapse of most types of Christian belief and activity took place in many European urban communities, sundering that close, almost umbilical relationship between city and Christianity dating back to the late Roman era. As well as a drastic fall of church attendance from around the 1960s, there was growing indifference to religious rites of passage and to the local church (linked perhaps to the erosion of neighbourhood identity), and a loss of belief in a personal God. The decline of religious belief was most marked in the Nordic countries, less common in the Mediterranean region (outside Spain). Among the various influences were rising urban living standards, comprehensive welfare and medical services, greater personal mobility, and improved education. Not that religion completely deserted the European city. Ethnic minorities from Asia and North Africa brought a kaleidoscope of mosques and temples, sometimes located in former Christian churches: in 2000, for instance, the British city of Leicester had twelve Muslim mosques and ten Hindu temples, many of them full to overflowing at prayer time. In Russia, the collapse of Communist rule triggered a revival of the Orthodox Church: at St Petersburg, after 1989, about ninety churches were returned to church control and most were restored, while a further forty new churches were constructed, mainly in the suburbs.

II

Along with the Christian faith, education has been another cornerstone of urban identity since the medieval era. For the nineteenth-century bourgeoisie, the education of their children became a prime concern and form of class label, and this encouraged the growth of secondary schooling (often at Church or private institutions), leading on to university studies. One result was the marked increase in number and size of urban universities before and after the First World War. Municipal councils frequently played a part in the founding or expanding of higher education institutions, particularly in the creation of science departments.

Lower-class take-up of education was more sluggish. Literacy levels, normally rising in the eighteenth century, dipped or stagnated after 1800, as urbanization and immigration from the countryside accelerated and social conditions deteriorated. At the industrial town of Mulhouse, only 28 per cent of male conscripts in 1841 could read, and in Mediterranean cities illiteracy rates remained above 80 per cent. Even among the better paid, attitudes to schooling were ambivalent. Parisian artisans often demanded education as a right but were less certain what kind of education they wanted. Schooling was often seen as being manipulated by the ruling classes for social control purposes. Compulsory free education was introduced by the Prussian state in 1825, but initially lower-class interest, as at Cologne, was erratic. In the difficult decades of the early nineteenth century, poorer families depended on child labour to make ends meet and few could afford to send their sons to be taught: as a result, schools sometimes stood half empty. In 1851, only half of London children living in the Southwark area attended elementary schools, though after the 1870 Education Act the figure climbed to 69 per cent, and at the turn of the century had reached 85 per cent.

By 1900, the introduction of compulsory schooling in European states, together with improved living conditions and reduced child mortality, launched a general advance in urban educational standards. In many cities, expenditure on schooling snowballed, while urban illiteracy rates fell sharply, to below 10 per cent in most North and West European countries; here, basic literacy was increasingly replaced as a job qualification by the number of years of schooling. In East European and Mediterranean cities, the process was slower, but by the 1930s nearly 90 per cent of Polish and

Russian townspeople were literate, and, in the most urbanized regions of Italy, the figure was around 95 per cent.

After the Second World War, higher education was opened up to the children of ordinary townspeople. As we noted in Chapter 13, a massive growth of universities took place—virtually all located in towns. In most countries (except England) recruitment had a strong regional bias and so reinforced the city in its wider hinterland. If during the post-war era universities were often viewed as semi-detached from their urban communities, mainly funded by states, at the end of the century many city and academic authorities sought to develop closer partnerships, particularly through the establishment of science and business parks. The large armies of students in university towns were often crucial in supplying the demand and labour for new cultural entertainments, ranging from nightclubs and bands to alternative comedy.

III

While religion and education remained long-standing elements in the cultural equation of the modern city, the nineteenth century saw an efflorescence of secular entertainments, notably music performances, the theatre, museums and art galleries, and libraries and associations. Shedding their earlier identification with Courts and elites, these were often run on a commercial basis and were heavily targeted at a bourgeois clientele. Most important was public music-making. Classical music concerts multiplied in number and scale and became highlights of the civic cultural scene. Famous soloists like the violinist Paganini toured European cities and towns by train, playing to rapt audiences. Charles Hallé began his first season of concerts at Manchester in 1858 and their rapid success led to them being copied in other British cities. By 1913, Paris heard 700 concerts a year, and after the war the figure more than doubled. Already established in English towns during the eighteenth century, music festivals flourished in Victorian Britain, patronized by middle-class audiences eager to hear large-scale works. The Triennial Birmingham Festival hired Mendelssohn to conduct the premiere of his *Elijah* (1846), and later commissioned works from Bruch, Gounod, Dvorák, and Elgar. Similar events spread on the continent: for instance, Richard Wagner launched the Bayreuth festival in 1876 to showcase his operas, and performances were heard by the well-heeled Bavarian bourgeoisie as well as royalty.

Opera was still the most prestigious of all urban musical entertainments in the nineteenth century. In Germany and Italy, major cities acquired new opera houses, both to celebrate civic pride and as a fashionable meeting-place for local worthies. Composers like Verdi or Gounod wrote operas on melodramatic or sentimental themes to appeal to middle-class audiences—works which made both composers and soloists famous and rich (the great French tenor, Naudin, was paid 110,000 francs to sing in a Meyerbeer opera). From the late nineteenth century, the appeal was widened. Operettas were pioneered in Paris by Offenbach and the genre was quickly copied by Suppé, Strauss, Lehar, and others. Johann Strauss's light operettas, lively, sweetly plaintive, sometimes in the local dialect, were highly popular: the *Gypsy Baron* (1885) had over 300 performances in Vienna and 100 at Budapest before 1900; Lehar's *Merry Widow* (1905) was even more successful. In Britain, the comic operas of Gilbert and Sullivan had a similar success among wider middle-class audiences.

Public concert-going was matched by the growth of family performances, with many pieces of vocal and chamber music being specially written for them. Domestic music-making was encouraged by the growing factory production of pianos (including iron-framed and upright instruments), by the greater availability of sheet music, and by music teaching in schools, particularly for young women. In Vienna, many wealthier families arranged *musicales* on Sunday afternoon and invited young musicians to take part.

Urban theatre likewise steadily broke away from noble and Court patronage. In Italian cities, under Austrian rule, various new theatres were opened in the early part of the century. In Berlin, as in many other German centres, the main theatres were still under Court control up to the 1840s, but official controls declined after the 1848 Revolution and less exclusive theatres sprang up. Theatres spread from the metropolitan centres to a wide spectrum of towns. English and Danish country towns had them by the early nineteenth century, French cities like St Etienne and Marseille acquired municipal theatres in 1853 and 1882, and local councils in the Ruhr built civic playhouses in the years before 1900. Frequently, they were a source of civic pride—a Bordeaux councillor called the Grand Theatre there the glory of the city—and received municipal subsidies. In Eastern Europe, theatres were often linked to national as well as civic politics.

Prague's national theatre after 1868 reflected a heightened sense of Czech identity; Latvian and Russian theatres were opened at Riga to compete with the German playhouse of the German-speaking elite; and Tallinn's Estonian theatre had a similar purpose. Most theatres filled their stalls with middle-class audiences, but large playhouses were built with cheap seats for skilled workers and the like. Traditional street theatre, performed by itinerant entertainers, came under pressure from the authorities in the nineteenth century and was forced by police regulations to move indoors, initially to taverns. From the 1860s, music halls became popular in European cities (London had 200), often developing out of drinking premises.

Cabinets of curiosities—private collections of artefacts—were already established in capital cities by the seventeenth century, often owned by rulers, nobles, or associations like the Royal Society. Public museums began in the eighteenth century with the British Museum, founded on a voluntary basis in 1753, and the Louvre Museum first opened to the public in 1793. However, the main development of museums took place during the nineteenth century, first in metropolitan centres and later spreading to provincial towns. England had fifty municipal museums by 1887; a decade later, fourteen major Dutch cities, mostly in the north and west of the country, possessed museums—a mixture of state, provincial, and municipal institutions. Indicative of growing pride in the national heritage, the museum movement also mirrored bourgeois concerns with education and the need to civilize the urban lower orders. No less important, museums, with their ornate premises in town centres, were part of the projection of civic patriotism against urban rivals.

Art galleries, often on the same site or nearby, developed in a similar fashion. The opening of the Louvre as an art gallery as well as museum served as the model for a series of new public galleries. Leading the way in Germany, Ludwig I of Bavaria inaugurated the Glypothek (sculpture gallery) at Münich in 1830, followed by the Pinakothek (art gallery) in 1836, and Neue Pinakothek in 1853. In the second half of the century, galleries proliferated in provincial towns, usually established by town councils. Ambitious to combat the perceived spiritual poverty of industrializing towns through education in aesthetics, art galleries also promoted artists, visitors, and the art trade. Foreign students and artists flocked to Münich's galleries and art life became integral to the city's cultural identity in the late nineteenth century. Art exhibitions became popular (one at Münich in 1869 attracted over 100,000 people), and the number of art dealers multiplied. Paris had

130 in 1911 and over 200 a couple of decades later; Berlin had eighty private art galleries in the 1920s. Important artistic communities flourished in the major cities (Münich had nearly 1,200 artists by the 1890s). Many artists depicted urban or suburban scenes, and copies of their work were widely circulated in prints, art books, and (after the 1860s) postcards. Though town views date from the fourteenth century, for the first time multiple images of urban life, particularly of the European capitals, became indelibly printed in the public consciousness across the continent and beyond.

Urban images were multiplied and transmitted by the growth of the commercial media. Whereas the earlier printing industry had been heavily, though not exclusively, concentrated in state capitals, during the nineteenth century the relaxation of censorship controls, soaring urban demand, and advances in printing technology led to an important dispersal to provincial towns. By 1900, a thriving trade was found even in smaller towns, like Valence in France (20,000 inhabitants) whose eight printers turned out a great mixture of newspapers, magazines, and other publications for local and regional consumption. The growth of newspapers initially catered for the bourgeoisie. At Basel, in the 1840s, three new papers were set up and played a part in that city's political liberalization. The bourgeois press tended to reflect class preoccupations with business, politics, and culture in town and region. As education and living standards improved for the lower classes, the end of the century saw a spate of cheaper popular papers. Before the First World War, Warsaw had fourteen dailies and sixty-one weekly newspapers, buoyed up by the large increase in circulation. Budapest saw a similar upsurge of the cheap boulevard press: by 1900, news-stands offered twenty-two daily papers for sale. Popular prints not only catered for the insatiable public interest in crime and scandal, but also manipulated nationalist and racist sentiments.

Public libraries were slower to advance. Paris had twenty-three public reading rooms in 1819 and 118 in 1893, but members had to pay a small subscription. The situation was the same with the Working Men's Institutes in British towns. Popular needs were ignored. At Maidstone's town library, loans were confined to local taxpayers (or those sponsored by one): in 1893, borrowers numbered 687 (just over 2 per cent of the population). In the Ruhr region, Dortmund had a municipal library in 1886, but most towns only got one after 1900.

One problem for public libraries was the competition from commercial libraries and those run by voluntary associations. Though clubs and societies evolved in West European cities (mainly in England) in the Enlightenment period, it was during the nineteenth century that they became one of the essential elements of urban cultural life. From the 1830s and 1840s, a growing range of voluntary associations proliferated in continental cities, often male-dominated on the British model. At Cologne, various English-style clubs were established about 1830; Budapest had 80 societies by 1848, while Nordic cities about this time enjoyed a flowering of political, language, missionary, philanthropic, and temperance associations, as well as mutual aid and social clubs. How do we explain this associational success? Firstly, clubs were at the heart of bourgeois networking with many businessmen and traders belonging to several societies: at Mulhouse in Alsace, for example, 15 per cent of the population, mainly the middle class, were members of a mosaic of associations. Secondly, as we saw in Chapter 14, they brought together different middle-class groups in neutral space. Thirdly, associations helped to articulate the wider educational and intellectual interests of the bourgeoisie. Lyon, in 1903, had thirty societies of this type, ranging from medical, learned, and architectural societies to those promoting fine arts, photography, and education, while Moscow had societies for antiquities, historic records, natural history, music, the arts, and public improvement (thus the Association of Russian Doctors organized numerous congresses to disseminate medical advances). Fourthly, almost every European town supported its own associational repertoire, which contributed to a specific local identity, though by 1900 more and more clubs and societies had national affiliations. In the cities of Eastern and Northern Europe, voluntary networks became influential vehicles for mobilizing nationalist sentiment. In Finland, for example, Fennomanians used the Finnish educational society, temperance organizations, voluntary fire brigades, and trade unions for national mass organization. Finally, associational growth was encouraged by press liberalization, increased legal recognition (in France, 1901; Russia, 1906; Germany, 1908), and, after the 1890s, reduced working hours, and the growing ability of people to pay the membership fees.

IV

Though the bourgeoisie defined the new cultural agenda of the nineteenth-century city, ordinary townsmen retained their loyalty to more traditional activities. As we noted above, popular religiosity remained fairly high until the end of the century, often focused on neighbourhood churches. Again, the popular tavern or drinking-house was not only important, as we saw, for the urban service sector, but remained central to male and neighbourly sociability. As the number of premises increased, so did their functions: it was said that nineteenth-century French cafés 'were meeting places for friends ... There one read the newspaper and discussed the news ... played cards or billiards ... or found a job ... [Here] one commemorated happy events, birthdays, or retirement. One held meetings of social and political groups there'. For a while, at least, taverns provided a home for new-style cultural activities (such as clubs and sports), though by the inter-war period, as noted in Chapter 14, the number and role of popular drinking premises was on the wane.

Before 1900, the better-off lower classes were emulating the new cultural activities of the affluent, benefitting not just from improved living standards but greater leisure time. Artisan mutual-aid and political societies had been common earlier, but in the late nineteenth century there was a groundswell of working-class voluntary associations. Initially sponsored by churches, employers, and political parties, they were soon taken over and run by ordinary townspeople. In Germany, working-class choral societies flourished: around 1892, the three hundred or so lower-class societies had only 9,000 members, but by 1914 lower-class membership equalled that of their middle-class counterparts. British cities had growing numbers of working men's clubs from the 1870s which steadily threw off their links with the middle class and offered a galaxy of political, educational, sporting, and entertainment activities (including amateur dramatics and variety shows), often expressing a new sense of class autonomy. Within a generation, lower-class membership of associations was on a par with that of higher social groups. Among the most numerous and popular kinds of association were sports clubs.

Organized competitive sports such as cricket and horse-racing began in England, particularly in London, during the eighteenth century (see Chapter 10), under the lead of elite and middle-class organizations, and this remained the scenario until the mid-nineteenth century. Three developments occurred after the 1850s. In the first place, new competitive sports emerged. Traditional neighbourly or street football was transformed in large measure by the middle classes into football and rugby and organized through national associations. Other urban sports invented around this time included hockey, athletics, golf, lawn-tennis, and cycling, almost invariably run by middle-class organizations. Second, a number of the new sports (together with older ones like cricket) were taken up by ordinary townspeople. Initially, the new sports were promoted by churches or firms as a way of weaning the working class from traditional sociability and educating them into a middle-class sense of discipline. But popular interest rapidly gained its own momentum: for example, at Battersea Park in South London in 1904–5, about 70,000 people played tennis, 22,000 cricket, and 16,000 football.

The third development was that the new sports spread quickly across the Channel to other European cities. Paris had athletics clubs by the 1880s and football clubs the following decade, while rugby was adopted in south-west France at Bordeaux, Pau, and Bayonne. German cities boasted rowing, cycling, and alpine clubs among others, just as St Petersburg acquired clubs for tennis, hockey, rowing, and skating. If the original initiative usually came, as in Britain, from the affluent classes, popular participation grew. The First World War and its armies of young men played an influential role in the mass popularization of competitive sports in European cities. No less important were rising living standards, reduced working hours, and improved public transport. Strong official support for sport as a prescription for working-class health, and inter-city competitions and national and international events (the Olympic Games in Stockholm, 1912, and Berlin, 1936; the Workers' Olympiads in Prague, 1921, and Vienna, 1931) fuelled extensive media and public interest. By the 1930s, competitive sports had become a mainstream leisure activity in European cities, attracting all social classes and growing numbers of young people and women (a quarter of the membership of German sports clubs was female).

V

Commercialization became steadily more pervasive in sport, and in other leisure fields. From the 1890s, cycling races (including the Tour de France after 1903) were sponsored by cycle manufacturers and sports newspapers. In England, the 1880s witnessed the rapid rise of professional football clubs in major cities, with paid players and coaches, that culminated in the formation of the Football League in 1888. In Germany, professional boxing acquired a similar mass following in all the major cities, its popularity fanned by newspapers, cinema, and radio broadcasts.

Among other commercial entertainments, dancing was increasingly emancipated from its traditional neighbourhood roots and its connection to public drinking-houses. By 1925, all the major British towns had purpose-built dance halls, run by private companies, like the Palais de Dance at Hammersmith, where bands played the Charleston and other American-style dance music. But it was cinema that became the leading commercial and mass entertainment. Already, by 1914, Vienna had over 100 cinemas and Budapest just under that figure. In German cities, the number of cinemas rose fivefold between 1910 and 1928, and in the 1930s virtually every significant town across Europe had one or more picture houses, with large audiences. Thus, Liverpool (population 850,000) had sixty-nine cinemas with seating capacity for 1.3 million customers a week. Though cinemas at first reflected local tastes and attracted socially segmented clienteles, by the 1930s new cinema buildings and talkie films were targeting a more homogeneous audience, including adolescents escaping parental supervision, young women, and middle-class and working-class customers. About 1946, two thirds of British teenagers went at least once a week to their local picture house. Though city authorities often tried to regulate and censor films, cinemas became part of national chains (in some countries) and often showed international (mainly Hollywood) films. All this presented serious challenges to local cultural identity.

The same erosion of a local cultural identity occurred through other developments during the inter-war era. First, there was the growing popularity among urban families of outdoor holidays, either at one of the seaside resorts or in the countryside, encouraged by improved living standards, cheap travel, and heavy advertising by seaside towns and transport companies. Camping became popular side by side with sunbathing. Town councils and voluntary bodies organized camping holidays for the disadvantaged, particularly children. A second breakthrough stemmed from the rapid spread and popularity of radios; by the 1930s, it was said the wireless had 'become a very general adjunct of the amenities of working-class life in London'. Nationally produced, normally transmitted from the capital, radio broadcasts tended to strengthen the domestic family setting, but widened the window to national and international trends and standards in culture and leisure. Older urban institutions, whether churches, music concerts, museums, or theatres, struggled to compete with the new mass entertainments.

VI

After the Second World War, the move towards cultural convergence in European cities was maintained, a process that was promoted by rising living standards, further reductions in work hours, rapidly expanding travel, the success of the commercial entertainment sector, and heavy advertising. From the 1960s, radio was challenged by the spread of television and within a decade or more TV sets had become an essential part of the equipment of the urban home: by 1980, nine in ten French households had one. Among other mass entertainments, cinemas went into decline after the 1960s before recovering sharply in the 1990s due to the growth of new multiple-screen film complexes. Everywhere, cinema programmes came to be dominated by imported American films: even in France, with its strong film industry, 58 per cent of films projected (in 1989) were of North American origin.

A growing mass interest in organized sport for personal health and fitness emerged. In the late 1960s, over one in ten male Londoners (and up to 17 per cent of teenage boys) took part in cricket, football, and other sport in parks, while the following decade about half the residents of Helsinki were actively engaged in outdoor sports. Sports clubs became the leading type of voluntary association and a democratization of sport took place as hitherto largely middle-class games such as golf and tennis became less exclusive, and women became prominent in a number of sports. Fuelling the expansion of organized sport was increased public expenditure, often channelled into new sports complexes in suburban districts.

Sports clubs were only part of the continuing growth of voluntary associations in European cities, including (from the 1970s) many green, radical, ethnic, charitable, and leisure organizations. Associations remained at the heart of neighbourhood and community networking, sociability, identity, and integration. During the 1980s and 1990s, between 38 and 43 per cent of the residents of bigger German cities belonged to societies—not only sports clubs but also religious, musical, and environmental associations. Likewise, in Swedish cities, up to 29 per cent of town dwellers were members of one or more associations and around one in ten people were active in them. The end of the Communist system set off an explosion of voluntary associations in Russia: for instance, the provincial city of Tambov and its district had over 200 societies in 2000, many of them locally based and ranging from veteran and cultural organizations to the ubiquitous sports clubs. Little evidence exists that European towns experienced that catastrophic fall in associational activity found in North American cities towards the close of the twentieth century.

European cultural life was ever more influenced by commercialism. In the case of sport, the last decades of the twentieth century saw a breakthrough in the level of commercial investment and sponsorship. Professional League football in London, commercial from the late nineteenth century, became dominated by a few highly successful clubs, often owned and staffed by foreigners, with matches played in lavish new stadia and increasingly watched by international audiences of television viewers. A similar trend developed in major European cities from Hamburg to Milan and Barcelona. Other sports followed the same direction, with rugby, athletics, and cricket in Britain moving towards more professional and commercial organizations, and a growing emphasis on bigger stadia and television viewing. In the Nordic cities, ice-hockey fans enjoyed revamped stadia and match spectacles, such as high-kicking cheer leaders, on the American model. Golf spread to many European towns, where courses were usually established by private clubs or international companies: in greater Berlin, for instance, a dozen new courses opened in the years 1990–6.

Paradoxically, despite the trends towards commercialization and internationalization, the last years of the twentieth century were marked by increased cultural pluralism in European cities. In part, this was driven by commercial and technological developments, but it also reflected new tastes and fashions in urban life. Thus, there was an important spread of local radio stations and cable TV channels, carrying predominantly local news and opinion and catering for a wide range of social, ethnic, and cultural interests. In the Netherlands, the number of local radio and TV stations rose from forty-one in 1984 to 367 in 1994; a few years later, Londoners could hear up to fourteen local commercial radio stations. In sport, there was a turn away from competitive, organized activity to more informal, individualistic, and experiential pursuits. Jogging was probably the first of the new sports of this type, imported from the United States and quickly spreading to European cities during the 1970s. By the 1990s, however, jogging was being overshadowed by event running (such as marathons), often identified with particular cities but sustained by commercial sponsorship. Meanwhile, new sports like orienteering, rock-climbing, and skateboarding enjoyed growing urban popularity, often among young people.

What about urban ceremony? As we know, popular rituals and traditions were still resilient in working-class neighbourhoods at the start of the twentieth century, and though they may have declined in subsequent decades, because of reduced religiosity, municipal regulations, and urban expansion, they enjoyed a spectacular resurgence on the streets of many European towns at the close of the Second World War. At the Liberation of France in 1944, crowds, street theatre, parades, songs, and rough music rituals took over public spaces from the Nazis in Paris and other cities, while street singing and dancing swept British towns at the end of the war. If these were largely spontaneous events, the later twentieth-century city welcomed a calvacade of organized festivals and carnivals. In Britain, London's Notting Hill Carnival (established 1965) was the first of a series of new-style events. The Rotterdam Summer Festival, officially established in 1994, attracted nearly a million people at the end of our period. Even small towns joined in, places like Beziers in southern France with its *corrida* festival, or Hultsfred in southern Sweden, which since 1986 has hosted the biggest pop, rock, and metal festival in the country. The number of popular events has risen markedly across Europe, with thousands by the 1990s. Some events have been linked to ethnic minorities (like Leicester's Festival of Lights), but commercial promotion has played a key part, along with a new concern by cities to market themselves—locally, nationally, and beyond—to attract tourists and other visitors.

VII

Urban marketing has a long tradition, as we observed in earlier chapters. After the mid-nineteenth century, states and metropolitan authorities joined together to mount international exhibitions, cities competing with each other in the extravagance of the staging. One of the first, the Great Exhibition at London's Crystal Palace in 1851, which attracted 6 million visitors, had an industrial focus, but later ones showcased the arts, new architecture, the exotic, and imperialism, as well as urban innovations like electric lighting. An English visitor to the 1878 Paris exposition exclaimed: 'everything on the visit struck me amazingly ... The exhibition must affect everyone with the greatest wonder'. Though nationalist pride was always a marketing priority, the urban dividends were extensive, stimulating tourism and national and international visibility. Paris was the queen of expositions, organizing no fewer than eight between 1855 and 1937 (that of 1889 saw the opening of the Eiffel Tower), but other important exhibitions were held at Vienna in 1873, Turin in 1902, and Stockholm in 1930. By the 1920s, competition to organize one had become so fierce that an international agreement had to be made to regulate their number.

In the late twentieth century, however, European cities showed a diminished appetite for staging international exhibitions, preferring place promotion through other events. The end of our period witnessed mounting rivalry between cities to serve as the venue for mega-events, like the European football championships or Olympic Games (eight bidders for the 2000 games, eleven for 2004), and to become a European Capital of Culture (in a competition launched by the European Commission in 1985). In addition to the economic dividends (discussed in Chapter 13), they were viewed as invaluable for raising a city's international status. By the later twentieth century, many European councils recognized cultural strategies as an essential tool of urban marketing. While commercial interests were often involved, a high proportion of costs were paid from city budgets.

Bigger cities often devised multiple place strategies for different markets. Through different municipal agencies, Amsterdam advertised both as the historic city of Rembrandt and the Dutch Golden Age, and as the home of youth culture, heavy drinking, permissive sex, and drugs. In a similar way, Manchester in the 1990s sold itself as the gay capital of Britain, but also as a leading centre for the arts and music with many new facilities (the Lowry Arts Centre, the Imperial War Museum North, and the Bridgewater Concert Hall). Other towns have sought to emulate aspects of metropolitan policy. In Britain, in the early 1990s, 42 per cent of town councils had adopted policies to encourage public art, including outdoor sculptures. Decayed port cities like Marseille, Liverpool, and Bilbao have inaugurated art galleries and museums, while the old industrial town of Lahti in southern Finland funded a beautifully designed, acoustically brilliant, concert hall by the lake (Sibelius Talo, opened 2000) to house its internationally famous Lahti Symphony Orchestra.

Cultural marketing, place promotion, and mass tourism have generated contradictions of identity for European cities and towns at the end of the period. In smaller historic towns, the daily influx of visitors may lead to congestion and overcrowding, forcing local people to retreat into a 'back region' away from the tourist gaze. In some places, it has led to mounting tension between the rhetoric of heritage and conservation and the cultural lives of ordinary people. In bigger cities, the problems have been less intense but heavy expenditure on prestige projects, sometimes at the expense of education or social services, has raised questions about whose community the city represents.

VIII

Such contradictions and tensions of urban cultural identity between outsiders and insiders, between different groups of townspeople, between the local, national, and international city, were not exclusive to the late twentieth century. In the nineteenth century, bourgeois ascendancy, with its optimistic assertion of 'civilizing' urban values, served to mask the divisions within urban communities. As we have seen, traditional cultural activity at the popular level was regulated and, wherever possible, driven out of sight. Already, Balzac wrote of Paris in the 1830s as an unfathomable ocean, restless, disaggregating, and, in the novels of Charles Dickens, where the central image of the metropolis was of contrasts and juxtapositions, popular social and cultural life was often depicted as a peripheral, comic, grotesque world more akin to Africa than Europe. Reading their magazines and journals, the middle classes of mid-century Budapest could experience, vicariously and in sanitized form, both the fashionable social world of the dandy and the chaotic underworld of the poor with its brothels, bars, dark streets, and other criminal scenes. By the late nineteenth century, the exploration of the city was the role of fictitious detectives like Conan Doyle's Sherlock Holmes investigating bizarre crimes in dark London suburbs or opium dens, while the genre of literary *flâneur* was transformed from an early nineteenth-century Balzacian figure, enthusiastically observing the modern city ('To wander about Paris—adorable and delicious existence!') to a Flaubertian stroller, drifting through an increasingly vast metropolis, with a sense of dispossession and estrangement. Yet the cultural image of the European city before 1900 that was projected in literature and art was broadly optimistic, ranging from the entertaining fairyland (*fin de siècle* Paris—where Impressionist painters airbrushed out images of factory chimneys) to the global business metropolis (London, with its choking smog depicted as an early morning mist) and the imperial parade ground (Vienna).

Urban optimism really began to run out of steam towards the end of the nineteenth century as a new mood of pessimism arrived that began explicitly to recognize the contradictions of the modern city. A clutch of novelists and political thinkers, artists, film-makers, and sociologists began to highlight the polarities of the city: the contrast between the respectable city overground, and the city underground, with its hidden labyrinth of poor living in cellars, its new sewer, water, and electricity systems, and functional subway lines; the contrast between the city of light—with its brilliantly lit stores, cafés, and boulevards—and the city of darkness, with the slums and backstreets of the poor, of prostitutes and criminals; the contrast between the hectic, mechanized city centre and the calm rusticated suburbs.

In Germany, the vision of the modern city by Oswald Spengler and Expressionist and New Realist writers was especially apocalyptic—the monster city out of control, threatening national identity and civilization. But in countries like England, a more nuanced anti-urbanism was interleaved with rural nostalgia. Elsewhere, the picture was mixed. Italian Futurists called for the destruction of ancient cities like Venice but their replacement by Modernist metropoles. In Finland, an emphasis on nature was complemented by a vision of the progressive planned city. In Soviet Russia, anti-urbanism in the 1920s led to schemes for the destruction of imperialist cities, only soon to be replaced by a new glorification of urban-industrial growth in the 1930s. Already, before the Second World War, anti-urbanism was on the wane in much of Europe. The rise of the International Modern movement of architects and planners, increasingly influential in the 1930s, combined a rejection of the values and historical traditions of the nineteenth century with a proclamation of the cultural primacy of the city, through its planned landscape.

IX

Throughout the modern era, changes in the urban landscape refracted the complex cultural, political, and other currents of the European city. This becomes evident as we examine in turn the public spaces, private housing, growth of planning and, finally, post-Modernist developments of the period. For much of the nineteenth century the civic bourgeoisie, in league with the state and expanding business sector, reshaped the built environment in accordance with three concerns: the development of housing for the better off, the reconstruction of city centres, and the creation of designed green space. We already noted, in Chapter 14, how spacious, ornate villas proliferated in the suburbs of British, and, to a lesser extent, continental towns during the nineteenth century, while the latter also saw the construction of comfortable apartment blocks for middle-class families. Apartment blocks of this type were often integrated into the redevelopment of the public space of the central city.

The remodelling of the central districts of cities was affected by a variety of factors. One was the problem of traffic congestion and (in many places) obsolescence of city fortifications. Another was the imperative to find space for railway stations and yards and for the construction of new town halls, courthouses, and other municipal offices needed by an expanding urban government. A further pressure came from the burgeoning of the service sector in town centres and the profusion of purpose-built shops, hotels, banks, and insurance offices. Political changes also had an impact, particularly in capital cities: in Paris, for instance, the revolutions of 1830, 1848, and 1871 all reconfigured the landscape to match the altered structures of power. Finally, the urban landscape had to be remodelled to accommodate the growing panorama of bourgeois cultural institutions—from new churches to concert halls and theatres.

Large, new central districts emerged in towns, distinguished by monumental administrative, commercial, and cultural edifices, many of which from the 1890s were floodlit. Capital cities witnessed the most extensive redevelopment. In Brussels, the creation of a new royal and government centre after independence (1830) involved the large-scale demolition of old housing and successive waves of new construction. Haussmann's rebuilding of central Paris under Napoleon III was the most comprehensive and ambitious attempt in any European city to create an administrative quarter for the regime, along with commercial and bourgeois residential districts—a project that was only completed under the Third Republic. The Parisian model was copied on a lesser scale across Europe, the new metropolitan spaces often combining imperial, national, and civic symbols. The Viennese Ringstrasse, a wide avenue 4 kilometres long, lined by vast squares, heavy mansions, and resplendent public buildings anointed in a mixture of historicist styles (Renaissance Revival museums, Baroque Parliament, Neo-Gothic city hall) celebrated state power and greatness, but within a generation much of the residential area had been taken over by the Viennese bourgeoisie. In the Balkan capitals of Athens, Bucharest, Belgrade, and Sofia drastic reconstruction took place—encompassing Western-style palaces, public buildings, and boulevards—to eradicate all traces of Ottoman rule.

Progress in Europe's provincial towns depended on municipal budgets and economic development, but by 1914 most cities and towns of any standing had laid out new central areas whose architecture increasingly fixed their image and identity, counterbalancing the growing spatial sprawl. Those country towns that failed to modernize in this way were reckoned to be old-fashioned and backward. As we noted in Chapter 12, European urban improvement, like other cultural developments, had a ripple effect outside Europe—affecting colonial and neo-colonial cities from the Americas to Asia and Australasia.

Central districts of European towns acquired not only new buildings, but also a growing range of green spaces. When Zagreb in Croatia was redeveloped after the 1880s, the city planned an elaborate arrangement of public edifices and parks with the aim of creating 'a green horseshoe'. During the nineteenth century, municipal parks proliferated, first in West European cities and then spreading to other regions. Planned green spaces became necessary as the old natural areas of cities—common fields, orchards, wasteland, and the like—were swallowed up for housing or factory construction. Initially, municipal elites designed ceremonial squares and a variety of ornamental parks and gardens, often in middle-class areas, with extensive flower beds and exotic vegetation. Though gardening styles varied between the formal French and the variegated English, parks tended to be highly regimented, fabricating illusions of solitude and social tranquillity, places for the bourgeoisie to promenade and the lower classes to learn good manners. Parks were also seen as essential natural 'breathing spaces' in a pathological city. But the vision of nature in the city was highly controlled, compared to the natural world of the countryside which was still often perceived as wild, romantic, and threatening.

From the later nineteenth century evolved a more pluralistic vision of green space in the city. New types of space appeared: less formal, more natural parks, often called people's parks, for sport and other relaxation; small neighbourhood parks in lower-class districts to combat environmental degradation; and, by the First World War, garden allotments and sports grounds (discussed in Chapter 16). This pluralism was matched, as we have noticed, by a new, more nostalgic, benign perception of nature outside the city, by the greater incorporation of the countryside, through day trips, rambling and camping, into urban social life. Into the twentieth century much of the design of urban green space reflected the elite agenda of disciplining, reforming, and improving the lower classes, but this was only part of the picture. Ordinary people, including young people, women, and workers often regarded and used green space subversively—for drinking, for sex, and for cleaning carpets and hanging out laundry.

The expansion of lower-class housing in nineteenth-century cities owed everything to small builders, speculative developers, the building cycle and land market, and little to public provision. The condition of most housing of this kind was desperately poor, whether located in inner-city slums, tenement areas next to industrial plants, or in shanty-towns on the outskirts. By the 1880s and 1890s, the housing crisis, along with the mounting urban sprawl, was seen to threaten not only the social stability of European cities but their sense of community and identity.

Various international planning movements from the turn of century were part of the response. Though Ebenezer Howard's idea of the Garden City was influenced by American writers (notably Henry George), the concept of new urban communities set in a benign countryside was essentially European. Model towns were established in England at Letchworth (1903) and Welwyn (1920), and Howard's ideas spread quickly on the continent, promoted by international conferences and competitions, and the work of societies of planners and architects like the French Societé des Cités Jardins (1903) or the Russian Garden City Society based in St Petersburg (1914). Initially, Howard's ideas were mainly adapted and implemented as bourgeois garden suburbs, in peripheral areas where land was cheap and the social and environmental problems of the big city kept at bay. During the inter-war period, garden suburbs continued to spread—from Helsinki to Athens—and housed not only bourgeois families but also the lower classes, frequently in social housing estates constructed or subsidized by municipalities.

If the garden suburb was one planning response to the perceived crisis of the European city, another was offered by the International Modern Movement. Here, the vision was less one of installing the town in nature, than of incorporating nature—in the form of spaces of greenery—into the urban grand design, a panoramic design which was ruled by geometric spaces and high-rise buildings and deliberately emptied of historical reference. A range of strategies were on offer: at one end, Le Corbusier's Voisin Plan for Paris (1925) which envisaged replacing many of the buildings on the Right Bank with skyscrapers and giant expressways; at the other,

Stockholm's Functionalist adaption of Modernist ideas to create modestly-scaled apartment blocks in new green suburbs such as Hammarbyhöjden and Traneberg (which also incorporated some of Howard's ideas).

The Modern Movement had only limited impact on Europe's urban landscape before the Second World War, but its strong organization—manifested in international conferences (for instance, London in 1935, Paris in 1937, and Stockholm in 1939), exhibitions and visits by experts—gave a powerful impetus to the growth of planning legislation and municipal planning. Piecemeal planning of cities had occurred since the medieval period, usually of elite areas, and from the early nineteenth century there were more extensive projects, as at Hamburg after the fire of 1842 or in Haussman's central Paris. But, in the early twentieth century, planning legislation arrived, led by the British Town and Country Planning Act of 1909 and the Prussian Wohnungsgesetz of 1918 that allowed bigger cities to introduce urban zoning. Most countries adopted similar legislation over the next two decades, and in Soviet Russia urban planning became a tool of political and economic restructuring (as, for instance, in the Modernist-style 'Masterplan for the Reconstruction of the City of Moscow', approved by Stalin in 1935). Modernism also boosted the status of architects and planners as urban prophets. Architects like Geddes and Abercrombie in Britain, Wagner in Germany, and Saarinen and Alto in Finland became influential figures, visionaries, and prophets, who promoted both Modernist buildings and planning, and enjoyed close links to city politicians and property developers.

City centres were often badly affected by the military destruction of the Second World War. However, the threat to the integrity and identity of central districts was compounded by large-scale redevelopment and traffic schemes in the decades of rapid commercial expansion after 1945. Such schemes were mainly the brainchild of Modernist architects in cooperation with city engineers, local politicians, and builders. One example of this was at Coventry in the British Midlands where a Modernist city architect, Donald Gibson, persuaded the city council to take advantage of the damage by German bombing (90 per cent of the core area) to design a new city centre with Modernist shopping precincts, strict zoning of land use, traffic segregation, and elevated ring roads. Even without extensive war damage, British cities like Bristol, Sheffield, Leeds, and Newcastle experienced wholesale redevelopment of their centres in the 1960s, with an emphasis on free-flow traffic, tower blocks, and pedestrian walkways. In Stockholm,

Modernist redevelopment plans for the city centre dating from the 1930s were implemented after the war, involving the clearing of old residential areas and the erection of an ugly multi-storeyed commercial complex. Even smaller towns underwent elements of Modern-style remodelling, their main streets blighted by the insertion of low-grade facades and flat-roofed premises. East European cities fared no better: Communist Social Realist planning often involved the construction of wide boulevards and heavy monumental buildings that betrayed the footprints of Western Modernism.

Modernist influence—utopian in inspiration, democratic in vision, too often authoritarian in implementation—was no less powerful in the development of large-scale social housing estates during the post-war era. Taking advantage of new industrial building methods, including prefabrication and standardization, as well as site mechanization (the advent of tower cranes), and responding to the acute political and media pressure for new modern housing to shelter growing populations, multi-storey housing blocks were erected rapidly, frequently in peripheral locations with poor communications. In Stockholm, the so-called Million Housing programme moved away from the earlier small apartment buildings to high-rise blocks at Tensta, Kista, and elsewhere. In France, Modernist 'Grandes Ensembles'—massive, industrially constructed tower blocks—were parachuted on to the periphery of great and small towns alike: at Nîmes they housed 20,000 inhabitants. Beset by a slum crisis, Glasgow raced to erect new apartment blocks. Quality controls were poor and the multi-storeyed towers and deck-access housing suffered from deterioration, poor maintenance, and vandalism, and rapidly turned into new slums. Similar problems affected Modernist-style housing developments in Soviet bloc cities such as East Berlin. Not all such developments were a failure. The suburb of Tapiola in western Helsinki, built in the 1950s and 1960s, combined both garden suburb and Modernist influences and was praised as 'Europe's most convincing effort in new town planning'; but the later forest suburbs in the Helsinki area proved less successful.

From the end of the 1960s, the golden age of the planned city, the city as planned panorama, was largely over, as the post-war economic boom evaporated, urban populations started to decline, city budgets lost their bounce, and environmental groups and local residents fought and defeated a number of high-visibility redevelopment schemes, such as those for Kungsträdgården in Stockholm, the Covent Garden Market in London, and the Käpylä garden suburb in Helsinki. Given urban development pressure, growing environmental anxiety from this time about the de-greening of the countryside, as well as the way that the multiplying car trips and summer cottages of town dwellers increasingly conflated town and countryside, it was not surprising that urban green spaces from parks to private gardens and sports grounds were increasingly seen as a valuable natural resource—to be preserved and studied (urban biotope studies pioneered by the Berlin ecologist Herbert Sukopp date from the 1970s). From the same time, building conservation was progressively recognized in national legislation. Architects and planners lost their previous infallibility as urban visionaries and planning became less comprehensive, more project based, and, in theory, more accountable. In Britain, planning controls were liberalized from the 1980s, but the most dramatic decline of urban planning occurred in Russian cities after 1990, where speculative developers in cahoots with local politicians subverted controls on historic buildings and green space.

In the last decades of the twentieth century, the urban landscape, like urban culture as a whole, has become more diverse. The end of the Modernist hegemony led to a jumble of styles replete with pseudo-historical references, creating a sense of theatricality. If usage of old leisure spaces such as parks and sports grounds has declined, indoor sports halls and private golf courses have multiplied. Increased privatization of urban space has occurred, most notably in the spread of shopping malls and entertainment complexes, often on the outskirts of towns; these are frequently controlled by private security firms and have limited integration with the local area. Another type of privatized space involved office-block developments in new business districts (for instance, Canary Wharf in East London) with their own access and security controls. However, gated suburban communities, common in the United States, had made little impact on European cities by 2000.

Post-war reconstruction, suburbanization, and private commercial de-velopments posed major challenges to the cultural vitality of city centres. At the end of the twentieth century, municipal policies sought to combat these challenges: through conservation and restoration policies like the Temple Bar scheme in central Dublin or the Finlayson redevelopment project in Tampere, and securing designation for historic areas as UNESCO world heritage sites; through the construction of prestigious cultural buildings; through a permissive policy towards popular entertainment facilities such as bars and nightclubs, and through aggressive urban marketing which has frequently portrayed the city centre as totemic of the city community as whole.

Thus, in spite of the many upheavals we have described during the nineteenth and twentieth centuries, the cultural role and landscape of European cities and towns remained as crucial at the close of the period as in earlier times for offering a sense of identity and cohesion to townspeople, as well as projecting the urban image to the wider world. And here in this chapter we have seen how vital municipal authorities have been in promoting cultural identity, whether in the creation of the new cultural matrix of the Victorian city, in urban planning, or in the new generation of cultural marketing at the end of the twentieth century. In the next chapter, we turn to examine in detail the wider functioning and changes of urban governance in the modern and contemporary era.

16

Governance 1800–2000

Political developments in the modern European city were defined and challenged by a set of paradoxes rooted in preceding centuries: a strong sense of municipal identity and communalism but a municipal government structure in which effective power was concentrated in a relatively few hands; significant civic autonomy, but where there was always tension with the centralizing authority of the state; intense political rivalry with other cities but also the need for inter-city cooperation. At the same time, the nineteenth and twentieth centuries saw many fundamental changes to urban governance. One was the opening up of municipal politics in a way that swept aside the old closed elites and introduced, first, a bourgeois ascendancy and then, after the end of the nineteenth century, more democratic representation. Another change was the massive expansion of civic administration, involving increased functions, personnel, and expertise. No less important was the mounting impact of state consolidation and later of international integration—not least with the advent of the European Community (later European Union).

As in earlier periods, one has to recognize the specificity of political trends. At the municipal level, the quality and character of city leadership (and its policies) could make a vital difference in administrative outcomes. Also critical were variations between countries (affected by national politics) and between different urban regions, with their distinctive phases of urban and economic growth. Institutionally, it may be useful to distinguish the different legal and administrative 'families' in modern Europe, in part the effect of the French Revolution: thus, a Napoleonic system of civil law, embracing France, the western Mediterranean and Low Countries; alongside smaller British, German, Scandinavian, and East European legal systems.

Trends in urban governance can be examined in three main phases: the first covering the period until the last decades of the nineteenth century, a time of inadequate municipal adaptation to accelerating urban growth; the second up to the Second World War, an era of extensive political reform and municipal expansion; the third covering the later half of the twentieth century when municipal activity was initially boosted by state growth, but then from the 1980s ran into financial and other problems.

I

In the nineteenth century, continuing a process evident during the previous century, central governments steadily imposed the political agenda for cities, and established the framework for urban governance. Despite the conservative reaction after 1815, a number of institutional and legal reforms of the Napoleonic era survived the downfall of the Emperor. In France, the new hierarchy of administrative towns set up in the 1790s remained, as did the reform of town councils that gave the dominant vote to the bourgeoisie. The Prussian city ordinance of 1808, conferring new powers on municipalities, was revised in 1831, and was extended to the new territories annexed to Prussia. In England, hitherto largely unaffected by reform, the 1832 Reform Act assured the middle classes the leading position in urban representation in Parliament, and three years later the Municipal Corporations Act established elected town councils (replacing the old system of cooption) and provided a framework for the funding and management of basic urban services. Ancient local privileges were abolished without many new urban powers being granted, but the key outcome was middle-class control of municipal government through narrow electorates: for instance, at Birmingham only 3 per cent of the inhabitants, at Leeds 10 per cent.

On the continent, liberal bourgeois anger at conservative regimes, combined with growing artisan militancy and popular destitution, provoked demonstrations and risings after 1830, reaching a climax in 1848. Then large protesting crowds poured on to the streets of major cities, such as Paris, Berlin, Vienna, Milan, Naples, Budapest, and Stockholm (where eighteen people were killed and hundreds injured). If the immediate government response was usually repressive, including the banning of political parties and imposition of strict censorship, in the longer term governments sought to ally with the urban bourgeoisie against the threat of popular and radical forces. In 1845, the Prussian government introduced into Rhineland cities a three-class franchise system under which real civic power was exercised by a wealthy bourgeois minority: and this scheme was extended, step by step, with some resistance, to the rest of the Prussian territories. At the same time, all the other German states before 1918 operated a census-biased franchise system against the working classes. In France, interference by government *préfets* continued into the late nineteenth century, but middle-class town councils put up resistance and enjoyed considerable effective power. In Austria, feudal jurisdictions were finally suppressed and municipal autonomy was recognized, while Swedish municipal and parliamentary reform produced a franchise restricted to about 20 per cent of adult males.

Despite its internal divisions, the bourgeoisie's ascendancy in municipal politics was entrenched, a process reinforced by their power in economic and social life. Often, as at Hamburg, the new political and business leadership overlapped. At Cologne, there was an influx of new middle-class leaders from outside the city, while at Valencia a revamped bourgeoisie, half of them outsiders, took charge of the city and set out to modernize it. In Eastern Europe, middle-class political leadership was slower to evolve. St Petersburg's city government remained under aristocratic as well as merchant control, and only later in the century did the upper bourgeoisie increase their influence. But in many European cities a bourgeois-dominated public sphere emerged after mid-century—structured by political clubs and other associations, political parties, newspapers, shared cultural activities, and a growing role in municipal government.

II

Pressure built up in the early nineteenth century for town councils to intervene more actively to deal with the growing army of problems, created by accelerating urbanization and high levels of immigration: specifically, problems related to public order and crime, public health and environmental degradation; and social welfare.

Whether a real increase in crime occurred in European cities during the early nineteenth century is uncertain, but clearly there was a strong middle-class perception of enhanced disorder in cities, particularly in the suburbs, a perception linked to recurrent radical agitation, strikes, and popular social unrest. This chimed with government concerns after the

French Revolution to keep a grip on public order, not least in capital cities. Following eighteenth-century innovations in Paris and Berlin, state-controlled police forces were established in many capitals. London had its own civilian police force, under the control of the Home Secretary, from the 1820s. The French model of state military police, the gendarmes (institutionalized by Napoleon), was copied in a number of countries, including Prussia (Berlin had a state police force after 1812), Bavaria, and Piedmont. In provincial towns, by comparison, policing was mainly left to the municipalities, and here bourgeois parsimony and localism retarded institutional progress. In France, municipal forces were set up in 1789, with *commissaires de police* appointed in 1795. Responsible to state *préfects* but financed by towns, the police faced conflicting pressure from both sides. In German provincial towns, police forces increased slowly: for instance, Aachen in the 1830s had only nine constables and three officers for a population of 40,000; indeed, the incidence of police declined, relatively, in industrializing centres like Krefeld. In England, provincial towns maintained only small municipal forces in the 1830s (many with fewer than five men) and up to the 1850s ratios of police to population varied greatly from one town to another; national legislation only came in 1856. Though the bourgeoisie rallied to the police in times of crisis, communal consent was widely lacking. Typically, at Graz in Austria, an observer noted, 'the police cannot expect any assistance from these inhabitants'. However, the obvious failures of the urban police during the 1848 revolutions and fears of renewed political upheaval, plus the growing political cooperation between states and bourgeoisie, opened the door to expanded urban policing by the 1860s and 1870s.

Public health and environmental problems of major cities were already identified by the 1820s. In France, hygienists, often doctors in Paris and Lyon, promoted investigation and debate about health, sanitation, and housing, while similar studies were published by British sanitarians like the physician Southwood Smith. There was growing collection and analysis of social statistics. Devastating cholera outbreaks from the 1830s, as well as other epidemics, triggered mounting public anxiety, bordering on panic, over the apparently lethal stench of sewage and the danger of epidemic streets—nests of infection—that might threaten the whole community. Yet the official response was narrow. The British public health movement, led by Edwin Chadwick, stuck mainly to sanitary reform and other countries largely followed the British example. After the great fire at Hamburg in

1842, William Lindley, a friend of Chadwick, was hired to construct a combined water supply and sewage plant in that city. In London, the Metropolitan Board of Works built a new sewage system in the 1850s, though the outlets in the Thames were not far enough downstream. In Paris, Haussmann proposed a dual water supply and sewage system as in London, but only the first was installed and the old system of cesspools cleansed by street scavengers survived in the French capital until the 1880s. Berlin adopted a combined system in the 1870s. Outside Western Europe reforms arrived even more slowly. In Moscow, improvement only took place at the end of the century, while in Lisbon repeated proposals for reform came to almost nothing before the 1880s. In provincial towns, innovation trailed behind that of the metropolitan centres, and even in the bigger cities poor suburban districts rarely received sanitation or clean water much before 1900.

Other types of environmental reform in the first part of the century were small-scale and self-serving. Concerned to clean up respectable central districts, magistrates often removed abattoirs, cemeteries, and polluting industries to poorer suburbs. Lower-class housing was left to the private market despite all its failings, not least because middle-class landlords did well out of renting tenement properties.

General urban improvement, encompassing street widening, the construction of new boulevards, river embankment, parks, and the like, followed a similar trajectory, only sporadic development taking place before the 1850s and 1860s. Innovations were frequently left to private or commercial interests, like the embellishment of the public promenade at Lisbon after 1833 that was paid for by private subscriptions. In numerous instances initiatives came from landowners with an eye for a profit. Thus, land for municipal parks was often given by building developers aware that a fashionable green space would push up the value of their property in the vicinity. Public intervention in urban improvement only really got going after the 1850s and 1860s—inspired by Haussmann's work in Paris.

In terms of social welfare, with many early nineteenth-century communities overwhelmed by growing numbers of poor, jobless workers and rural refugees, the failure of the municipal response was critical. At root was the widespread and disastrous fragmentation of responsibility for relief. In French cities, aid for the poor and sick was handled by a mixture of civic agencies, religious charities, and bourgeois societies. In Nordic cities, voluntary agencies were left to carry the main burden of welfare provision. In Belgian towns, the Catholic St Vincent de Paul Society was one of the most active relief agencies, but it could only aid a small proportion of the poor—at Antwerp one or two thousand people, a fraction of those in need. Public agencies were no more effective. In England, poor law boards, set up under legislation in 1834 and packed with bourgeois worthies, were obliged to economize on relief; only after the 1860s was the system reformed to deal with urban conditions. Public charity bureaux in Belgian towns, beset by shortages of funds, could relieve just half of the needy. In Germany, the town of Elberfeld pioneered a system of poor relief using middle-class volunteers as relief workers, a money-saving model that was copied in other German towns.

Municipal action in the first part of the nineteenth century was constrained not only by the parsimony and limited ambition of bourgeois civic leaders, influenced by laissez-faire ideas rather than old-style paternalism, but by other factors. One was the ineffectiveness of local administration beset by nepotism and clientage, and the small size of civic bureaucracies (Turin, for example, had only 100 officials in 1867 for a population of over 180,000). Second, and no less fundamental, was the long-standing problem of urban finances. In many communities, municipal revenues depended on traditional taxes and city rents, and councils faced difficulty in borrowing. Issuing bonds to pay for Haussmann's rebuilding of central Paris was exceptional at the time. In Lisbon, major civic improvement after the 1880s was only made feasible by the compulsory purchase of building land, the profits from subsequent housing development going into city coffers to fund public works. In Germany, city councils enjoyed significant fiscal autonomy, but elsewhere municipal finances were cramped by state policy. Unwilling to give cities freedom to organize their own resources, governments perversely refused to transfer sufficient funds to enable them to carry out necessary urban improvements. In this sense, neither the allocation of resources nor the delivery system for services functioned well.

By the 1870s and 1880s, the failure of many city councils to respond effectively to the many social, environmental, and other problems spawned by urbanization led, as we saw in Chapters 14–15, to a growing perception of urban crisis that was widely shared at both the national and local level. However, before the end of the century a new phase of urban governance had begun.

III

Behind the new municipal advance was more than the need to reverse the deterioration in urban conditions. From Britain, pioneered at Birmingham by Joseph Chamberlain, emerged the concept of municipal socialism, through which urban infrastructure investment was used to boost the efficiency and profitability of local firms. Entwined with this was an emphasis on municipal pride and competition with other cities. In this new context, leading businessmen became directly and energetically involved in municipal governance. By the turn of the century, additional impetus for municipal action derived from popular politics, reflecting the rise in working-class education and living standards, and measures for municipal and parliamentary enfranchisement across Europe. Thus, the universal male franchise was introduced in Germany and France in 1871, and in Norway in 1898, while more limited reform was passed in Britain in 1884. No sudden transformation of municipal governance occurred. At Birmingham, the municipal electorate still comprised only 19 per cent of the city's population in 1911; at Leeds it was 20 per cent. In German cities, despite a wider franchise, the tiered voting system ensured the affluent still held on to the reins of power. Worse, in Russian cities like Moscow, entrepreneurs tightened their grip on the city *duma* in the decades before 1914. Nonetheless, around the turn of the century came an upsurge of socialist parties, trade union activity, or both, in many countries. By 1918, or soon after, universal suffrage had been widely introduced which offered a new legitimacy to European urban government.

Before the First World War working-class representation on town councils was minimal, but after 1918 it steadily progressed, linked to rising levels of electoral participation in municipal elections: at Toulouse, for instance, the rate rose to 77 per cent in 1925 and 80 per cent ten years later. Even so, one should not exaggerate the extent of political change at the civic level. In many communities there was considerable stability of council personnel and a measure of consensus politics.

After the 1870s, municipal government steadily expanded. In addition to the local momentum for change, central governments, anxious at the threat to social and political stability from urban problems, supported greater municipal intervention. National legislation gave backing to urban welfare and education services and other initiatives, albeit with a limited, often ad hoc allocation of resources. However, municipal finances also benefited from tax reform, and the growing ability to issue bonds and undertake other forms of borrowing, underwritten by municipal trading. In Britain, capital formation by local authorities accounted for 95 per cent of all public investment in the years 1870–1914; and on the eve of the First World War council debt amounted to £656 million. Step by step, town councils assumed a decisive role both in the allocation and delivery of new urban services that reached a high proportion of the community. Once again, cities became—as they had been earlier, for instance, in the sixteenth century—laboratories where public policy was developed and tested.

As we know (see Chapter 14), concerns about crime tended to subside in the later nineteenth century and this doubtless reflected a variety of economic and social factors, as well as administrative developments. Nonetheless, the increased scale, organization, and professionalism of urban policing played its part. In British cities, the number of police increased nearly threefold between 1861 and 1911 and the cost of policing quadrupled over the same period. In Germany, reduced state control after 1865 over urban policing (outside Berlin) drove urban communities to expand their own forces. As usual, capital cities attracted the heaviest policing, due to government fears and state funding: in Paris, the number almost trebled in the half-century before the First World War. In the provinces, the picture stayed highly variable, often reflecting funding and local conditions. In British industrial cities like Sheffield and Leeds the size of the police force roughly doubled between 1871 and 1911, but in others like Middlesbrough and Bradford the increase was around threefold.

In general, policing became more organized and professional through the creation of detection departments, the use of informers, improved training, and better wages and equipment. There was increased targeting of specific criminal groups like juvenile delinquents, known offenders, or professional gangs rather than the lower classes in general, which led in some cities to fewer assaults on the police and greater public consent and cooperation. Also important here was the way that the police were increasingly drawn into enforcing municipal regulations on a range of issues, from public health to traffic offences, that interested the respectable working classes. True, the police were still involved, often brutally, in the suppression of strikes and legitimate political protest, but by the early twentieth century urban policing was no longer seen just as an arm of bourgeois control.

Equally important, social welfare became a key concern of the new municipal interventionism. After 1871, German towns (except for Bavaria) adopted the Prussian model of municipal support for all two-year residents, and by 1914 about sixty German cities had inaugurated unemployment schemes and in some cases unemployment insurance. In Danish cities like Copenhagen, where charities still dispensed the large majority of relief up to the 1870s, there was a fivefold increase in public welfare expenditure during the next decades. In France, places like Marseille and Lyon doubled their civic expenditure on welfare in the years 1890–1909. Legislation in Russia transferred responsibility for poor relief to municipal authorities, but the actual growth of provision was slow and in some cities non-existent. In Britain, the poor law boards and voluntary sector still dominated welfare services up to the First World War, but crucially in 1908 the state took charge of old-age pensions, After the war, many welfare functions devolved on British councils, including maternity and child welfare services, and (in 1929) poor relief: in the years 1918–39, municipal expenditure on welfare services constituted 40 per cent of the national total (though the voluntary sector was still significant in British towns up to 1939).

Housing remained one of the most acute social problems in European cities, but municipal action was limited before 1914. In major British cities like London and Liverpool, where considerable slum clearance was carried out by local authorities, new construction was left mainly to the private sector: up to the First World War, less than 1 per cent of urban housing was owned by councils or charities. In Swedish and Danish towns, philanthropic bodies were more active in new housebuilding, while in the Netherlands, France, and Germany housing or building associations had a greater role, backed by municipalities.

In Western Europe, especially, housing problems were exacerbated by the First World War, which marked a turning point in public provision of social housing. In Britain, the 1919 Housing Act subsidized for the first time large-scale council housing, though some councils were more active than others. Liverpool constructed almost 38,000 houses in the 1920s and 1930s, half of all the new housing in the city. Beset by a huge refugee problem after the war, the city of Vienna (under Social Democrat control) turned to erecting massive suburban housing estates. In Sweden, Stockholm council supported workers' self-build housing in the 1920s, but after the Great Depression opted for Functionalist housing estates for the lower classes.

Turning to environmental problems, the public health movement, well organized by the 1860s, continued to put its focus on sanitary reform, linked to the supply of clean water. The greatest advances were in Western and Northern Europe, whereas in the Mediterranean and Eastern Europe improvement was tardy and uneven. One of the worst examples was Naples, mired in filth and deprivation (up to 90,000 inhabitants living in underground hovels), and with only 1 per cent of the municipal budget spent on sanitation: little wonder that a major cholera outbreak swept the city as late as 1910—11. But cities like Naples were becoming exceptions to the general rule. By 1900, public health officials also targeted hygiene and cleanliness in the home, with a growing emphasis on the role of mothers. As urban medical services expanded during the late nineteenth century, the municipal role increased. In Britain, legislation in 1929 gave borough councils extensive responsibilities, particularly over hospitals. In the capital, for instance, the London County Council took over sixty hospitals and institutions, and hospital expenditure rose sharply.

In other fields, municipal intervention was patchy. In German cities like Darmstadt and Mannheim one finds the emergence, in fits and starts, of an urban industrial policy to deal with chronic pollution through relocating industries to the outskirts. By comparison, the critical problem of smoke pollution caused by domestic fuel was not tackled until the 1950s (after the London Smog of 1952). Problems of food adulteration and contamination that badly hit lower-class consumers also attracted less regulation—often because of hostility from food suppliers. In British towns, municipal controls made a considerable impact after 1899, but in Spain, despite the establishment of municipal laboratories, lack of funding meant that inspections of suppliers were sporadic and ineffectual up to the 1930s.

Linked to public health was the growing provision of parks and other green spaces for public leisure and recreation. As we saw in Chapter 14, from the late nineteenth century competitive sports became increasingly popular, first among the middle classes and then among ordinary townspeople. One outcome was a major increase of municipal recreation areas. Old parks were converted, at least in part, into sports grounds, and new recreation fields were opened. In London, the county council boasted of 'fine new lidos and athletics tracks; more and better playing fields and bowling greens; [and] municipal golf courses'. At the same time, private provision was widespread, including golf courses, private tennis clubs and courts, and company sports grounds. In Helsinki, by comparison, most of the expansion of sports areas was the result of municipal action. In 1919, a special Sports Committee was established by the city to supervise developments; twenty years later, the city had eighty-six outdoor sports grounds. Public–private partnerships were common, the city constructing the sports spaces but leaving maintenance to sports clubs or workers' associations. As well as sports areas and school playing fields, town councils in Northern Europe promoted the spread of allotment gardens and campsites on the edge of cities and beyond, so that ordinary townspeople, and children especially, could benefit from the open air. German cities like Leipzig had extensive allotment gardens before 1900, promoted by the Schreber Association, and the idea spread quickly to cities in the Nordic countries, Russia, and elsewhere.

This emphasis on children was closely linked to the impressive expansion of education under municipal control. As we noted in Chapter 13, expenditure on city schools rose strongly, and there was also growing civic support for universities and research institutes, with the aim of improving urban economic performance.

Another major area of municipal intervention concerned transport and public utilities. Rapid urban and economic growth in the late nineteenth century almost overwhelmed existing transport services, buses and tramways, mostly run by private companies. Mounting traffic congestion snarled up town centres, and there was growing popular demand for cheap travel. The main breakthrough came in the 1890s. The city of Halle in Germany acquired control of its tramway in 1891 and introduced electrification; three years later Glasgow followed suit, took over the manufacture and repair of trains, introduced cheap fares for workmen, and before the end of the decade had a fully electrified and integrated tramway system. In the Netherlands, a municipal horse-drawn tramway was established at Amsterdam in 1875, followed by the first electrified line at The Hague in 1890. By 1904, 174 European cities owned tramways and two thirds of them operated them; seven years later, the proportion had reached 90 per cent. In Paris, the first section of the metro was opened in 1900 but only extended to the suburbs in 1929. An integrated public transport system was established at Berlin in 1929, and London had its Passenger Transport Board four years later. As in other areas, municipal control was most advanced in Western (and Northern) Europe. For example, in 1926 a consortium of German cities was involved in setting up the airline Lufthansa. Elsewhere,

municipal intervention was a good deal less. In Spanish cities, like Madrid
and Barcelona, the new transport services were run by foreign companies
and the same was true in Eastern Europe: in Russia, Belgian firms ran half
the country's electric tramways up to the Revolution.

As well as public transport, major cities from the later nineteenth century,
led by those in Western Europe, began a policy of taking over utilities like
gas, water, and electricity. The big attraction of municipal trading was that
it generated substantial profits that could be used to underwrite municipal
borrowing, not least for infrastructure improvement. Initially, gas supply
was largely in the hands of private monopolies, but, by 1885, 30 per cent
of British undertakings were under local authority control, and by the First
World War the proportion had risen to nearly 40 per cent. At this time, all
the major Dutch cities had municipal undertakings and three-quarters of
those in German cities were under municipal control. German cities also
led the way over electricity generation. In 1884, Berlin gave permission
for the German Edison Company to provide lighting for a large area of
the capital, and after 1900 there was increasing standardization of power
transmission: by 1907, over 80 per cent of German electricity works were
run by municipalities. Water supply went in the same direction. By 1914,
the United Kingdom had 326 municipal enterprises (against 200 in private
hands); municipal ownership in Germany had reached 90 per cent; and
all the Swedish waterworks were under council control. In other parts
of Europe, however, private companies remained widespread up to the
inter-war period.

IV

Up to the Second World War, an important part of urban services continued
to be supplied by non-municipal providers: voluntary organizations of
different kinds as well as private firms. Nonetheless, municipalities were
directly responsible for a growing share of service delivery. How was this
achieved? One key development was the growing size and professionalism
of the civic bureaucracy. At Düsseldorf, for instance, the cadre of city
employees rose from only fifty in 1850 to 6,000 by 1914. Numbers
continued to augment in the inter-war era. Toulouse, with 2,074 municipal
employees in 1912, had over 3,000 by 1937; Helsinki, with 3,737 staff in

1931, employed 5,686 a decade later. The design and implementation policy was undertaken by a new generation of professional specialist officials, whose expert status was reinforced by technical training, the growth of professional organizations and qualifications, and increasing international contact and innovation transfer through conferences, study tours abroad, and the like. Professionalization of this type offered officials a defence against the corrupt pressures of old-style political clientage.

New city departments proliferated. In the planning field, city architects and engineers often had considerable power and influence, working hand in glove with leading politicians and developers. Decisions were regularly taken behind closed doors with little public consultation. In some countries, planning was aided by the municipal ownership of development land. In German cities, after 1900, city officials gained the power to reserve land for public services and to purchase land for the community: thus, Freiburg owned three-quarters of the land in its jurisdiction. The same policy was adopted in Nordic cities.

A second factor behind improved civic effectiveness was the extension of administrative jurisdictions to keep pace with or even ahead of urban and suburban growth. European cities launched a wave of annexations before and after the First World War. Though the jurisdiction of the London County Council, established in 1888, was soon encircled by a sea of suburbia outside its control, the annexations at Leeds and Birmingham (1911), and Edinburgh (1920), were more successful. On the continent, Lisbon increased its administrative area by 50 per cent (1886), Vienna incorporated its suburbs across the Danube (1890), a greater Berlin authority was set up in 1920, and, in Eastern Europe, Prague benefited from a major extension of its limits, in 1922, that increased its territory eightfold. Annexations were invaluable in helping to plan and provide integrated services for expanding urban populations, and also in generating additional urban revenues.

Third, by the 1930s, municipal capacity to provide additional services was undoubtedly aided by the improved position of municipal finances. This was because of greater financial transfers by states to councils; state-backed municipal bonds and borrowing; and increased local revenue from municipal trading and local taxes. Still, there could be significant constraints, such as government monetarist policies or economic recession, as in the early 1930s. At Vienna, for instance, the Great Depression triggered rapidly rising unemployment and demand for welfare payments at a time of falling tax revenues, forcing a massive retrenchment of social benefits.

Growth in municipal services varied markedly across Europe, most advanced in Western Europe but also relatively strong in Nordic countries such as Sweden where a substantial increase in urban welfare provision occurred under the Social Democrats during the 1930s. Local leadership could be decisive. In the Paris suburbs, Henri Sellier, the Socialist mayor of Suresnes, inspired the construction of a cité-jardin of 2,500 housing units, innovative schools, swimming pools, and city dispensary.

If this was particularly ambitious, a new preoccupation was apparent among city governments to provide services not just for the affluent minority (as in the nineteenth century), but for all the citizenry. Fundamental was the evolution of a new kind of relationship between urban authorities and central government. Mutual antagonism and fear, dating back to the early modern period, was replaced by a degree of partnership as state governments relied on local councils (and other local interest groups) to implement broadly liberal political agendas.

Even so, there were major exceptions. Under Soviet rule, centralized state or party control over municipal policy-making became more and more intrusive in Russia, causing the erosion of local decision-making and the fragmentation of policy implementation at the urban level, along with the rigging of elections and the repeated purges of city officials under Stalin. In places like Moscow, the outcome was a polarized world of two cities—one in which the elite *nomenklatura* had access to luxurious apartments, lavish services, and other facilities, and another in which ordinary inhabitants occupied barrack housing and had minimal access to necessities (sewage provision actually declined). In Germany, the rise of the Nazis ensured municipal politics became polarized and political conflict on the streets widespread. Once in power, the Nazi regime undermined local urban power and authority through arrests of local politicians.

V

The Second World War (with its unprecedented mobilization of state resources), the post-war economic recovery, and the spread of international cooperation set the parameters for urban political development in democratic Europe after 1945. National governments, empowered by new social welfare agendas, greater financial resources, and enlarged bureaucracies, intervened in most aspects of urban life and their principal instrument was the municipality. In Soviet bloc countries, centralization also expanded, driven mainly by Communist party agendas. Across Europe, the balance of power between city and state changed. Town governments usually lost a good deal of their earlier say in the allocation of urban services, but still played a vital role in the delivery of a greatly expanded range of them. As we saw in Chapter 14, councils were heavily implicated in the major post-war housing programmes. Council participation in the expansion of health, education, and leisure services was equally important. In Helsinki, for instance, municipal expenditure on sport and leisure grew fivefold in the post-war era, and doubled again in subsequent decades.

Exemplifying the major expansion of municipal administration and expenditure after the war was transport policy, as cities struggled to cope with the soaring number of motor cars and trucks and all the congestion and environmental hazards they created, including growing air and noise pollution. In the 1950s and 1960s, new roads, including urban motorways (for instance, in Paris or Birmingham), and car park construction were the main priorities, while public transport tended to decline (as in London and Copenhagen). The oil crises of the 1970s triggered a number of moves to upgrade mass transport, which involved new or extended metro systems in Lyon, London, and Helsinki. Falling oil prices and municipal cutbacks during the 1980s tilted the balance back in favour of private transport, and parking restrictions became the main instrument of traffic control; even in Soviet Moscow, mass transit failed to keep pace with population growth. Continuing urban decentralization and the rapid growth of commuting exacerbated the problem: by about 2000 over half of all the jobs in twenty major European cities depended on commuting, frequently by car. In response to the traffic pressure, many communities enlarged the pedestrian areas of their central districts; a number of cities in France and Britain revived their tram systems; and Stockholm and London pioneered congestion charging. The outcomes have been highly variable. In Nordic cities, subsidized public transport ensured that only about 35 per cent of Helsinki and Copenhagen residents drove to work in spite of high levels of car ownership. By contrast, in Sheffield, with similar levels of car ownership, 82 per cent went to work by car, and in Athens only a quarter of residents used public transport.

The rapid growth of urban programmes after the Second World War generated the need both for expanded municipal facilities and a growing civic bureaucracy. Modernist municipal buildings multiplied across Europe: it is difficult to think of a town without one or more. Leeds, for instance, acquired a range of new public buildings, among them a police headquarters, central baths, civic centre, ambulance station, and fire brigade headquarters. The increase of bureaucrats was no less striking. At Toulouse, the number of city employees rose from 3,000 before the war, to 8,700 in 1980. In Britain, local authority employment (predominantly in cities) rose by a half in the years between 1957 and 1972. Especially powerful were the new urban planning departments created after the war, where staffing levels rose quickly. Led frequently by Modernist architects and working closely with local politicians and commercial developers, planning departments were heavily engaged in the major redevelopment of town centres, and large-scale housing projects in the suburbs, as well as traffic management. Already, by the 1970s (see Chapter 15), growing public resistance built up to planning schemes, reflecting a wider feeling that council bureaucrats were too powerful and too close to commercial interests.

A further factor fuelling the expansion of urban administration was the sustained growth of financial resources. At French cities like Toulouse and Besancon, municipal expenditure rose four- or fivefold between 1960 and 1980; at Helsinki, the level more than trebled over the same period, with continuing expansion into the early 1990s. As already noted, civic budgets benefited from growing transfers from the state, albeit with variations between countries: in the Netherlands, in the early 1980s, 81 per cent of municipal revenue came from government sources, compared to 66 per cent in Italy and less than 30 per cent in France and Germany. During the post-war era, local tax revenues were also boosted by the economic upturn, mounting consumption, and rising property values.

Yet, if the post-war era was a dynamic one for municipal administration, several problems became evident. One was the way that councils (outside the Soviet bloc) tended to become more partisan and less consensual, as national party conflicts fuelled division at the local level. While municipal politics in Soviet Europe was undermined by electoral fraud and purges, elsewhere legitimacy was weakened by the slow erosion of electoral participation rates. Here, the decline was most evident in West European countries, and less sharp in Nordic cities: in major German cities, the average rate fell from 73 per cent in 1975–9 to 57 per cent in the mid-1990s, with a similar trend in French cities, whereas in Stockholm rates remained above 80 per cent until the mid-1990s.

Another growing problem was the way that suburbanization and economic growth was increasingly taking place outside municipal limits, posing a long-term threat to urban control and the urban fiscal base. Unlike earlier in the century, only a relatively small number of cities and towns, among them Moscow, Helsinki, and Prague, managed to extend their boundaries in the post-war era: at Helsinki, the annexations of 1946 and 1966 almost quadrupled the city area (to 177 sq km in 1970). Elsewhere, efforts to erect enlarged metropolitan authorities usually failed: the Greater London Council established in 1966 was closed down in 1985, leaving in its stead a mosaic of 272 administrative agencies; Rotterdam's Rijnmond Metropolitan Authority (1964), incorporating twenty-three neighbouring communes, had limited authority and was wound up in 1986; in Denmark, the council for the capital city, created in 1974, was eventually suppressed in 1989, and replaced by ad hoc arrangements within the Copenhagen agglomeration. In France, a number of metropolitan 'communities' were established in 1966 (for example, at Lille), which brought together several local municipalities, but initially they ran up against fierce local opposition. Generally, suburban communities resisted incorporation in civic jurisdictions because of their higher costs and taxes, and the loss of local identity.

In sum, municipal expansion after the Second World War was constructed on less than secure bases. Growing dependence on state financial transfers involved the necessary acceptance of government policy agendas. Urban autonomy suffered. In France, the Modernist housing estates, the 'Grandes Ensembles', constructed in the Paris suburbs and other provincial centres were imposed by the state with little concern for local circumstances or communal limits. In Britain, post-war town councils lost a raft of established powers over health care (after the launch of the National Health Service in 1948), public utilities (following the nationalization of electricity and gas, 1947–8), and (in the case of boroughs) education and planning (due to local government reform in 1970). Nationalization of municipal utilities and public transport was widespread in West European and Nordic countries. In Eastern Europe, Russian occupation involved the imposition of Soviet policies and the widespread eclipse of municipal authority, for instance, over urban planning.

VI

The 1970s and 1980s marked a watershed for the governance of European cities, as for the urban economy. Firstly, conservative financial policies threatened reductions in government funding for urban programmes, just at the time when municipal budgets were often suffering from the manufacturing downturn. The problem was particularly serious in Italian and British cities. In the early 1980s, Italian municipalities lost 13 per cent of their revenues; in Britain, the Thatcher government not only curbed state funding to cities but also stopped city councils increasing local taxation as an alternative. In Finnish cities, the financial problems came at the end of the decade and start of the 1990s.

Secondly, municipalities experienced a crucial upheaval in political relationships with the state. In Britain, central government greatly extended its control over town councils, undermined municipal autonomy, and transferred civic responsibilities to non-elected organizations such as Urban Development Corporations and Enterprise Zones, with a serious effect on municipal capacity to deliver urban services. Conversely, in a number of other countries, national governments gave increased autonomy to town councils. In Sweden and Finland, this was a real transfer of power, affecting social, health, and education services that employed more than three-quarters of municipal workers. In France and Italy, devolution policies were more cosmetic. In France they generated multi-partnerships between state, regions, and cities, together with an infinite complexity of procedures, agreements, and programmes, such as the Societés d'Economie Mixte (1983) and Zones Franches Urbaines (1996). As the French Cours des Comptes observed in 2001, 'the energy spent making this sophisticated system of meetings, exchanges and negotiations work would have been better used making operations concrete'.

A third change marked the growing political activity and militancy of voluntary organizations. Disputes over planning policies gave an initial stimulus to radical and environmental groups that went on to exploit economic and social problems caused by the decline of industrial employment. In the 1970s, radical movements in German cities, including squatter groups and cooperatives, offered new ideas on housing and opposed the large-scale redevelopment of inner-city areas. They also criticized existing state and municipal structures. In French and Scottish cities, like

Roubaix and Glasgow, radical activists allied with local residents angry over redevelopment and housing issues. In Spanish cities, neighbourhood associations inspired the opposition to Francoist town councils in the 1970s, while voluntary organizations for the homeless attracted widespread support in France.

How did European cities and towns respond to these changes in the political landscape? A minority of councils, particularly in Britain (Sheffield, Birmingham, London) sought to increase municipal expenditure, particularly on social welfare, to boost employment and offset state reductions. Such moves were defeated by a determined and hostile Thatcher government. More often, councils went down the road of attempting to pare costs but maintain services through a range of privatization policies. Policies of this kind were pioneered in North American cities from the 1960s and introduced to Europe in the 1980s, principally via international conferences. Much remains to be discovered about this privatization campaign, but everything suggests that heavy pressure came from conservative governments (as in Britain) concerned 'to roll back the state' for ideological reasons, and from right-wing economic theorists, consultants, private companies, and banks. Towns in Britain and France (often led by those with conservative councils) were in the van of the adoption of privatization schemes; other West European cities and councils elsewhere followed more cautiously, though most by the 1990s had introduced some degree of privatization or contracting-out of municipal services.

Strategies varied between countries. In Britain, the government compelled town councils to privatize a large part of their housing stock, and to sell publicly owned utilities to the private sector. After 1988, councils had to put out to competitive tender basic services such as waste disposal or public transport. In French cities, competitive tendering became the norm with a growing range of urban services contracted-out to a few large companies; councils were left merely to regulate their activities as best they could. In Germany, semi-private agencies were established to carry out urban services, and, in Nordic cities, the policy was to set up public–private partnerships to undertake new initiatives. In Finland, partnerships of this type were engaged in the large-scale redevelopment of town centres for commercial purposes. The results boosted rents and commercial profits and benefited affluent consumers, without necessarily being in the interest of local residents. On the other hand, despite privatization, municipal employment has been broadly stable: in Nordic cities such as Helsinki the trend remained upward into the 1990s; in British cities, where a decline occurred earlier in that decade, the number of local authority workers was rising again by its close.

Another development saw civic governments at the close of the twentieth century foster closer ties with the private sector than in the immediate post-war era. In some ways this marked a reversion to the nineteenth-century situation, but with a significant difference: now private companies were often international or global firms rather than local or regional ones. As councils became more business friendly, planning controls were relaxed to facilitate major developments. Also related, the privatization of public utilities and deregulation policies, combined with the arrival of new technologies, led to the de-standardization of urban services, reversing the trend pioneered by municipalities (and states) from the end of the nineteenth century. Services either deteriorated or fragmented. Thus, television, telephone, and Internet services became segmented, with high-quality facilities frequently reserved to a minority paying additional access charges. In other fields, such as waste management or public transport, it is arguable that radical management policies have suffered and services have become less integrated and effective. In Britain, where the privatization of municipal bus companies mostly led to the creation of a few giant monopoly companies and a sharp decline in bus journeys, in those few cities where competition actually functioned, as in Oxford, travellers faced a chaotic overlapping of services.

Furthermore, later twentieth-century city councils not only rebuilt bridges to the private sector, but also sought to incorporate voluntary groups into the political process. Voluntary organizations were frequently used to implement municipal services to reduce costs and to tailor provision more closely to the needs of residents. In German cities, citizen groups and the like were involved in local initiatives on housing and unemployment. In British cities, the provision of social housing was turned over to housing associations. One problem with this strategy was that voluntary organizations became professionalized, and sometimes politicized, and so detached from the ordinary residents they were supposed to represent. They also became too dependent on council policy and funding and, when town councils imposed financial cuts, organizations tended to engage in private lobbying and infighting rather than mobilizing to secure greater public support.

Again, town councils endeavoured to take account of the opinions of residents more effectively, not just via voluntary organizations but through wider forms of consultation. Planning processes in many European cities by the 1980s and 1990s incorporated some form of audit of public opinion. In Swedish and Finnish cities, public consultation became a formal part of the planning procedure. Consultation processes of this type proved problematic, however, given the complex concerns and self-interests of local residents. Thus, recent detailed research on the development of the Vuosaari area of Helsinki in the 1990s concluded that consultation was more pro-forma than real.

What, then, was the condition of urban governance at the end of the twentieth century? At worst, it risked turning into a political morass occupied by competing groups of municipal politicians and bureaucrats, voluntary organizations, residents, and commercial interests. However, in numerous cities, it proved possible to build coalitions of business groups, non-governmental organizations, and local residents to support council initiatives directed at economic growth. At Turin, a political corruption crisis in 1993 led to a new strategic plan for the city promoted through the Torino Internazionale Association that brought together all the councils, chambers of commerce, universities, and other key partners in the conurbation with the aim of reviving the city as a dynamic economic centre. One initiative involved cultural strategies (discussed in Chapter 15): this led to the staging of the Winter Olympics near the city in 2006. Another approach targeted the creation of an innovative environment, extending beyond the older ideas of city universities or science parks to a vision covering the wider city. At Helsinki, in 2003–4, the city council led the way in creating an innovation strategy for the metropolitan region, reinforcing collaboration between the region's councils and universities, national agencies, and the private sector. A joint company, Culminatum, was founded to promote research, the consolidation of expertise clusters, and integrated support for innovative research and development, including the new concept of Living Laboratories. Here, the strategy took advantage of the Finnish system of urban autonomy, supported by extensive fiscal resources. In 2004, the Helsinki region was rated the European leader in competitiveness and creativity.

Too often, European cities at the end of the twentieth century were seen as locked in fierce competition with one another. Inter-city competition and rivalry has, of course, been a strong feature of European urban development since the Middle Ages, but in the 1980s and 1990s rivalry was fanned by state policy (establishing national competitions for government funding), economic upheavals, and the pressures of the international market. As we have observed, this environment contributed to a rush of urban marketing, heavy investment in prestigious infrastructure projects, and competition for international recognition.

However, the close of the century saw greater cooperation between urban communities. At the local level, this sometimes involved adjoining centres cooperating to overcome the fragmentation of services and long-term planning problems that flowed from suburbanization and de-centralization. In Sweden, cooperation between cities led in 1992 to the creation of the Stockholm-Mälär Regional Council with extensive responsibilities for trade and industry, the environment, and infrastructure. At Frankfurt, a similar partnership developed with neighbouring communities for specific administrative purposes. In the Lille area, formal metropolitan cooperation begun in the 1960s was yielding major dividends by the 1990s. Such arrangements proved more successful than attempts at metropolitan annexation on the nineteenth-century model: at Ljubljana, in Slovenia (1994), and Berlin (1996) suburban communities defeated proposed metropolitan extensions.

Inter-urban cooperation at the international level has been encouraged by the European Union. As a result, various consortia of European cities were established to lobby on issues of urban policy, to exploit opportunities for funding, and to disseminate innovations and best practice between urban governments. EUROCITIES, founded in 1986 by six cities, fostered networking, research, and cooperation among a hundred communities and organized a large programme of conferences and publications, as well as funding its own office in Brussels; POLIS (sixty-five cities) concentrated on transport and environmental issues; ENERGIE-CITÉS brought together over 150 municipalities and other groups to develop initiatives on energy management.

From a wider perspective, the European Union after the 1980s presented considerable challenges as well as opportunities for European cities and their leaders. Neo-liberal economic policies exacerbated the plight of traditional urban manufacturing centres (encouraging delocalization, preventing protectionist support), and contributed only marginally to the growth of new advanced technology sectors. On social exclusion and related social problems, the Union's policies proved stronger on rhetoric than content (for example, the Urban II programme 2000—6 under the URBAN Community Initiative provided 728 million euros funding for seventy European cities—only six from the Nordic countries). On the other hand, the Union's environmental policies strengthened the hand of civic authorities in promoting sustainability and green policies on waste management, public transport, and urban regeneration. In addition, heavy Union investment in transport, communications, and other infrastructure enhanced inter-city networking, upgraded urban capacity, particularly in Eastern Europe and the Mediterranean, and so promoted urban integration Europe-wide. Here, and in other ways, the European Union may be seen as helping to complete a pan-European urban system.

VII

How successful European cities and towns have been politically in managing their many problems at the end of our period has depended in considerable measure on the extent of urban autonomy and the quality of civic leadership. In general, bigger urban centres, including major regional cities have done best: smaller centres with minimal political clout have done less well. But important variations are visible across Europe. In Northern Europe, the Nordic cities have taken advantage of their considerable levels of political and financial autonomy to promote new economic growth while ensuring relatively high levels of social cohesion. In Western Europe, German cities, with significant political freedom, have enjoyed some success with their social policies. In contrast, British towns, their autonomy systematically attacked by conservative governments, have faced greater difficulty in managing their economic and social problems. Here, metropolitan centres like Birmingham, Manchester, and Glasgow have done better at marketing themselves as major cultural, shopping, and social centres, though the dividends have been selective. Social problems have deteriorated in these cities, with recurrent issues of drugs, violent crime, and deprivation in inner-city areas.

In the Mediterranean region the picture has been varied. In Spain, leading cities have benefited from the high level of regional autonomy and have undertaken major commercial, infrastructure, and touristic investment, as in the case of Barcelona, Toledo, Bilbao, and Seville. In Portugal, lack of coordination in metropolitan government at Lisbon has led to serious inefficiency and financial problems. Among the Italian cities, Turin has proved successful in responding to its industrial decline, but Milan, like many other communities, has suffered from issues of decision-making, corruption, and problems of infrastructure development. At Athens, issues of clientage and municipal–state relations have retarded the city's prosperity. In Eastern Europe, cities have slowly recovered their autonomy since 1990 but serious political problems have remained. Political reform has sometimes led to municipal fragmentation.

VIII

As Chapters 12–16 have demonstrated, the nineteenth and twentieth centuries wrought the transformation of urban Europe. Though Western Europe led the way in the urbanization process, other regions increasingly caught up, and by the late twentieth century most parts of Europe had the majority, sometimes the great majority, of their inhabitants resident in towns. Virtually all layers of the urban order experienced long-term growth, including regional centres and some small towns, but the trend was biased towards bigger cities. Capital cities, both old and new, consolidated their ascendancy in national urban networks, but they were joined in the nineteenth century by major industrial and port towns. In 1900, these comprised 57 per cent of the largest thirty European cities, their presence especially notable in Western Europe. By comparison, the other main types of specialist towns multiplying in the period—military towns and the hundreds of spa and seaside towns—were a lot smaller. In the later twentieth century, many big centres, including industrial and port cities, suffered from a stagnation or loss of population, due to demographic decentralization and contraction of manufacturing and dock employment. Arguably this has tended to rebalance the urban network more towards traditional medium-size regional centres and smaller towns.

Powering urban growth, particularly during the nineteenth and early twentieth century, was extensive industrialization, as production mechanized, diversified, and became ever more focused on towns. In West European cities, especially, there was an upsurge of large-scale factory production, but this was only part of a dual industrial system in which workshop output remained important across European cities. During the later twentieth century, small-scale output experienced a renaissance with the spread of new high-technology, consumer, and engineering industries, at a time when old large-scale manufacturing was in decay. As we discovered, however, industrialization was only one of the economic engines of European urban expansion. From the late nineteenth century, the service sector experienced a massive take-off, covering retailing, finance, the professions, public utilities, cultural and leisure industries, and tourism and local government. In the late twentieth century, financial services, tourism, and the entertainment sectors became essential pillars helping to stabilize European urban economies after the manufacturing crisis of the 1970s and 1980s.

Socially, the period was no less crucial, resolving many of the problems that had beset European cities since the medieval era and before. Not only was there a conquest of epidemic disease, as urban mortality rates fell below rural ones, but hitherto excluded or marginalized populations of cities—women, lower-class people, the elderly, and young—became more integrated into the urban community, though the process was still incomplete at the end of the period. Class formation was a striking phenomenon. If the nineteenth century saw the rise of the urban middle class as a powerful social, political, and cultural force in many cities, eclipsing the role of traditional elites, by the inter-war era, their social ascendancy was challenged by a new working-class identity, reflecting improved living standards, education, and political awareness. However, in the late twentieth century, the urban working class was transformed by new social opportunities created by social welfare and post-war affluence, by suburbanization, and by the decline of traditional blue-collar jobs and unions from the 1980s. Class boundaries and distinctions were also elided by the growth of mass entertainments.

Culturally, cities became the dominant European player, sweeping aside their old competitors—the Courts and countryside. Religious belief remained a powerful force into the early twentieth century, but there was a decisive shift toward secular activities, including music-making, the theatre, arts, and clubs and societies, drawing on the cultural innovations of the Enlightenment city. Initially, the impetus came from the bourgeoisie who were concerned to promote class identity, civic pride, and the social disciplining of the lower classes. But, from the end of the nineteenth century, commercialism, alongside growing popular demand, gained the upper hand and fed the growth of the popular press, cinema, radio, and sports, which appealed to a wider mass market. In many ways, urban cultural life reached its zenith in terms of the range and vitality of its local activity in the early part of the twentieth century. Ultimately, as part of the commercialization process, cultural life lost much of its distinctive urban identity and became subsumed in national and international trends. But, in the last years of the twentieth century, city leaders sought to revive the distinctive cultural role of cities through cultural initiatives and marketing. Changes in the landscape reflected similar trends. As we have seen, the nineteenth-century emphasis was on developing city centres as a stage for bourgeois cultural, political, and economic aspirations. In the twentieth century, the growth of suburbs and social housing, along with city centre redevelopment, was increasingly shaped by national and international planning movements. Finally, at the end of the period, there has been an attempt by civic fathers to restore the distinctive townscape through cultural and other prestige building projects in city centres.

Municipal leaders had a key role in shaping the development of their communities in the modern period. In the early nineteenth century, municipal parsimony and conservatism combined to continue the tradition of limited civic government inherited from the early modern era, as cities palpably failed to grapple with the deficit of services and infrastructure created by mounting urbanization. However, from the end of the century, municipal government enjoyed something of a golden era in terms of the allocation and delivery of a growing range of services for the large proportion of inhabitants. Here, it was buttressed by a closer partnership with central government, improved civic finances, and an expanded bureaucracy. Especially in the years after 1945, European cities were the main proving grounds for large-scale increases in social welfare, health, education, and social housing. In the later twentieth century, the encroachment of state power, financial cutbacks, and privatization policies reduced the power of the municipality and created a more pluralistic system of urban governance, involving voluntary organizations, commercial interests, and (in theory) local residents.

The urban transformation of Europe was never a smooth process. In the early nineteenth century, urban and industrial expansion occurred at the expense of the most vulnerable, marginalized members of the community—the labouring poor, recent migrants, children, and lower-class women. Widespread social deprivation was matched by environmental degradation. In the late twentieth century, the crisis in urban manufacturing led to heavy unemployment and serious social distress, especially in metropolitan cities and industrial towns. Urban problems were exacerbated by the decentralization of populations, reductions in social welfare provision, and heavy ethnic immigration. Social deterioration became acute in inner-city and out-of-town social housing estates (particularly in Western Europe), areas that tended to attract not only the unemployed but also the elderly, vulnerable families, and ethnic migrants at the end of the twentieth century.

The upheavals of the 1970s and after had wider implications for the European urban order. In general, West European cities, long the urban pace-setters, proved less creative in managing the economic and social problems than their counterparts in outer Northern Europe with their often greater levels of civic autonomy and urban initiative, and more effective investment in new industries, high-quality education, and social provision. Without large-scale manufacturing sectors, Mediterranean cities apparently shrugged off the economic and social problems in the short term but failed—with the notable exception of Spain—to capitalize fully on the opportunities to modernize their urban structure. In Eastern Europe, the decline of urban manufacturing contributed to the eventual collapse of Soviet rule after 1989, followed by a broad if sometimes slow urban recovery.

Yet, for all these continuing variations in performance across the continent, there can be no doubt about the underlying resilience and capacity of many European cities and towns in the twentieth century to resolve and bounce back from crises. By 2000, many urban economies had generally come to grips with de-industrialization and mounting global competition through a decisive expansion of their service functions and, in some countries, advanced manufacturing sector. At the start of the new century, the various regional urban networks across Europe were starting to coalesce and form, arguably for the first time in our period, a truly European urban system. Of the Four Horsemen of the Apocalypse that had so blighted the lives of medieval and early modern citizens, only war continued to disfigure European cities into the late twentieth century, and even here the crises caused by military devastation, as in the two world wars and Balkan wars, were overcome, by historic standards, relatively quickly. In the final chapter of this book, we need to try and explain the success of European cities in maintaining their resilience, effectiveness, and coherence in a global society.

17

Conclusion

I n the year 2000, Europe was still one of the most heavily urbanized continents in the world, only outranked by the great city systems of North and South America (see Table 17.1).

As this book has revealed, the making of urban Europe since the early Middle Ages was a slow and complex process with sudden rushes of expansion, but also numerous changes of gear and losses of momentum. Urban decline after the disintegration of the Roman Empire in the West was only slowly reversed in the eighth and ninth centuries, but by the high Middle Ages the rate of urban growth was as high as at any time before the nineteenth century, only to be followed by widespread urban deceleration after the Black Death. Renewed growth in the sixteenth century was succeeded again by decline over the next century, before urban recovery began in the fifty years or so before the French Revolution. Setbacks as a result of the revolutionary wars were soon reversed and the locomotive of urbanization built up inexorable steam from the mid-nineteenth century, turning Europe definitively urban after the Second World War, though with renewed problems and setbacks, including the decline of specialist cities, in the later twentieth century.

Table 17.1. Urbanization rates across the world in 2000

	Percentage urban %
Africa	36.2
Asia	37.1
Australasia/Oceania	70.5
Europe	71.7
Latin America and Caribbean	75.4
North America	79.1

Source: *UN World Urbanization Prospects* 2005

Despite this volatility of urban change, a number of the underlying forces shaping the evolution of European cities have emerged in this book. It is these dynamic forces that need to be recapitulated before we turn to a comparative evaluation of European urban achievements in a global context.

I

Throughout this book, we have emphasized the regional imperative. During the medieval period and into the sixteenth century, the Mediterranean cities, particularly those of the western Mediterranean, forced the pace of change. Drawing on their early start in the ancient world, they managed to overcome the many threats and setbacks of the late Roman and early medieval period to enjoy sustained growth, affluence, significant civic autonomy, and cultural revival by the thirteenth century. In spite of the late medieval economic recession, north Italian cities were in the van of the Renaissance in art, architecture, and literature. But, by the sixteenth century, the towns of Western Europe had started to catch up, led first by the cities of the Southern Netherlands, and then after the revolt against Spain by Dutch cities. When the Dutch golden age faded, other West European cities took charge. As we saw in Chapter 7, London and Paris, capital cities of powerful states, became leading commercial hubs and beacons of the Enlightenment, while British provincial towns along with urban centres in the Southern Netherlands (after 1830 Belgium), France, and Germany began to industrialize and expand. In the nineteenth century, Western Europe's urban primacy was underpinned not only by the growth of large-scale manufacturing and a burgeoning service sector, but also by innovation in infrastructure investment, planning, social policy, and cultural life. However, as we argued in the last part of this book, during the twentieth century other urban regions closed the gap on Western Europe, and at the end of the century it was the cities and towns of outer Northern Europe—from Ireland to the Eastern Baltic—that often set the pace in economic, political, and cultural creativity.

Urban regional trends were determined by a host of factors. Up to the nineteenth century, advances in agrarian productivity were of key significance, affecting the early medieval revival of Italian cities and the expansion of West European ones during the high Middle Ages, while improvements in agriculture in Britain, the Low Countries, and other parts of Western Europe enabled, by improving food supply and releasing labour from the land, the new surge of urbanization in that region in the eighteenth century. Agrarian (and transport) advances in North America, in the late nineteenth century, unlocked much of Europe's dependence on domestic agriculture and helped release the wider urban transformation across the continent during the twentieth century. Changes of direction in trade were no less critical: the rise of overland trade with the Middle and Far East that aided the precocious development of medieval Italian and Spanish cities; the dramatic rise of Atlantic and Asian commerce from the seventeenth century that lubricated the economic development of West European cities; and the new directions in trade at the end of the twentieth century, that advantaged North and East European countries and cities closer to Asian markets.

Industrial specialization played its part too. From the end of the eighteenth century, West European cities built their industrial take-off on the exploitation of fossil fuels and other mineral resources in their regions, that enabled the growth of extensive, mechanized, factory production and the rise of specialist manufacturing towns. But this was only one specific phase in Europe's urban development. In the Middle Ages, industrial specialization, producing a range of luxury and more basic products, provided the key to the manufacturing success of the north Italian and later Flemish cities, while in the early modern period craft specialization created dynamic industrial regions in the Western Netherlands and in England. In the late twentieth century, industrial specialization has often been linked, notably in Northern and Mediterranean Europe, to the growth of small-scale, dispersed, and flexible manufacturing production in advanced technology, communications, and media. The specialist workshop—not the factory—has been the abiding ingredient of Europe's manufacturing success over the centuries.

We have also examined how the service sector has been crucial to Europe's urban advance. In the late Middle Ages, the Renaissance was, above all, a service revolution encouraging the growth of new professions, like law and medicine, new retailing and victualling trades, new schools, universities, and printing presses—inaugurating indeed the first information age: such developments played a key part in Mediterranean cities and to a lesser extent elsewhere in helping cushion the effects of the economic instability of the late Middle Ages. The Enlightenment, too, was heavily geared to the introduction, initially in West European centres, of a new generation of service trades, from concert promoter to theatre manager, from bookseller to engineer, and, in the late nineteenth century, West Europe's urban hegemony was buttressed, as we saw in Chapter 13, by an explosion of the tertiary sector. Little wonder that the main urban response to the manufacturing crisis of the late twentieth century has been focused on the further elevation of the service city.

Power has been another vital determinant of urban development since the Middle Ages. Located as the Western Mediterranean was at the heart of the world's first command economy, the Roman Empire, it was paradoxical that when Roman power in the West collapsed, it was the political vacuum created by the battles of Pope and Emperor, Christian and Muslim rulers, that enabled the ascent of the Italian city-states and powerful Iberian cities in the high Middle Ages. After the Reformation, the rise of nation-states had a more negative effect, as towns were ruthlessly exploited and squeezed as milch cows for royal military and strategic ambition, yet, by the eighteenth century, Enlightenment rulers in Western Europe promoted the economic interests of their capitals, ports, and other key towns, even if their political autonomy was curtailed. In the later nineteenth century, the success of West European cities was underpinned by the trend towards greater partnership between powerful expansive states and effective city government, though that partnership started to become unbalanced in the later twentieth century.

Cultural changes, too, have been of critical significance in shaping urban fortunes. Given the extensive (if degraded) infrastructure and sense of urban identity inherited from the Roman era, it is hardly surprising that it was the Mediterranean cities that first re-established in the high Middle Ages the powerful cultural voice and ascendancy of cities over the countryside, attracting clergy, landowners, writers, architects, and artists to celebrate and promote urban cultural life. In Western Europe during the eighteenth century Enlightenment values, increasingly fed by commercialization and the affluence of urban elites, promoted the modernization of European urban culture, representing traditional rural life as backward and old-fashioned and laying the foundations for the international fame and influence of West European cities in the late nineteenth century. In the late twentieth century, as we have seen, municipal councils have fought to market the cultural image of their communities in the battle to obtain global recognition.

Of course, the dynamism of European towns and cities stemmed not just from structural factors, whether external or internal. The recurrent volatility of European communities has yielded dividends. Frequently, new bursts of urban energy, new shifts in direction, and new phases of innovation have come in response to periods of crisis. The late medieval crisis of demographic decline, falling demand, and problems of urban manufacturing also stimulated important innovations. Economically, it triggered the growth of new specialist, often luxury industries, and the emergence of the service sector already noted. Eager to attract affluent outsiders to town, civic leaders made environmental improvements with piped water supplies and paved streets and street cleaning, as well as marketing themselves through plays, pageants, and town bands. This onrush of innovation set the compass for many European towns into the early modern era. In a similar fashion, the social, political, and environmental upheavals of the early and middle decades of the nineteenth century, as European communities were swamped by demographic and industrial growth, played an equally vital part in the wave of administrative, social, and other reforms broadly associated with municipal socialism. In the later twentieth century, the crisis of European manufacturing employment helped propel a shift not only towards a service economy, but also towards increased civic cooperation with the private sector, and heavy municipal sponsorship of urban marketing. Arguably, such developments offered a springboard for the recovery of many European cities at the end of the period.

What were the mechanics in helping European cities to generate effective responses to crises? And why did some cities prove more responsive than others? Throughout this book, we have seen how immigration has exercised a key role in replenishing the population and labour market of cities hit by demographic crises, whether as a result of epidemics or due to war. But immigrants have also contributed to the diffusion of innovation, as in the spread of new textile trades in Italian cities in the thirteenth century, or in the transfer of British technology to continental cities in the nineteenth century. The influx of landed immigrants with their tower houses transformed the landscape of high medieval Italian cities, just as noble newcomers helped transmute eighteenth-century cities like London and Paris into places of high fashion and enlightenment. Urban elites were frequently reinvigorated by a wave of outsiders. In the late twentieth century, as in earlier centuries, ethnic migrants have often brought essential trades and skills to European cities. Those cities which have gained most from their migrant influxes have been those like medieval Venice and Barcelona, seventeenth-century Amsterdam and Georgian London, and some of the modern Nordic cities which have been tolerant enough, often through active municipal policies, to welcome newcomers and encourage them to enter into the urban mainstream, whether in business, politics, or cultural life.

An under-researched theme is the role of female migrants in helping to revitalize urban economies. In the late Middle Ages, the influx of women into towns may well have contributed, through their cheap flexible labour, to the advent of new service trades. During the eighteenth century, high levels of female immigration in West European cities may have promoted not only the tertiary sector but also new kinds of manufacturing process. Women up to the end of the nineteenth century were generally marginalized from the urban mainstream, but this did not stop them having a creative influence on urban society. Affluent women in Italian Renaissance cities performed a vital part, through their interest in fashion, in stimulating demand for new luxury and retailing trades. Smart women in Enlightenment cities became prominent actors both in the consumption of public culture—from music concerts to the theatre and art exhibitions—and in the reshaping of the urban household with a growing female emphasis on gendered space, privacy, and cleanliness. Women in the twentieth-century city were at the forefront of new ideas on green space—on neighbourhood parks, allotment gardens, and children's play areas—as cities struggled to cope with the social costs of industrial urbanization.

Over the centuries, there has been a constant dialogue in European cities between social and other pressures and creativity. High levels of immigration and mobility in cities, along with widespread poverty, have often generated real problems of urban dislocation, social polarization, and political tension. Frequently, cities responded strongly to problems of this kind by fabricating a whole series of stratagems for reinforcing a sense of urban identity. Those early symbols of urban status—walls and churches—were regularly rebuilt, and by the fifteenth century they were joined by a repertoire of municipal buildings, including town halls and market houses. New cultural buildings also sprang up in Enlightenment cities, but it was in the late nineteenth century, in response to rapid urban growth and social and political unrest, that one sees the marshalling in city centres of a battery of grandiose buildings—from museums to railway stations—to guard and reassert civic identity and cohesion. Urban upheavals in the later twentieth century also triggered a wave of new monumental public and commercial buildings: Berlin's Potsdamer Platz, with its architectural extravaganza of shopping arcades, high-rise office blocks, and transport facilities, was designed in the 1990s to reunify the two halves of a divided post-war city. Cities and towns at the end of our period further sought to strengthen urban identity and market the urban place through the promotion of international events, popular festivals, and other entertainments—following a policy dating back, as we have seen, to the late Middle Ages.

Resources, along with financial and political autonomy, are clearly vital for funding urban marketing and other strategies, which have been devised in response to the many challenges facing cities. In the medieval period, it was no accident that it was the wealthy city-states of northern Italy with their high degree of financial and political autonomy that were most effective in extracting trade privileges from kings and emperors, or projecting their urban image through a kaleidoscope of public buildings. In the late twentieth century, Nordic cities (and those in Germany) which enjoy extensive municipal independence have proved relatively successful in promoting new economic development, as well as maintaining social cohesion. By itself, municipal autonomy is no guarantee for success, as is evident from the stagnation of many of the German imperial cities or Italian city-states like Venice during the eighteenth century. Autonomy needs to be combined with imaginative civic leadership. Here, from our survey, it would seem that open, cosmopolitan town magistracies, willing to learn from elsewhere and embrace change, have been most successful in advancing their cities. Time and again, we have seen how the quality of urban leadership is a vital factor in the success or otherwise of European urban communities.

Competition from other cities has been a major challenge for many European urban communities since the Middle Ages, whether one thinks of the battles between the Italian city-states of the twelfth and thirteenth centuries or the conflicts between textile towns during the early modern era, or the fierce rivalry among contemporary cities to win the right to stage international events or spectacles. Yet such competition has often been a way by which communities defined their own identity as well as being stimulus for improvement and renewal. Along with competition has come emulation, whether in the establishment of communes in Mediterranean and West European cities after the eleventh century, in the rebuilding of town churches during the Counter-Reformation, in the installation of street lighting, pavements, and street cleaning in eighteenth-century cities, or the rapid diffusion of ideas of public infrastructure and utilities at the end of the nineteenth and start of the twentieth centuries. Moreover, as we have regularly observed, competition has been tempered by or conjoined with inter-city collaboration, which has often provided a vital boost to urban development, enabling cities to overcome external pressures and challenges. Among the most important developments of this kind have been the German city leagues of the Middle Ages, the informal network of Dutch cities forming the Randstad during the seventeenth century, and the later twentieth-century European urban consortia that support the dissemination of innovation and best practice among member cities.

In sum, what has been striking about European cities and towns in our period is the way that the challenges and threats to urban development—high mobility, economic downturns, problems of urban identity, issues of political autonomy, and inter-urban competition—have often been used creatively by communities, particularly the most successful ones with strong imaginative leaderships, to strengthen their identity and improve their performance. Creativity and innovativeness—with new ideas transmitted across the urban network through a range of vectors including migrants, universities, voluntary associations, publications, professional activities, international exhibitions, and conferences, as well as municipal action—have indeed been one of the distinctive features of European cities to the present time.

II

Certainly, European cities are confronted with many challenges in a globalizing environment. Interaction with the non-European world is not new, as we have seen throughout this book, but in the past it often had a selective, regional bias. In the Middle Ages, commercial centres, particularly in the Mediterranean, enjoyed a range of trading, demographic, and cultural connections with the Arab world and, via the overland route, to Asia, while Islamic rule left its influence on the architecture and art of Iberian cities. From the fifteenth century, the Ottoman military advance in the Balkans and Eastern Europe had a powerful effect on the pattern, economy, and landscape of towns in those regions, just as in Western Europe burgeoning European exploration and trade from the sixteenth century across the Atlantic and Pacific lubricated the prosperity of Atlantic port cities, created markets for urban manufactures, exported European-style towns and settlers particularly to the Americas, and opened the door to a flood of imported consumer goods from chinaware to cotton, from sugar to tea, as well as creating the first fashion for Asiatic styles. In the nineteenth and early twentieth centuries, interaction intensified, and reshaped the European urban economy and cultural life (from American films to bamboo furniture), while European global hegemony spawned a host of European colonial and neo-colonial cities across Africa and Asia. Since the 1960s, many European towns have been transformed both by the impact of Asian imports on European manufacturing and by the influx of population from developing countries.

At the start of the twenty-first century, European cities appear increasingly overtaken on a number of key criteria by their counterparts in Asia and the Americas. If Europe still remains one of the most urbanized continents, this record may soon be eclipsed in the wake of the torrential growth of cities elsewhere. Of the world's hundred largest agglomerations only eight were located in Europe in 2005 (against eighteen in 1975), and in 2015 it is projected that the figure will decline to just five. Again, Europe, according to some estimates, has only about four of the world's global city regions—greater London, greater Paris, the Randstad, and greater Frankfurt—compared to large numbers in Asia and Latin America. In terms of global economic activity, the track record of European cities appears only moderately successful. Not only have they lost a major part of their basic manufacturing capacity to new production centres in the developing world, but, in finance, where Europe's cities dominated the scene into the early twentieth century, only London, Zürich, Geneva, and Paris figured among the top ten world cities in 2007, and among the leading fifty cities the significant majority were non-European. As for gross domestic product, only London and Paris appear in the top decennial, though thirty European cities—including not just capital cities but leading regional centres like Birmingham, Lyon, and Münich—are well represented in the top 100 world cities.

On the other hand, in many sectors, the achievements of the European urban order remain impressive. In terms of the number and diversity of towns—ranging from multi-functional capital cities to regional centres, smaller communities, and specialist towns—Europe has a much denser network than any other continent, a nascent urban system based on strong national and regional economies, relatively efficient, pan-European transport and communication links, and powerful support from the European Union for greater integration. In the United States and Japan, in the 1990s, about three-quarters of the urban population resided in cities of more than 200,000 people, against 56 per cent in Europe (and 40 per cent of the total population). Clearly, the longevity of the European urban network dating back to the high Middle Ages, and in some regions much longer, is of fundamental importance for its multi-layered density and strength.

With regard to their physical extent, European cities are now largely overshadowed by those in Latin America or Asia, which, since the late twentieth century, have witnessed relentless urban sprawl, sometimes doubling their size in a couple of decades. Of the thirty-eight world agglomerations, covering an area of more than 3,000 square kilometres, only one or two European cities figure in the list. But, as we know, spatial size can spawn many problems not least for governance and urban coherence. Many large cities in the United States, where most growth since the 1940s has been concentrated in an ever-widening ring of suburbs, leaving stagnant or collapsing city cores, are administered by a multitude of local authorities, beset by fiscal problems, unable to put the urban humpty dumpty back together again. In Latin America, the enormous sprawling *barrios* are often outside municipal control: at Rio de Janeiro, over 80 per cent of the population lives beyond the municipal borders. Though some recent advances have occurred in urban autonomy and civil society, urban governance in developing countries is too often blighted not only by fragmentation but also by corruption and a lack of financial and other resources. As a result, issues such as urban poverty, unemployment, crime, and environmental degradation, including air pollution, water quality, and toxic wastes, have overwhelmed many city administrations. By contrast, most European cities and towns, in spite of the late twentieth-century trend towards decentralization, have remained physically cohesive with vital and dynamic city cores and generally effectual urban government

Again, while European citizens are rightly concerned at the growth of new slums, deprived inner-city and peripheral estate areas, with their chronic problems of social exclusion and crime, these bear no comparison with the areas of poverty and social difficulty in the cities of Latin America or South-East Asia, where up to half the inhabitants may be below the poverty level at times, many of them living in illegal shanty-towns.

Despite strong economic growth, globalization and conservative economic policies have often yielded the middling classes and workers meagre dividends. In North American cities, the middle classes are more likely to experience downward social mobility than upward movement, and there has been mounting economic and social polarization. By contrast, for many European cities the role of social welfare transfers and education remain crucial for containing poverty levels and ensuring a measure of social mobility and social cohesion.

In sum, many of the key achievements of the European city of the later nineteenth and twentieth centuries—effective municipal governance, the provision of infrastructure, utility, and welfare services for the large part of the urban population, planned green areas—remain largely intact, despite some moves at the end of the twentieth century to dismantle them or roll them back. In terms of quality of life, European cities perform very well: here, seven of the top ten global cities in 2007 were European, and half of the top fifty were from the same continent. In the case of the key indicators of health and sanitation, European cities again figure prominently in global rankings, with the Nordic cities led by Helsinki (ranked third globally) doing especially well. In terms of attractiveness, European cities remain world leaders. Of the top fifty international destinations for tourist arrivals in 2006, nearly half were European cities, with London in the global lead.

In a new world order of rising population, affluence, and environmental constraints, Europe's compact, effectively governed, environmentally conscious, heavily networked cities and towns, collaborating as well as competing, creative and innovative, have much to offer. Given adequate levels of funding and public support, as in the Nordic countries, all the signs are that this European urban model not only works, but is highly successful in generating economic and cultural dynamism. Thus, the long history of European cities since the fifth century may well help to determine their future in the twenty-first century.

Select Bibliography

Items of special or general importance are starred (*)

1. Introduction

General Surveys

Bairoch, P. *Cities and Economic Development from the Dawn of History to the Present*, (transl. C. Braider, London, 1988)

*Bairoch, P. et al. *La population des villes européennes 800–1850* (Geneva, 1988)

Hall, P. *Cities in Civilization* (London, 1998)

Hohenberg, P., and Lees, L. H. *The Making of Urban Europe 1000–1950* (2nd edition, London, 1995)

*Pinol, J-L., ed. *Histoire de l'Europe urbaine* (2 vols, Paris, 2003)

Methodology and Literature

Clark, P. 'The City', in P. Burke, ed., *History and Historians in the 20th Century* (Oxford, 2002), pp. 37–54

Manninen, A. et al. 'Urban History Research-Dynamic in Europe today' (Britain, Italy, Netherlands, Sweden, Germany), *Helsinki Quarterly, 3/2002* (2002): 3–41

Rodger, R. ed. *European Urban History: Prospect and Retrospect* (Leicester, 1993)

Ancient Period

Amery, C., and Curran, B. *The Lost World of Pompeii* (London, 2002)

Coulston, J., and Dodge, H., eds. *Ancient Rome: The Archaeology of the Eternal City* (Oxford, 2000)

Drinkwater, J. F. *Roman Gaul: The Three Provinces 58 BC–AD 260* (London, 1983)

Finley, M. I. 'The Ancient City: From Fustel de Coulanges to Max Weber and Beyond', in B. D. Shaw and R. P. Saller, eds, *Economy and Society in Ancient Greece* (London, 1981), pp. 3–23

Mattingly, D. J. *An Imperial Possession: Britain in the Roman Empire 54 BC–AD 409* (London, 2006)

Osbourne, R., and Cunliffe, B., eds. *Mediterranean Urbanization 800–600 BC* (Oxford, 2005)

Potter, T. W. *Roman Italy* (London, 1987)

Wacher, J. S. *The Towns of Roman Britain* (London, 1975)

Whittacker, C. R. 'Do Theories of the Ancient City Matter?', in T. J. Cornell and K. Lomas, eds, *Urban Society in Roman Italy* (London, 1995), pp. 9–26

PART I: 400–1500

General Surveys/Collected Volumes

Coulet, N., and Guyotjeannin, O., eds. *La ville au Moyen Âge* (Paris, 1998)

*Ennen, E. *The Medieval Town* (transl. N. Fryde, Amsterdam, 1979)

Heers, J. *La ville au Moyen Âge en occident* (Paris, 1990)

Nicolas, D. *The Growth of the Medieval City: From Late Antiquity to the Early 14th Century* (London, 1997)

Nicolas, D. *The Later Medieval City 1300–1500* (London, 1997)

_____ *Urban Europe 1100–1700* (Basingstoke, 2003)

Simms, A., and Clarke, H. B., eds. *The Comparative History of Urban Origins in non-Roman Europe: Ireland, Wales, Denmark, Germany, Poland, and Russia from the Ninth to the Thirteenth Century* (Oxford, 1985)

National/Regional Surveys

Christie, N., ed. *From Constantine to Charlemagne: An Archaeology of Italy AD 300–800* (Aldershot, 2006)

Fevrier, P-A. *Le développement urbain en Provence de l'époque romain à la fin du XIVe siècle* (Paris, 1964)

Holt., R., and Rosser, G., eds. *The English Medieval Town: A Reader in English Urban History 1200–1540* (London, 1990)

*Jones, P. J. *The Italian City-State* (Oxford, 1997)

*Menjot, D. *Les espagnes médiévales 409–1474* (Paris, 1996)

*Palliser, D. M., ed. *The Cambridge Urban History of Britain: I: 600–1540* (Cambridge, 2000)

Renouard, Y. *Les villes d'Italie de la fin du Xe siècle au début du XIVe siècle* (Paris, 1969)

Individual Cities/Towns

Barron, C. M. *London in the Later Middle Ages* (Oxford, 2004)

Carrère, C. *Barcelone: Centre économique á l'époque des difficultés 1380–1462* (Paris, 1967)

Carter, F. W. *Trade and Urban Development in Poland: An Economic Geography of Cracow, from its Origins to 1795* (Cambridge, 1994)

Epstein, S. A. *Genoa and the Genoese 958–1528* (London, 1996)

Herlihy, D. *Pisa in the Early Renaissance* (New Haven, 1958)

_____ *Medieval and Renaissance Pistoia: the Social History of an Italian Town 1200–1430* (New Haven, 1967)

Lane, F. C. *Venice: A Maritime Republic* (Baltimore, 1973)

Nicholas, D. *The Metamorphosis of a Medieval City: Ghent in the Age of the Arteveldes 1302–1390* (Leiden, 1987)

2. Urban Trends 400–1500

Andersson, H. 'Urbanisation', in K. Helle, ed., *Cambridge History of Scandinavia: I* (Cambridge, 2003), pp. 312–42

Austin, D., and Alcock, L., eds. *From the Baltic to the Black Sea: Studies in Medieval Archaeology* (London, 1990)

*Brogiolo, G. P., and Ward-Perkins, B., eds. *The Idea and Ideal of the Town between Late Antiquity and the Early Middle Ages* (Leiden, 1999)

*Christie, N., and Loseby, S. T., eds. *Towns in Transition* (Aldershot, 1996)

Clarke, H., and Ambrosiani, B. *Towns in the Viking Age* (revised edition, London, 1995)

Dahlbäck, G. 'The Towns', in Helle, ed., *Cambridge History of Scandinavia: I* (Cambridge, 2003), pp. 611–34

Dollinger, P. *The German Hansa* (transl. and ed. D. S. Ault and S. H. Steinberg, London, 1970)

Guidoni, E. *La ville européenne: Formation et signification du quatrième siècle* (Brussels, 1981)

Hilton, R. H. *English and French Towns in Feudal Society: A Comparative Study* (Cambridge, 1992)

Hodges, R., and Hobley, B., eds. *The Rebirth of Towns in the West AD 700–1050* (London, 1988)

Holt, R. 'What if the Sea Were Different? Urbanization in Medieval Norway', in C. Dyer et al., eds., *Rodney Hilton's Middle Ages* (Oxford, 2007), pp. 132–47

Mitchell, K., and Wood, I., eds. *The World of Gregory of Tours* (Leiden, 2002)

Nilsson, L., and Lilja, S., eds. *The Emergence of Towns: Archaelogy and Early Urbanization in Non-Roman, North-West Europe* (Stockholm, 1996)

Samsonowicz, H. 'Les villes d'Europe centrale à la fin du Moyen Âge', *Annales E.S.C.*, 43 (1988): 173–84

Slater, T.R., ed. *Towns in Decline AD 100–1600* (Aldershot, 2000)

Tikhomirov, M. *The Towns of Ancient Rus* (transl. from the 2nd Russian edition, Y. Sdobikov, Moscow, 1959)

*Verhulst, A. *The Rise of Cities in North-West Europe* (Cambridge, 1999)

*Wickham, C. *Framing the Early Middle Ages: Europe and the Mediterranean 400–800* (Oxford, 2005)

3. Economy 400–1500

Blockmans, W. B., and Prevenier, W. *The Promised Lands: The Low Countries under Burgundian Rule 1369–1530* (transl. E. Fackelman, Philadelphia, 1999)

Blondé, B., et al., eds. *Buyers and Sellers: Retail Circuits and Practices in Medieval and Early Modern Europe* (Turnhout, 2006)

Boone, M., and Prevenier, W., eds. *La draperie ancienne des Pays-Bas* (Leuven, 1993)

Campbell, B. M. S., et al. *A Medieval Capital and its Grain Supply* (London, 1993)

Carrère, C. *Barcelone, centre économique à l'époque des difficultés 1380–1462* (Paris, 1967)

Constable, O. R. *Trade and Traders in Muslim Spain* (Cambridge, 1994)

Eliassen, F-E., and Ersland, G. A, eds. *Power, Profit, and Urban Land: Landownership in Medieval and Early Modern Northern European Towns* (Aldershot, 1996)

Keene, D. *Survey of Medieval Winchester* (Oxford, 1985)

*Körner, M., ed. *Destruction and Reconstruction of Towns* (vols 1–2, Berne, 1999)

Marshall, R. K. *The Local Merchants of Prato* (London, 1999)

Spufford, P. *Money and its Use in Medieval Europe* (Cambridge, 1988)

Thomas, A. *The Painter's Practice in Renaissance Tuscany* (Cambridge, 1995)

Unger, R. W. *Beer in the Middle Ages and the Renaissance* (Philadelphia, 2004)

*Uytven, van, R. *Production and Consumption in the Low Countries 13th–16th Centuries* (Aldershot, 2001)

*Wee, van der, H. *The Low Countries in the Early Modern World* (Aldershot, 1993)

4. Social Life 400–1500

Brodman, J. W. *Charity and Welfare: Hospitals and the Poor in Medieval Catalonia* (Philadelphia, 1998)

*Carlier, M., and Soens, T., eds. *The Household in Late Medieval Cities: Italy and North Western Europe Compared* (Leuven, 2000)

*Cohn, S. K. Jr. *The Laboring Classes in Renaissance Florence* (New York, 1980)

Dillard, H. *Daughters of the Reconquest: Women in Castilian Town Society 1100–1300* (Cambridge, 1984)

Dyer, C. *Standards of Living in the Later Middle Ages: Social Change in England c.1200–1520* (Cambridge, 1989)

Farmer, S. A. *Surviving Poverty in Medieval Paris: Gender, Ideology, and the Daily Lives of the Poor* (London, 2002)

Geremek, B. *The Margins of Society in Late Medieval Paris* (transl. J. Birrell, Cambridge, 1987)

Gerven, van, J. 'War, Violence and an Urban Society: The Brabantine Towns in the Later Middle Ages', in W. P. Blockmans et al., ed., *Secretum Scriptorum: Liber Alumnorum Walter Prevenier* (Leuven, 1999), pp. 183–212

Henderson, J. *Piety and Charity in Late Medieval Florence* (Oxford, 1994)

*Howell, M. C. *Women, Production and Patriarchy in Late Medieval Cities* (Chicago, 1986)

Little, L. K., ed. *Plague and the End of Antiquity: The Pandemic 541–750* (Cambridge, 2007)

Lynch, K. A. *Individuals, Families, and Communities in Europe 1200–1800: The Urban Foundations of Western Society* (Cambridge, 2003)

Martines, L. *The Social World of the Florentine Humanists* (London, 1963)

Zorzi, A. 'Controle Social, Ordre Public et Repression Judiciare à l'Epoque Communale', *Annales E.S.C.*, 45 (1990): 1169–88

5. Culture and Landscape 400–1500

Arnade, P. J. *Realms of Ritual: Burgundian Ceremony and Civic Life in Late Medieval Ghent* (London, 1996)

Boucheron, P. *Le pouvoir á batir: Urbanisme et politique édilitaire à Milan XIVe–XVe siècles* (Rome, 1998)

Crouzet-Pavan, E. *Venise: Une invention de la ville (XIIIe–XVe siècle)* (Seyssel, 1997)

Flynn, M. *Sacred Charity: Confraternities and Social Welfare in Spain 1400–1700* (Basingstoke, 1989)

Goldthwaite, R. A. *Wealth and the Demand for Art in Italy 1300–1600* (London, 1993)

Grendler, P. F. *Schooling in Renaissance Italy: Literacy and Learning 1300–1600* (London, 1989)

Holmes, G. *Florence, Rome and the Origins of the Renaissance* (Oxford, 1986)

Lecuppre-Desjardin, E. *La ville des cérémonies* (Turnhout, 2004)

Leguay, J-P. *L'eau dans la ville au Moyen Âge* (Rennes, 2002)

Rosser, G. 'Solidarités et Changement Social. Les Fraternités Urbaines Anglaises à la fin du Moyen Âge', *Annales E.S.C.*, 48 (1993): 1127–43

Slater, T. R., and Rosser, G., eds. *The Church in the Medieval Town* (Aldershot, 1998)

Tracy, J. D., ed. *City Walls: The Urban Enceinte in Global Perspective* (Cambridge, 2000)

*Ward-Perkins, B. *From Classical Antiquity to the Middle Ages: Urban Public Building in Northern and Central Italy* AD 300–580 (Oxford, 1984)

6. Governance 400–1500

Bensch, S. P. *Barcelona and its Rulers 1096–1291* (Cambridge, 1995)

*Boone, M., and Prevenier, W., eds. *Finances publiques et finances privées au bas Moyen Âge* (Leuven, 1996)

Brady, T. A. Jr. *Turning Swiss: Cities and Empire 1450–1550* (Cambridge, 1985)

Bulst, N., and Genet, J-P., eds. *La ville, la bourgeoisie et la genèse de l'état moderne* (Paris, 1988)

Finlay, R. *Politics in Renaissance Venice* (London, 1980)

Lunenfeld, M. *Keepers of the City: The Corregidores of Isabella I of Castile 1474–1504* (Cambridge, 1987)

Menjot, D., and Pinol, J-L., eds. *Enjeux et expression de la politique municipale (XIIè–XXè siècles)* (Paris 1997)

Mundy, J. H. *Liberty and Political Power in Toulouse 1050–1230* (New York, 1954)

Powers, J. F. *A Society Organised for War: The Iberian Municipal Militias in the Central Middle Ages 1000–1284* (London, 1988)

Prevenier, W. 'Officials in Town and Countryside in the Low Countries: Social and Professional Developments from the 14th to the 16th Century', *Acta Historiae Neerlandicae*, 7 (1974): 1–17

Reynolds, S. *Kingdoms and Communities in Western Europe 900–1300* (Oxford, 1984)

*Rigaudière, A. *Gouverner la ville au Moyen Âge* (Paris, 1993)

*Tilly, C., and Blockmans, W. P., eds. *Cities and the Rise of States in Europe A.D. 1000 to 1800* (Oxford, 1994), chs. 2–6

PART II: 1500–1800

General Surveys / Collected Volumes

Clark, P., ed. *The Early Modern Town* (London, 1976)

*Clark, P., ed., *Small Towns in Early Modern Europe* (Cambridge, 1995)

*Cowan, A. *Urban Europe 1500–1700* (London, 1998)

Friedrichs, C. R. *The Early Modern City 1450–1750* (London, 1995)

Hohenberg, P. M., and Lees, L. H. *The Making of Urban Europe 1000–1950* (2nd edition, London, 1995)
Livet, G., and Vogler, B., eds. *Pouvoir, ville et société en Europe 1650–1750* (Paris, 1983)
*Meyer, J. et al. *Etudes sur les villes en Europe occidentale* (2 vols, Paris, 1983)

National/Regional Surveys
Barry, J., ed. *The Tudor and Stuart Town* (London, 1990)
*Benedict, P., ed. *Cities and Social Change in Early Modern France* (London, 1989)
*Borsay, P., ed. *The Eighteenth Century Town* (London, 1990)
Borsay, P., and Proudfoot, L., eds. *Provincial Towns in Early Modern England and Ireland* (Oxford, 2002)
*Clark, P., ed. *Cambridge Urban History of Britain: II: 1540–1840* (Cambridge, 2000)
Clark, P., and Slack, P., eds. *Crisis and Order in English Towns 1500–1700* (London, 1972)
*Corfield, P. J. *The Impact of English Towns 1700–1800* (Oxford, 1982)
*Lepetit, B. *The Pre-Industrial Urban System in France* (transl. G. Rogers, Cambridge, 1994)
Miller, J. *Urban Societies in East-Central Europe, 1500–1700* (Aldershot, 2008)
Sandberg, R. 'The Towns, the Urban System and the State in Early Modern Sweden', in K. Stadin, ed., *Society, Towns and Masculinity: Aspects on Early Modern Society in the Baltic Area* (Stockholm, 2001) pp. 63–83
*Schilling, H. *Die Stadt in der Frühen Neuzeit* (Munich, 1993)
Stadin, K., ed. *Baltic Towns and their Inhabitants* (Stockholm, 2003)
Todorov, N. *The Balkan City 1400–1900* (London, 1983)

Individual Communities
Amelang, J. S. *Honored Citizens of Barcelona* (Princeton, 1986)
Beachy, R. *The Soul of Commerce: Credit, Property and Politics in Leipzig 1750–1840* (Leiden, 2005)
Beier, A. L., and Finlay, R., eds. *London 1500–1700: The Making of the Metropolis* (London, 1986)
Burke, P. *Venice and Amsterdam: A Study of 17th-Century Elites* (London, 1974)
Clark, P., and Gillespie, R., eds. *Two Capitals: London and Dublin 1500–1840* (Oxford, 2001)
Dreyfus, F. G. *Sociétés et mentalités à Mayence [Mainz] dans la seconde moitié du XVIIIe siècle* (Paris, 1968)
Farr, J. R. *Hands of Honor: Artisans and their World in Dijon 1550–1650* (London, 1988)
*Friedrichs, C. R. *Urban Society in an Age of War: Nördlingen 1580–1720* (Princeton, 1979)
Garden, M. *Lyon et les Lyonnais au XVIIIe siècle* (Paris, 1975)
Goubert, P. *Beauvais et le Beauvaisis de 1600 à 1730* (Paris, 1960)
*Roche, D. *The People of Paris* (transl. M. Evans, Leamington Spa, 1987)
*Schwarz, L. D. *London in the Age of Industrialisation* (Cambridge, 1992)

SELECT BIBLIOGRAPHY 377

7. Urban Trends 1500–1800

*Benedict, P., ed. *Cities and Social Change in Early Modern France* (London, 1992), chs. 1, 3, 7

Clark, P., and Lepetit, B., eds. *Capital Cities and their Hinterlands in Early Modern Europe* (Aldershot, 1996)

*De Vries, J. *European Urbanization 1500–1800* (London, 1984)

Eliassen F-E., et al., eds. *Regional Integration in Early Modern Scandinavia* (Odense, 2001)

*François, É. 'The German Urban Network between the 16th and 18th Centuries: Cultural and Demographic Indicators' in A. van der Woude et al., eds, *Urbanization in History: A Process of Dynamic Interactions* (Oxford, 1990), pp. 84–100

Garrioch, D. *The Making of Revolutionary Paris* (London, 2002)

Granasztói, G. 'L'urbanisation de l'éspace danubien (1500–1800)', *Annales E.S.C*, 44 (1989): 379–99

*Lawton, R., and Lee, R., eds. *Population and Society in Western European Port Cities c.1650–1939* (Liverpool, 2002)

Maczak, A., and Smout, C., eds. *Gründung und Bedeutung kleinerer Städte im nördlichen Europa der frühen Neuzeit* (Wiesbaden, 1991)

Perrie, M., ed. *The Cambridge History of Russia: I* (Cambridge, 2006), chs. 13, 25

*Reher, D. S. *Town and Country in Pre-Industrial Spain: Cuenca 1550–1870* (Cambridge, 1990)

*Ringrose, D. R. *Madrid and the Spanish Economy 1560–1850* (Berkeley, 1983)

Stobart, J., and Raven, N., eds. *Towns, Regions and Industries: Urban and Industrial Change in the Midlands c.1700–1840* (Manchester, 2005)

Thompson, I. A. A., and Casalilla, B. Y., eds. *The Castilian Crisis of the 17th Century* (Cambridge, 1994)

Wrigley, E. A. 'Urban Growth and Agricultural Change: England and the Continent in the Early Modern Period', in Borsay, ed., *The Eighteenth-Century Town*, pp. 39–82

8. Economy 1500–1800

Barbour, V. *Capitalism in Amsterdam in the 17th Century* (Baltimore, 1950)

Berg, M., ed. *Markets and Manufacture in Early Industrial Europe* (London, 1991)

Blondé, B., et al., eds. *Retailers and Consumer Changes in Early Modern Europe* (Tours, 2005)

Calabi, D. *The Market and the City* (transl. M. Klein, Aldershot, 2004)

Crossick, G., ed. *The Artisan and the European Town 1500–1900* (Aldershot, 1997)

Epstein, S. R., ed. *Town and Country in Europe 1300–1800* (Cambridge, 2001)

Farr, J. F. *Artisans in Europe 1300–1914* (Cambridge, 2000)

Fox, R., and Turner, A. eds. *Luxury Trades and Consumerism in Ancien Régime Paris* (Aldershot, 1998)

Hanne, G. *Le travail dans la ville: Toulouse et Saragosse, des lumières à l'industrialisation* (Toulouse, 2006)

Heeres, W. G., et al., eds. *From Dunkirk to Danzig: Shipping and Trade in the North Sea and the Baltic 1350–1850* (Hilversum, 1988)

*Prak, M., et al. *Craft Guilds in the Early Modern Low Countries* (Aldershot, 2006)

Pullan, B. *Crisis and Change in the Venetian Economy in the 16th and 17th Centuries* (London, 1968)

Scott, T. *Regional Identity and Economic Change: The Upper Rhine 1450–1600* (Oxford, 1997)

Wee, van der, H. *The Low Countries in the Early Modern World* (transl. L. Fackelman, Aldershot, 1993)

9. Social Life 1500–1800

Amelang, J. *The Flight of Icarus: Artisan Autobiography in Early Modern Europe* (Stanford, 1998)

Boulton, J. *Neighbourhood and Society: A London Suburb in the 17th Century* (Cambridge, 1987)

Brennan, T. E. *Public Drinking and Popular Culture in 18th-Century Paris* (Princeton, 1988)

Clark, P. *The English Alehouse: A Social History 1200–1830* (London, 1983)

Clark, P., ed. *The European Crisis of the 1590s* (London, 1985)

Clark, P. 'Improvement, Policy and Tudor Towns', in G. W. Bernard and S. J. Gunn, eds, *Authority and Consent in Tudor England* (Aldershot, 2002), pp. 233–48

Clark, P., and Souden D., eds. *Migration and Society in Early Modern England* (London, 1987)

Fehler, T. G. *Poor Relief and Protestantism: The Evolution of Social Welfare in 16th-Century Emden* (Aldershot, 1999)

Friedrichs, C. R. 'German Town Revolts and the 17th-Century Crisis', *Renaissance and Modern Studies*, 26 (1982): 27–51

Garrioch, D. *The Formation of the Parisian Bourgeoisie 1690–1830* (London, 1996)

Houston, R. A. *Social Change in the Age of Enlightenment: Edinburgh 1660–1760* (Oxford, 1994)

Jones, C. *Charity and Bienfaisance: The Treatment of the Poor in the Montpellier Region 1740–1815* (Cambridge, 1982)

Kaplan, S. L. 'Les corporations, les "faux-ouvriers", et le faubourg St Antoine au XVIII siècle', *Annales E.S.C.*, 43 (1988): 453–78

Landers, J. *Death and the Metropolis: Studies in the Demographic History of London 1670–1830* (Cambridge, 1993)

Lindemann, M. *Medicine and Society in Early Modern Europe* (Cambridge, 1999)

Österberg, E., and Lindström, D. *Crime and Social Control in Medieval and Early Modern Swedish Towns* (Uppsala, 1988)

Pardailhé-Galabrun, A. *La naissance de l'intime: 3000 foyers parisiens XVIIe–XVIIIe siècles* (Paris, 1988); [*The Birth of Intimacy: Privacy and Domestic Life in Early Modern Paris* (transl. J. Phelps, Oxford, 1991)]

Roeck, B. *Eine Stadt in Krieg und Frieden: Studien zur Geschichte der Reischsstadt Augsburg zwischen Kalenderstreit und Parität* (Göttingen, 1989)

Ruggiu, F-J. *Les élites et les villes moyennes en France et en Angleterre (XVIIe–XVIIIe siècles)* (Paris, 1997)

Sherwood, J. M. *Poverty in 18th-Century Spain: The Women and Children of the Inclusa* (Toronto, 1988)

Slack, P. *The Impact of Plague in Tudor and Stuart England* (Oxford, 1990)

Soly, H., and Thijs, A. K. L., eds. *Minorities in Western European Cities (Sixteenth–Twentieth Centuries)* (Brussels, 1995)

10. Culture and Landscape 1500–1800

Bogucka, M. 'Townhall as Symbol of Power: Changes in the Political and Social Functions of the Gdansk Town Hall till the End of the 18th Century', *Acta Poloniae Historica*, 75 (1997): 27–38

*Borsay, P. *The English Urban Renaissance: Culture and Society in the Provincial Town 1660–1770* (Oxford, 1989)

Borsay, P. *The Image of Georgian Bath 1700–2000* (Oxford, 2000)

Clark, P. *British Clubs and Societies 1500–1800: The Origins of an Associational World* (Oxford, 2000)

Cowan, B. W. *The Social Life of Coffee: The Emergence of the British Coffeehouse* (London, 2005).

De Mare, H., and Vos, A., eds. *Urban Rituals in Italy and the Netherlands* (Assen, 1993)

Dooley, B., and Baron, S. A., eds. *The Politics of Information in Early Modern Europe* (London, 2001)

François, E. *Protestants et catholiques en Allemagne: identités et pluralisme: Augsbourg 1648–1806* (Paris, 1993)

Gee, M., and Kirk, T., eds. *Printed Matters: Printing, Publishing and Urban Culture in Europe in the Modern Period* (Aldershot, 2002)

Grendler, P. F. *Schooling in Renaissance Italy* (London 1989)

Guillery, P. *The Small House in Eighteenth-Century London* (London, 2004)

*Hsia, R. P-C. *Social Discipline in the Reformation: Central Europe 1550–1750* (London, 1989)

*Jacob, M. C., and Mijnhardt, W. M., eds. *The Dutch Republic in the 18th Century: Decline, Enlightenment and Revolution* (London, 1992)

McVeigh, S. *Concert Life in London from Haydn to Mozart* (Cambridge, 1993)

Mommsen, W. J., et al., eds. *The Urban Classes, the Nobility and the Reformation* (Stuttgart, 1979)

Mulryne, J. R., et al. *Europa Triumphans: Court and Civic Festivals in Early Modern Europe* (2 vols, Aldershot, 2004)

Quéniart, J. *Culture et société urbaines dans la France de l'Ouest au XVIIIe siècle* (Paris, 1978)

Records of Early English Drama (multiple volumes, Toronto, 1979–)

Roper, L. *The Holy Household: Women and Morals in Reformation Augsburg* (Oxford, 1989)

*Schilling, H. *Religion, Political Culture and the Emergence of Early Modern Society* (Leiden, 1992), chs 5–6

Schneider, R. A. *Public Life in Toulouse 1463–1789* (London, 1989)

Spufford, M. 'Literacy, Trade and Religion in the Commercial Centres of Europe', in K. Davids and J. Lucassen, eds., *A Miracle Mirrored: The Dutch Republic in European Perspective* (Cambridge, 1995), pp. 229–82

Tittler, R. *Architecture and Power: The Town Hall and the English Urban Community c.1500–1640* (Oxford, 1991)

Wall, C. *The Literary and Cultural Spaces of Restoration London* (Cambridge, 1998)

11. Governance 1500–1800

Beik, W. *Urban Protest in 17th-Century France* (Cambridge, 1997)

Cerutti, S. *La ville et ses métiers. Naissance d'une language corporatif (Turin XVIIe–XVIII siècle)* (Paris, 1990)

Cowan, A. *The Urban Patriciate: Lübeck and Venice 1580–1700* (Cologne, 1986)

*Davids, K., and J. Lucassen, eds. *A Miracle Mirrored: The Dutch Republic in European Perspective* (Cambridge, 1995), chs 3–4

Diefendorf, B. B. *Paris City Councillors in the 16th Century* (Princeton, 1983)

Hittle, J. M. *The Service City: State and Townsmen in Russia 1600–1800* (Cambridge, Mass., 1979)

Hochmuth, C., and Rau, S., eds. *Machtträume der frühneuzeitlichen Stadt* (Constance, 2006)

Mulryne, J. R., et al. *Europa Triumphans: Court and Civic Festivals in Early Modern Europe* (Aldershot, 2004)

Prak, M. 'Identité urbaine, identités sociales. Les bourgeois de Bois-le-Duc au XVIII siécle', *Annales E.S.C.*, 48 (1993): 907–33

Reinhard, W. *Power Elites and State Building* (Oxford, 1996)

Robbins, K. C., *City on the Ocean Sea: La Rochelle 1530–1650* (Leiden, 1997)

Rogers, N. *Whigs and Cities: Popular Politics in the Age of Walpole and Pitt* (Oxford, 1989)

Sweet, R. *The English Town 1680–1840* (Harlow, 1999)

*Tilly C., and Blockmans, W. P., eds. *Cities and the Rise of States in Europe, A.D. 1000 to 1800,* (Oxford, 1994), chs 7–10

PART III 1800–2000

General Surveys/Collected Volumes

Beauregard, R. A., and Body-Gendrot, S., eds. *The Urban Moment: Cosmopolitan Essays on the Late 20th Century City* (London, 1999)

*Lees, A., and Lees, L. H. *Cities and the Making of Modern Europe 1750–1914* (Cambridge, 2007)

*Schmal, H., ed. *Patterns of European Urbanisation since 1500* (London, 1981)

National/Regional Surveys

*Bater, J. H. *The Soviet City: Ideal and Reality* (London, 1980)

*Daunton, M., ed. *The Cambridge Urban History of Britain: III: 1840–1950* (Cambridge, 2000)

Guérin-Pace, F. *Deux siècles de croissance urbaine: La population des villes françaises de 1831 á 1990* (Paris, 1993)

Johnson, J. H., and Pooley, C. G., eds. *The Structure of 19th-Century Cities* (New York, 1982)

Johnston, W. M. *The Austrian Mind: An Intellectual and Social History 1848–1938* (London, 1972)

*Morris, R. J., and Rodger, R., eds. *The Victorian City: A Reader in British Urban History 1820–1914* (London, 1993)

*Sagnes, J., ed. *La ville en France aux XIXe et XXe siècles* (Beziers, 1997)

Waller, P. J. *Town, City and Nation: England 1850–1914* (Oxford, 1983)

Individual Cities

*Ayçoberry, P. *Cologne: Entre Napoléon et Bismarck, la croissance d'une ville rhénane* (Paris, 1981)

*Bater, J. H. *St Petersburg: Industrialization and Change* (London, 1976)

*Bell, M., and Hietala, M. *Helsinki: The Innovative City: Historical Perspectives* (Helsinki, 2002)

Bradley, J. *Muzhik and Muscovite: Urbanization in Late Imperial Russia* (London, 1985)

*Evenson, N. *Paris: A Century of Change 1878–1978* (London, 1979)

Lukacs, J. *Budapest 1900* (London, 1988)

Merriman, J. M. *The Red City: Limoges and the French 19th Century* (Oxford, 1985)

Nash, D., and Reeder, D., eds. *Leicester in the Twentieth Century* (Stroud, 1993)

Roncayolo, M. *Les grammaires d'une ville: essai sur la genèse des structures urbaines à Marseille* (Paris, 1996)

Ruble, B. A. *Leningrad: Shaping a Soviet City* (Oxford, 1990)

Sarasin, P. *La ville des bourgeois: Élites et société urbaine à Bâle dans la deuxième moitié du XIXe siècle* (Paris, 1998)

Syrjämaa, T. *Constructing Unity, Living in diversity: A Roman Decade* [Rome in the 1870s] (Helsinki, 2006)

Van Dijk, H. *Rotterdam 1810–1880* (Schiedam, 1976)

12. Urban Trends 1800–2000

Anderson, S. C., and Tabb, B. H., eds. *Water, Leisure and Culture: European Historical Perspectives* (Oxford, 2002)

Andersson, H., et al., eds. *Change and Stability in Urban Europe* (Aldershot, 2001)

Baranowski, S., and Furlough, eds. *Being Elsewhere: Tourism, Consumer Culture, and Identity in Modern Europe and North America* (Ann Arbor, 2001)

Borsay, P., et al. *New Directions in Urban History: Aspects of European Art, Health, Tourism and Leisure since the Enlightenment* (Münster, 2000)

Commerçon, N., and George, P., eds. *Villes de transition* (Paris, 1999)

De Bailly, A., and Huriot, J-M., eds. *Villes et croissance: Théories, modèles, perspectives* (Paris, 1999)

Demazière, C. *Entreprises, développement économique et espace urbain* (Paris, 2000)

Diefendorf, J. M., ed. *Rebuilding Europe's Bombed Cities* (London, 1990)

Duham, G., et al., eds. *Paris—Berlin: Regards croisés sur deux capitales européennes* (Paris, 2000)

Dupart, M. C., and Chaline, C., eds. *Le port, cadre de ville* (Paris, 1998)

Falk, T. *Urban Sweden: Changes in the Distribution of Population: The 1960s in Focus* (Stockholm, 1976)

Fedor, T. S. *Patterns of Urban Growth in the Russian Empire during the 19th Century* (Chicago, 1975)

Gordon, G., ed. *Regional Cities in the United Kingdom 1890–1980* (London, 1986)

Hall, P., and Hay, D. *Growth Centres in the European Urban System* (London, 1980)

*Hall, T., ed. *Planning and Urban Growth in the Nordic Countries* (London, 1991)

Hamm, M. F., ed. *The City in Late Imperial Russia* (Bloomington, 1986)

Jarrasé, D. *Les thermes romantiques: bains et villégiatures en France de 1800 à 1850* (Clermont-Ferrand, 1992)

Jensen-Butler, C., et al., eds. *European Cities in Competition* (Aldershot, 1997)

Jouret, B. *Définition spatiale du phénomène urbain bruxellois* (Brussels 1972)

Kalb, D. *Expanding Class: Power and Everyday Politics in Industrial Communities, The Netherlands 1850–1950* (London, 1997)

Laborie, J-P., and Renard, J., eds. *Bourgs et Petites Villes* (Toulouse, 1997)

*Lawton, R., and Lee, R., eds. *Population and Society in Western European Port Cities c.1650–1939* (Liverpool, 2002)

Leontidou, L. *The Mediterranean City in Transition* (Cambridge, 1990)

Nilsson, L. *Den urbana transitionen: Tätorterna i svensk samhällsomvandling 1800–1980* (Stockholm, 1989)

Pereira, P. T., and Mata, M. E., eds. *Urban Dominance and Labour Market Differentiation of a European Capital City: Lisbon 1890–1990* (Dordrecht, 1996)

Prévélakis, G. *Athènes: Urbanisme, culture et politique* (Paris, 2000)

Pumain, D., and St-Julien,T., eds. *Urban Networks in Europe* (Paris, 1996)

Reif, H. *Die Verspätete Stadt: Industrialisierung, städtischer Raum und Politik in Oberhausen 1846–1929* (Cologne, 1993)

Spence, N., et al. *British Cities: An Analysis of Urban Change* (Oxford, 1982)

*Sutcliffe, A., ed. *Metropolis 1890–1940* (London, 1984)

Teuterberg, H. J., ed. *Urbanisierung im 19. und 20. Jahrhundert* (Cologne, 1983)

Tilly, L. A. *Politics and Class in Milan 1881–1901* (Oxford, 1992)

Walton, J. K. 'Seaside Resorts and their Hinterlands in Western Europe and the Americas, from the late 18th Century to the Second World War', *Storia del Turismo: 2003* (2004): 69–87

13. Economy 1800–2000

Accampo, E. A. *Industrialization, Family Life, and Class Relations: St Chamond 1815–1914* (London, 1989)

Cassis, Y. *Capitals of Capital: A History of International Financial Centres 1780–2005* (transl. J. Collier, Cambridge, 2006)

Castells, M., and Himanen. P. *The Information Society and the Welfare State: The Finnish Model* (Oxford, 2002)

*Cheshire, P. C., and Hay, D. G. *Urban Problems in Western Europe: An Economic Analysis* (London, 1989)

Crossick, G., ed. *The Artisan and the European Town 1500–1900 (Aldershot, 1997)*

Crossick, G., and Haupt, H-G., eds. *Shopkeepers and Master Artisans in 19th-Century Europe* (London, 1984)

Damette, F. *La France en villes* (Paris, 1994)

Elmhorn, C. *Brussels: A Reflexive World City* (Stockholm, 2001)

Gaillard, J. *Paris, la ville 1852–1870* (Paris, 1977)

Jacobs, M., and Scholliers, P., eds. *Eating Out in Europe* (Oxford, 2003)

King, A. D. *Global Cities: Post-Imperialism and the Internationalization of London* (London, 1990)

*Körner, M., ed. *Destruction and Reconstruction of Towns* (3 vols, Berne, 1999–2000)

Lancaster, W. *The Department Store: A Social History* (London, 1995)

Lequin, Y. *L'usine et le bureau* (Lyon, 1990)

McKay, J. P. *Tramways and Trolleys: The Rise of Urban Mass Transport in Europe* (Princeton, 1976)

Miller, M. B. *The Bon Marché: Bourgeois Culture and the Department Store 1869–1920* (London, 1981)

Millward, R. *Private and Public Enterprise in Europe: Energy, Telecommunications and Transport 1830–1990* (Cambridge, 2005)

Mironov, B. 'Les villes de Russie entre l'Occident et l'Orient (1750–1850)', *Annales E.S.C.*, 46 (1991): 705–33

Neufeld, M. J. *The Skilled Metalworkers of Nuremberg: Craft and Class in the Industrial Revolution* (London, 1989)

Pasleau, S. *Industries et populations: L'enchaînement des deux croissances à Seraing au XIXe siècle* (Geneva, 1998)

Reid, D. *The Miners of Decazeville: A Geneaology of Deindustrialization* (London, 1985)

Ward, S. V. *Selling Places: The Marketing and Promotion of Towns and Cities 1850–2000* (London, 1998)

White, H. P. *The Continuing Conurbation: Change and Development in Greater Manchester* (Farnborough, 1980)

14. Social Life 1800–2000

Alter, G. *Family and the Female Life Course: The Women of Verviers, Belgium 1849–1880* (London, 1988)

Berlanstein, L. R. *The Working People of Paris 1871–1914* (London, 1984)

Body-Gendrot, S. *The Social Control of Cities? A Comparative Perspective* (Oxford, 2000)

Brunet, J-P. *Une banlieue ouvrière: St-Denis 1890–1939* (Lille, 1982)

Chinn, C. *They Worked All their Lives: Women of the Urban Poor 1880–1939* (Manchester, 1988)

Daunton, M. J. *House and Home in the Victorian City* (London, 1983)

Engel, B. A. *Between the Fields and the City: Women, Work and Family in Russia 1861–1914* (Cambridge, 1994)

Evans, R. J., ed. *The German Working Class 1888–1933: The Politics of Everyday Life* (London, 1982)

Gravesteijn, S. G., et al., eds. *Timing Global Cities* (Utrecht, 1998)

Hanagan, M. P. *Nascent Proletarians: Class Formation in Post-Revolutionary France* (Oxford, 1989)

Henriksson, A. *The Tsar's Loyal Germans: The Riga German Community, Social Change and the Nationality Question 1855–1905* (New York, 1983)

Hilden, P. *Working Women and Socialist Politics in France 1880–1914: A Regional Study* (Oxford, 1986)

_____ *Women, Work and Politics: Belgium 1830–1914* (Oxford, 1993)

Jordansson, B., and Vammen, T., eds. *Charitable Women: Philanthropic Welfare 1780–1930: A Nordic and Interdisciplinary Anthology* (Odense, 1998)

*Kocka, J., and Mitchell, A., eds. *Bourgeois Society in 19th-Century Europe* (Oxford, 1993)

*Lis, C. *Social Change and the Labouring Poor: Antwerp 1770–1860* (London, 1986)

MacGregor, S., and Pimlott, B., eds. *Tackling the Inner Cities: The 1980s Reviewed, Prospects for the 1990s* (Oxford, 1990)

Madanipour, A., et al., eds., *Social Exclusion in European Cities* (London, 1998)

Martens, A., and Vervaeke, M., eds. *La polarisation sociale des villes européennes* (Paris, 1997)

Morris, R. J. *Class, Sect and Party: The Making of the British Middle Class, Leeds 1820–1850* (Manchester, 1990)

Musterd, S., et al. *Multi-Ethnic Metropolis: Patterns and Policies* (Dordrecht, 1998)

Prunty, J. *Dublin Slums 1800–1925: A Study in Urban Geography* (Dublin, 1999)

Sassen, S. *The Global City* (2nd edition, Princeton, 2001)

Sassen, S. *Cities in a World Economy* (2nd edition, London, 2000)

*Sewell, W. H. *Structure and Mobility: The Men and Women of Marseille 1820–1870* (Cambridge, 1985)

15. Culture and Landscape 1800–2000

*Abrams, L. *Workers' Culture in Imperial Germany: Leisure and Recreation in the Rhineland and Westphalia* (London, 1992)

Auslander, L. *Taste and Power: Furnishing Modern France* (London, 1996)

Bastéa, E. *The Creation of Modern Athens* (Cambridge, 2000)

Borsay, P. *A History of Leisure: The British Experience since 1500* (Basingstoke, 2006)

Borsay, P., et al., eds. *New Directions in Urban History: Aspects of European Art, Health, Tourism and Leisure since the Enlightenment* (Münster 2000)

Boyer, M. C. *The City of Collective Memory: Its Historical Imagery and Architectural Entertainments* (London, 1994)

Brooks, H. A., ed. *Le Corbusier* (Princeton, 1987)

*Clark, P., ed. *The European City and Green Space: London, Stockholm, Helsinki and St Petersburg 1850–2000* (Aldershot, 2006)

Deland, M. *The Social City: Middle-Way Approaches to Housing and Suburban Governmentality in Southern Stockholm 1900–1945* (Stockholm, 2001)

*Ferguson, P. P. *Paris as Revolution: Writing the 19th-Century City* (London, 1994)

*Gee, M., et al., eds. *The City in Central Europe: Culture and Society from 1800 to the Present* (Aldershot, 1999)

Greenhalgh, P. *Ephemeral Vistas: The Expositions Universelles, Great Exhibitions and World's Fairs 1851–1939* (Manchester, 1988)

*Gunn, S. *The Public Culture of the Victorian Middle Class* (Manchester, 2000)

Hanák, P. *The Garden and the Workshop: Essays on the Cultural History of Vienna and Budapest* (Princeton, NJ, 1998)

Holt, R. *Sport and Society in Modern France* (London, 1981)

McLeod, H. *European Religion in the Age of Great Cities 1830–1930* (London, 1995)

*McLeod, H. *Piety and Poverty: Working-Class Religion in Berlin, London, and New York 1870–1914* (London, 1996)

*McLeod, H., and Ustorf, W., eds. *The Decline of Christendom in Western Europe 1750–2000* (Cambridge, 2003)

Miller, M. J. *The Representation of Place: Urban Planning and Protest in France and Great Britain 1950–1980* (Aldershot, 2003)

Nikula, R. *Focus on Finnish Twentieth Century Architecture and Town Planning* (Helsinki, 2006)

Olsen, D. J. *The City as a Work of Art: London, Paris, Vienna* (London, 1986)

Prendergast, C. *Paris and the Nineteenth Century* (Oxford, 1992)

Ross, C. 'Mass Culture and Divided Audiences: Cinema and Social Change in Inter-war Germany', *Past and Present,* 193 (2006): 157–95

Rotenberg, R. *Landscape and Power in Vienna* (London, 1995)

*Schlör, J. *Nights in the Big City: Paris, Berlin, London 1840–1930* (London, 1998)

Schorske, C. E. *Fin-de-Siècle Vienna: Politics and Culture* (New York, 1981)

*Waller, P. J., ed. *The English Urban Landscape* (Oxford, 2000)

Wheeler, R. F., et al. [Special issue on Sport and Leisure], *Journal of Contemporary History,* 13 (1978)

Whitehand, J. W. R., and Carr, C. M. H. *Twentieth-Century Suburbs: A Morphological Approach* (London, 2001)

Williams, S. C. *Religious Belief and Popular Culture: A Study of the South London Borough of Southwark c.1880–1939* (Oxford, 1999)

16. Governance 1800–2000

Berlière, J-M. *Le Monde des Police en France* (Brussels, 1996)

Borraz, O. *Gouverner une ville: Besançon 1959–1989* (Rennes, 1998)

Claval, P., and Sanguin, A-L., eds. *Métropolisation et politique* (Paris, 1997)

*Cohen, W. B. *Urban Government and the Rise of the French City: Five Municipalities in the 19th Century* (Basingstoke, 1998)

*Colton, T. J., *Moscow: Governing the Socialist Metropolis* (London, 1995)

*Dagenais, M., et al., eds. *Municipal Services and Employees in the Modern City* (Aldershot, 2002)

*Daunton, M., ed. *The Cambridge Urban History of Britain: III: 1840–1950* (Cambridge, 2000), ch. 9 *et passim*

Emsley, C. *Crime, Police and Penal Policy: European Experiences 1750–1940* (Oxford, 2007)

*Emsley, C., and Weinberger, B., eds. *Policing Western Europe: Politics, Professionalism, and Public Order 1850–1940* (London, 1991)

Ferreira da Silva, Á. 'Running for Money: Finance and Municipalisation in Lisbon (1850–1914)', in A. Giuntini, et al., eds., *Urban Growth on Two Continents in the 19th and 20th Centuries: Technology, Networks, Finance and Public Regulation* (Granada, 2004), pp. 87–116

Fuchs, R. G. *Poor and Pregnant in Paris* (New Brunswick, N.J., 1992)

Gabriel, O. W., and Hoffman-Martinot, V., eds. *Démocraties urbaines* (Paris, 1999)

Hietala, M. *Services and Urbanization at the Turn of Century: The Diffusion of Innovations* (Helsinki, 1987)

*Jacobs, B. D. *Fractured Cities: Capitalism, Community and Empowerment in Britain and America* (London, 1992)

*Ladd, B. *Urban Planning and Civic Order in Germany 1860–1914* (London, 1990)

Lees, A. *Cities, Sin, and Social Reform in Imperial Germany* (Ann Arbor, 2002)

Le Galès, P. *Le retour des villes européennes* (Paris, 2003)

Lorrain, D., and Stoker, G., eds. *La privatisation des services urbains en Europe* (Paris, 1995)

*Menjot, D., and Pinol, J-L., eds. *Enjeux et expressions de la politique municipale (XIIe–XXe siècles)* (Paris, 1997)

Mouritzen, P. E., ed. *Managing Cities in Austerity: Urban Fiscal Stress in Ten Western Countries* (London, 1992)

Nevers, J-Y. 'Du cliéntélisme à la technocratie, cents ans de démocratie communale dans une grande ville Toulouse', *Revue Francaise de Science Politique*, 33 (1983): 428–54

[OECD] *Managing and Financing Urban Services* (Paris, 1987)

Pinson, G. 'Political Government and Governance: Strategic Planning and the Reshaping of Political Capacity in Turin', *International Journal of Urban and Regional Research*, 26 (2002): 477–93

Rootes, C.. ed., *Environmental Protest in Western Europe* (Oxford, 2003)

*Smith, M. P., and Feagin, J. R., eds. *The Capitalist City: Global Restructuring and Community Politics* (Oxford, 1987)

Spencer, E. G. *Police and the Social Order in German Cities: The Düsseldorf District 1848–1914* (De Kalb, 1992)

Index